Manual of Online Search Strategies
Volume II

Dedicated to the memory
of
Kathy Armstrong
1951–1998

Manual of Online Search Strategies

Third Edition
Volume II: Business, Law, News and Patents

Edited by
C.J. Armstrong
and
Andrew Large

Gower

Published by
Gower Publishing Limited
Gower House
Croft Road
Aldershot
Hampshire GU11 3HR
England

Gower Publishing Company
131 Main Street
Burlington VT 05401–5600 USA

British Library Cataloguing in Publication Data
Manual of online search strategies. – 3rd ed.
    Vol. II: Business, law, news and patents
    1. Online bibliographic searching – Handbooks, manuals, etc.
    2. Information storage and retrieval systems – Business –
    Handbooks, manuals, etc. 3. Information storage and
    retrieval systems – Law – Handbooks, manuals, etc.
    4. Information storage and retrieval systems – Patent
    documentation – Handbooks, manuals, etc.
    I. Armstrong, C. J. (Christopher J.) II. Large, J. A.
    025.5'24

ISBN 0 566 08304 3

Library of Congress Cataloging-in-Publication Data
Manual of online search strategies / edited by C.J. Armstrong and Andrew Large.– 3rd ed.
    p. cm.
    Includes bibliographical references and index.
    ISBN 0–566–07990–9 (set) – ISBN 0–566–08303–5 (v. 1) – ISBN 0–566–08304–3 (v. 2)
    – ISBN 0–566–08305–1 (v. 3)
    1. Online information resource searching–Handbooks, manuals, etc. 2. Online
information resource searching–United States–Handbooks, manuals, etc. I. Armstrong,
C.J. II. Large, J.A.

ZA4060.M36 2000
025.5'24–dc21

                                                                                    00–025154

Typeset in Times by Bournemouth Colour Press, Parkstone and printed in Great Britain by MPG Books Limited, Bodmin.

Contents

List of figures   vii
List of tables   xi
Notes on contributors   xiii
Preface   xv
Acknowledgements   xix

1   Search strategies: some general considerations   1
Chris Armstrong and Andrew Large
Information seekers   1
Technologies   4
Database differences between vendors   10
Controlled versus natural-language searching   11
Interfaces   13
Search evaluation   14
Database evaluation   17

2   Patents   23
Edlyn S. Simmons
An introduction to patents   23
Patent data fields   33
Patent databases   49
Other databases that include patents   122
Databases offering information about patents   124
Patent litigation databases   126
Selecting a database   127
Selecting a host system   136

3   Business and economics   141
Jacqueline Cropley and Gwenda Sippings
Expansion of the market   141
New product development   142

The need for multiple systems   147
Types of business information and sources   158
Evolving products   209
Market predictions   213

4   News and current affairs   **217**
Peter Chapman
Introduction   217
Definitions   217
Background   217
Considerations   218
Electronic sources   219
Traditional online sources   222
CD-ROMs   226
The World Wide Web   227
Search strategies   233
Sample search: Louise Woodward   236
Conclusion   240

5   Law   **243**
John Williams
Introduction   243
Legal material   244
LEXIS   248
The Central Computer and Technology Agency Government
Information Service   252
JUSTIS online and on CD-ROM   255
Current legal information   257
FINDLAW   258
The Legal Information Institute   260
Conclusion   260

Database index   263
Subject index   275

List of figures

1.1   Opening directory on YAHOO!   6
1.2   Excerpt from the opening screen of the AUSTRALIAN
    BIOLOGICAL RESEARCH NETWORK   7
1.3   SOCIAL SCIENCE INFORMATION GATEWAY (SOSIG)   8
1.4   Failure of controlled language   12
1.5   French-language interface to EXCITE   18
1.6   SYSTRAN translation software on ALTAVISTA   19
2.1   US patent no. 5,046, 659: front page   25
2.2   DERWENT WORLD PATENTS INDEX record: Questel-Orbit
    file DWPI   51
2.3   DERWENT PATENT CITATION INDEX: STN file DCPI   58
2.4   INPADOC family and status record: DIALOG file 345   63
2.5   CLAIMS US patents: Questel-Orbit file IFIUDB   70
2.6   CLAIMS CURRENT PATENT LEGAL STATUS: Questel-Orbit
    file CRRX   74
2.7   LEXPAT: LEXIS-NEXIS   76
2.8   US PATENTS FULLTEXT: DIALOG file 654   79
2.9   USPATFULL: STN   84
2.10   QPAT search screen   87
2.11   QPAT search results   88
2.12   INTELLECTUAL PROPERTY NETWORK Boolean
    Search screen   89
2.13   INTELLECTUAL PROPERTY NETWORK Search Results
    screen   90
2.14   USPTO Manual Advanced Search screen   91
2.15   USPTO Manual Search Results screen   92
2.16   EUROPEAN PATENTS FULLTEXT: DIALOG file 348   95
2.17   PCTPAT citation: Questel-Orbit file PCTPAT   100
2.18   PATOS: STN file PATOSEP   102
2.19   PATDPA: STN   106
2.20   JAPIO: DIALOG file 347   108

2.21   APIPAT: DIALOG file 353   110
2.22   WORLD PATENTS INDEX/APIPAT: Questel-Orbit file WPAM   112
2.23   MARPAT citation: STN file MARPAT   115
2.24   PHARMSEARCH record: Questel-Orbit file PHARM   118
2.25   DRUG PATENTS INTERNATIONAL: Questel-Orbit file DPINNS 121
2.26   GENESEQ citation: STN file DGENE   123
3.1   REUTERS BUSINESS BRIEFING search   146
3.2   REUTERS BUSINESS BRIEFING results   146
3.3   Dun & Bradstreet's WHO OWNS WHOM search   159
3.4   Dun & Bradstreet's WHO OWNS WHOM results   159
3.5   Dun & Bradstreet's WHO OWNS WHOM family tree view   160
3.6   COMPANIES HOUSE DIRECT   160
3.7   PRIMARK GLOBAL ACCESS search   163
3.8   PRIMARK GLOBAL ACCESS search results   165
3.9   PRIMARK GLOBAL ACCESS search results filings   165
3.10   PRIMARK GLOBAL ACCESS search results Extel Report   166
3.11   CAROL company reprint selection   166
3.12   EXPERIAN LINK screens   171
3.13   FT PROFILE search   175
3.14   FT PROFILE search results   177
3.15   WASHINGTON POST business screen   178
3.16   MAID PROFOUND search   181
3.17   MAID PROFOUND search results summary   182
3.18   MAID PROFOUND selected search results   183
3.19   MAID PROFOUND Alert Manager   186
3.20   MAID PROFOUND stock quotes   186
3.21   EMMA initial search specification   188
3.22   EMMA search results   189
3.23   EMMA company record printout   191
3.24   LEXIS-NEXIS search   194
3.25   LEXIS-NEXIS KWIC view results   194
3.26   LEXIS-NEXIS full view results   195
3.27   DRI RISK MANAGEMENT search   202
3.28   DRI RISK MANAGEMENT search results in graphical format   203
3.29   BRIDGE CHANNEL real-time screen   205
3.30   Citicorp homepage screens   208
4.1   UKNEWS: command-driven interface   222
4.2   FT Profile Infoplus menu-driven interface   223
4.3   FT Discovery Windows-based interface   224
4.4   NEXIS basic Windows interface   225
4.5   NEXIS Freestyle end-user interface   225
4.6   Chadwyck-Healey's 'Freeway' interface   226
4.7   Chadwyck-Healey's *Times* interface   227
4.8   Televisual Data interface   228
4.9   *The Times* on the Web   229

4.10	*The Telegraph*	229
4.11	Story links on the *Boston Globe*	230
4.12	Added value information on *The Times*	230
4.13	DialogWeb entry page	231
4.14	Front page of PAPERBOY site	232
4.15	YAHOO! news	232
4.16	*The News Tribune's* report on the Woodward case	238
4.17	Louise Woodward's local news site	239
4.18	Results of an ALTAVISTA search on 'Louise Woodward'	239
5.1	GIS Organisational Index	253
5.2	Crown Prosecution Service Web site	254
5.3	FINDLAW Web site	259

List of tables

2.1   Country coverage of patent databases   28
5.1   JUSTIS databases   255

Notes on contributors

Chris Armstrong is Managing Director of Information Automation Ltd (IAL), a consultancy and research company, established in 1987 in the library and information management sector. Prior to this he worked as a Research Officer at the College of Librarianship Wales/Department of Information and Library Studies, University of Wales, Aberystwyth. In 1993, following several projects which pointed to a need for action in the area of database quality, IAL set up the Centre for Information Quality Management (CIQM) on behalf of The Library Association and the UK Online User Group; the Centre continues to monitor database quality and work towards methodologies for assuring data quality to users of databases and Internet resources. The company's Web site can be found at <URL http:/www.i-a-l.co.uk/>. Chris Armstrong publishes in professional journals and speaks at conferences regularly. He is a Fellow of the Institute of Analysts and Programmers and a member of the Institute of Information Scientists, the UK Online User Group and The Library Association. He maintains close contact with the Department of Information and Library Studies and is currently Director of its International Graduate Summer School.

Peter Chapman is Head of Electronic Information Services for Newsquest (NE) Ltd, the publishers of *The Northern Echo*. His role is to manage the provision of electronic information sources within the company and to organize the company's electronic publications – the feeds of the newspaper's contents to various database hosts and the publication of the Web site <URL http://www.thisisthenortheast. co.uk>. Before taking up his current post, Peter was Chief Librarian of *The Scotsman*. Besides being the founding Chairman of the National Association of News Libraries, he was also for many years first Secretary and then Chairman of the Association of UK Media Librarians.

Jacqueline Cropley is a Consultant currently specializing in information and knowledge management and information technology. She has also worked for a number of financial and professional organizations, in charge of information and marketing functions. The introduction and exploitation of business and economic databases has been a recurrent theme throughout her career. She publishes and lectures widely on information technology, marketing and business issues. She is also a Member of the British Library Advisory Council, Honorary Treasurer of The Library Association and a Member of the Council of the Institute of Information Scientists.

Andrew Large is the CN-Pratt-Grinstad Professor of Information Studies at the Graduate School of Library and Information Studies, McGill University, Montreal, Canada. As well as editing earlier editions of the *Manual of Online Search Strategies* and Unesco's *World Information Report* (1997), he has authored several books, the most recent being *Information Seeking in the Online Age* (1999). He is also joint editor of the quarterly *Education for Information*. He has published widely on a variety of information science themes and acted as consultant for both national and international organizations.

Edlyn S. Simmons is a Section Head in Business Intelligence Services at the Procter & Gamble Company in Cincinnati, Ohio, USA. For many years previously, she was Manager of the Patent Information Group in the Patent Department of Hoechst Marion Roussel Inc. She gained BS and MS degrees in chemistry from the University of Cincinnati, and is a registered US patent agent. She is past chair of the Patent Information Users Group and a member of the American Chemical Society Divisions of Chemical Information and Chemistry and the Law and of the Cincinnati Intellectual Property Law Association. She has published and spoken extensively in the fields of chemical and patent information.

Gwenda Sippings is Head of Information, London at Clifford Chance, a major international law firm. She is directly responsible for central information services to lawyers and their clients, and provides information consultancy and management support to practice area and international office information partners and their staff and services. Over the last five years, she has been heavily involved in the evaluation and procurement of electronic information sources for the firm, and monitored the impact of the Internet on changes to products and services.

John Williams is Professor of Law and Head of the Department of Law at the University of Wales, Aberystwyth. He is the author of a number of books on the law and social welfare including *Social Services Law* (Tolley, 1996) and *Mental Health Law* (Fourmat, 1990). In addition, he has written articles on a wide range of legal matters, including elder abuse, law and technology, and child law. He was a member of the Human Fertilisation and Embryology Authority and chaired its Information Committee. He is an active member of the Citizens' Advice Bureaux and is a past chair of the North Wales CAB Area Committee. He is an enthusiastic advocate of the greater use of information technology in legal education and was one of the original members of the United Kingdom's Law Technology Centre.

Preface

Despite the development of more friendly, attractive and helpful interfaces, a declining emphasis on time-related charges that placed a premium on familiarity and expertise, and more imaginatively packaged information, the need remains for know-how if the numerous and expanding electronic information resources are to be exploited effectively. This third edition of the *Manual of Online Search Strategies*, as with the earlier editions, sets itself the task of offering to the searcher – whether an information professional or otherwise – sound advice on database selection, search service selection and search strategy compilation in order to maximize the chances of finding the best information available for a given task. In a range of subject fields, experienced searchers pass on to the reader the benefits of their daily familiarity with electronic information resources, whether available from dial-up online services, CD-ROMs or the Internet.

This third edition of the *Manual of Online Search Strategies*, unlike its predecessors, has been divided into three separate volumes rather than appearing as a single entity. This decision has been necessitated by the growth in size of the contents – itself a reflection of the continued information explosion. This volume contains five chapters: Business, Law, Patents, News and Current Affairs, as well as an introductory chapter on Search Strategies. Volumes I and III deal with the Sciences (Chemistry, the Biosciences, Agriculture, the Earth Sciences and Engineering and Energy), and with the Humanities, the Social Sciences, Education and Citation Indexes, respectively.

The location, in this particular volume, of the chapter on Patents deserves some explanation. A topic like patent information could legitimately have been included in any of the three volumes, and there are especially persuasive arguments for including it in Volume I on the Sciences. Nevertheless, it has been placed in this volume because of the close links between patent information and business; a second reason is that several of the chapters in Volume I also refer to patent databases where relevant.

The most obvious differences between the third and second editions of the *Manual*, apart from the breakdown into multiple volumes, are the slightly amended chapter divisions and the inclusion of Internet-based information resources alongside dial-up online and CD-ROM services. The latter requires little explanation, so dramatic has been its impact, especially of the World Wide Web, since the publication of the last edition in 1992. The major changes in the coverage of the chapters included in this volume are the treatment of all law information in one single chapter instead of in two chapters divided by place of information origin – Western Europe or North America – and the same for business information. When the two earlier editions were published the databases in these two fields seemed sufficiently different in Western Europe from North America to demand a different author expertise and attract a different readership. Growing globalization suggests that now this distinction has much less validity and both law and business can be treated in one chapter apiece.

Similar provisos regarding content must be made about the third edition as were offered for the earlier two editions. This is not an introductory textbook on information retrieval; apart from some advice offered in the opening chapter it is assumed that readers will have a basic familiarity with accessing and finding information from electronic sources (skills, in any case, somewhat less necessary with today's more user-friendly systems). Authors have been given free rein to select information sources and services for their chapters, guided by their familiarity with them. It has never been the intention to list absolutely every source or service that might conceivably be used in a search (itself an impossible task if the *Manual* is to be confined to realistic dimensions). The authors of this volume are drawn from Canada, the UK and the USA, and this inevitably influences their selections. Nevertheless, sources and services from elsewhere are by no means ignored in the following pages. Perhaps the most thorny issue with publications of this type is currency: it would be pointless to deny the rapid rate of change in the electronic information sector. Every effort has been made by the authors, editors and publisher to ensure that the content is as up-to-date as possible on publication.

Information sources, let alone information services, cannot neatly be compressed into the chapter division used by the *Manual* (or any other subject division, for that matter). Inevitably, many databases and services are mentioned in more than one chapter. It is hoped that the indexes in each volume will enable the reader to pursue specific titles across the chapters.

It is never simple to compile a book involving two editors, one publishing editor and 17 authors scattered across two continents and several countries. Notwithstanding the marvels of modern telecommunications, at times one dreams of a real meeting around a non-virtual table. It is to the credit of the many people involved in the production of this book that it has seen the light of day without that particular dream being realized. We remain very grateful for the promptness and courteousness unfailingly exhibited by all the authors. Special thanks must be offered to Suzie Duke of Gower Publishing, who did all and more than could be expected of a publishing editor.

While this *Manual* was struggling to emerge, another battle was being waged. Kathy Armstrong, who had followed with a lively interest work on all the editions of the *Manual*, was fighting her own battle with a courage and fortitude that none of her family or friends will ever forget. This edition is dedicated to her memory.

Chris Armstrong, Bronant, Wales, UK
Andy Large, Montreal, Quebec, Canada
September 2000

Acknowledgements

We should like to acknowledge the support of the various information providers and services who have kindly given permission to reproduce their content in the third edition of the *Manual of Online Search Strategies*. Copyright over all figures and searches remains with the individual producers.

Chapter 1

Search strategies: some general considerations

Chris Armstrong and Andrew Large

The subsequent chapters in the *Manual of Online Search Strategies* discuss in detail the strategies that can successfully be used to retrieve digitized information in a wide range of subject areas. However, more general topics common to all areas are assembled in this opening chapter, rather than being duplicated throughout the book. The objective here, then, is to provide introductory comments on the users of information systems – the information seekers – and the variety of technologies that can now be used to offer digitized information to those seekers. It also reminds seekers that the same database may differ in content or structure from platform to platform or even from vendor to vendor. Subsequent chapters discuss the specific indexing characteristics of many databases; in this chapter some general points are made about the relative merits of searching on assigned controlled terms as against natural-language terms as found in the database documents themselves. The interface to any retrieval system is a crucial determinant both of user satisfaction and success, so interface design criteria are very briefly reviewed. Finally, the chapter discusses the important topics of search and database evaluation.

Information seekers

There is a tendency to discuss information seekers as if they are a homogeneous group. In reality, of course, each seeker is an individual who brings to the workstation a particular set of personal characteristics, subject knowledge and retrieval skills as well as a unique information need; all of these influence the search outcome. Nevertheless, it is both practical and useful to sort them into categories according to certain broadly defined characteristics.

The most common characteristic relates to the seekers' level of experience in information retrieval. Applying this measure, seekers can broadly be categorized as novice or experienced. Unfortunately, no generally accepted criteria have been formulated to assist in this distinction. Borgman (1996) suggests that an information seeker requires three layers of knowledge:

- conceptual – to convert an information need into a searchable query
- semantic – to construct a query for a given system
- technical – to enter queries as specific search statements.

An experienced searcher, therefore, would be someone possessing such knowledge and able to implement these three actions. This begs the question, of course, as to *how* such tasks might be assessed and judged as well or badly performed. Hsieh-Yee (1993) offers more specific criteria: novice searchers are non-professional searchers who have little or no search experience and have not taken courses in online searching or attended relevant workshops provided by librarians or system vendors; experienced searchers are professional searchers who have at least one year of search experience and have either taken courses on online searching or attended workshops provided by system vendors. This definition, equating novice with non-professional (or end user) and experienced with professional, suggests that only the latter can become experienced. While user studies do indicate that many non-professionals are not especially effective when searching, it is a sweeping statement to suggest that only professional searchers can attain expertise, and that this is achieved only by taking courses or attending workshops. Extensive information seeking on the World Wide Web, and discussion of this activity in popular magazines and on radio and television, is providing a level of familiarity (if not always expertise) with information retrieval among diverse user groups regardless of formal instruction. Despite the definitional problems, the terms 'novice' and 'experienced' recur in discussions of information seeking.

A related distinguishing characteristic is between an information professional (or information intermediary) – the person who conducts a search on behalf of a client – and an end user – the person who actually wants the information to answer a specific need (as we have just seen, Hsieh-Yee uses this characteristic to distinguish between the novice and the experienced). This distinction was especially valid when most online searching was conducted by intermediaries – librarians or other information specialists – rather than by the actual information requester. Information professionals were considered experienced users, as was generally the case, and end users were novices who conducted searches rarely and with little or no preliminary training (often also true). Much searching is now undertaken by end users – a consequence in large part of simpler retrieval interfaces and a wider range of accessible information on CD-ROM and the World Wide Web.

Information seekers can also be categorized by a variety of other criteria. Do they have a thorough knowledge of the subject in which that search is to be conducted (whether novice or experienced, end user or intermediary)? The subject specialist's search is likely to be different from the non-specialist's because, for example, the former will have a greater awareness of the subject's terminology, and therefore be better placed to select suitable search terms. The specialist should be better at selecting the most suitable sources for the search, which has become increasingly difficult as electronic information resources proliferate. The specialist should also be able to judge the relevance of retrieved information and adjust a search strategy if this seems appropriate.

Many user studies have investigated young adult information seekers in the context of a university library. Most researchers are located in university departments, and the most obvious and accessible subjects for their studies are to be found on their own doorsteps. It would be difficult to argue, however, that university undergraduates necessarily represent a cross-section of information system users in general. More recently, greater interest has been shown in other user groups. A prime example is children, who increasingly use online information systems both in school and from their homes. Do systems that have been designed for adults work just as effectively for children, or do the different cognitive skills and knowledge bases of children demand information systems that have been specially designed with this specific user group in mind? The same might be said of users at the opposite age spectrum. Elderly citizens are likely (for the time being, at least) to be less familiar with computers, to have poorer eyesight and less precise hand movements than their juniors. Should this make a difference, for example, to the kinds of interfaces provided by the OPAC or Web site?

Seekers might also be differentiated by their search objective: are they trying to find absolutely everything that is available on a topic, even if only tangentially linked to it, or only a little information directly on the topic? These distinctions will almost certainly affect the search strategy, and perhaps the choice of database.

Finally, psychological factors such as attitude, motivation and cognitive style can differentiate users (or even the same user on different occasions), although attempts to measure their impact on search outcome have proved far from conclusive. As in other types of human performance, it is extremely difficult reliably to isolate individual characteristics that can then be tested for an effect on searcher performance. Fidel and Soergel (1983), for example, identified over 200 variables that could come into play when investigating searching.

Some studies have failed to find a clear, positive relationship between search experience and search results. Lancaster *et al.* (1994), for example, compared CD-ROM searches on a bibliographic database by graduate student end users and skilled university librarian intermediaries. The librarians were able to find, in total, more relevant records on the database than the students, but a higher percentage of the records retrieved by the students were judged relevant by them. The greatest problem encountered by the students was failure to identify and use all the terms needed to perform a more complete search; they were less successful in identifying synonyms than the librarians. Hsieh-Yee (1993) found, however, that search experience positively affected search behaviour, especially when the experienced searchers had some subject knowledge relevant to the topic of the search. They used more synonyms and tried more combinations of search terms than novices.

Many studies have commented on the positive evaluations typically made by end users of their own search results, and questioned whether such optimism is really justified (see, for example, Lancaster *et al.*, 1994; Martin and Nicholas, 1993). Sanderson (1990) considered that no matter how user-friendly the system, end users need clear directions to help them get the best results; training programmes should emphasize system capabilities and the kind of information that can be obtained, and should include hands-on sessions in which users are taught how to do basic searches.

Technologies

Digital (or electronic) information can now be found using several related, but distinct, technologies. Remote online information systems, accessible via dial-up telecommunication networks (typically only to users who have signed a contract with the system) remain important purveyors of databases. Examples of such systems are DIALOG, DIMDI and STN. The first public demonstration of such an interactive retrieval system was made by the System Development Corporation in 1960, and until the late 1980s these online systems dominated the digital information market.

In the 1980s libraries began to replace their card catalogues with Online Public Access Catalogues (OPACs). Unlike the traditional online systems, whose use was largely confined to information professionals, OPACs were intended for all library users. Another development of the late 1980s was the CD-ROM, an optical rather than a magnetic data storage medium. Although data could not be deleted from or added to a CD-ROM (as is the case with magnetic storage media), the CD-ROM proved to be a cheap and efficient medium for publishing digital information, thereby extending the market from the institutional to the domestic setting. Increasing numbers of CD-ROMs are purchased to be used on home-based personal computers for recreational purposes (in many cases the CD-ROMs contain games rather than 'information' *per se*).

Technology developments have continued into the 1990s. In their early days, CD-ROMs could not be networked, or if this was possible then response times were severely degraded. Institutional exploitation of CD-ROM technology was greatly facilitated by the emergence of networked versions of many CD-ROM titles. CD-ROMs also have been joined by related optical storage devices that greatly extend the quantity of data that can be stored on a single disc (the Digital Video Disc/Digital Versatile Disc or simply DVD-ROM, for example, can accommodate around seven times more data than a CD-ROM); data can now be added to a disc so it is not just read-only (the introduction of CD-R – CD Recordable – for example, allowed institutions or individuals to create their own CDs and therefore to store locally created data on this medium).

Undoubtedly, the most dramatic development of the 1990s, however, has been the rapid growth of the Internet, and especially the World Wide Web that makes statistics outdated by the time they are collected. In late 1999, however, one Web search engine – ALTAVISTA – claimed to index 250 million pages (Notess, 2000) while INKTOMI, in January 2000, had over 1 billion documents in its database, each relating to a unique page (Inktomi, 2000). And not even the largest engines are able to index anything like the entire Web.

Web search engines can either be general, such as AltaVista <URL http://www. altavista.digital.com/> or NORTHERNLight <URL http://www. northernlight.com/>, attempting to provide access to the Web as a whole, or specialized, such as AL IDRISI <URL http://www.alidrisi.com> (in this case, Arabic-language pages) or WAITER.COM <URL http://www.waiter.com/cgi-bin/SCMMOS/RegSys/AutoRegHome.cgi> dealing with take-out food delivery. An increasing number of search engines cover a specific country or region, such as SearchUK <URL http://www.searchuk.com/> or NZ EXPLORER <URL http://nzexplorer.co.nz/> (for over 250 000 Web pages in New Zealand).

At the other extreme, meta search engines like DogPile <URL http://www. dogpile.com/index.html> or MetaCrawler <URL http://www.metacrawler.com/ index.html>, search simultaneously on multiple regular search engines (useful because no single engine, including the very largest general ones, in practice indexes more than a part of the entire Web). Hock (1999) advises that these meta-engines are most useful when searching for a single, very rare word or when it is not important that all the relevant records are found (because most of the meta-engines only return between ten and 30 pages from each target engine, and do not employ sophisticated search syntax such as Boolean term matching, even if the user enters them),

Web search engines should be distinguished from Web directories, the best known of which is YAHOO! (see Figure 1.1). These directories provide hierarchical menus of subjects that can be used to narrow a search, but will only give access to a fraction of the Web.

The Web has made digital information an everyday fact of life for millions of people across the globe. In part, it has provided an alternative platform for the kinds of databases that previously were only found on traditional online systems, OPACs or CD-ROMs. But it has also extended the type of information that can be accessed digitally by enabling practically any institution or individual to create a Web site from which information can be disseminated around the world. Virtual libraries such as the AUSTRALIAN BIOLOGICAL RESEARCH NETWORK (ABREN) Virtual Library <URL http://abren.csu.edu.au/abren/library/Organisation.html> and gateways such as the SOCIAL SCIENCE INFORMATION GATEWAY (SOSIG) <URL http://sosig.ac.uk/> are just two examples (see Figures 1.2 and 1.3).

It is interesting to see these changes mirrored in the various editions of the *Manual of Online Search Strategies*. The first edition, appearing in 1988, was confined to traditional dial-up online systems. By the second edition, in 1992, CD-ROMs also occupied a prominent place in most of the chapters. The most casual perusal of this third edition will reveal the central role now being played by the World Wide Web, alongside traditional online systems and CD-ROMs.

Many databases are now available on more than one technology – dial-up online system, CD-ROM and the Web, as well as other possibilities such as diskette or magnetic tape – and from more than one supplier. For example, the MEDLINE database is found on several online systems (including LEXIS-NEXIS, OCLC FirstSearch, Ovid Online, DIALOG, DataStar, and STN), as CD-ROMs from, for example, SilverPlatter, and in at least two Web versions (PubMed

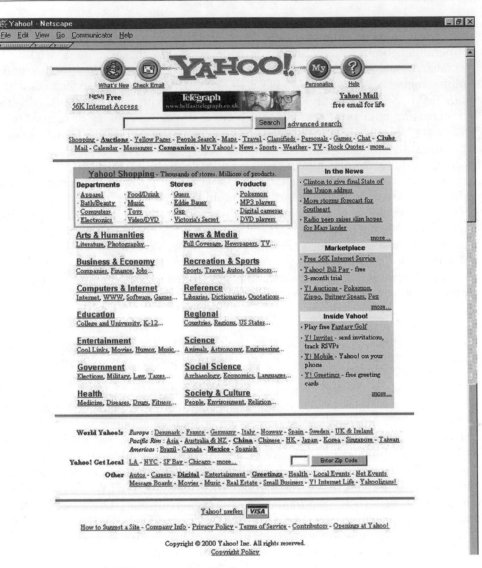

Figure 1.1   Opening directory on YAHOO!

and INTERNET GRATEFUL MED), as well as being available on tape for local installation. Some database producers, such as the National Library of Medicine, have long made their products available themselves over dial-up routes or on CD-ROM; the Web has encouraged many more, like the Institute for Scientific Information (ISI), to follow suit.

When a database is available via several technologies, how should a choice between them be made? Both the traditional online systems and the World Wide Web require the use of a data transmission network to connect the user's workstation with the database server. Response times can be variable depending

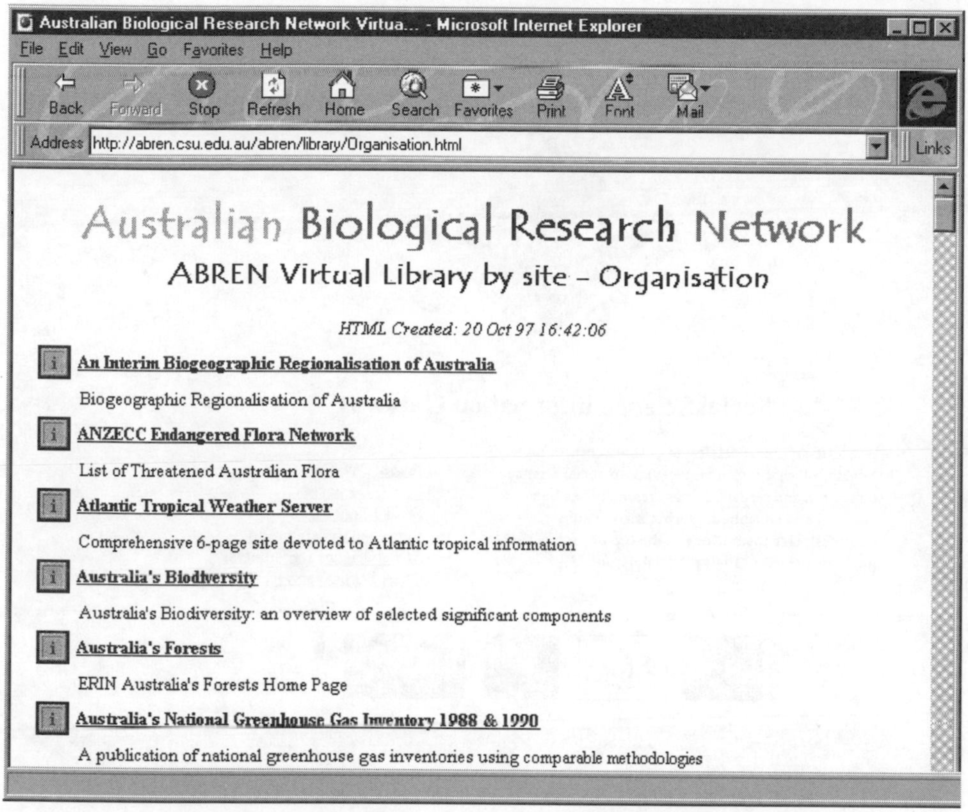

Figure 1.2   **Excerpt from the opening screen of the AUSTRALIAN BIOLOGICAL RESEARCH NETWORK**

on network use (for example, from Europe the use of North American-based hosts tends to be faster in the morning – when most North Americans are in bed rather than hunched over their computers – than in the afternoon or early evening). The use of graphics on Web versions of databases can enhance database content compared with traditional online versions, but also slow down data transmission. CD-ROMs and leased tapes (as well as OPAC searching within the OPAC's home library) normally eliminate the need for long-distance data transmission.

Although interface dialogue modes – command languages, menus of various kinds, and direct manipulation or an object-oriented interface (an interface that provides a visual environment for the dialogue between user and computer) – are not strictly related to individual technologies, in practice command searching has been associated with traditional systems, whereas menus and direct manipulation techniques have been more common with CD-ROMs and now the Web. Vendors such as The Dialog Corporation do offer menus on their traditional online version as well as commands, and commands on their Web version as well as menus, but experienced command-mode users may still find the online version preferable to the Web version because it is easier to view the search developing in a linear

Figure 1.3   SOCIAL SCIENCE INFORMATION GATEWAY (SOSIG)

sequence (although it must be conceded that familiarity also plays a big part – searchers who have learned their skills in one mode will tend to cling to it through habit and familiarity).

Pricing structures differ between the various platforms, which in turn can encourage somewhat different search strategies. Traditionally the online systems charged largely according to connect time – the duration of a search from an initial system log-on to a final system log-off. This pricing structure placed a premium on short searches, which in turn favoured experienced, professional searchers who could quickly find the desired information, and a command-driven interface which in the hands of such an experienced searcher is faster than a menu-driven or even a direct manipulation interface. In contrast, CD-ROMs incurred no incremental costs when a search was undertaken. Like a book or a serial, the CD-ROM was obtained either by direct purchase or by subscription independently of the number of times used. CD-ROMs were therefore more hospitable to novice or occasional searchers and could employ user-friendly menus even if these proved much slower than commands. Although Web searching does involve a connect charge (in the form of a charge for an agreed number of hours connect time over a given period of time – typically a month), this is so small in practice as to be largely or entirely discounted, and therefore, as with CD-ROM searching, professional expertise is less needed. In the case of certain vendors that offer Web services, such as DIALOG, a connect charge is incurred to the vendor as well as the Internet provider. Such connect time, however, is only measured when the host computer is actually occupied with the search; as the client workstation logs on and off the host server, the counter is switched on and off, thus allowing the searcher to pause for thought within a search at no connect cost – a luxury never afforded by the traditional online systems.

A major drawback with the CD-ROM is that its data cannot be updated except by issuing a new disc. A new CD-ROM disc cannot really be updated more frequently than every three months or so. This poses no problems for databases containing rather static information that does not require frequent updating, such as encyclopedias. Where more regular updating is required – monthly, weekly, daily or even real-time – online and Web services have a clear advantage. For example, someone searching to establish whether a particular invention has already been patented will want to ensure that the database is as up-to-date as possible (Volume II, Chapter 2). For this reason, a CD-ROM may be searched for retrospective information, but its online equivalent searched for the most recent updates. Increasingly, hybrid CD-ROMs are appearing that allow an initial disc search to be updated from a dial-up online or Web connection. Examples include Microsoft's ENCARTA and World Books' MULTIMEDIA ENCYCLOPEDIA.

Dial-up online systems and CD-ROM search engines typically offer similar options: Boolean term matching, stem truncation (usually only right-handed – masking the end of the word so that all words beginning with that word stem will be found – although DIMDI also offers left-hand – to find all words *ending* in the search term), embedded truncation (to mask letters within words in order, for example, to find both 'woman' and 'women'), adjacency (or proximity) searching (to locate words next to or close to each other as phrases), and field searching. Increasingly, the Web search engines are also providing these features, although fields are much less formally defined on a typical Web page. One advantage that remains with the online systems is the ability to store and re-use if necessary sets retrieved earlier in the search, although some Web interfaces to an existing online service (for example, Ovid) also now offer this option. The Web search engines offer an additional feature – ranking of retrieved documents. Whereas the online systems and CD-ROMs have normally displayed any retrieved data records in chronological sequence – the last ones to have been added to the database in any retrieved set will be the first displayed on the screen – Web engines attempt to rank by probable relevancy (to the initial query) the most relevant retrieved documents being displayed first. Such ranking typically relies on various techniques such as word frequency occurrences in the query, the retrieved documents and the Web as a whole (Stanley, 1997), location of words on the page and the number of links to the page.

The World Wide Web, with its intra- and interdocument hypertext links, provides a navigational tool that facilitates database browsing in contrast to database searching. Boolean-driven retrieval systems are not hospitable to browsing. They are designed to divide a database into two parts – one that contains those records matching the search statement, and the other which contains all the other non-matching records in the database. Yet many users do not begin with such a clear view of their information requirements that they can formulate a sharp search statement. For these users it can prove very productive to browse the database (or a part of it), looking for potentially interesting material. Hypertext allows this to take place. The danger in such systems, as exemplified by the Web, is that the browser becomes disorientated – lost, so to speak – in a tangle of linked sites. Navigational aids such as the back, forward, bookmark and search history facilities on a Web browser are intended to minimize such problems.

Traditional online systems, unlike CD-ROMs or the Web, cannot provide multimedia graphics, still images, video, animation, or sound clips. Such graphic capabilities are invaluable in many information fields.

Database differences between vendors

This diversity of delivery leads to a very important observation, and one that is explored much more fully in the following chapters: database content and/or structure can differ from one medium to another, or one vendor to another. It is therefore important that the user be aware of the different configurations of the same database title that might be encountered in the market.

Tenopir and Hover (1993) have established seven criteria by which to compare differences between the same database mounted by different vendors:

- The first criterion is update frequency. INSPEC, for example, was then updated weekly on Orbit but bi-weekly on DataStar; PSYCINFO was updated quarterly on the SilverPlatter CD-ROM but monthly by several online vendors.
- Second, database time coverage can vary. CAB ABSTRACTS was then available from DIALOG since 1972 but on DataStar only since 1984.
- Third, pricing formulae for the same database can vary greatly: connect time, flat fee charge, payment per retrieved record, and so on.
- Fourth, a database may be searchable as one big file or as several files. MEDLINE, for example, was then available on DIALOG as one huge file (and therefore easier to search in its entirety), while on NLM it was broken down by date into several separate files (making it therefore easier to search for, say, records only appearing in the most recent few years).
- Fifth, database content can vary. For example, although the CHEMICAL ABSTRACTS database is available on several online systems, only the version on STN includes abstracts as well as the bibliographical citation. Dissertations are to be found in the online versions of PSYCINFO, but not on the PSYCLIT CD-ROM equivalent. A full-text omnibus news database may include items from different source publications in its various versions; if a vendor already offers a newspaper title as a separate database, then records from that paper may not be added to the omnibus version carried by that vendor.

- Sixth, value-added support features like online thesauri, document delivery, cross-file searching and so on, will not be available from all vendors.
- Seventh, records in the same database may be structured and indexed differently by various vendors.

On the Web, the search engines index pages according to different principles as well as offering different search capabilities. For example, ALTAVISTA, EXCITE and NORTHERNLIGHT attempt to index every page on a site while INFOSEEK, LYCOS and WEBCRAWLER only index sample pages. Several offer truncation, but WEBCRAWLER and LYCOS, for example, do not. Sullivan (1998) has compiled useful comparative data for seven major search engines, and Hock (1999) offers tips on searching eight major Web engines.

Controlled versus natural-language searching

Many databases continue to offer the information seeker a choice between conducting a search using the words found in the records themselves – titles, abstracts or complete texts – or using index terms that describe the content of the record while not necessarily using the natural-language words found within it. In most cases such index terms have been assigned by a human indexer and have been chosen from a list of controlled terms representing the subject area of the particular database. Web sites (other than those few that contain organized databases which utilize controlled vocabulary) do not include controlled index terms, although in some instances the site creator may have added metadata at the beginning of the document, which can include uncontrolled keywords that seek to encapsulate its content. As this is not uniformly or exclusively used by search engines for indexing purposes it is currently of questionable benefit. Furthermore, an unscrupulous site developer can deliberately add keywords of little or no relevance to the site's content just so as to attract users (a practice termed 'spamming'). The absence of indexing on most Web sites is considered by many information professionals, at least, as a grave weakness and one reason why large numbers of irrelevant documents are so often retrieved in a Web search.

When a database does offer the choice between a search on the natural-language terms found within the records themselves, and a search limited only to the index terms assigned to those records (often called descriptors), which option should the searcher choose? Natural-language searching offers the opportunity to search for the actual words and phrases employed by the author. It also provides more words on which to search, as typically a record will not be assigned more than a handful of descriptors whereas the words in a full-text article may number in the thousands. In subject areas where the vocabulary is volatile, controlled vocabulary cannot keep pace with change; only by searching on natural language can the latest terminology be applied.

From the database producer's point of view, indexing is an expensive proposition. The benefits therefore must be considerable to justify the extra work

Title	Journal	Issue	London (Eng)	Fires	Subways	Fires-Great Britain	Great Britain
UK police doubt arson caused fatal subway fire	Calgary Herald	Nov 21,1987	■	■	■		
Reports say (London) subway fire warnings were ignored	Calgary Herald	Nov 22,1987	■	■	■		
Full inquiry ordered into (London subway) tragedy	Calgary Herald	Nov 20,1987	■	■	■		
Fire safety on subway questioned	Globe and Mail	Nov 20,1987	■	■	■		
Swift spread of flames in station baffles London subway officals	Globe and Mail	Nov 20,1987	■	■	■		
London subway bans smoking, tobacco ads	Globe and Mail	Nov 25,1987	■	■	■		
Raging fire claims 32 in (London) subway	Calgary Herald	Nov 19,1987	■	■	■		
Police don't suspect arson in subway fire	Montreal Gazette	Nov 21,1987	■	■	■		
"Coctail" of gases suspected in subway fire	Globe and Mail	Nov 21,1987	■	■	■		
35 killed, 80 hurt in UK subway fire	Globe and Mail	Nov 19,1987	■		■		
Killer fire (in London subway) sparks ban on smoking	Calgary Herald	Nov 25,1987			■		
Subway inferno kills 32:"catastrophe" strikes London underground	Halifax Chronicle Herald	Nov 19,1987	■				
(London) subway fire inquiry announced	Winnipeg Free Press	Nov 20,1987	■	■	■		
Britain to hold public inquiry into subway fire that killed 30	Montreal Gazette	Nov 20,1987	■	■	■		
32 dead in London subway blaze	Montreal Gazette	Nov 19,1987	■	■	■		
Escalator carried commuters into inferno of flames, smoke	Toronto Star	Nov 19,1987	■	■	■		
UK fire chief says blaze began on subway escalator	Toronto Star	Nov 20,1987	■	■	■		
Escalator problems cited in subway fire	Toronto Star	Nov 21,1987	■	■	■		
Flaming horror in London subway (King's Cross)	Macleans	Nov 30,1987			■	■	■
An inferno in the London Underground	Newsweek	Nov 30,1987			■	■	■
Escalator to an inferno: panic and death in London's Underground	Time	Nov 30,1987			■	■	■
Total occurrence of each descriptor			17	15	20	3	3

Source: Jacsó (1992). Reproduced by permission.
Figure 1.4   Failure of controlled language

involved in preparing the database. The greatest advantage offered by indexing is the control that it imposes over the inconsistencies and redundancies in natural language. The synonyms (and near synonyms) so frequently encountered in all languages can be represented by just one index term, thus removing the searcher's need to enter all possible synonyms in order to be certain that the actual word used by the author has been entered. A few carefully chosen controlled terms can also summarize the main subjects dealt with in a record, thereby allowing the searcher to find records that are central to a particular subject rather than minor referents (the words chosen for the title may also accomplish this objective, but titles, especially in the humanities and social sciences, are not always descriptive of the actual content). A list of controlled terms may also be very helpful to a searcher who is unfamiliar with the subject area of the database and finds it difficult to formulate a search unaided using natural-language terms. Controlled terms from a well-organized thesaurus can help with hierarchical or generic searches. For example, someone looking for information on dogs might expect that all records dealing with individual breeds will have been indexed with the generically higher term 'dogs'; a natural-language search, to be comprehensive, might have to include the names of individual breeds in case the authors themselves only mentioned the breed and not the species. Of course, if the searcher opts for controlled language then confidence is placed in the reliability and the consistency of the database's indexers. It is not an easy task to take an article and determine which, say, ten terms from a controlled list should be chosen to represent the subject matter of the article. Figure 1.4 shows that controlled languages are still at the mercy of the human indexer.

Interfaces

Most of the interfaces discussed in the following chapters rely on graphical devices: windows, pull-down and pop-up menus, buttons and icons. A dwindling number of CD-ROMs and OPACs, as well as traditional online systems, rely on non-graphical, DOS-based interfaces. Shneiderman (1998) lists several benefits for the user of graphical interfaces:

- control over the system
- ease of learning the system
- enjoyment
- encouragement to explore system features.

At the same time, unless designed with some care, graphic devices can seem little more than gimmicks, and their initial novelty value can soon dissipate. Furthermore, users unfamiliar with graphical interfaces can find them confusing and forbidding. It is all too easy to produce cluttered and confusing screens containing too much visual information. Careful screen layout, restrained use of colour and consistency in the application of graphical devices will all help to produce an effective, rather than a baffling, interface. Many guides to sound interface design are available (see, for example, Galitz, 1997; Mandel, 1997; Shneiderman, 1998), but unfortunately, as in other areas of human endeavour, it is often easier to propose, than to follow, guidelines. Head (1997) provides a useful discussion of graphical interfaces specifically directed at online information services.

Search evaluation

The *Manual of Online Search Strategies* provides guidance on how to conduct most effectively searches for information in a variety of subject areas. It is therefore important to discuss how a successful search might be measured, so as to differentiate it from an unsuccessful search. How can search performance be evaluated?

The first large-scale tests of information retrieval systems began in the late 1950s at the Cranfield College of Aeronautics in England. The Cranfield Projects employed two measurements for an information retrieval system: recall and precision. The assumption behind these measures is that the average user wants to retrieve large amounts of relevant materials (producing high recall) while simultaneously rejecting a large proportion of irrelevant materials (producing high precision).

Recall and precision

Recall is a measure of effectiveness in retrieving all the sought information in a database – that is, in search comprehensiveness. A search would achieve perfect recall if every single record that should be found in relation to a specific query is indeed traced. It is normally expressed in proportional terms. The recall ratio in any search can theoretically be improved by finding more and more records; in fact, 100 per cent recall can always be achieved by retrieving every single record in the database, including all the irrelevant alongside the relevant ones, although this defeats the purpose of a retrieval system. Clearly, a parallel measure is required to work alongside recall, which will take account of the false hits produced. This measure is called precision. It assesses the accuracy of a search – that is, the extent to which the search finds only those records that should be found, leaving aside all records that are not wanted. A search would achieve perfect precision if every single record retrieved in relation to a specific query were indeed relevant to that query. Precision, like recall, is normally expressed in proportional terms.

The Cranfield tests found an inverse relationship between recall and precision. As attempts are made to increase one, the other tends to decline: higher recall can only be achieved at the expense of a reduction in precision. As a strategy is implemented to retrieve more and more relevant records there is a tendency also to retrieve growing numbers of irrelevant records; recall is improved but precision worsened. As a strategy is implemented to eliminate irrelevant records there is a tendency also to eliminate relevant ones; precision is improved but recall worsened. There is a common sense logic to this inverse relationship that has been demonstrated in many, but not all, evaluation tests.

Criticisms of recall and precision measures

Despite the widespread use of recall and precision as measures of search effectiveness, a number of criticisms can be made. First, recall and precision offer an incomplete evaluation of information retrieval, at least from the average searcher's point of view. Searchers may want to maximize both recall and precision, but what about other factors such as the expense involved in completing the search, the amount of time taken, and the ease of conducting it? A retrieval system might give impressive recall and precision ratios yet be costly, slow and frustrating.

Secondly, recall depends on the assumption that a user wishes to find as many relevant records as possible. In practice, users may not always want a search that finds everything, but instead opt for a search that retrieves just a few highly relevant items. In such cases, precision alone is the only measure of retrieval effectiveness. Many Web searchers, for example, are likely to find themselves in this situation; high recall in many cases will simply overwhelm the searcher.

Thirdly, to measure recall it is necessary to know the total number of relevant records in the database, retrieved and not retrieved. But how can the number of relevant non-retrieved records in the database be established? In the case of the very small test databases sometimes used for evaluation experiments, it is feasible to examine all the documents and thus to determine which are, and which are not, relevant to any particular search query. Considerable doubt has been expressed, however, about the validity of extrapolating search results from these test databases to the much larger databases typically encountered in real searches. The constantly changing content on the Web, as well as the vast size of the 'database', make recall measurement especially problematic. Clarke and Willett (1997) have proposed, however, a methodology for measuring recall, as well as precision, in order to evaluate the effectiveness of search engines.

The most serious criticisms of precision and recall measures, however, concern the reliability of the crucial concept underlying both – relevance. How is relevance to be determined, and by whom? Experimentally, relevance judgements have typically been based on a match between the subject content – the 'aboutness' – of a retrieved record and the initial query that stimulated the search. In the Cranfield tests, for example, the subject content of the query and the subject content of the records were compared by subject experts to decide whether a retrieved record was relevant or not. Many searches are now conducted by end users and not, as in earlier days, by information intermediaries. This means that the person judging the retrieved results as they are displayed is the ultimate user of the information, who may bring various subjective elements into play. A bibliographic record, for example, might be judged relevant on the basis of its author, the series in which it appears, its recency, local availability and so on, as well as on its subject content. On the other hand, would a retrieved document that the seeker has already read be considered relevant, even if directly related to the subject? Lancaster and Warner (1993) prefer to distinguish between relevance and a related concept – pertinence. They define pertinence as the relationship between a document and a request, based on the subjective decision of the person with the information need. They argue that pertinence decisions are essential to the evaluation of operating (rather than trial) information retrieval systems serving real users who have real information needs. Harter (1992) proposes the term 'psychological relevance' for records that suggest new cognitive connections, fruitful analogies, insightful metaphors or an increase/decrease in the strength of a belief. He argues that records about a topic may in fact prove less important to the user than relevant records which are not on the topic but that allow new intellectual connections to be made or cause other cognitive changes in the user. Furthermore, he believes that such a view of psychological relevance is inconsistent with the notion and utility of fixed relevance judgements and with traditional retrieval testing as exemplified by the Cranfield tests and their successors.

Nevertheless, most information retrieval experts do agree that subject aboutness is still the principal criterion used in judging relevance. A search system can only be judged in terms of whether it is able to match the user's information need as expressed in the search strategy with the stored data. The additional facility to screen out from the retrieved records those that the user has already read may well be a highly valuable feature, but the failure of a system to undertake this extra step cannot reasonably be invoked to judge the performance of the system at *retrieving* relevant information.

Another problem with relevancy is that judgements about one record may be influenced by other records that have already been examined. After examining nine totally irrelevant documents, a tenth one might be considered relevant, but had this tenth record been viewed after seeing nine highly relevant ones it might have been judged irrelevant. This emphasizes, of course, the binary nature of relevancy judgements for recall and precision purposes: there is no place for the fairly relevant, or the marginally relevant, or even the extremely relevant. A record is accepted as relevant or rejected as irrelevant.

Spink and Greisdorf (1997) argue that researchers should question the assumption that users always even need the most highly relevant items. At the outset of an information-seeking process a user's information problem is often ill-defined. The retrieved items considered highly relevant may well provide users with what they already know: as they are likely to equate strongly with the current state of the user's information problems, they may only reinforce the current state of the information problem. Items that are only 'partially relevant' may then play a greater role in shifting the user's thinking about the information problem, providing new information that leads the user in new directions towards the ultimate resolution of the information problem.

Unfortunately, the critics of recall/precision measures are unable to proffer any alternative quantitative evaluation technique. Yet everyone does agree that the ability to evaluate information retrieval is crucial. All this suggests that recall and precision ratios as reported in experimental studies should be treated as relative, rather than absolute, indicators. The measures of recall and precision based on estimates of relevance remain valid evaluation parameters even if their precise measurement in experimental studies is problematic. In evaluating strategies and reacting to preliminary results during an interactive search, for example, the concepts of recall and precision are extremely useful to help the searcher decide on strategy adjustments. A small number of hits may suggest a need to broaden the search to improve recall, even if this adversely affects precision. A search with higher recall but a large percentage of irrelevant records is a prime target for strategy adjustments to improve precision, even if at the expense of lower recall.

Making judgements during a search on the relevance of intermediate results and then using these judgements to revise the search strategy is termed 'relevance feedback'. Some information retrieval systems do not simply rely on the searcher to initiate such feedback. The system itself may automatically search, for example, to find more records that share index terms with records already retrieved and judged relevant by the user.

Database evaluation

No matter how sophisticated is the information seeker or powerful the retrieval system, the resulting information from a search will ultimately depend on the database quality: the accuracy, completeness, authority and currency of its information, and the reliability of its indexing. Unfortunately, database quality cannot be taken for granted. Information stored in electronic format is inherently no more nor less reliable or accurate than other kinds of information. A few years ago, when much electronic information had been transcribed at the keyboard from hard copy originals, many typographical errors were detected in all kinds of databases. These errors not only affected data use but also data retrieval; only by similarly misspelling the term in the search would the record containing the misspelled word be found. More data are now generated at the outset electronically, and scanning equipment is more reliable, but errors are still to be found in databases.

Technically, electronic data can be updated more easily and quickly than, say, printed information. Many databases are updated monthly, weekly, daily or even in real time. Nevertheless, it should not be assumed that electronic information is always current. A number of online encyclopaedias, for example, contain data long since superseded even by print sources. Typically, online or Web-based sources are updated more frequently than CD-ROM or print equivalents (if these also exist), but occasionally technical problems have reversed this dictum.

The Internet, in particular, has highlighted the problems of data reliability. There is no umbrella organization to ensure data accuracy, currency or consistency, or to vouch for the authority of the data. Now that anyone can create a Web site there is no longer an established publishing process to ensure some kind of quality control through, for example, market pressures or academic refereeing. It can be difficult to assess the validity of much data available on the Web, although some search engines claim to exercise judgement when deciding whether

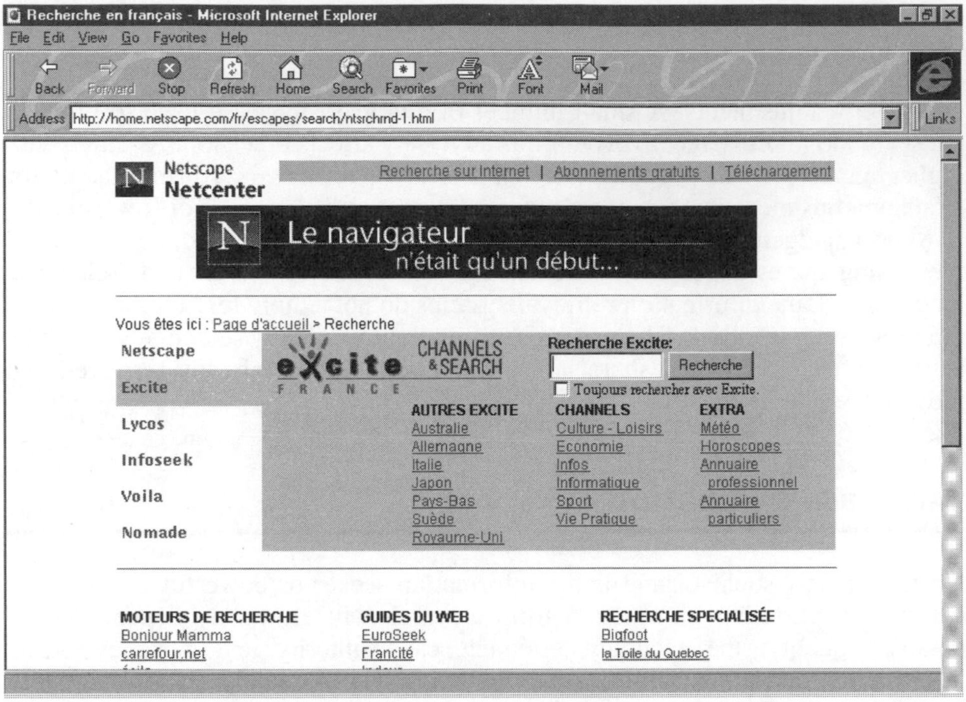

Figure 1.5   French-language interface to EXCITE

or not to provide access to sites from their hierarchical indexes, and some provide evaluation scores based on an assessment of 'quality'. The ephemeral nature of much Web material also means that what can be found today may have vanished or been transformed by tomorrow. In Volume I, Chapter 5 on the biosciences, for example, Frank Kellerman cites the example of the GENOME database from Johns Hopkins School of Medicine which had a short-lived life on the Web before being withdrawn. The ephemeral nature of much Web content is now posing very considerable bibliographic problems.

Although the Web is dominated by English-language information, pages in other languages are now being added proportionately faster than the English-language sites. Many problems remain in accessing, on the Web, information in a language unknown to the searcher (Large and Moukdad, 2000) but the reality of a truly worldwide service, free from language barriers, is getting a little closer. The provision, by many Web search engines, of interfaces in languages other than English, for example, is a welcome sign. Figure 1.5 shows the French-language interface from EXCITE. It is now possible to input search terms in other languages and to confine the resulting search either to sites in that language or to sites originating in a country using that language. ALTAVISTA goes one step further by allowing a search term in one language to be translated automatically into the corresponding term in a second language (although currently only between

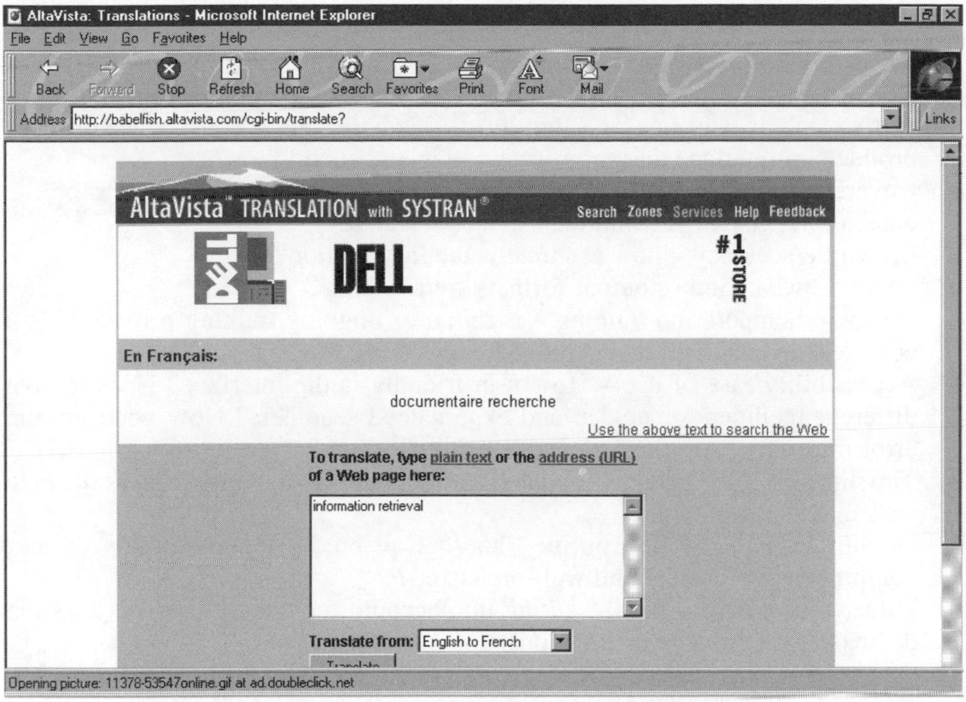

Figure 1.6   SYSTRAN translation software on ALTAVISTA

English, on the one hand, and French, German, Italian, Portuguese or Spanish on the other) prior to a Web search. In Figure 1.6 the term 'information retrieval' has been translated into French by SYSTRAN, the machine translation software employed by ALTAVISTA: the correct French phrase requires an inversion of word order from the English original: 'recherche documentaire' rather than 'documentaire recherche' as SYSTRAN has it (although this does not matter in a Web search unless the two words are to be searched together as a phrase).

The recurrent issues concerning pornography and hate literature further complicate discussions concerning Internet content. This is likely to prove especially controversial where certain user groups, and especially children, are involved. Some libraries have experimented with various proprietary site-blocking software, but the results generally prove unsatisfactory, failing to block some material deemed unacceptable while excluding other material to which exception is not taken.

Evaluation criteria

Evaluation criteria for databases have been proposed by a number of authors, and there is a large measure of agreement about these. One influential evaluation checklist was formulated in 1990 by the Southern California Online User Group (Basch, 1990):

- Consistency – does the database maintain consistency in coverage, currency and so on? If it is one of a family of databases, how consistent are these products in interface design, update policy and such like?
- Coverage/scope – does the coverage/scope match the stated aims of the database; is coverage comprehensive or selective?
- Error rate/accuracy – how accurate is the information?
- Output – what kind of output formats are available?
- Customer support and training – is initial or ongoing training provided? Is a help desk available during suitable hours?
- Accessibility/ease of use – How user-friendly is the interface? Does it have different facilities for novice and experienced searchers? How good are the error messages? Are they context-sensitive?
- Timeliness – is the database updated as frequently as it claims, and as the data warrant?
- Documentation – is online and/or printed documentation clear, comprehensive, current and well-organized?
- Value to cost ratio – finally, taking into account the above features, does the database give good value for money?

Anagnostelis and Cooke (1997) propose somewhat more detailed evaluation criteria to be applied to Web-based databases – in this case, specifically for comparison of various MEDLINE database services on the Web:

- authority of the service provider as well as the database
- content – coverage and currency
- retrieval mechanism – general search features, free-text searching, natural-language queries, thesaurus searching, command searching, display and output
- ease of interface use
- unique features
- help and user support.

Similar evaluation criteria can be found in Tenopir and Hover (1993) who specifically discuss comparison of the same database available on different systems, and from the Organising Medical Networked Information (OMNI) Consortium (1997), which is involved, among other tasks, with the evaluation of MEDLINE Services on the Web. The SOCIAL SCIENCE INFORMATION GATEWAY has prepared a detailed list of criteria used by various eLib Gateway projects (including OMNI as well as SOSIG itself), while Bartelstein and Zald (1997), and Tillman (1997) also provide valuable insights. A longer discussion can be found in Cooke (1999).

References

Anagnostelis, B. and Cooke, A. (1997), 'Evaluation criteria for different versions of the same database – a comparison of Medline services available via the World Wide Web', *Online Information '97: Proceedings of the 21st International Online Information Meeting, London, 9–11 December 1997*, Oxford: Learned Information, 165–179.

Bartelstein, A. and Zald, A. (1997), *Unwired R545: Teaching Students to Think Critically about Internet Resources: A Workshop for Faculty and Staff.* Available at <URL http://weber.u.washington.edu/~libr560/NETEVAL/index.html>.

Basch, R. (1990), 'Measuring the quality of data: report of the Fourth Annual SCOUG Retreat', *Database Searcher,* **6** (8), 18–23.

Borgman, C. L. (1996), 'Why are online catalogs still hard to use?', *Journal of the American Society for Information Science,* **47** (7), 493–503.

Clarke, S. J. and Willett, P. (1997), 'Estimating the recall performance of Web search engines', *Aslib Proceedings,* **49** (7), 184–189.

Cooke, A. (1999), *A Guide to Finding Quality Information on the Internet: Selection and Evaluation Strategies*, London: Library Association Publishing.

Fidel, R. and Soergel, D. (1983), 'Factors affecting online bibliographic retrieval: a conceptual framework for research', *Journal of the American Society for Information Science,* **34** (3), 163–180.

Galitz, W. O. (1997), *Essential Guide to User Interface Design: An Introduction to GUI Design Principles and Techniques*, New York: Wiley.

Harter, S. P. (1992), 'Psychological relevance and information science', *Journal of the American Society for Information Science,* **43** (9), 602–615.

Head, A. J. (1997), 'A question of interface design: how do online service GUIs measure up?', *Online* **21** (3), 20–29.

Hock, R. (1999), *The Extreme Searcher's Guide to Web Search Engines: A Handbook for the Serious Searcher*, Medford, NJ: CyberAge Books. Updated at <URL http://www.onstrat.com/engines/>.

Hsieh-Yee, I. (1993), 'Effects of search experience and subject knowledge on the search tactics of novice and experienced searchers', *Journal of the American Society for Information Science,* **44** (3), 161–174.

Inktomi (2000), Inktomi WebMap. Available at <URL http://www.inktomi.com/webmap/>.

Jacsó, P. (1992), *CD-ROM Software, Dataware and Hardware: Evaluation, Selection, and Installation*, Englewood, Colorado: Libraries Unlimited.

Lancaster, F. W., Elzy, C., Zeter, M .J., Metzler, L. and Low, Y. M. (1994), 'Searching databases on CD-ROM: comparison of the results of end-user searching with results from two modes of searching by skilled intermediaries', *RQ,* **33** (3), 370–386.

Lancaster, F. W. and Warner, A. J. (1993), *Information Retrieval Today*, Arlington: Information Resources.

Large, A. and Moukdad, H. (2000), 'Multilingual access to Web resources: an overview', *Program*, **34** (1), 43–58.

Mandel, T. (1997), *The Elements of User Interface Design*, New York: Wiley.

Martin, H. and Nicholas, D. (1993), 'End-users coming of age? Six years of end-user searching at the Guardian', *Online and CDROM Review,* **17** (2), 83–89.

Notess, G.R. (2000), *Search Engine Statistics: Database Total Size Estimates.* Available at <URL http://www.notess.com/searchstats/sizeest.shtml>.

OMNI Consortium. (1997), *Medline on the Internet.* Available at <URL http://www.omni.ac.uk/general-info/internet_medline.html>.

Sanderson, R. M. (1990), 'The continuing saga of professional end-users: law students search Dialog at the University of Florida', *Online,* **14** (6), 64–69.

Shneiderman, B. (1998), *Designing the User Interface: Strategies for Effective Human–Computer Interaction*, (3rd edn), Reading: Addison-Wesley.

Social Science Information Gateway (nd), *Quality Selection Criteria for Subject Gateways.* Available at <URL http://sosig.ac.uk/desire/qindex.html>.

Spink, A. and Greisdorf, H. (1997), 'Partial relevance judgements during interactive information retrieval: an exploratory study', in C. Schwartz and M. Rorvig (eds), *ASIS '97: Proceedings of the 60th ASIS Annual Meeting, Washington, D.C., November 1–6, 1997.* Volume 34. Medford: Information Today, 111–122.

Stanley, T. (1997), 'Search engines corner: moving up the ranks', *Ariadne,* **12**. Available at <URL http://www.ariadne.ac.uk/issue12/search-engines/>.

Sullivan, D. (2000), *Search Engine Features for Webmasters.* Available at <URL http://searchenginewatch.com/webmasters/features.html>.

Tenopir, C. and Hover, K. (1993), 'When is the same database not the same? Database differences among systems', *Online,* **17** (4), 20–27.

Tillman, H. N. (1997), *Evaluating Quality on the Net.* Available at <URL http://www.tiac.net/users/hope/findqual.html>.

Chapter 2

Patents

Edlyn S. Simmons

An introduction to patents

Patents reside at the intersection of technology, law and commerce as governmental guarantees that companies and individuals who develop new products and processes may take legal action to prevent others from manufacturing, selling or using their inventions. A patent describes the invention, identifies its owner and specifies the limits of the grant of exclusivity. Thus patents are valuable sources of information about advances in science and technology, about the research interests of businesses and individuals, and about the legal limits to one's own business activities. Patents are uniquely valuable sources of information about the ownership of inventions: inventions that are claimed in patents cannot be used without authorization from the patent owner while the patent is in force. They are invaluable sources of information about technology, and most of the information can be used in research without infringing the patent. They are also rich stores of information about businesses; they identify the areas of research and development activity in industry and thereby facilitate the prediction of market changes.

Patents contain vast stores of practical scientific and engineering information – much of it unique. Research is often missing from the journal literature, for many inventors refuse to teach the world about discoveries that have not been protected by a patent. It is not unusual for corporations to delay submission of manuscripts to scientific journals until after a patent application has been published, and many manuscripts submitted to journals are refused publication because they do not meet a referee's standards of scientific sophistication. Patent applications are published by most countries about 18 months after they are filed. They are subject to screening on the basis of national security considerations in most countries, but they are normally published promptly without any other editing or restriction. As a result, a large share of research and development is described first in patents, or indeed only in patents. By combining the technical information in patents with the names of inventors and corporate patent owners it is possible to track the research and business interests of companies and other institutions. With the addition of legal status information it is also possible to determine which products and processes are being emphasized by competitors and which have been abandoned. Most importantly, of course, patents tell us which products and processes are the exclusive domain of others.

The word 'patent' refers to the grant of patent rights and also to the patent specification – the document that describes the invention. The front page of the specification of US patent 5,046,659 is illustrated in Figure 2.1. A patent is a form of intellectual property. The grant of a patent by a national government gives the owners of the invention the right to exclude others from making, using or selling the item invented and the right to sell or license those rights to others. The property rights are granted for a limited time and are confined to the product or process claimed in the patent specification. Patent rights are limited by the scope of the allowed claims, by the geographical borders of the granting country and by the obligation to pay maintenance fees during the life of the patent. Patent terms are not renewable; they can be extended beyond the statutory expiration date in some countries only under very special circumstances. The owner of a patent has the right to practise the invention only to the extent that he or she does not infringe other patents while doing so. When it is necessary to practise inventions claimed in earlier patents in order to practise the invention claimed in a later patent – for example, to use a patented pigment in a newly patented paint formulation – the earlier patents are said to 'dominate' the invention, and the patent owner must obtain a licence from the owner of the dominating patent to avoid infringement. Patent rights are defended from infringers through civil court suits.

One right that is not conferred by the grant of a patent is a copyright on the patent specification itself. It is the claimed invention that belongs to the patent owner, not the words used to describe it. Governments grant patents in order to encourage innovation and to encourage the spread of knowledge. The right to exclude others is balanced by a requirement that the invention be described fully in a published patent specification. To obtain a patent, the inventors are required to file a patent application that consists of a specification describing the invention, an oath or declaration signed by the applicants and an application fee. The term 'patent application' is commonly used to refer either to the act of applying for a patent or to the text of the patent specification. In most countries, no patent is granted until the application has been examined to determine whether the claimed invention is new, useful and inventive as the terms are understood in the patent laws of that country, but in most countries the patent specification is published before the examination proceedings are begun, usually 18 months after the original filing or priority date.

Published applications are often referred to as 'patents', although many of them never mature into granted patents. Many inventions claimed in patent applications are found to be unpatentable during examination and others are abandoned because they are discovered not to be worth further development. In many countries the application may be abandoned before examination is begun by failing to submit a formal request for examination. Most patent applications that

United States Patent [19]

Warburton

[11] ' **Patent Number:** **5,046,659**

[45] **Date of Patent:** **Sep. 10, 1991**

[54] **LATCHING STRUCTURE FOR FOOD CONTAINER**

[75] Inventor: **Richard T. Warburton,** Canandaigua, N.Y.

[73] Assignee: **Mobil Oil Corporation,** Fairfax, Va.

[21] Appl. No.: **611,576**

[22] Filed: **Nov. 13, 1990**

[51] Int. Cl.^{5} **B65D 1/22**
[52] U.S. Cl. **229/2.500;** 220/4.22;
220/4.23; 220/4.24; 220/339
[58] **Field of Search** .... 229/2.5 R, 2.5 EC;
220/4.1, 4.2, 4.3, 4.21, 4.22, 4.23, 4.24, 306, 339,
315, 352

[56] **References Cited**

U.S. PATENT DOCUMENTS

2,706,065	4/1955	Stone	220/4.21
3,149,747	9/1964	Burgess	220/4.21
3,234,077	2/1966	Reifers et al.	229/2.5 EC
3,565,146	2/1971	Arnolds	220/4.23
3,771,712	11/1973	Richards	229/2.5 EC
4,030,850	6/1977	Hyde	220/306

4,193,496	3/1980	Barratt	206/380
4,333,580	6/1982	Sweigart, Jr.	220/4.21
4,512,474	4/1985	Harding	220/4.23
4,576,330	3/1986	Schepp	229/44

FOREIGN PATENT DOCUMENTS

1117491	2/1982	Canada .	
1418897	12/1974	United Kingdom .	
1602694	11/1981	United Kingdom	220/4.24
2118142	10/1983	United Kingdom	229/2.5 R

Primary Examiner—Stephen P. Garbe
Assistant Examiner—Christopher McDonald
Attorney, Agent, or Firm—Alexander J. McKillop; Charles J. Speciale

[57] **ABSTRACT**

Latching structure for thermoformed plastic containers for food and the like wherein the lid and base of the containers are each provided with mating male and female elongated elements where the locking takes place at the end of the elongated elements rather than along the sides of these elements.

12 Claims, 7 Drawing Sheets

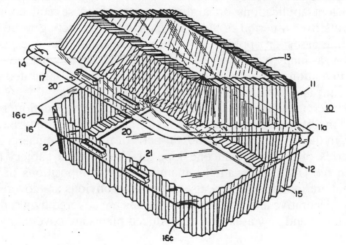

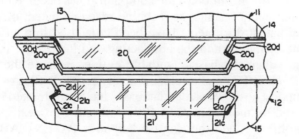

Figure 2.1   US patent no. 5,046,659: front page

do result in granted patents are amended during examination, changing the scope of the claims and even the details of the supporting disclosure. Patent databases commonly index the published application, assuming in doing so that the application contains all of the information that will appear in the issued patent.

Patents have legal effect only within the country that grants them, and each country has its own patent laws which are occasionally amended. There are variations from country to country both in the kinds of invention that may be patented and in the breadth of the claims that are allowed. Differences among the laws of various countries are diminishing as the national patent laws of World Trade Organization member states are amended to conform to the requirements of the General Agreement on Tariffs and Trade (GATT), but most patents now in force were filed before the laws were amended. In some countries, for example, new chemical compounds could not be claimed and are protected by claims directed to methods of synthesis and, in many countries, pharmaceutical agents and methods of treating disease may not be patented. Some countries allow patent claims to be written in broadly generic language, so as to cover embodiments of the claim language that are not exemplified in the patent specification, while other countries restrict the claims to the exemplified species. There is also great variability in the patent office procedures of the various countries. An inventor who files patent applications on a single invention in several countries often obtains patents over a period of several years, each protecting a different claim scope. In some cases, an application will result in more than one patent from a single country, as many patent offices restrict each patent to what they consider to be a single invention, requiring that the original claims be separated into two or more divisional applications. Patent laws in most countries do not permit the applicant to insert new information into a pending patent application, but do allow the filing of modified applications. The resulting documents may be 'patents of addition' or, in the USA, 'continuations-in-part' of the original patent application. Some countries offer more than one kind of patent, each subject to different standards. In the USA, for example, manufactures, compositions of matter and processes that are found to be new, useful and non-obvious are covered by utility patents; new, decorative and non-obvious designs are covered by a separate series of design patents; and new asexually reproduced plants are covered by a series of plant patents.

In the years since the invention of the computer it has become increasingly easy to find information about patents, as machine-readable patent office records and computer-typeset patent documents have been converted into an ever-increasing number of patent databases, and the abstracting and indexing services that index patents have made their databases available online. Because the US Patent and Trademark Office (USPTO) makes electronically readable files of US patent data available for a modest cost, US patent databases have proliferated on conventional online services and on the Internet. In 1997 full-text European patent databases also began to proliferate, and the English-language PATENT ABSTRACTS OF JAPAN began to appear on the Internet. While searching the full text of patents makes it possible to find specific terminology in patent documents, it does not simplify searches for chemical compounds, mechanical drawings, electrical wiring diagrams or descriptions written in general terms, all of which are characteristic of patents. Controlled indexing is necessary for meaningful retrieval in all but the most casual searches of patent databases.

Patent databases include many kinds of document, not all of them having the legal force of granted patents. Recognizing the various types of documents was made somewhat easier by the work of an organization called ICIREPAT, which developed a series of internationally recognized codes for identification of patent data. ICIREPAT country codes (now replaced by a nearly identical list of ISO codes) are two-letter codes for country names. A list of current and discontinued country codes applied to the countries whose patents are indexed by online databases may be found in Table 2.1. INID numbers, Internationally Agreed Numbers for the Identification of Data (formerly called ICIREPAT Numbers for the Identification of Data), are placed on the cover page of patents so that it is possible to tell what names and numbers signify without being able to read the language of the patent. There are also 'patent kind' codes that identify the type of patent document. These codes consist of a letter, sometimes followed by a number, and the meaning of a particular code depends upon the laws of the country issuing the document. The first publication of a patent in the regular series of utility patents is usually identified by the letter A, sometimes followed by a numeral. Patents republished after examination are usually labelled B, also sometimes followed by a number. There are also codes for design patents and 'utility models', for patents of addition and for 'inventors' certificates', which were issued as alternatives to patents in some communist countries. Lists of the kinds of patent issued by the various countries may be found in the manuals issued by EPIDOS, the European Patent Information and Documentation Systems of the European Patent Office, in the World Intellectual Property Organization (WIPO) *Patent Information and Documentation Handbook*, in Derwent's *Global Patent Sources*, in the publication *Patent Information from Chemical Abstracts Service Coverage and Content*, and in the *Manual of Patent Examining Procedures* of the US Patent and Trademark Office, as well as on the Web sites of many patent offices and database producers.

Legally valid patents can be obtained only on inventions that have not been described in a printed publication before the effective filing date of the patent application, so it is important to file a patent application on a useful discovery before publishing a description of it anywhere else. On the other hand, if one wishes to reserve the right to practise an invention without patenting it, one has only to publish a description of it before anyone else has a chance to file a patent application on it. This can be done with a publication in a scientific journal, but there are also publications devoted specifically to 'defensive disclosures'. Two of these, *Research Disclosures* and *International Technology Disclosures*, are abstracted by Derwent Information Ltd in DERWENT WORLD PATENTS INDEX. The *IBM Technical Disclosure Bulletin* is available on the IBM Intellectual Property Network (see Addendum). Published patent applications that are abandoned before grant also serve as defensive publications. In the USA a programme for the publication of Defensive Publications has been superseded by

Table 2.1 *Country coverage of patent databases*

COUNTRY, (TREATY)	ISO CODE	WPI	INPADOC	APIPAT*	CA SEARCH	ESP@CENET**	OTHER DATABASES
ALBANIA	AL						
ALGERIA	DZ						
ANTIGUA & BARBUTA	AG						
ARGENTINA†	AR	1974–6	1973–91	*		1973–	
ARIPO: INDUSTRIAL PROPERTY ORGANIZATION FOR AFRICA	AP		1984–			ALL/ALL	
ARMENIA (EA)	AM						
AUSTRALIA	AU	1963–69 1982–	1973–	*	1967–	1973–	
AUSTRIA (EPO)	AT [OE]	1975–	1969–	1982–	1967–	1975–/1920–	
AZERBAIJAN (EA)	AZ						
BARBADOS	BB [BD]						
BELARUS	BY						
BELGIUM (EPO)	BE	1963–	1964–	1964–	1967–	1964–/1920–	CLAIMS: 1950–79
BENIN (OAPI)	BJ [DA]						
BOSNIA & HERZIGOVINA	BA		1998–				
BRAZIL	BR	1975–	1973–	1982–	1976–	1973–	
BULGARIA	BG		1973			1973–	
BURKINA FASO (OAPI)	BF [HV, UV]						
CAMEROON (OAPI)	CM [KA]						
CANADA	CA	1963–	1970–	1964–	1967–	1970–	
CENTRAL AFRICAN REPUBLIC (OAPI)	CF [ZF]						
CHAD (OAPI)	TD [TS]						
CHINA	CN	1985–	1985–	1985–	1986–	1985–	CHINAPATS 1985–
CONGO (OAPI)	CG [GF]						
COSTA RICA	CR						
CROATIA†	HR		1994–			1994–	
CUBA	CU		1974–95			1974–	
CYPRUS (EPO)	CY		1975–			1975–	

Country	Code						Databases
CZECH REPUBLIC	CZ	1993–	1993–	1993–	1993–	1993–	
CZECHOSLOVAKIA (EPO)	CS	1975–93	1973–93	1982–93	1967–92	1973–1993	
DENMARK	DK	1974–	1968–	1982–	1967–	1968/1920–	
DOMINICA	DM						
EGYPT†	EG [ET]	1976–	1976–			1976–	
ESTONIA	EE						
EURASIAN PATENT OFFICE	EA	1996–	1996–			1996–	
EUROPEAN PATENT OFFICE	EP	1978–	1978–	1978–	1979–	1978–/1978–	EPAT: 1978–; EPO Register: 1978–; PATOSEP: 1978–; EP FULLTEXT: 1978–; EUROPATFULL: 1995–; PHARMSEARCH: 1983–
FINLAND	FI [SF]	1974–	1968–	1982–	1967–	1968–	
FRANCE (EPO)	FR	1963–	1968–	1964–	1967–	1968/1920–	FPAT: 1969–; CLAIMS: 1950–79; PHARMSEARCH: 1961–73, 1983–
GABON (OAPI)	GA						
GAMBIA (ARIPO)	GM						
GEORGIA	GE						
GERMANY, EAST†	DD [DL] (EG)	1963–	1973–	1983–	1967–94	1973–	
GERMANY, FEDERAL REPUBLIC (EPO)	DE [DT] (DS, GE)	1963–	1967–	1964–	1967–	1967–/1920–	PATDPA: 1968–; PATOSDE: 1968–; CLAIMS: 1950–79; PHARMSEARCH: 1992–
GHANA (ARIPO)	GH						
GRANADA	GD						
GREECE (EPO)	GR		1977–94			1977–	
GUINEA (OAPI)	GN						
GUINEA-BISSAU (OAPI)	GW						
HONG KONG†	HK	1976–	1976–			1976–	
HUNGARY	HU	1973–	1973–	1982–	1967–	1994–	
ICELAND	IS	1975–					
INDIA	IN	1975–94	1975–94	1967–81	1967–	1975–	

Table 2.1 *cont'd*

COUNTRY, (TREATY)	ISO CODE	WPI	INPADOC	APIPAT*	CA SEARCH	ESP@CENET**	OTHER DATABASES
INDONESIA	ID						
IRELAND (EPO)	IE [EI]	1963–69 / 1995–	1973–	1982–		1973–/1996–	
ISRAEL	IL	1975–	1968–	1982–	1967–	1968–	
ITALY (EPO)	IT	1966–69 / 1977–	1973–	1982–	1967–75	1973–/1978–	ITALPAT: 1983–
IVORY COAST (OAPI)	CI						
JAPAN	JP (J#) [JA]	1963–	1973–	1968–	1967–	1973–/1980–	JAPIO: 1976– PATOLIS: 1955–
KAZAKHSTAN (EA)	KZ						
KENYA (ARIPO)	KE		1975–89			1975–	
KOREA, NORTH	KP [KN]						
KOREA, SOUTH	KR [KS]	1986–	1978–	1986–		1978–	
KYRGYZSTAN (EA)	KG						
LATVIA	LV		1994–			1994–	
LESOTHOL (ARIPO)	LS						
LIBERIA	LR						
LIECHTENSTEIN (EPO)	LI						
LITHUANIA	LT		1994–			1994–	
LUXEMBOURG (EPO)	LU	1984–	1960–	1984–		1960–/1945–	
MACEDONIA	MK						
MADAGASCAR	MG [MD]		1973–94			1973–	
MALAWI (ARIPO)	MW		1953–89				
MALAYSIA	MY						
MALI (OAPI)	ML [MJ]						
MALTA†	MT						
MAURITANIA (OAPI)	MR [MT]		1967–				
MEXICO	MX	1997–	1981–95	1995–		1981–	
MOLDOVA (EA)	MD		1994–			1994–	
MONACO (EPO)	MC		1975–			1975–/ALL	
MONGOLIA	MN [MO]		1972–89			1972–	

Country		Code						Notes
MOROCCO		MA						
MOZAMBIQUE		MZ						
NETHERLANDS	(EPO)	NL	1963–	1964–	1964	1967–	1964–/ALL	CLAIMS : 1950–79
NEW ZEALAND		NZ	1992–	1978–	1992–		1979–	
NIGER	(OAPI)	NE						
NORWAY		NO	1974–	1968–	*	1967–	1968–	
OAPI: AFRICAN INTELLECTUAL PROPERTY ORGANIZATION		OA		1993–96			1966–/ALL	
PATENT COOPERATION TREATY	(PCT)	WO (WP)	1978–	1978–	1978–	1979–	1978–/1978–	PCTPAT: 1978– PATOSWO: 1983 PHARMSEARCH: 1989–
PHILIPPINES†		PH [RP]	1992–	1975–94	1994–		1975–	
POLAND	(EPO)	PL [PO]		1973–	*	1967–	1973–	
PORTUGAL		PT	1974–	1976–	1982–		1976–/1980–	
ROMANIA	(EA)	RO [RU]	1975–	1973–95	1982–	1967–	1973–	
RUSSIA		RU	1993–	1993–97	1993–	1993–	1993–	
SAINT LUCIA		LC						
SENEGAL	(OAPI)	SN						
SIERRA LEONE	(ARIPO)	SL						
SINGAPORE		SG	1995–	1983–	1995–	1996–	1993–	
SLOVAKIA		SK	1993–	1993–	1993–		1992–	
SLOVENIA		SI	1992–	1992–			1971–	
SOUTH AFRICA		ZA (SA)	1963–	1971–	1964–	1968–	1968–/1968–	
SPAIN	(EPO)	ES	1983–	1968–	1982–	1967–		
SRI LANKA		LK [CL]						
SUDAN	(OAPI)	SD						
SWAZILAND	(ARIPO)	SZ						
SWEDEN	(EPO)	SE [SW]	1974–	1968–	1982–	1967–	1969–/1920–	
SWITZERLAND	(EPO)	CH (SW)	1963–	1969–	1982–	1967–		
TAIWAN, REPUBLIC OF CHINA†		TW	1993–		1993–			
TAJIKISTAN	(EA)	TJ						
TANZANIA	(ARIPO)	TZ						
TOGO	(OAPI)	TG [TO]						

Table 2.1 *concluded*

COUNTRY, (TREATY)	ISO CODE	WPI	INPADOC	APIPAT*	CA SEARCH	ESP@CENET**	OTHER DATABASES
TRINIDAD AND TOBAGO	TT						
TURKEY	TR		1973–97			1973–	
TURKMENISTAN (EA)	TM						
UGANDA (ARIPO)	UG						
UKRAINE	UA						
UNITED ARAB EMIRATES	AE						
UNITED KINGDOM (EPO)	GB (BR)	1963–	1969–	1964–	1967–	1969–/1920–	CLAIMS: 1950–79 PHARMSEARCH: 1992–
UNITED STATES	US	1963–	1968–	1964–	1967–	1968–/1920–	CLAIMS: 1950– USPATENTS: 1970– LEXPAT: 1975– PATFULL: 1975– USPATFULL: 1975– PHARMSEARCH: 1983–
USSR	SU (RU)	1963–	1972–97	1982–	1967–93	1972–	
UZBEKISTAN	UZ						
VIETNAM	VN		1984–97			1984–	
YUGOSLAVIA	YU		1973–92			1973–	
ZAMBIA†	ZM [ZB]		1968–94			1968–	
ZIMBABWE (ARIPO)	ZW [RH]		1980–95			1980–	

Notes

Country codes in brackets are obsolete ICIREPAT codes. Country codes in parentheses were used by Derwent Information Ltd prior to the adoption of standard country codes. The obsolete codes remain on printed records, but have been replaced by current codes in online databases. For Japanese patents, Derwent replaced the second character of the country code with the first digit of the publication year prior to 1992; this variant of the company code is still found in online databases and printed publications.

† Not a member of the Patent Cooperation Treaty as of March 2000.

* Countries not covered systematically. In addition, patents from some of the systematically covered countries may have been indexed in earlier years.

** Dates refer to bibliographic data. Where two years are shown, the second refers to displayable images.

Countries designated as members of the European Patent Organization, the Eurasian Patent Organization (EA), the African Regional Industrial Property Organization (ARIPO), the African Intellectual Property Organization (OAPI) or the Patent Cooperation Treaty may be found as designated states in the records of EP, EA, OA, AP and WO documents, whether or not those countries are indexed separately in a database.

a series of Statutory Invention Registrations which are published through the same channels as US patents and are included in some databases that index US patents.

Because any publication will prevent the grant of a valid patent, searches that aim to discover whether a prior publication will prevent the issuance of a patent must include not only patent databases but also databases dealing with the non-patent literature of the relevant technology. The state of technology before the filing of a patent application and the publications that describe it are referred to as the 'prior art'. In most countries, an invention that has not been described in a printed publication is unpatentable if the invention was used publicly before the patent application was filed. In most cases, public use is brought to the attention of the patent office or the courts by persons with inside information. It is very difficult to find information about prior public use by searching online, although in cases where prior use is suspected it may be possible to document it by searching the periodical literature. More important, from the point of view of a patent searcher, is the statutory requirement for non-obviousness or inventiveness. This requirement prevents the grant of a patent unless the claimed invention is sufficiently different from what is already known that a person of ordinary skill would not arrive at it through a simple modification of the nearest prior art product or process. It is often unnecessary to retrieve a reference that describes an invention in every detail to determine that the invention is likely to be unpatentable. Since the legal requirement for inventiveness or non-obviousness is applied differently in every country, however, an invention that is similar to one described in a published reference is likely to be patentable in some countries and not in others.

Patent data fields

Patents are more complex than other publications because they function both as technical documents and as legal documents. The information in a patent divides itself into three general kinds of data:

- bibliographic information identifying the document itself
- technical information describing the claimed invention
- and information about the history of the patent application with regard to its prosecution by the applicant's representative in the national or international patent office, and its legal status.

In searches for technical information alone, the bibliographic and technical information found in the patent specification is sufficient to answer any possible question. The bibliographical information on patents from a great many countries is available online, and all the information from the front page of the patents – bibliographic information, information about the patent office's prior art search, and abstract – as well as the text of the patent specification is available for a handful of major countries. If the searcher needs to know whether or not a patent is currently in force, however, legal status information is also needed. At the present time, it is possible to answer all questions about the current status of a patent from only a few countries by searching online. For patents issued by most countries, only limited information is available in the databases about changes in patent ownership, the expiry of patent terms or the lapse of patents prior to the end of their statutory terms. Some countries publish every change in the status of a pending patent application; some even announce the serial number, title and applicant before the specification itself is published. These announcements of filing, usually with the patent kind code A0, are not actually publications of the patent specification. Other countries, notably the USA, keep all details of pending patent applications secret until a patent is granted. In order to guess whether an American patent application on a particular invention has been filed it is necessary to search for equivalent applications published by other countries and estimate the likelihood that a corresponding application was filed in the USA. A change in the US law scheduled for late 2000 will result in the publication of pending applications equivalent to applications filed in other countries, although patent applications filed only in the USA will continue to be kept in secrecy until grant; this change will result in the publication of English-language versions of patent applications published by other countries 18 months after filing.

Bibliographic data fields

In patent databases, as in other bibliographic databases, the bibliographic data tell the searcher who wrote the cited publication, where it can be found and when it was published. But a patent is a legal document, and its bibliographic information also identifies the owner of the claimed invention and the extent of his or her rights.

Country or patent convention

Historically, patents are published by the patent-granting authority of a national government and have legal effect only in that country. Each patent document bears the name of the granting country and recent patent documents also bear a two-letter ISO code identifying the country. Current and obsolete ISO codes for the countries covered by the patent databases discussed in this chapter are listed in Table 2.1. Some databases use standard ISO codes to identify the patent country, but others – especially databases that are not devoted primarily to patents – identify the patent country by the full name of the country or an abbreviation that may or may not be ambiguous.

In recent years there has been a move toward international cooperation in the processing of patent applications. The Patent Cooperation Treaty (PCT), which came into force in 1977, provides for the filing of a single patent application in a single language to be processed by the patent offices of several countries. As of

2000, 107 countries had signed the treaty. PCT applications are published by WIPO 18 months after filing with the ISO code WO, but the published document is not a granted patent. Using the results of a single prior art search, each of the countries designated in the PCT application examines the application separately in its own language and issues a patent if the invention meets the national standards of patentability. The European Patent Convention created a centralized European Patent Office empowered to grant patents having effect in each of the member countries and enforced by the courts of each country. European patent applications are published in English, French or German with the ISO code EP 18 months after filing and, if the claimed invention is found to be patentable, republished after allowance with any amendments made during prosecution. Negotiations toward the creation of a European Community patent, enforceable by the European Union rather than the national courts, have taken place for many years, but the Union Patent had not come into being by 2000. In Africa there are similar regional patent offices: the African Intellectual Property Organization (OAPI), which provides for patents in 16 French-speaking countries, and ARIPO, the African Regional Industrial Property Organization, which provides for patents in 11 English-speaking countries. The Eurasian Patent Organization provides patents for most of the countries of the former Soviet Union.

Designated states

Applicants for patents who file PCT or European patent applications may elect to obtain patent coverage in as few or as many of the member countries as they desire. The selections, indicated on the patent application as 'designated states', define the geographical boundaries of the area for which protection is sought. PCT applications may designate some countries through national patent office procedures and others through the regional European Patent Office, OAPI, ARIPO and Eurasian Patent Office procedures. Patent databases usually provide a field to identify the designated states for WO and EP documents.

Document number and publication date

Patents and published patent applications are issued with a document number that is used in combination with the country name or ISO country code to identify it. This number and the date of publication are printed on the face of the document. Some countries, such as the USA and the UK, issue patents in single continuous series. Others issue a new series of patent numbers every year, with the year as part of the document number. Prior to 2000, Japanese patent applications used the Japanese Imperial year, representing the year of the reign of the Emperor. For patent documents published prior to 8 January 1989, the Imperial year refers to the Showa era and is equal to the Gregorian year minus 1925, the year before Emperor Hirohito was crowned. Patents published since the accession of Emperor Akihito refer to the Heisei era, equal to the Gregorian year minus 1988. Patents published during the first few months of the Heisei era were printed with the year 64, but are indexed with the 'correct' year designation 01.

Because some patent databases are produced by indexing data obtained from the patent gazettes or electronic databases published by the issuing patent offices, they include some patent numbers and publication dates for which no actual patent documents exist. These include notices of filing and national patent numbers assigned to designated states in PCT applications and European patents. The most conspicuous of these are Euro-PCT applications. The European Patent Office publishes all patent applications 18 months after their priority date, with the exception of European patent applications based on PCT applications that have already been published in English, French or German. The EPO assigns a patent number and date to those applications, but defines the published WO document as the patent specification.

Databases vary in the way they handle the various patent number formats. Some databases use a fixed field length for all patent numbers. The nine-character format used by Derwent until the end of 1990 was adapted to many of the other patent databases carried on Questel-Orbit and as a user-defined option in databases on STN and DIALOG. With the modification of Derwent's formats to accommodate twenty-first century dates, considerable confusion is likely. For patent numbers that incorporate the publication year, Derwent's patent number format placed the last two digits of the publication year at the front of the serial number. Beginning in 2000, the four-digit year number is used. Derwent's format incorporates the Imperial year for published Japanese applications issued before the Western year was substituted by the Japanese Patent Office in 2000, and the Western year for examined Japanese patent applications issued before the patent law was amended in 1995. This is to provide easily distinguishable series of publication numbers for published applications and granted patents. DIALOG has adopted a standard patent number format of its own, consisting of the ISO code followed by a space and the document number. The hosts that have adopted a standard format permit the searcher to use either the standard format or the format provided by the database producer. DIALOG automatically selects the standardized format for cross-file searching and STN searches all possible formats, while Questel-Orbit allows the searcher to select either format. As DIALOG does not reverse Derwent's formatting algorithm when reformatting patent numbers, cross-file searching between DERWENT WORLD PATENTS INDEX and other databases with the MAPPN command is relatively inefficient.

In indexing published patent applications, databases sometimes use the application serial number, rather than the publication number, to represent the document. This can cause serious problems in cross-file searching between databases with different input policies. No matter how carefully the vendor has standardized formats, for example, it will not be possible to cross an Austrian patent number between CA SEARCH and DERWENT WORLD PATENTS INDEX; the 'patent number' cited by DERWENT WORLD PATENTS INDEX is indexed by *Chemical Abstracts* as the application serial number if it is in the record at all. Searchers who fail to retrieve the correct patent by searching for a known number in the patent number field should try reformatting the number, searching in the application or priority number field or, if all else fails, searching a different database or host system.

Patent publication dates are very important in some countries; most patent applications filed in the USA before the 1995 patent law revisions and Canadian patents applied for prior to the 1989 patent law revisions, for example, had patent terms measured from the issue date. In most countries, however, the patent expiry date is calculated from the date of filing, and the publication date indicates only the date that the document became available to the public. The publication dates of patents retrieved as references in prior art searches are important in deciding the patentability of a claimed invention, as only patents published before the application was filed can be considered as references.

Patent kind or level of publication

A patent document number is not always sufficient to identify a particular patent. Some countries issue two or more series of documents with identical serial numbers, while others assign a unique serial number to a patent application and use the same number to identify the corresponding granted patent after it has been changed by amendment. Modern patent numbers have associated with them a one- or two-character ISO code that indicates the kind of patent or level of publication of the document. This code – a letter or a letter followed by a numeral – indicates whether the document is an announcement of filing, a published application, an examined patent, a patent granted after opposition, a patent of addition or a re-issued granted patent, and whether it is a utility patent, a utility model, a design patent or a plant patent, depending on the choices available in the country in question. The codes are defined separately for each country: an 'A' document in the USA is a granted patent, while an 'A' document in France is a published application.

The patent kind codes are not strictly bibliographic identifiers. Their main purpose is to indicate the legal status of the document. But the code is usually printed with the document number on the face of the patent and it is often an essential bibliographic element. In countries where the same document number follows a patent application through several levels of publication, the code (or an indication of the level it represents) is necessary for unambiguous identification of the patent document. An indication of the level of publication is essential for countries like Japan that use an identical numerical sequence to identify a patent application, an unrelated published specification and an unrelated examined patent.

Application number and date

Patent applications are assigned a serial number when they are filed. This serial number identifies the application in the patent office before it is published. Both the serial number and the application date are printed on the document. The date of filing is of great legal importance, as a valid patent will be granted only if the invention has not been described elsewhere prior to the application date. In most countries the term of the patent is calculated from the application date, the most common term being 20 years from filing to expiry. Databases that treat patents only as sources of technical information frequently omit application numbers and dates from their records.

Priority application number and date

Only one patent can be granted in each country for any invention, and in most countries the first applicant is entitled to that patent. Applicants for patents on a single invention in several countries that are members of international patent treaties such as the Paris Convention for the Protection of Industrial Property or the World Trade Organization can rely on the filing of a single application to establish the effective filing date in all of the countries. A convention priority date is established by filing an application in one country and making a formal claim for priority, based on that original filing, in applications filed within one year in other countries. The national application number and date of the original patent application appear on each of the resulting patents as the priority number and date. The original application, and any other application that is filed on the invention without claiming priority, are published without a priority number and priority date, but many patent databases treat the local application data as priority data in order to establish patent families. Most countries allow applicants to claim more than one priority. Databases generally index multiple priorities so that all of them can be used to search for members of a patent family.

Application numbers are printed on patents in a format characteristic of the country of publication. The priority application number may be printed in a different format when priority is claimed in another country, and it may appear in yet another format when the priority information is put into computer-readable form by a database producer and modified still further by the host system when it is offered online. The difficulty which this creates for searchers is largely due to the practice of treating the final two digits of the year as a part of the standardized priority application number format, compounded by the reloading of some files with formats converted to the four-digit year. When the priority application is Japanese, the Imperial year designation complicates the problem still further. Each of the records in Figures 2.18–2.22 (pp. 102, 106, 108, 110 and 112) describes a patent based on Japanese patent application number 06-134701, filed on 16 June 1994. The priority application number is represented in PATOSEP on STN as JP 94-134701, in PATDPA on STN as 1994-134701 in JAPIO in the Japanese Patent Office format without country code and in the DIALOG format JP 94134701, in APIPAT on DIALOG as JP 94134701, and in the WORLD PATENTS INDEX/APIPAT record on Questel-Orbit in the current Derwent format 1994JP-0134701. Searchers will sometimes notice that queries based on patent application numbers fail to retrieve the expected patents even though the numbers are formatted correctly for the database being searched. This usually means that no patent based on that priority has been issued in the countries covered by the database, but the possibility that the priority data have been indexed incorrectly should not be overlooked.

Patent family members

Patents that are filed in a number of countries on a single invention by a single applicant form families of equivalent patents. Such patents usually have the same technical information, although the claims may vary from country to country. Since each country requires that patent applications be filed in its official language, equivalent patents are useful as translations. In many countries the law permits applicants to claim more than one priority. To minimize the number of patents they index, databases fully analyse only the first patent on an invention to reach the indexers, referred to as the 'basic patent'. Patents are treated as equivalent family members when they claim the same priority application numbers as a patent that was indexed earlier or because they seem, to the indexer, to cover the same invention despite the absence of a common priority.

Because patent databases differ in their treatment of multiple priorities, in their policy towards intellectually identified equivalent patents and in the number of countries they index, the number of patents in a family may differ in the various databases that index its members. It is important to recognize the fact that 'equivalent' patent applications may differ considerably in content, either because the original specification was modified before the later applications were filed or because the various patent offices have required amendment of the applications after filing.

Patentee names

All patent documents bear the name and residence of the applicant who becomes the owner of the patent when it is issued. As units of property, patents may be sold or given to another by the original patentee and they may be owned jointly by two or more companies or individuals. All inventions have inventors, individuals or teams of individuals who conceived of the invention and reduced it to practice, but most inventions are made at the behest of the inventors' employers. Patent applications may be filed by the inventors or by the contractual owner of the invention, depending on the national laws and individual circumstances. In the USA, where the inventors are required to apply for the patent, many patents are assigned to the inventors' employer or financial backer prior to the publication of the patent document, and the name of the assignee as well as that of the inventor appears on the patent. Some countries categorize patentees, indicating whether the patent owner is, for example, a corporation or a foreign government. In most databases the patentee field indexes the patent assignee or corporate patent applicant listed on the face of the patent specification. Almost invariably, the indexed patentee is the original owner of the patent. Subsequent sale or reassignment of the patent is rarely indexed by patent databases. Changes of corporate name or affiliation, on the other hand, are tracked by some database producers, so that the record for a patent often will be found to identify the patent owner by a name different from the one on the face of the patent specification.

Some patent databases have established a series of patentee codes for organizations that have a substantial number of patents. These may be used to group all patents belonging to the various divisions of a corporation, as they are by Derwent, or each company name may have a unique code. The codes may or may not be continued when the name of the company changes. Some databases also use a list of standardized company names, applying the preferred form of the name along with, or instead of, a company code.

Inventors are not always identified on patent documents published by countries that treat the corporation as the patentee, and inventor names are not always indexed by patent databases. Therefore, a search for a patent claiming subject matter developed by a particular scientist or engineer will be incomplete if it requires that the inventor's name be present in the record of every patent it retrieves.

Cross-reference citation

Patent offices publish bulletins or gazettes in which they announce the publication of patent documents. The patent office gazette citation is not an essential bibliographic element, but it is cited in some patent databases. Databases based on abstracting services, such as DERWENT WORLD PATENTS INDEX, CA SEARCH and JAPIO, include the accession number or citation of the printed abstract in the online record. Cross-reference citations to these abstracting services are present in records in some of the other patent databases.

Technical data fields

Patents are required to describe the claimed invention in sufficient detail that it can be practised without undue experimentation by a hypothetical person of ordinary skill in the art to which the invention pertains. At the same time, patents are written with an eye toward the eventual need to defend them from infringers in the courts. In order to obtain protection for the broadest possible invention, patent agents and attorneys normally draft patent applications using generic language in place of specific language that would be easy for an infringer to design around. A patent will refer to a leg as a 'supporting means' and a housepaint as an 'exterior protective coating'. That kind of language is helpful when a competitor introduces a similar product or process using a cantilevered bracket or a varnish, but it complicates free-text searching enormously. A common form of generic description is the Markush structure, named after a patent applicant whose claims were approved in a landmark decision of the US Patent Office. Markush structures are usually employed in chemical patents; they consist of a central substructure and one or more groups of optional substructures.

Title

Patents are published with short titles in the language of the patent. These are often so general and so concise that they offer no clue about the details of the invention: 'Cleaning Composition' or 'Mining Apparatus', for example. Some patent databases translate the titles, augment the original titles with explanatory phrases, or replace the original title with a new one that summarizes the gist of the invention.

Abstract

Most countries now require that patent applications include an abstract that summarizes the invention. The abstract submitted by the applicant is of uncontrolled quality; it may be extremely vague or it may be a restatement of the broadest claim in the application as filed. It is nearly always in generic language and it seldom contains specific details.

Some database producers write their own abstracts. These may be longer than the ones supplied with the patent application and they commonly include specific language and examples taken from the body of the patent specification. Because each database indexes patents from its own point of view and in its own native language, the content of the abstracts it produces may differ markedly from the content of the author abstract and from the abstract produced for another database. In Figures 2.5 and 2.9 (pp. 70 and 84) the original abstract of US patent US 5,661,172 is reproduced in citations from the CLAIMS UDB and USPATFULL databases and in Figure 2.17 (p. 100) the abstract of equivalent PCT application, WO 95/01791, is reproduced; the DERWENT WORLD PATENTS INDEX and Chemical Abstracts' MARPAT abstracts of these patents in Figures 2.2 and 2.23 are more informative (see pp. 51 and 115).

Claims

Patent claims define the scope of the patent grant. A patent usually contains one or more broad generic claims and a series of narrower subgeneric and specific claims that cover embodiments of the broader claims. The broadest claim must be an independent claim – one that defines the invention fully, although it may be necessary to refer to the body of the specification for the limits of some of the generic language. The narrower claims are usually written as dependent claims, in which some of the features of the invention are defined by referring back to an earlier claim.

In published applications, the claims define the invention for which the applicant hopes to obtain protection. They often include unpatentable material. Granted patent claims have been examined for patentability and have often been amended after filing. Claims in a valid granted patent define a product or process that cannot be made, used or sold without the consent of the patent owner. Products and processes that are described in the patent and not claimed are not protected by the patent and can be used by the public unless they are claimed in some other patent in the same country. Within a family of patents filed by an applicant in several countries, the scope of the granted claims may vary widely. This occurs because the laws that define patentable subject matter and the standards for judging whether an invention is disclosed in sufficient detail to support a patent claim differ from one country to the next. If it is important to know whether your company is permitted to practise an invention disclosed in a patent, it is essential to obtain a copy of the granted patent document from the country in which you wish to do business.

Many sources of patent information that publish patent claims use only one or two of the claims, not all claims published in the document. The claim that is chosen is usually the first claim, which is conventionally assumed to be the broadest claim. In many cases, however, the patent contains several broad claims covering different aspects of the invention, such as a product and the process for making it, or a class of compounds and method for treating a disease with the compounds. In databases where a single 'main claim' is reproduced, one should never assume that the claim summarizes the patented invention in its entirety. If it is important to know the legal scope of a patent, the patent specification or a database that includes the text of all claims should be consulted.

Disclosure

The bulk of a patent specification is in the disclosure, which teaches how to make and use the claimed invention. A typical patent disclosure consists of: a description of the problem the claimed invention seeks to solve; a summary of the prior art; a detailed description of the claimed invention with definitions for all new or obscure terms; a general description of the ways the invention can be made and used; and examples of the production and use of specific embodiments of the generic invention. The disclosure usually teaches how to prepare sub-assemblies and chemical intermediates as well as the final product. Although patent abstracts and claims often contain only obscure generic language, the disclosure contains clear specific language. It is not unusual for a patent disclosure to contain speculative or prophetic examples describing embodiments of the invention that were never made. These are educated guesses and they are sometimes in error.

It is in their treatment of prophetic disclosures that national patent examining procedures and patent databases differ most widely. The patent claims may be allowed to issue as filed or the applicant may be required to delete the unexemplified scope from the patent claims before grant. Likewise, the abstract or indexing prepared by the database may either include the 'paper examples' or the database's indexing policy may require that they be ignored. Thus, the content of the patent claims will differ significantly from country to country, and the depth of indexing will differ significantly from database to database.

Drawings

Electrical and mechanical patents normally contain pages of drawings for the claimed invention. The parts of the drawings are identified by reference symbols, and the disclosure explains what the drawings depict in terms of the reference symbols. Chemical structures are usually integrated into the disclosure and claims. The drawings and chemical structures are an essential part of the patent disclosure, but until patent databases became available on the Internet, they were especially difficult to depict online. The first-page drawings from recent PCT applications are available on the *PCT Gazette* on the Internet at <URL http://pctgazette.wipo.int>. Exemplary patent drawings for German patents are provided in PATDPA and for French patents are provided in FPAT. Drawings from US patents can be displayed on LEXIS-NEXIS and in the US patent image collections discussed later. Exemplary images can be displayed in most versions of JAPIO. While the STN mounting of the CAS database contains drawings of chemical structures from some patents, these are the illustrations used in the printed *Chemical Abstracts* publication and may not correspond to structures shown in the abstracted patents. Exemplary drawings and chemical structures provided in the DERWENT WORLD PATENTS INDEX database are also taken from the printed versions of the *World Patents Index*. Chemical structures illustrated in MARPAT and in the Merged Markush Service, the auxiliary chemical structure database for DERWENT WORLD PATENTS INDEX and PHARMSEARCH, are notations that represent the indexing conventions and do not necessarily correspond to structures shown in the patents. Each database has its own procedures for dealing with drawings in the abstracts and claims that are not reproduced in the online record. The database may ignore the structure, translate the structure into a linearized form that can be shown in the print-out, reproduce only alphanumeric substructures, or refer the reader to the printed patent specification. Differences in the way drawings are treated can make a significant difference to the amount of information available in the online record and in its cosmetic appearance, as can be seen by comparing the treatment of the chemical structure diagram shown in US 5,661,172 and its equivalents by DERWENT WORLD PATENTS INDEX, IFIUDB, USPATFULL, and PHARMSEARCH in the records reproduced in Figures 2.2, 2.5, 2.9 and 2.24 (pp. 51, 70, 84 and 118).

Drawings and chemical structure diagrams are available in patent databases that provide images of patent documents. Images of all US patents issued since 1790 are available from the Corporate Intelligence Service and MicroPatent, which also have collections of a wide selection of international patents for downloading.

Images of US patents issued since 1974 are available in the CHEMICAL PATENTS PLUS database available from Chemical Abstracts Service on the World Wide Web, STN's US PATENTS FULLTEXT database, the US Patent and Trademark Office Web site, QPAT-WW, and DELPHION INTELLECTUAL PROPERTY NETWORK. Images of European patents and published applications, and of PCT applications are available from IBM, QPAT and MicroPatent. The European Patent Office offers a wide range of patent images over the ESP@CENET Web service. These include images from the international patent collection comprising the PCT Minimum Documentation file for the examination of patents and links to databases of the the most recent two years of patent applications published by each of the member countries. STN provides hyperlinks to the USPTO site and ESP@CENET from patent records using STN Express or its Internet interfaces. The Japanese Patent Office offers the images of recent Japanese patents via PATOLIS service.

Subject indexing

The technical content of patents is made more accessible to searchers through subject indexing applied by both the patent issuing authorities and some database producers. Patent information is found in two distinct types of databases: those that catalogue the patents of one or more countries as legal documents; and those that index patents as technical disclosures. Databases in the first group include INPADOC and the national patent databases. In these databases, the subject indexing is usually limited to patent classification codes and such words as happen to occur in the title, abstract and claims or the full text of the patent. Databases in the second group include DERWENT WORLD PATENTS INDEX, the CLAIMS UNITERM and COMPREHENSIVE databases, APIPAT, PHARMSEARCH, and many databases, such as CA SEARCH, that index both journal and patent literature in a technological field. These databases index the patent disclosure in considerable depth and some replace the original patent abstract with a comprehensive abstract based on the technical data present in the specification. The deepest indexing is applied to chemical patents; yet even databases that index chemical patents intensively provide relatively superficial indexing for patents without chemical aspects.

Patent classification codes

Patent indexing has traditionally been done in patent offices by means of hierarchical patent classification codes. The classification codes appear on the patent document and are used to identify the field of technology to which the patent belongs. The classification schemes were designed to subdivide the files of paper copies of patent documents used by examiners and searchers in the patent office search rooms. Patent classification systems are modified frequently to keep up with changes in technology.

Each national patent office has traditionally designed and used its own patent classification system. The national systems do not necessarily have similar guidelines for subdividing technologies and they do not use the same kinds of symbols to identify classifications. The most common national patent classification codes in patent databases are US classes, which are formatted as a three-digit numerical class code followed by a slash or hyphen and a subclass code consisting of from one to three numbers occasionally followed by a letter or by a decimal point and additional numerals. Patents are given a single 'original classification' and usually are given one or more 'cross-reference classifications'. The US patent classification system is under constant revision and, as the purpose of the system is to provide a useful arrangement of the patents on the shelves of search rooms, file copies of the patents are moved to their new places and the indexes are revised when new classifications are assigned to existing patents. The printed patent specification is not changed, of course, when a patent is reclassified: some databases change the records of reclassified patents while others retain the original classification codes.

WIPO designed an International Patent Classification (IPC) system for patents that has been adopted by most of the industrially advanced countries of the world. Even countries that continue to use the national classification system as the basis for the organization of the patent search files print a corresponding IPC classification on the patent documents. Although the IPC is used by most countries, they do not all follow the same guidelines for applying the codes and they do not all use the finest divisions of the classification system. Patents with identical claims may be classified differently in each country in which the patent application was filed.

The IPC, in the format ANNA-NNN/NN, where A represents a letter and N represents a numeral, represents a hierarchical system in which each successive character narrows the definition of the invention. Some countries index patents only to the four-character subclass level, while others use the full IPC. In searching, it is usually necessary to truncate IPC codes unless the level of specificity used by the country of interest is known. A hybrid system of classification has been introduced for more specific indexing of patents; countries that use the hybrid system append indexing codes in the format NNN:NN to IPC codes for some technologies. The IPC has been revised six times since it was introduced in 1968 and, at the time of writing, is in its seventh edition. Some patent offices and some databases, but not all, identify the edition of the IPC used in classifying a patent. The European Patent Office has reclassified all of the patents in its search documentation files according to its own standards, using a somewhat modified version of the IPC, known as ECLA, and has made the resulting index of reclassified patents available in the EDOC database which was recently merged into Questel-Orbit's PLUSPAT. Although ECLA codes are used within the EPO for searching; the codes themselves are not printed on European patent documents.

Database-supplied indexing

Patent databases run the gamut in the depth of indexing supplied by their producers. Many patent databases have no information in their records that is not present in the patent document, and many contain no more than the original text of the title, the abstract and a single claim. A few patent databases – notably DERWENT's WORLD PATENTS INDEX, APIPAT and the CLAIMS UDB and CDB – index the entire patent specification by means of controlled thesaurus terms and chemical compound coding. The deepest indexing is provided at great expense, so it is not surprising that access to such indexing is usually restricted to organizations that have paid a subscription fee for access and is made available to non-subscribers, if at all, at a higher cost or for limited connect time. Indexing is common in databases produced from literature-abstracting services that include patents because of their technical content. Many of these databases are described in other chapters of the *Manual*. As an especially large proportion of the records in the online versions of *Chemical Abstracts*, are patents, it is discussed in this chapter as a major patent database, as well as in Chapter 4 of Volume I.

Prosecution history and legal status data fields

After a patent application is filed in a national patent office its legal status changes frequently. Prosecution history information is extremely valuable to those who are interested in the commercial exploitation of the invention claimed in the patent. If a valid patent grant is in force, the use of the patented invention can lead to a lawsuit. If the patent has lapsed or if the patent application has been abandoned, the invention is freely available.

Prior art search results

Patent examiners search the 'prior art' for patents or other publications that disclose or suggest the claimed invention in each patent application. The examiner notes in the patent application file citations to the most pertinent references found in the search, and some patent offices print the citations on the patent document when it is published. If the document is a granted patent, the cited references describe 'related art'; if the examiner had discovered a reference that described the claimed invention, the applicant would have been required to amend the claims before the patent was granted. If the document is a published application, some of the cited references may describe exactly the same product or process being claimed, and the application may never mature to a granted patent. Search reports made for European patent applications and PCT applications are issued as documents separate from the published application itself and are not always available when the published application is indexed by a database.

Cited references are useful in searches for technical information as they represent the most relevant prior publications on the claimed subject matter found by a skilled searcher. Even more useful are citing references – those later patents in which the patent examiner has cited a publication known to be relevant to the search in progress. Patent examiners still rely heavily on manual searches of patent documents, so they often cite valuable references that are not retrievable online in any other way, especially patents published before the online era. Conversely, some cited references relate to aspects of the citing patent that are irrelevant to the subject of the search in progress. Examiners' citations are also used as statistical indicators of patenting trends.

The patent classifications searched by the examiner are printed on the face of US patents as the field of search to indicate the scope of the examiner's search. It is not customary to publish any information about the additional non-patent sources of information that may have been used, although the references that were found are cited on the document.

Prosecution details

Before a patent is granted, the application passes through a number of stages in its prosecution. Monitoring the progress of a patent application can provide useful information to potential licensees or competitors. As of 2000, no information about the status of a US patent application is available to the public before the patent is issued, but the title and applicant of newly filed patent applications and/or progress in the prosecution of published applications are treated as public records in some countries. In many countries, before the application is examined, the applicant must make a formal request for examination of the application. Patent examiners issue office actions in which they report the results of the prior art search, make any necessary comments on the format of the application, and either allow or reject the claims. The applicants may abandon the application or file amendments, and they may file documents containing data supporting the patentability of the claimed invention. Applications that have been finally rejected by the examiner may be appealed to the courts, which eventually issue decisions on the patentability of the invention. In many countries, the public is invited to oppose the grant of a patent on an invention during a period of time after the examined patent specification is published. The usual route of publication for patent prosecution information is the printed patent office gazette. Increasingly, patent offices are making patent status information available online.

Amendments and certificates of correction

Many patent databases obtain information about the technical content of patents from published patent applications. But after a patent application has been filed and before a patent has been granted, the scope of the claims and the content of the supporting disclosure are often changed by amendment. Published applications therefore differ from the patent that eventually protects the claimed invention. In some countries the granted patent may be changed radically, either through the deletion of material found not to be pertinent to the allowed claims or through the addition of supporting data that were not in the application when it was filed. Patent databases do not usually index granted patents in sufficient depth to identify the changes wrought by amendments. If the legal scope of a patent indexed from the published application is important, it is essential to obtain a copy of the granted patent specification.

When a patent is published, errors are sometimes found in the document. In the USA, these can be corrected through the issuance of a Certificate of Correction. The existence of a Certificate of Correction is not noted in most patent databases.

Patent term lapse or extension

Patents expire at the end of their statutory term. The expiry date does not appear on the face of the patent, so it does not appear in patent databases. The expiry date is generally calculated by adding the length of the statutory term to the date from which that country measures patent terms. Calculating the expiry date of US patents is complicated by a change in patent law that defines the term of patents published prior to 8 June 1995, as the longer of 17 years from the date of grant and 20 years from the earliest filing date. Anticipated expiry dates have been added to the CLAIMS US patents databases.

Most of the world's patent laws require that periodic fees be paid to maintain a patent in force throughout its entire statutory term. Failure to pay these fees causes the patent to become void. Most patent databases do not record the lapse dates of patents, although the fact that a particular patent is no longer in force is of the greatest importance.

Sometimes a patentee gives up the right to some or all of the claims in the patent, either by dedicating the patent to the public before it expires or by disclaiming the unwanted claims. In the USA some patent applications are found to be so closely related to other, commonly owned, patents, that they are allowed to issue only on condition that the resulting patent expires no later than the related patent. In such cases, a terminal disclaimer – a statement that the patentee's rights will expire on a date earlier than the end of the statutory patent term – appears on the face of the patent. Although the patent becomes partly or wholly ineffective as of the disclaimer date, many patent databases do not record that information.

Patents may also be nullified as the result of a court decision. Although the decisions may be published in legal databases, the invalidation of the patent is not commonly reported in patent databases.

In some countries it is also possible to obtain an extension of a patent if it can be shown that the patentee was prevented from exercising its rights. Until recently, the only patent term extensions available in the USA covered pharmaceutical, medical and agricultural products kept from the marketplace by government regulatory delays, and the extension applies only to the approved product and not to the entire scope of the patent. Patents subject to a 20-year term may also be extended if the grant of the patent has been delayed by protracted patent appeals or interferences. European patents, and national patents issued by European countries and covering pharmaceutical products whose marketing was delayed by governmental approval processes, are extended through the issuance of Supplementary Protection Certificates. US patent term extensions and SPCs are recorded in patent databases that cover post-issuance actions, and information about patent term extensions may be available online in government regulations or business news databases. Patent term extensions issued by other countries are less likely to be reported in online databases.

Patent examiner and applicant's representative

Patents usually record the name of the patent attorney or agent who represented the patentee in the prosecution of the patent and sometimes record the name of the patent examiner who examined the patent application. This information may be useful to persons who are planning strategies for a patent suit or who are evaluating the persons involved for employment opportunities, but it is not important for searches into the technical content of the patent.

Patent databases

Patent databases have been mounted on the major search services since the dawn of the online era, and both the number of databases and the amount of information searchable and displayable in established databases has increased markedly over the years. The expansion of the World Wide Web resulted in the introduction of many additional patent databases during the late 1990s. As many of these databases were introduced only a short time before this was written, it is likely that major changes will be made in their availability, cost and features. Searchers are advised to refer to database documentation, especially online Help screens, to confirm the current file content and search capabilities.

Patent databases can be subdivided on the basis of their content and their availability. The simplest databases consist of information provided by patent offices – bibliographic information, international and national patent classification codes, patent status information and original text. Most of those databases contain data from a single patent-issuing authority, and many of them contain the full text of the patent specification. Searching the full text of a patent specification does not guarantee that all relevant patents will be retrieved. Searches for common terms inevitably retrieve an enormous volume of irrelevant material because the full text of the specification is reproduced. Obscure information is as accessible as significant information because the vocabulary in patents is completely uncontrolled. And because most full-text patent databases cover the entire scope of science and technology, text terms with more than one definition are likely to retrieve patents that are completely unrelated to the subject matter of the search.

Furthermore, searchers must use more than one language for retrieval of information from databases containing the text of European patents, PCT applications and patents published by multilingual countries. On the other hand, full-text databases are particularly good places to find patents dealing with brand names and generic drug names, and for specific plants, animals or microorganisms, as the biosystematic name can normally be used as an unambiguous search term. More informative databases contain indexing and abstracts provided by database producers; most databases in this category include patents from many patent-issuing authorities. The added value provided by database producers comes at a higher price, but searching is greatly facilitated by the application of controlled indexing across patents from many countries. Patent searching is also facilitated by the availability of multiple patent databases on a single search service. The major patent databases are mounted on one or more of STN International, DIALOG, or Questel-Orbit, where they may be accessed through multifile search capabilities and sorted with duplicate identification, grouping and removal commands. Comprehensive searching is not possible in those patent databases that are available from direct connections or individual World Wide Web sites. Most of these are limited to a single country's patents, have no controlled indexing, and provide answers only in strict chronological order or in the order prescribed by a proprietary relevance-ranking algorithm.

The data fields contained in major patent databases are summarized in the following sections. Databases are illustrated by a sample citation in full format from one of the host files or by the search and answer screens from proprietary search software. The print field tags shown in the figure appear in brackets in the discussion of the corresponding data elements; the illustrated field tags may not be applicable to the database on a different host. The figures illustrate citations from only a few patent families, so that the differences in record content can be seen readily. FR 2,707,166, and equivalent patents US 5,661,172 and WO 95/01791 are shown in Figures 2.2, 2.4, 2.5, 2.9, 2.17, 2.23 and 2.24 (pp. 51, 63, 70, 84, 100, 115 and 118); US 5,046,659, EP 557, 436 and equivalent patents are shown in Figures 2.3, 2.6, 2.7, 2.8, 2.16 and 2.22 (pp. 58, 74, 76, 79, 95 and 112); EP 687,807, JP 08-004521 and equivalents are shown in Figures 2.18 and 2.22 (pp. 102 and 112). The results of searches for the drug deslorelin in five different databases are shown in Figures 2.10–2.15, 2.25 and 2.26 (pp. 87–92, 121 and 123).

DERWENT WORLD PATENTS INDEX

The DERWENT WORLD PATENTS INDEX (DWPI) database produced by Derwent Information Ltd, covers the technological content of patents from 40 patent-issuing authorities and invention disclosures from two defensive publication journals. The database was designed to give access to the technical information in patents, not to provide bibliographic documentation of every patent in the database. For that reason, each record represents a family of patents that claim a single invention. The database corresponds to a complex of subscription

```
1/1 DWPI -  (C) Derwent- image
 AN   - 1995-054161 [08]
 XA   - C1995-024591
 TI   - Compsns. contg. efaroxan for treatment of
         neurodegenerative diseases – such as cognition loss,
         Alzheimer's disease, etc.
 DC   - B02
 PA   - (FABR ) FABRE MEDICAMENT SA PIERRE
 IN   - BRILEY M, COLPAERT F, IMBERT T
 NP   - 10
 NC   - 22
 PN   - FR2707166      A1   19950113 DW1995-08 A61K-031/415       8p *
         AP: 1993FR-0008497 19930709
       - WO9501791      A2   19950119 DW1995-09
         AP: 1994WO-FR00841 19940707
         DSNW: AU CA JP NZ US
         DSRW: AT BE CH DE DK ES FR GB GR IE IT LU MC NL PT SE
       - AU9472308      A    19950206 DW1995-18 A61K-031/415
         FD: Based on WO9501791
         AP: 1994AU-0072308 19940707
       - WO9501791      A3   19950309 DW1996-12 A61K-031/415
         AP: 1994WO-FR00841 19940707
       - AU-688346      B    19980312 DW1998-22 A61K-031/415
         FD: Previous Publ. AU9472308; Based on WO9501791
         AP: 1994AU-0072308 19940707
       - EP-707477      A1   19960424 DW1996-21 A61K-031/415 Fre
         FD: Based on WO9501791
         AP: 1994EP-0921698 19940707; 1994WO-FR00841 19940707
         DSR: AT BE CH DE DK ES FR GB GR IE IT LI LU MC NL PT SE
       - NZ-268914      A    19990629 DW1999-31 A61K-031/415
         FD: Based on WO9501791
         AP: 1994NZ-0268914 19940707; 1994WO-FR00841 19940707
       - US5661172      A    19970826 DW1997-40 A61K-031/415       2p
         FD: Based on WO9501791
         AP: 1994WO-FR00841 19940707; 1996US-0581516 19960111
       - EP-707477      B1   19991117 DW1999-53 A61K-031/415 Fre
         FD: Based on WO9501791
         AP: 1994EP-0921698 19940707; 1994WO-FR00841 19940707
         DSR: AT BE CH DE DK ES FR GB GR IE IT LI LU MC NL PT SE
       - JP08512305     W    19961224 DW1997-10 A61K-031/415       9p
         FD: Based on WO9501791
         AP: 1994WO-FR00841 19940707; 1995JP-0503865 19940707
 PR   - 1993FR-0008497 19930709
 CT   - EP-486385; EP--71368; US4855308
         6.Jnl.Ref
 IC   - A61K-031/415 C07D-405/04
 AB   - FR2707166 A
         The use of efaroxan of formula (I) and its derivs, salts,
         racemates, and isomers in medicaments for the treatment of
         neurodegenerative diseases, their progression, cognition
         loss, and especially the evolution of Alzheimer's disease,
```

Figure 2.2   **DERWENT WORLD PATENTS INDEX record: Questel-Orbit file DWPI**

as well as the disease itself, is new. R1 = H or 1-6C
alkyl; R2 = H, CH3, Cl, Br, or F; R3 = H, CH3, OH, CH3O,
Cl, Br or F.
USE - Efaroxan (I; R1 = ethyl; R2, R3 =
2,3-dihydroxy) is described in GB2102422 as an
anti-depressant and anti-migraine agent. Compounds of
formula (I) are also described in WO 92/05171 as
anti-diabetics and potassium channel blockers.   (Dwg.0/0)

```
IC     - A61K-031/415  C07D-405/04
EQAB - US5661172 A
         Method for the treatment of Alzheimer-like senile
         dementia, pre-Alzheimer's syndrome, and progressive
         supranuclear palsy, comprises administering an amount of a
***
MC    - CPI: B06-A01 B14-J01A4
UP     - 1995-08
UE     - 1995-09; 1995-18; 1996-12; 1996-21; 1997-10; 1997-40; 1998-22; 1999-31;
         1999-53
M2     - *01* D012 D016 D021 D022 D023 D100 F012 F522 H401 H441
         H541 H601 H602 H603 H608 H641 H642 M1 M116 M210 M211 M212
         M213 M214 M215 M216 M231 M232 M233 M240 M272 M280 M281
         M282 M283 M320 M412 M511 M521 M530 M540 M630 M640 M650
         M781 M800 M903 M904 P446 P448 P451 P625 9508-11801-U
CN     - 9508-11801-U
FN     - WPF15SH1.GIF
```

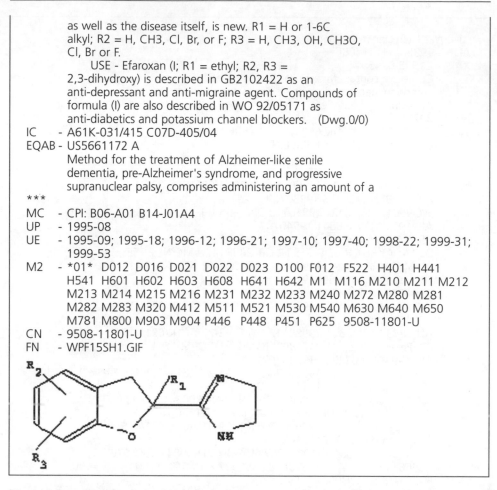

Figure 2.2 concluded

services: the 13 sections of the *Chemical Patents Index* (CPI, formerly known as the *Central Patents Index*), the three sections of the *Electrical Patents Index* (EPI) and the two sections of *General and Mechanical Patents Index* (GMPI). Subscribers may purchase print, microfilm, CD-ROM and magnetic tape versions of abstracts, indexes and complete specifications. They are given access to special in-depth coding for online retrieval and discounted rates for online searches. The database is mounted on STN, Questel-Orbit and DIALOG. It was announced in early 2000 that DERWENT WORLD PATENTS INDEX would become available through the DELPHION INTELLECTUAL PROPERTY NETWORK. Patents indexed by Derwent during the last three weeks can also be searched for limited bibliographic information in the Derwent Web site, <URL http://www.derwent.co.uk/>. Figure 2.2 shows the record for the patent family based on FR 2,707,166, from Questel-Orbit's file DWPI. Additional records showing DERWENT WORLD PATENTS INDEX data fields can be found in

Figures 2.3 and 2.22 (pp. 58 and 112).

Derwent began the database in 1963 with patents from 15 countries in the field of pharmaceuticals, and has gradually increased the scope of coverage over the years. Abstracts were printed on punched cards and all the indexing was represented by punch coding. Indexing has been expanded greatly, but the constraints of the punched card system are still evident in the fixed field formats that became the *de facto* standard for online systems as hosts converted patent data in other databases to Derwent's formats either as the only searchable format or as an alternative to the format provided by the database producer. Derwent has revamped its data processing system, enlarging the data fields so that those data elements that have historically been truncated can be entered in full. Although the changed formats will be apparent in Derwent's current products, it is possible that the host systems will not have been able to convert the online databases to the new formats, even though much effort has been expended to standardize patent data formats for all databases on each host system.

Patents from various countries are not treated equally, being divided for depth of indexing into 'major' and 'minor' countries. Indexing is based on the earliest publication of the patent specification in a covered country, the indexed patent being treated as the basic patent and later patents as equivalent. The patents indexed for the database are the first published document in each country. For some major countries, the examined patent is also indexed. Patent families are defined by the latest priority application cited on the patent documents. Patents that do not claim priority are sometimes made equivalent to other patents on the basis of their technical content, date of filing and ownership. Abstracts [AB] are prepared for basic patents and were included for equivalent granted patents from the UK, Germany, the European Patent Office and the USA [EQAB] prior to 1998.

The patent country code for basic and equivalent patents is searchable on the DERWENT WORLD PATENTS INDEX database both alone and in combination with the publication number. The standardized patent number used for cross-file searching is in a fixed nine- or 11-character format [PN]. The one- or two-character ISO code that indicates the level of publication is appended to each patent number in the patent family. Designated states for European and PCT documents are searchable and are printed as a subfield following the patent number, and a language field is also present in records that include these documents. Document numbers and Derwent's entry week are indexed for both basic and equivalent patents. The entry week corresponds to the week the patent was processed for the database, not to the date the document or its abstract was published. The 'number of patents' field [NP], which gives only the number of entries in the [PN] field, and the number of countries field [NC], which represents the number of countries the patents cover as national patents or designated states, are provided to give an indication of the breadth of coverage chosen by the applicant. Application numbers other than priority application numbers have been indexed only since 1984, and they were originally indexed only for basic patents and selected equivalent patents. The application number of the priority application, or the national application number if priority is not claimed, is indexed as a priority [PR], as are earlier and later applications relied on to establish filing dates of continuing applications. The national application numbers of patents that have been indexed as equivalent on the basis of technical content are also searchable as priorities. Application numbers were originally cross-file searchable in a fixed 11-character format, which resulted in the deletion of the first digit of serial numbers from countries; those having serial numbers with more than six digits have been indexed in full since 1992. Publication dates of basic and equivalent patents are provided in the PN field for patents indexed since 1974, and information about the filing details of patents – for example, the identities of corresponding regional patents or divisional status – have been provided since 1992.

Derwent's indexers use a thesaurus of standard company names for major patentees, and also integrate the more complete company name thesaurus used by INPADOC into the Derwent system. In addition to company names, Derwent uses a four- or five-character company code to index patent owners [PA], which can be found in a manual or through a patentee code look-up facility on Derwent's World Wide Web site. In the early punch code-based years, the company code was the only searchable patentee name, and standard codes were assigned to all patentees. Later, rules were developed for the assignment of non-standard codes to patentees without large patent portfolios, and standard codes are now used only for major patenting organizations. New standard company codes are added rather infrequently as Derwent has no regular procedure for identifying new companies with significant patent activity. Since non-standard codes are applied to more than one patentee, searches using these codes do not give precise answers. Codes are maintained when organizational name changes take place and, in most cases, recognized corporate affiliates are assigned the code belonging to the parent organization. In cases where equivalent patents name different patent assignees, all appropriate company codes and names are indexed. The patentee name field is of limited length; abbreviations are used and names are often truncated. It is best to use the **Neighbor** or **Expand** command to locate possible truncated forms of names and to check for the company code in the printed or Web-based *Company Code Manual*. Individual inventor names [IN] appear in the online database; for older patent families they are not in the corresponding printed abstract. Inventor names have been indexed only since 1978 and are taken only from basic documents other than Japanese patents, so a 'NO POSTINGS' message in a search for a patent by a particular inventor should never be taken as evidence that the invention has not been patented.

Accession numbers in DERWENT WORLD PATENTS INDEX [AN] refer to the entire patent family and take the form ####-X####X, where # is a numeral and X is either a letter or a numeral. The first four digits refer to the entry year of the basic patent and correspond to the terminal letter that designated the year of publication from 1970 to mid-1983. Prior to 2000, accession numbers used a two-digit year designation, and searchers should be aware that references to Derwent patent families are likely to show the accession number in the older format. Before a unified chemical patents service was established in 1970, Derwent produced three separate patent services: FARMDOC, with accession numbers terminating in F; AGDOC, with accession numbers terminating in G or H; and PLASDOC, with accession numbers terminating in P or Q. Dummy year designations were assigned to records from these three services, so that the year '1966' corresponds to all 'pre-CPI' pharmaceutical patents, '1967' corresponds to agricultural patents, and '1968' corresponds to polymer patents. Because the records were created from three independent databases, there are two or three records for some families of patents from the pre-CPI era. The Questel-Orbit DWPI file has accession numbers with the dummy year '1965' assigned to records incorporated into the file through the merger of the APIPAT file with DWPI. Related accession numbers are reported in the XR field for some patent families, but they are not provided for most of these pre-CPI records. Throughout most of its history, Derwent's system for assigning equivalent patents to families assigned them only to one of the multiple pre-CPI records; if a full patent family is needed it is necessary to search for a second record based on the same priority or having overlapping patent families. Since 1983, Derwent has assigned two series of secondary accession numbers in addition to the primary accession numbers. These are in the format ####-C##### for chemical patents [XA] and ####-N##### for non-chemical patents.

Derwent abstractors write descriptive titles [TI] for all basic patents. The titles of all but the earliest records include an indication of the inventive concept stressed in the patent specification. Abstracts are available online for most patent families. Derwent produces two kinds of abstracts for chemical patents: short abstracts are published in *Alerting Bulletins*, and longer documentation abstracts of basic chemical patents are published a few weeks later in *Documentation Abstracts Journals*; only the alerting abstracts are online. The Extended Abstract text present in *Documentation Abstracts* has been available in separate subscriber-level files since 1999. The printed abstracts include drawings and chemical structures and describe the invention in terms of them. Drawings and chemical structures are omitted from the online record of early basic patents and a single drawing or chemical structure record is available for recent basic patents [FN], but the verbal descriptions of the symbols in the drawings are online. Abstracts are not written for most basic patents from 'minor' countries or for non-chemical Japanese patents, although the expanded titles are often sufficient to allow retrieval. The notation 'NoAbstract' appears in the title of unabstracted patents to allow their exclusion from sets of records whose abstracts are to be printed. In addition to the title and abstract text, additional words are added to the online file if they are thought to be likely search terms. A thesaurus of heavily posted terms has been devised, and the preferred form of a significant title term is searchable in addition to the form that appears in the text. The title, abstract and index terms are written, with British spelling, as summaries of the entire patent specification. The novel features of the claims are stressed, but the claims are not reproduced verbatim except as the abstracts of some equivalent patents granted before 1998.

International Patent Classification codes [IC1] are indexed from the basic patent, and additional IPC codes are added to the online record when they are found in equivalent patents. Derwent assigns IPC codes to patents published without IPC codes and to non-patent references indexed from *Research Disclosure* and *International Technology Abstracts*. Derwent also applies several of its own indexing schemes to patents. The Derwent Classification Codes [DC], used for subdividing technologies in the printed abstract books, are useful for limiting searches to a general field. Use of the more precise special coding schemes is limited to subscribers. There is a system of 'Manual Codes' [MC]: hierarchical classification codes designed to sort printed documents for manual searching. A polymer code is used for patents classified in Section A (PLASDOC) of CPI; a chemical fragmentation code [M2] is applied to patents in Sections B, C and E, known as FARMDOC, AGDOC and CHEMDOC respectively. Derwent registry numbers have been applied to a few thousand common chemical compounds since 1981. Since 1987 most chemical structures in patents indexed in Sections B, C and E have been indexed for the MERGED MARKUSH SERVICE (MMS) structure file using Markush DARC software to provide topological storage and retrieval of both generically defined chemical structures and specific compounds. MMS is available only on Questel-Orbit, but Markush DARC compound numbers [CN] are searchable on all hosts. In 1999 Derwent introduced a new Derwent Chemistry Resource with searchable structures of specific and generic compounds. The Derwent Chemistry Resource provides supplemental information to the MERGED MARKUSH SERVICE on Questel-Orbit and is searchable with Messenger software in the DWPI file on STN.

Patents cited as references in European and PCT patent applications [CT] published before 1998 are indexed, but patents cited in other countries and journal references are not. The grant of a patent based on an indexed published application is indicated by the additional posting of a B- or C-level document among the equivalent patents. US re-issue patents and re-examined patents are indexed as equivalents to the original patent.

DERWENT WORLD PATENTS INDEX is updated weekly with bibliographic information, abstracts, IPC codes and subscriber manual codes. The remainder of the subscriber coding is added to the records several weeks after the bibliographic data. Patent families are updated whenever new equivalent patents are found. New information is taken from the weekly CPI, EPI and GMPI publications, and update codes correspond to the volume number of the printed abstract books. The actual publication date of the patents added to the file in a particular week varies from country to country; for example, week 2008 contains UK patents published during the first week of February 2000, and patents published in other countries from one week to several months later.

Questel-Orbit has retained all of Derwent's fixed-length fields and employs them as cross-file searchable formats in other patent databases. DIALOG and STN allow searching and display of records in Derwent format, but they reformat Derwent's patent, priority and application numbers for cross-file searching into standard DIALOG and STN formats by separating the country code and serial numbers. In DIALOG format the numerical sequence can be searched separately from the bound format of the country code, number and year. If one has an application serial number without an associated year of filing, this is a welcome improvement, but because DIALOG's format does not reverse Derwent's modifications to published patent numbers, some cross-file searches do not retrieve the correct documents in other databases. To address this problem, the **MAPPN** command converts Japanese patents to both the Imperial year and the Gregorian year for cross-file searches, resulting in the retrieval of unrelated patents as false drops when a database coincidentally contains the same serial number for a different level of publication. STN's **SELECT** and **TRANSFER** commands routinely generate all appropriate patent number formats for cross-file searching.

Derwent Patent Citation Index

The DERWENT PATENT CITATION INDEX database, (DPCI), produced by Derwent Information Ltd, covers patent and literature citations from the patents in DERWENT WORLD PATENTS INDEX. DERWENT PATENT CITATION INDEX was designed to provide information about the relationships among patents on the basis of citations made by examiners during examination, and to give access to related information in earlier patents cited by examiners and inventors as well as to later patents that have cited a patent. The original file design included both inventors' and examiners' citations from 16 patent-issuing authorities. In 1997 the database was redesigned, and later updates include only examiners' citations from European, PCT, British, US, Japanese and German patents, which made up 90 per cent of the original cited references. Unlike other patent citation databases, each record represents a family of patents that claim a single invention and lists the cited and citing references for the entire patent family in a single record, including both patent and non-patent literature references. The database is mounted on STN and DIALOG. Figure 2.3 shows the record for the patent family based on US 5,046,659 from STN's file DPCI.

A DERWENT PATENT CITATION INDEX record contains the bibliographic fields present in the corresponding DERWENT WORLD PATENTS INDEX records, primary and secondary accession numbers [AN, DNN], title [TI], Derwent class [DC], inventor names [IN], patentee names and codes [PA], number of patent countries [CYC], individual patent numbers, publication and entry dates, language, International Patent Classification codes [PI], application numbers and dates [ADT], priority numbers and dates [PRAI], International Patent Classification codes [IC, ICM, ICS] and file segments [FS]. The national and IPC [IC] codes forming the examiners' fields of search [EXF] are provided, as are counts of all citation data [CTCS] for use in statistical evaluations. Cited references include lists of cited patents [CDP] for each patent in the Derwent family, segmented into those cited by the inventor and those cited by the examiner. Later issued citing patents [CGP] are likewise segmented into citations of each patent family member by the inventor and examiner of the later patents. Patent citations include the patent number and Derwent primary accession number and the patentee and inventors named in the Derwent record; for cited patents that are

```
L2    ANSWER 1 OF 1  DPCI  COPYRIGHT 1998 DERWENT INFORMATION LTD
AN    91-287645 [39]  DPCI
DNN   N91-220122
TI    Latching structure for food container - has lid and base provided
      with mating male and female latching elements.
DC    Q32 Q33
IN    WARBURTON, R T
PA    (MOBI) MOBIL OIL CORP; (VISA) VISKASE CORP
CYC   15
PI    US 5046659   A  910910 (9139)*
      WO 9208649 A1 920529 (9224)  EN   23 pp      B65D001-26
          RW: AT BE CH DE DK ES FR GB GR IT LU NL SE
           W: CA
      EP   557436   A1 930901 (9335)  EN   13 pp      B65D001-26
        R: BE DE FR GB IT NL
      US   5046659  B1 940222 (9408)         3 pp      B65D001-22
      EP   557436   A4 950412 (9613)
      EP   557436   B1 970409 (9719)  EN   15 pp      B65D043-16
        R:  BE DE FR GB IT NL
      DE   69125615 E  970515 (9725)                   B65D043-16
ADT   US 5046659 A US 90-611576 901113; WO 9208649 A1 WO 91-US8437 911112;
      EP 557436 A1 WO 91-US8437 911112, EP 92-900796 911112; US 5046659 B1
      US 90-611576 901113;   EP 557436 A4 EP 92-900796           ; EP 557436 B1
      WO 91-US8437 911112, EP 92-900796 911112; DE 69125615 E DE 91-625615
      911112, WO 91-US8437 911112, EP 92-900796 911112
FDT   EP 557436 A1 Based on WO 9208649; EP 557436 B1 Based on WO 9208649;
      DE 69125615 E Based on EP 557436, Based on WO 9208649
PRAI  US 90-611576   901113
IC    ICM B65D001-22; B65D001-26; B65D043-16
      ICS B65D021-02; B65D043-02
FS    GMPI


EXF   EXAMINER'S FIELD OF SEARCH  UPE: 971007
-------------------------------------------------


IC    EP 557436   A4 950412
      A44B; A45C; B65D
      EP 557436   B1 970409
      B65D043-16


CTCS CITATION COUNTERS
------------------------------------

PNC.DI   0          Cited Patents Count (by inventor)
PNC.DX   22         Cited Patents Count (by examiner)
IAC.DI   0          Cited Issuing Authority Count (by inventor)
IAC.DX   5          Cited Issuing Authority Count (by examiner)

PNC.GI   2          Citing Patents Count (by inventor)
PNC.GX   17         Citing Patents Count (by examiner)
IAC.GI   2          Citing Issuing Authority Count (by inventor)
IAC.GX   3          Citing Issuing Authority Count (by examiner)
```

Figure 2.3   DERWENT PATENT CITATION INDEX: STN file DPCI

```
CRC.I        0          Cited Literature References Count (by inventor)
CRC.X        0          Cited Literature References Count (by examiner)

CDP  CITED PATENTS    UPD: 971007
---------------------------

     Cited by Examiner
     -----------------------

     CITING PATENT  CAT    CITED PATENT    ACCNO
     ----------------------------------------------------------------
     EP 557436    A1           US 2706065  A
                               US 3149747  A
                    IN:  BURGESS
                               US 4193496  A    80-C9554C/13
                    PA:  (BARR-I) BARRATT D C
                               US 4333580  A    82-H5478E/25
                    PA:  (ASPL-N) ASSOC PLASTICS INC
                    IN:  SWEIGART, R L
                               US 4512474       85-115728/19
                    PA:  (PLAS-N) PLASTOFILM IND INC
                    IN:  LEROY, A H
                               US 4576330       86-093524/14
                    PA:  (INLI-N) INLINE PLASTICS COR
                    IN:  SCHEPP, F
     EP 557436    A4   A       DE 2021350  A
                    PA:  (ISAP) ISAP SPA
                      A        DE 2461107  A    76-F9959X/27
                    PA:  (SCHO-I) SCHONFELD P
                      A        FR 1557699  A
                    PA:  JUNGWIRTH SOHN KG
                      A        FR 2429920  A    80-D2763C/15
                    PA:  (GODE-I) GODEY R
                      A        FR 2494175  A    82-41527E/21
                    PA:  (BOUR-N) SOC BOURGUIG PLAST
                    IN:  GONZE, A
                      XY       US 3565146  A    68-44064Q/00
                    PA:  (KALL) KALLE AG
                      Y        US 4771934  A    88-284871/40
                    PA:  (INLI-N) INLINE PLASTICS COR
                    IN:  KALMANIDES, D
     EP 557436    B1           DE 2021350  A
                    PA:  (ISAP) ISAP SPA
                               DE 2461107  A    76-F9959X/27
                    PA:  (SCHO-I) SCHONFELD P
                               FR 1557699  A
                    PA:  JUNGWIRTH SOHN KG
                               FR 2429920  A    80-D2763C/15
                    PA:  (GODE-I) GODEY R
*
*
*
```

Figure 2.3   cont'd

```
        US 5046659  A              CA 1117491  A   82-C1916E/09
                         PA:  (MAYL-N) MAYLED/INTINI DESIG
                         IN:  INTINI, T
                                 GB 1418897       75-N6417W/52
                         PA:  (WADD) PLASTONA WADDINGTON LTD JOHN
                                 GB 1602694       81-L8047D/46
                         PA:  (KEYE-N) KEYER HUNTSMAN LTD
                         IN:  DICK, J A
  *
  *
  *

        WO 9208649  A1             US 2706065  A
                                   US 3149747  A
                         IN:  BURGESS
                                 US 4193496  A   80-C9554C/13
                         PA:  (BARR-I) BARRATT D C
                                 US 4333580  A   82-H5478E/25
                         PA:  (ASPL-N) ASSOC PLASTICS INC
                         IN:  SWEIGART, R L
                                 US 4512474       85-115728/19
                         PA:  (PLAS-N) PLASTOFILM IND INC
                         IN:  LEROY, A H
                                 US 4576330       86-093524/14
                         PA:  (INLI-N) INLINE PLASTICS COR
                         IN:  SCHEPP, F


CGP  CITING PATENTS     UPG: 970819
----------------------------


     Cited by Inventor
     ----------------------


     CITED PATENT    CITING PATENT   ACCNO
     -----------------------------------------------
     US 5046659  A   CA  2119979  A   95-107408/15
                         PA:  (WILE-I) WILEY J M
                         IN:  WILEY, J M
                         US  5515993  A   96-250693/25
                         PA:  (TENC) TENNECO PLASTICS CO
                         IN:  MCMANUS, M W


     Cited by Examiner
     ----------------------


     CITED PATENT    CAT     CITING PATENT   ACCNO
     ------------------------------------------------------------------
     US 5046659  A              EP 544429   A1 93-177200/22
                         PA:  (MOBI) MOBIL OIL CORP; (VISA) VISKASE CORP
                         IN:  FRITZ, J A; HANSEN, D P
                         A       EP 661217   A3 95-232792/31
                         PA:  (BEKH-I) BEKHIET F
                         IN:  BEKHIET, F
```

Figure 2.3   cont'd

Figure 2.3   concluded

not in DERWENT WORLD PATENTS INDEX only the patent number and other data in the citation are given. For patents having non-patent literature citations, the cited references are provided in the format shown in the patent document.

INPADOC

INPADOC is a database of bibliographic patent information originally compiled by the International Patent Documentation Center (INPADOC), formerly an agency of the Austrian Patent Office and WIPO, and now produced by the European Patent Office. Data on patents published by 67 patent offices are forwarded to Vienna and reformatted for entry into the database and the weekly *INPADOC Patent Gazette*. The starting date for coverage varies, as each country began submitting data to INPADOC at a different time and some countries have submitted retrospective data. Bibliographic data differ somewhat from country to country because some countries omit certain information from the records that they provide to INPADOC. Although the database is updated weekly, the update schedule varies from country to country. Information is added to the INPADOC computer whenever it is received from the contributing patent offices, with a lag time of a few days or many months after publication of the patents, depending on the country.

INPADOC is searchable on the INPADOC PFS/PRS service in Vienna, operated by the European Patent Office, the Japanese PATOLIS system, LEXIS-NEXIS, MicroPatent, Questel-Orbit, DIALOG and STN, but the database differs radically according to the individual host. Although the data in INPADOC is the same on all hosts, records are organized quite differently. INPADOC has a file of patent status information on Austrian, Belgian, Brazilian, British, Danish, Dutch, European Patent Office, Finnish, French, German, Hungarian, Irish, Italian, Lithuanian, Monacan, PCT, Portuguese, Spanish, Swedish, Swiss and US patents.

The history of the progress of the patent application through the patent system of each country is tracked, but the data are not always current. Status information for the patent family is searchable in the INPADOC database on DIALOG; on STN, MicroPatent and LEXIS-NEXIS, legal status information is displayable but not directly searchable. On Questel-Orbit legal status data are segregated into the LEGSTAT database, where they may be searched directly. Legal status information is displayable in the ORBIT INPADOC file only by using the **FAMSTAT** command after a search has been carried out.

As mounted in Vienna, the INPADOC PFS/PRS is a patent family database, searchable only by means of patent number, application and priority data, and yields a list of all patent documents in the file with a common priority. Titles, names, IPCs and dates are printable, but not searchable. A fee is charged for each family searched. A search using the INPADOC computer is not exclusively a computer search. Online searches of the database are monitored by INPADOC staff members in Vienna, who back up each search with a manual search that sometimes identifies additional, equivalent non-priority patents. Searchers who attempt to use an unacceptable query are notified by INPADOC that they have made an error.

DIALOG's file 345 also permits searching for families without generating a search fee. An INPADOC record on DIALOG is stored as a complete family; the charge for displaying a record is determined by the format chosen for the display. DIALOG records can be printed in tabular format. Individual 'country families' can be extracted from the record for less expensive display using the standard ISO country code to designate the display format. The record for the 'patent basic' can also be displayed inexpensively, but unfortunately the earliest patent entered into a family is often the announcement of an unpublished patent application filing, and titles are often meaningless. A full citation from DIALOG file 345 of the patent family that includes FR 2,707,166, complete with the legal status information, is shown in Figure 2.4.

Patent country and number are indexed for each patent using the ISO country code and the document number; the patent kind code and publication date are also provided. Designated states are listed in the record of European and PCT documents, with separate lists of WO documents for countries designated for a national patent and those designated for coverage by a European or other regional patent. A separate record is provided for each level of publication of a patent document, but not every country provides INPADOC with the details of all levels of publication. INPADOC's Manual 002 lists the types of patents documented by each country; the manual can be downloaded from the EPO Web site, <URL http://www.european-patent-office.org/>. Each record carries the full patent kind code, which is necessary to identify the latest version of the document for countries in which the various levels of publication keep the same number. Later publications of the same patent in countries that assign different numbers to the various levels of publication can be correlated with the earlier publications through the application number. Each record bears the local application number and date as well as priority application numbers and dates. The national

DIALOG(R)File 345:Inpadoc/Fam.& Legal Stat
(c) 2000 EPO. All rts. reserv.

12171184
Basic Patent (No,Kind,Date): FR 2707166 Λ1 19950113 <No. of Patents: 013>
Patent Family:

Patent No	Kind	Date	Applic No	Kind	Date
AT 186640	E	19991215	EP 94921698	A	19940707
AU 9472308	A1	19950206	AU 9472308	A	19940707
AU 688346	B2	19980312	AU 9472308	A	19940707
DE 69421705	C0	19991223	DE 69421705	A	19940707
EP 707477	A1	19960424	EP 94921698	A	19940707
EP 707477	B1	19991117	EP 94921698	A	19940707
FR 2707166	A1	19950113	FR 938497	A	19930709 (BASIC)
FR 2707166	B1	19950929	FR 938497	A	19930709
JP 8512305	T2	19961224	JP 94503865	A	19940707
NZ 268914	A	19990629	NZ 268914	A	19940707
US 5661172	A	19970826	US 581516	A	19960111
WO 9501791	A2	19950119	WO 94FR841	A	19940707
WO 9501791	A3	19950309	WO 94FR841	A	19940707

Priority Data (No,Kind,Date):
    FR 938497   A   19930709
    WO 94FR841   W   19940707

PATENT FAMILY:
AUSTRIA (AT)
    Patent (No,Kind,Date): AT 186640 E 19991215
        VERWENDUNG VON EFAROXAN UND DESSEN DERIVATEN ZUR HERSTELLUNG EINES
        ARZNEIMITTELS ZUR BEHANDLUNG NEUROGENERATIVER ERKRANKUNGEN (German)
        Patent Assignee: PF MEDICAMENT (FR)
        Author (Inventor): COLPAERT FRANCIS (FR); BRILEY MICHAEL (FR);
        IMBERT THIERRY (FR)
        Priority (No,Kind,Date): FR 938497 A 19930709
        Applic (No,Kind,Date): EP 94921698 A 19940707
        Addnl Info: 707477 19991117
        IPC: * A61K-031/415
        CA Abstract No: * 122(13)151400U
        Derwent WPI Acc No: * C 95-054161
        Language of Document: German

AUSTRIA (AT)
    Legal Status (No,Type,Date,Code,Text):
        AT 186640 R 19991215 AT REF CORRESPONDS TO EP-PATENT
                            (ENTSPRICHT EP-PATENT)
                            EP 707477 P 19991117

AUSTRALIA (AU)
    Patent (No,Kind,Date): AU 9472308 A1 19950206
        USE OF EFAXORAN AND ITS DERIVATIVES FOR THE PRODUCTION OF DRUGS FOR
        TREATING NEURODEGENERATIVE DISEASES (English)
        Patent Assignee: PF MEDICAMENT

Figure 2.4   INPADOC family and status record: DIALOG file 345

Author (Inventor): COLPAERT FRANCIS; BRILEY MICHAEL; IMBERT THIERRY
Priority (No,Kind,Date): FR 938497 A 19930709; WO 94FR841 W
  19940707
Applic (No,Kind,Date): AU 9472308 A 19940707
IPC: * A61K-031/415
Derwent WPI Acc No: * C 95-054161
Language of Document: English
Patent (No,Kind,Date): AU 688346 B2 19980312
  USE OF EFAXORAN AND ITS DERIVATIVES FOR THE PRODUCTION OF DRUGS FOR
    TREATING NEURODEGENERATIVE DISEASES (English)
  Patent Assignee: PF MEDICAMENT
  Author (Inventor): COLPAERT FRANCIS; BRILEY MICHAEL; IMBERT THIERRY
  Priority (No,Kind,Date): FR 938497 A 19930709; WO 94FR841 W
    19940707
  Applic (No,Kind,Date): AU 9472308 A 19940707
  IPC: * A61K-031/415
  CA Abstract No: * 122(13)151400U
  Derwent WPI Acc No: * C 95-054161
  Language of Document: English

CANADA (CA)
  Legal Status (No,Type,Date,Code,Text):
    CA 2166781 P 19960108 CA REFW CORRESPONDS TO PCT
                    APPLICATION (ENTSPRICHT PCT ANMELDUNG)
                    WO 9501791 P

GERMANY (DE)
  Patent (No,Kind,Date): DE 69421705 C0 19991223
    VERWENDUNG VON EFAROXAN UND DESSEN DERIVATEN ZUR HERSTELLUNG EINES
      ARZNEIMITTELS ZUR BEHANDLUNG NEUROGENERATIVER ERKRANKUNGEN (German)
    Patent Assignee: PIERRE FABRE MEDICAMENT BOULOG (FR)
    Author (Inventor): COLPAERT FRANCIS (FR); BRILEY MICHAEL (FR);
      IMBERT THIERRY (FR)
    Priority (No,Kind,Date): FR 938497 A 19930709; WO 94FR841 W
      19940707
    Applic (No,Kind,Date): DE 69421705 A 19940707
    IPC: * A61K-031/415
    CA Abstract No: * 122(13)151400U
    Derwent WPI Acc No: * C 95-054161
    Language of Document: German

GERMANY (DE)
  Legal Status (No,Type,Date,Code,Text):
    DE 69421705 P 19991223 DE REF CORRESPONDS TO (ENTSPRICHT)
                    EP 707477 P 19991223

EUROPEAN PATENT OFFICE (EP)
  Patent (No,Kind,Date): EP 707477 A1 19960424
    USE OF EFAXORAN AND ITS DERIVATIVES FOR THE PRODUCTION OF DRUGS FOR
      TREATING NEURODEGENERATIVE DISEASES (English; French; German)
    Patent Assignee: PF MEDICAMENT (FR)
    Author (Inventor): COLPAERT FRANCIS (FR); BRILEY MICHAEL (FR);

Figure 2.4   cont'd

IMBERT THIERRY (FR)
Priority (No,Kind,Date): WO 94FR841 W 19940707; FR 938497 A
19930709
Applic (No,Kind,Date): EP 94921698 A 19940707
Designated States: (National) AT; BE; CH; DE; DK; ES; FR; GB; GR; IE;
IT; LI; LU; MC; NL; PT; SE
IPC: * A61K-031/415
CA Abstract No: * 122(13)151400U
Derwent WPI Acc No: * C 95-054161
Language of Document: French
Patent (No,Kind,Date): EP 707477 B1 19991117
USE OF EFAXORAN AND ITS DERIVATIVES FOR THE PRODUCTION OF DRUGS FOR
TREATING NEURODEGENERATIVE DISEASES (English; French; German)
Patent Assignee: PF MEDICAMENT (FR)
Author (Inventor): COLPAERT FRANCIS (FR); BRILEY MICHAEL (FR);
IMBERT THIERRY (FR)
Priority (No,Kind,Date): WO 94FR841 W 19940707; FR 938497 A
19930709
Applic (No,Kind,Date): EP 94921698 A 19940707
Designated States: (National) AT; BE; CH; DE; DK; ES; FR; GB; GR; IE;
IT; LI; LU; MC; NL; PT; SE
IPC: * A61K-031/415
CA Abstract No: * 122(13)151400U
Derwent WPI Acc No: * C 95-054161
Language of Document: French

EUROPEAN PATENT OFFICE (EP)
Legal Status (No,Type,Date,Code,Text):
EP 707477   P   19930709   EP AA   PRIORITY (PATENT
                                     APPLICATION) (PRIORITAET (PATENTANMELDUNG))
                                     FR 938497 A 19930709
EP 707477   P   19940707   EP AA   PCT-APPLICATION
                                     (PCT-ANMELDUNG)
                                     WO 94FR841 W 19940707
EP 707477   P   19940707   EP AE   EP-APPLICATION
                                     (EUROPAEISCHE ANMELDUNG)
                                     EP 94921698 A   19940707
EP 707477   P   19960424   EP AK   DESIGNATED CONTRACTING
                                     STATES IN AN APPLICATION WITH SEARCH REPORT
                                     (IN EINER ANMELDUNG BENANNTE VERTRAGSSTAATEN)
                                     AT BE CH DE DK ES FR GB GR IE IT LI LU MC NL
                                     PT SE
EP 707477   P   19960424   EP A1   PUBLICATION OF APPLICATION
                                     WITH SEARCH REPORT (VEROEFFENTLICHUNG DER
                                     ANMELDUNG MIT RECHERCHENBERICHT)
EP 707477   P   19960911   EP 17Q   FIRST EXAMINATION REPORT
                                     (ERSTER PRUEFUNGSBESCHEID)
                                     960725
EP 707477   P   19961211   EP RIN1   INVENTOR (CORRECTION)
                                     (ERFINDER (KORR.))
                                     COLPAERT, FRANCIS ; BRILEY, MICHAEL ; IMBERT,
                                     THIERRY

Figure 2.4   cont'd

```
        EP 707477          P    19991117    EP AK      DESIGNATED CONTRACTING
                                            STATES MENTIONED IN A PATENT SPECIFICATION:
                                            (IN EINER PATENTSCHRIFT ANGEFUEHRTE BENANNTE
                                            VERTRAGSSTAATEN)
                                            AT BE CH DE DK ES FR GB GR IE IT LI LU MC NL
                                            PT SE
        EP 707477          P    19991117    EP B1      PATENT SPECIFICATION
                                            (PATENTSCHRIFT)
        EP 707477          P 19991117       EP REF     IN AUSTRIA REGISTERED AS:
                                            (IN AT EINGETRAGEN ALS:)
                                            AT 186640 R 19991215
        EP 707477          P 19991223       EP REF     CORRESPONDS TO:
                                            (ENTSPRICHT)
                                            DE 69421705   P    19991223
FRANCE (FR)
    Patent (No,Kind,Date): FR 2707166 A1 19950113
        UTILISATION DE L'EFAROXAN ET DE SES DERIVES POUR LA FABRICATION DE
            MEDICAMENTS DESTINES AU TRAITEMENT DE MALADIES NEURODEGENERATIVES ET
            LEUR PROGRESSION . (French)
    Patent Assignee: PF MEDICAMENT (FR)
    Author (Inventor): FRANCIS COLPAERT; MICHAEL BRILEY; THIERRY IMBERT
    Priority (No,Kind,Date): FR 938497 A 19930709
    Applic (No,Kind,Date): FR 938497 A 19930709
    IPC: * A61K-031/415
    Derwent WPI Acc No: ; C 95-054161
    Language of Document: French
    Patent (No,Kind,Date): FR 2707166 B1 19950929
        UTILISATION DE L'EFAROXAN ET DE SES DERIVES POUR LA FABRICATION DE
            MEDICAMENTS DESTINES AU TRAITEMENT DE MALADIES NEURODEGENERATIVES ET
            LEUR PROGRESSION . (French)
    Patent Assignee: PF MEDICAMENT (FR)
    Author (Inventor): FRANCIS COLPAERT; MICHAEL BRILEY; THIERRY IMBERT
    Priority (No,Kind,Date): FR 938497 A 19930709
    Applic (No,Kind,Date): FR 938497 A 19930709
    IPC: * A61K-031/415
    CA Abstract No: * 122(13)151400U
    Derwent WPI Acc No: * C 95-054161
    Language of Document: French


FRANCE (FR)
    Legal Status (No,Type,Date,Code,Text):
        FR 9308497         AN 19950113 FR AGA       FIRST PUBLICATION OF
                                            APPLICATION (DELIVRANCE (PREM. PUB. DEMANDE
                                            DE BREVET))
                                            FR 2707166 A1 19950113
        FR 9308497         AN 19950929 FR AGA       SECOND PUBLICATION OF PATENT
        FR 2707166    B1 19950929
        FR 2707166         PN 19930709 FR AE        APPLICATION DATE (DATE DE
                                            LA DEMANDE)
                                            FR 938497 A 19930709
    ****
```

Figure 2.4   concluded

application number is duplicated in the priority field if no Convention priority is claimed. Patent applicant and assignee names are standardized for organizations with many patents. For countries that report them, inventor names are also present. The country of origin of the patentee and inventors is also present in the records of some countries' patents.

In addition to the bibliographic information relating to the patent documents themselves, INPADOC records contain cross-reference accession numbers for patents indexed in CHEMICAL ABSTRACTS, JAPIO or the DERWENT WORLD PATENTS INDEX. Cross-reference accession numbers are not provided for all equivalent patents in the family. Derwent accession numbers are represented in the form A##-######, where A represents the letter 'C' for patents classified in one of the chemical sections of the WORLD PATENTS INDEX database and 'G' for patents that are classified only in the electrical or general and mechanical sections. The numerical part of the accession number is Derwent's primary accession number; these Derwent accession numbers should not be confused with Derwent's secondary accession numbers which begin with the letters 'C' and 'N.'

The original title is given in its original language. Titles in non-Roman alphabets are translated into English. Some records have no titles; Japanese titles are provided as updates to the records after several months' delay. The International Patent Classification codes applied to the patents by the issuing patent office are listed. INPADOC contains neither abstracts nor additional indexing. The language of the document is provided if the issuing patent office provides the information.

The INPADOC databases on STN and Questel-Orbit have individual records for each patent publication. All bibliographical data are printable and searchable. Although it is possible to generate a patent family by searching for a priority number, this may or may not generate a full INPADOC family. INPADOC defines a patent family as any patent that shares one or more priorities with any other patent in the database. This is a very broad definition and provides families that often incorporate several different Derwent patent families, including some based on typographical errors.

The STN implementation of INPADOC stores data in individual patent records and generates appropriate family data automatically on the basis of the chosen display format. Formats are provided for individual patent publications, with or without patent status data, for compilations of all levels of publication for a patent for a given country and for the latest level of publication for a single country. These are available for less than the price of a full family display. All field labels are in English. Beginning in 1999, STN augments records from some countries with patent abstracts; the countries announced initially are the US and PCT signatories, as well as several other countries.

The INPADOC file on Questel-Orbit contains all the bibliographical and technical information in INPADOC's patent family database, but not the patent status information which is directly searchable in a separate LEGSTAT database. As in the INPADOC PFS/PRS, a surcharge is made for searches that generate patent families. In order to collect the surcharge, Questel-Orbit permits searches for patent family information only through special commands: **FAM** followed by the patent, application or priority number; **FPRI**, which generates the patent family through input of a priority application number; and **FPAT**, which locates equivalents to a patent number. A family search yields a set of records that may be manipulated further or printed in any available format. The **FAMSTAT** command also provides patent family information, displaying the patent status records as well as the bibliographic records for each patent in the family of any patent in an answer set; **FAMSTATE** displays only the English field labels. **FAMLIST** and **FAMLISTE** display separate lists of bibliographic and status information, the format used in the old ORBIT INPADOC file; **FAMINPD** displays only bibliographic records.

Questel-Orbit has augmented the PLUSPAT file with abstracts taken from the patents comprising the PCT Minimum Documentation collection and with the data formerly included in the EDOC database. EDOC was originally produced by INPI from data generated by the European Patent Office for use by its examiners. The file contained ECLATX classification codes and patent family information generated independently from the family data collected for the INPADOC database. Coverage of German patents begins in 1877, with other countries added over the years. Most of the patents in the European Patent Office files have been reclassified for the convenience of its patent examiners, using a refined version of the International Patent Classification code (ECLA) or, for some technologies, using the Netherlands' national patent classification code. The classification codes are applied in a consistent manner to all of the patents in the files, including those patents that were published before the IPC system was created. The EDOC data are especially useful for retrieving information about the status of Japanese patents issued before Japanese patent law changed in 1994, as they contain not only the numbers of patent applications published before and after examination, but also granted patent numbers which were omitted from other patent family databases.

CLAIMS

The CLAIMS family of databases, produced by IFI CLAIMS Patent Services, covers US patents issued since 1950. The CLAIMS BIBLIO/ABSTRACT database, the CLAIMS UNITERM database and the CLAIMS COMPRE-HENSIVE database are three parallel databases containing records of chemical patents from 1950, electrical and general or mechanical patents from 1963, and design patents from 1980 to the present. The bibliographic and text data of the BIBLIO/ABSTRACT database are included in full in both the UNITERM and COMPREHENSIVE databases. CLAIMS UNITERM also contains detailed indexing of chemical and chemically-related patents, including fragmentation coding of chemical compounds. CLAIMS COMPREHENSIVE, available by subscription only, indexes chemical and chemically-related patents with the same thesaurus of general terms used for the UNITERM database and provides more precise coding of chemical structures and linked indexing of the roles of the indexed substances. CLAIMS subscribers are encouraged to participate in the development of the database and the indexing system; changes and improvements are made, retrospectively in most cases, with every annual database reload. The databases are mounted on DIALOG, STN and Questel-Orbit. The CLAIMS family of databases also includes the CLAIMS/CITATION database on DIALOG and the CLAIMS/CURRENT PATENT LEGAL STATUS and CLAIMS REFERENCE files on DIALOG, STN and Questel-Orbit.

The CLAIMS databases are updated weekly (two days after publication of the patents) with all bibliographic data, abstract and claims. The original records are replaced monthly by edited records that have expanded titles, indexing and company coding. The entire database is reloaded annually with corrections; new citation counts and patent status flags, and updated patent classification codes and indexing. The full record of US 5,661,172 is shown in Figure 2.5 as it appeared in the IFIUDB file on Questel-Orbit. The CURRENT PATENT LEGAL STATUS record for US 5,046,659 is shown in Figure 2.6 (p. 74) as it appears in Questel-Orbit file CRXX. The reassignment and re-examination record is also shown in DIALOG format in Figure 2.9 (p. 84).

The CLAIMS databases index the patent number [PPN] and publication date, application [AP] and priority [PR] numbers and dates, with US application data in the priority field of patents not claiming foreign priority. For patents based on PCT applications, the PCT application number and bibliographic data relating to the published PCT application are provided [PPN]. Patent numbers of equivalent British, West German, Dutch, French and Belgian patents published up to 1979 are reported in the record of the corresponding American patent. The record also includes the number of claims, drawings and figures in the patent [NUM] and the anticipated normal expiry date of the patent [AEXD].

Inventor names [IN] are given with the state or city and country of origin, and assignee names and state or country of origin are indexed both as IFI standardized names and the names published on the patent document [PA]. The reel and frame of the original assignment record at the USPTO is provided [PIA]. CLAIMS applies five-digit numerical assignee codes [CC] and standardized company names to records for chemical and chemically related patents, and these codes are generally applied to other patents belonging to the same companies. The names associated with the codes are often changed when company names are found to have been changed, and the new names are posted retrospectively to the online files with subsequent reloads. When a patent is reassigned to a new owner, and the reassignment is recorded at the USPTO, a flag is added to the record for that patent and a record of the reassignment is added to the CLAIMS CURRENT PATENT LEGAL STATUS file.

In addition to the information relating to the patent documents themselves, CLAIMS records corresponding to patents that have been indexed by *Chemical Abstracts* are cross-referenced to the *Chemical Abstracts* accession number of the indexed patent, and CLAIMS records that correspond to patents indexed by

```
1/1 IFIUDB - (C) IFI
PN     - US 5661172  A  19970826  [US5661172 ]
TI     - USE OF EFAROXAN AND DERIVATIVES THEREOF FOR THE TREATMENT OF
         ALZHEIMER'S DISEASE ADMINISTERING A BENZOFURANYL IMIDAZOLE
         COMPOUND FOR IMPROVING MEMORY FUNCTIONS
IN     - Briley Michael /; Gaillac (FR)
         Colpaert Francis /; Castres (FR)
         Imbert Thierry  / CC  - 24251; Viviers-les-Montagnes (FR)
PA     - Fabre, Pierre Medicament /
         Boulonge (FR)
CC     - 24251
AP     - US58151696 19960111 [1996US-0581516]
PR     - FR938497 19930709 [1993FR-0008497]
PPN    - WO9501791 - 19950119 [WO9501791]
PAP    - WOFR9400841 19940707 [1994WO-FR00841]
PCLO   - 514402000
PCLF   - 514402000
IC1    - A61K-031/415
RP     - The Firm of Gordon W. Hueschen
EX     - Criares, Theodore J
AG     - 125
NUM    - NCLM=5 ; NDWG=0 ; NFIG=0
PIA    - Reel 008008 / Frame 0812
AEXD   - 2014-08-26
FS     - C
DT     - UTILITY
NCTG   - 000
CT     - US4855385, 1989.08, 514332000, Kester et al.
PCT    - PCT No. PCT/FR94/00841 Sec. 371 Date Jan. 11, 1996 Sec. 102(e) Date
         Jan. 11, 1996 PCT Filed Jul. 7, 1994 PCT Pub. No. WO95/01791 PCT Pub.
         Date Jan. 19, 1995
AB     - The present invention relates to the use of efaroxan and derivatives for
         the treatment of Alzheimer's disease.
MCLM - 1. Method for the treatment of Alzheimer-like senile dementia, pre-
         Alzheimer's syndrome, and progressive supranuclear palsy, in a mammal
         suffering therefrom, comprising the step of administering to the said mammal
         an amount of a compound selected from those of formula I
         - 2-R1,2-(2-IMIDAZOLIN-2-YL),R2,R3-2,3-DIHYDROBENZOFURAN
         - in which R1 represents hydrogen or linear or branched C1-C6 alkyl, R2
         represents hydrogen or methyl, chloro, bromo, or fluoro, and R3 represents
         hydrogen or methyl, hydroxyl, methoxy, fluoro, chloro, or bromo, and a
         therapeutically-acceptable salt thereof, a racemic mixture thereof, and an
         optically-active isomer thereof, which is effective for said purpose.
CLM    - 2. Method of claim 1, wherein R2 and R3 represent a hydrogen atom.
         - 3. Method of claim 1, wherein R1 represents an ethyl, n-propyl, or i-propyl
         group.
         - 4. Method of claim 2, wherein R1 represents an ethyl, n-propyl, or i-propyl
         group.
         - 5. Method of claim 1, wherein the compound is selected from the group
         consisting of:
         2-(2-ethyl-2,3-dihydrobenzofuranyl)-2-imidazoline,
```

Figure 2.5   CLAIMS US patents: Questel-Orbit file IFIUDB

2-(2-n-propyl-2,3-dihydrobenzofuranyl)-2-imidazoline, and 2-(2-i-propyl-2,3-dihydrobenzofuranyl)-2-imidazoline.

UN — General codes :
00097 ADMINISTERING; 00301 ANTIDEPRESSANTS; 01810 DRUGS; 02588 HEADACHES; 02976 ISOMERS; 03254 MAMMALS; 03584 NERVOUS SYSTEM DISORDERS; 04521 RACEMIC MIXTURES; 05828 UTILIZATION; 06232 PROCESS; 07599 LEARNING ENHANCEMENT; 08103 ALZHEIMER*S DISEASE; 10030 DRUGS/CT/

FCU — Fragment codes :
30003 ACYCLIC (P; 34210 FUSED OR BRIDGED RING (P; 34236 HETEROCYCLIC RING (P; 40001 BROMINE, ORGANIC; 40002 CHLORINE, ORGANIC; 40004 F AMINE SALT FG, INORGANIC ANION; 40070 F CN2 N=C-N; 40305 F HO HYDROXY FG, OH; 40417 F O ETHER FG; 40515 F X HALOGEN FG; 40516 FLUORINE, ORGANIC; 40537 R I C3N2 IMIDAZOLE RING; 40559 R II C4O.C6 ISOBENZOFURAN, PHTHALAN RING

Figure 2.5   concluded

Chemical Abstracts before mid-1979 contain CAS registry numbers. The STN version of the databases also has CAS registry numbers for patents indexed since 1979. This information is added to the records with other corrections and modifications in annual reloads.

The original titles [TI] are present in the database and are augmented by descriptive phrases in parentheses or separated by an underscore for patents published since 1971. The author abstract [AB] and the claims [MCLM, CLM] are present in the records. Chemical structures that occur in the claim printed in the *Official Gazette of the USPTO* are replaced in the online record by a linearized representation of the drawn structure. This allows the reader to visualize the structure without referring to the full text of the patent specification and allows structural features of the claim to be used as search terms.

The 'original' and cross-reference US patent classification codes [PCL] are present in all records. Each yearly reload includes any changes in patent classification announced by the USPTO, so that the classification codes in the database correspond to the latest revision of the classification system and are not the classification codes originally recorded at the time of publication. Records of patents published since 1971 also contain the International Patent Classification codes assigned at the time of publication by the USPTO [IC1]. IFI has used the USPTO Concordance to assign International Patent Classification codes to patents issued before such codes were applied to US patents, so that International Patent Classification codes can be used to search for patents published before the IPC system was created.

The UNITERM and COMPREHENSIVE databases contain extensive indexing for chemical and chemically-related patents. A thesaurus of general terms, extensively cross-indexed and frequently revised to accommodate new technologies, identifies general concepts, processes and substances. A fragmentation code is used to define the structure of specifically identified monomeric compounds, polymers and generic chemical structures from the examples and the claims of the patents. All general terms and fragment terms are identified by five-digit numeric codes and may be searched by the term name or code number [UN, FCU]. Common chemical substances are not indexed by fragmentation coding every time they occur, but are indexed through their own five-digit compound terms. One may discover whether a compound term exists by searching the separate CLAIMS REFERENCE or REGISTRY database with the fragmentation codes appropriate to the compound or with the name and/or molecular formula of the compound. In addition to the level of indexing supplied by the Uniterm database, CLAIMS COMPREHENSIVE provides further refinements of the chemical fragmentation coding system and a system of role identifiers that are linked to the fragment terms and to general terms that identify chemical substances. The roles indicate whether the compound is produced in the patent, used as a chemical intermediate, or present in some other role. For polymers, role identifiers link the coding for the structure of the polymer's monomeric unit with the type of polymeric structure being indexed.

The examiner's field of search [PCLF] is shown, as are the names of the applicant's representative [RP], the examiner [EX] and the USPTO art unit responsible for examining the patent application [AG]. All references cited by the examiner [CT] are printable, but cited US patent references can be searched only in the separate CLAIMS CITATION database, which is available only on DIALOG. Records in the BIBLIO/ABSTRACT, UNITERM and COMPREHENSIVE databases on all three hosts contain a flag [NCT] 'Cited in # Later Patents' to indicate whether a citation search would yield any references to the patent, but they do not identify the citing patents. The CLAIMS CITATION database is produced by Search Check Inc. and marketed by IFI. It indexes patents cited in US patents since 1947, the year the examiners' citations were first printed in US patents. There are three CLAIMS CITATION files, comprising patents issued from 1790 to 1946, from 1947 to 1970, and from 1971 to the present. A CLAIMS CITATION record consists of only a patent number and a list of cited or citing patents. US patents issued since 1947 are searchable and printable as citing and cited patents; those issued earlier can be searched only to determine whether they have been cited in patents published after 1946.

For re-issue patents and for patents that were filed as divisions, continuations or continuations-in-part of earlier patent applications, the CLAIMS record contains the application and/or patent numbers and dates of the parent applications. These related patents are retrieved automatically when the application or patent numbers are searched. Patents that have been republished after re-examination proceedings are flagged in the CLAIMS records and the re-examination certificate is indexed in the separate CLAIMS CURRENT PATENT LEGAL STATUS database. Flags are also provided for patents having a Certificate of Correction [DCOR]; the date of the certificate is given, but the text is not provided. Certificate of Correction information is originally indexed in the CURRENT PATENT LEGAL STATUS database and is moved to the bibliographic files in the annual database reloads, so both files may need to be searched to determine whether a Certificate of Correction was issued in recent months.

The CLAIMS CURRENT PATENT LEGAL STATUS (formerly CLAIMS REASSIGNMENTS AND REEXAMINATIONS) database includes the text of the re-examination certificate of all patents re-examined by USPTO (first issued in 1981) and the reassignment records of all patents whose change of ownership has been recorded with USPTO since 1980. Since late 1985, US patents have been subject to lapse for failure to pay periodic maintenance fees. The expiration dates of lapsed patents announced in the *Official Gazette* of the USPTO are reported in the CLAIMS CURRENT PATENT LEGAL STATUS file. Patents whose term has been extended under the Drug Price Competition and Patent Term Restoration Act of 1984, requests for re-examination or re-issue, disclaimers and dedications, and other post-issuance actions reported in the *Official Gazette* are also indexed. The database is updated weekly with data appearing in the *Official Gazette*, while reassignment data are updated bi-monthly. The record for a reassigned and re-examined patent, US 5,046,659 is reproduced in Figure 2.6. Each record contains the patent number and date [PN], the section of the *Official Gazette* in which it was included [PT], and the original assignee [PA]; each action is provided in a separate subfield [ACT]. The re-examination record contains the patent number and date, the name and address of the entity that requested re-examination, the dates and numbers of the re-examination request and certificate, and the result of the re-examination of the claims. An exemplary re-examined claim, showing the amendments, is reproduced in the record. Request data are provided as a separate action, and can be retrieved before re-examination has been completed. The reassignment record contains the date, reel and frame of the reassignment recordal record, the name of the assigner and the date of the reassignment, the name and address of the new assignee, and the name and address of a contact person or firm.

Companion CLAIMS files contain the registry of specific common compounds indexed for the UNITERM and COMPREHENSIVE databases, the US patent classification titles from the *Manual of Classification* and its Index, and the CLAIMS Thesaurus. All three of these are included in STN's IFIREF database; DIALOG's CLAIMS REFERENCE file includes the *Manual of Classification* and the CLAIMS Thesaurus, and the CLAIMS COMPOUND REGISTRY is a separate file.

PATINTELLIGENCE

The Corporate Intelligence PATINTELLIGENCE database contains the searchable full text of US patents from 1945 to the present and images of nearly all patents issued since the first US patent in 1790. Online access is available to subscribers through a dial-up or Internet connection using proprietary PATINTELLIGENCE software. A search screen has fields for entering patent numbers, application serial numbers, patent or non-patent cited references,

```
1/1    CRXX – (C) CLAIMS/RRX
AN  -  2179282
PN  -  US5046659   91.09.10
PA  -  Mobil Oil Corp
PT  -  M (Mechanical)
ACT -  19930322  REEXAMINATION REQUESTED
       Issue Date of O.G.: 19930601
       Reexamination Request Number: 90/003016
       Inline Plastics Corp., Milford, C

       19940222  REEXAMINED  CERTIFICATE B15046659, SEQUENCE 2232nd
       REQUEST - 90/003016, Inline Plastics Corp, Milford CT, US (93.03.22)
       CLAIM - AS A RESULT OF REEXAMINATION, IT HAS BEEN DETERMINED THAT: The
       patentability of claims 1-12 is confirmed. New claims 13-19 are added and
       determined to be patentable. 14. A container for food or other articles
       comprising: a lid having a horizontal flange extended around the
       periphery thereof, a base having a horizontal flange extended around the
       periphery thereof and adapted for engagement with the horizontal flange
       of said lid when said container is in closed condition, means for
       latching said lid to said base, said latching means including; at least
       one substantially rectangular male rib depending from said horizontal
       flange of said lid, the opposite ends of the said rib having outwardly
       extending shoulder structure, the sides of said rib being substantially
       straight. At least one substantially rectangular female recess in said
       flange of said base dimensioned to receive a cooperating said male rib in
       said led, the opposite ends of said female recess having inwardly
       extending shoulder structure adapted to mate with said outwardly
       extending shoulder structure of said male rib in said female recess being
       substantially straight, said ends of said male rib and said ends of said
       female recess being constructed and arranged to deflect with respect to
       each other so that when said male rib is pressed into said female recess
       said shoulder structure on said male rib will snap into position beneath
       said shoulder structure in said female recess and interlock therewith to
       latch said lid to said base, said cooperating male rib and female recess
       being in isolation from any other male rib or female recess of said
       latching means.
       19951226  REASSIGNED
       ASSIGNMENT OF ASSIGNOR'S INTEREST

       Assignor: MOBIL OIL CORPORATION DATE SIGNED: 11/17/1995

       Assignee: TENNECO PLASTICS COMPANY 1603 ORRINGTON AVENUE EVANSTON,
       ILLINOIS 60204

       Reel 7881/Frame 0871

       Contact: ARNOLD, WHITE & DURKEE RONALD B. COOLLEY P.O. BOX 4433 HOUSTON,
       TX 77210

UP  -  1999–00
```

Figure 2.6   CLAIMS CURRENT PATENT LEGAL STATUS: Questel-Orbit file CRRX

inventors, assignees, patent attorney or agent, patent examiner and examining art unit, original or current US classifications or international patent classification code and text terms. Searchers have the option of searching the front page or the full text of the patents in the database. Results can be downloaded as front-page information, full ASCII text, and images of any or all of the pages of the patents. The software permits the searcher to page through the images of patents in an answer set at a faster 'flip rate' than is possible with conventional search software or Internet connections. In addition to the patent as published, some post-issuance status change and citing patent information is provided.

LexPat

LexPat is produced by LEXIS-NEXIS as one of the libraries in the LEXIS-NEXIS databank. The LexPat library contains a full-text database of US patents published from July 1975 to the present, arranged as a file of design patents, a file of plant patents, a combined patents file, a file that indexes patents to their current US patent classification codes, the text of the *Manual of Classification*, and the text of the Index to the *Manual of Classification*. LEXIS-NEXIS also has the full text of European patents, the PATENT ABSTRACTS OF JAPAN database (JAPIO), INPADOC and the text of the *Manual and Index of the European Patent Classification*. The database is updated weekly. Figure 2.7 illustrates excerpts from the full citation for US 5,046,659 showing the bibliographic and examination information from the first page of the patent, post-issuance status change information, and a short passage from the Background of the Invention and Summary of the Invention sections of the disclosure.

As a full-text database, LexPat contains the document, application, and priority numbers and dates of all patents in the file and of all related patents and applications mentioned in the specification. The names and addresses of the inventors and assignees are included. For patents whose reassignment has been recorded, the name of the new assignee is also in the record. Corrections published in a Certificate of Correction are incorporated into the record.

The original title, abstract, disclosure and claims are searchable and printable in full. All US Patent Classifications and International Patent Classifications are present. The drawings published in the patent can be displayed as links in the patent record. Searchers are referred to the printed specification for chemical structure diagrams.

LexPat records include all the patent and literature citations made by the examiner as well as the field of search. The names of the examiner and the applicant's legal representative are both searchable and printable. Terminal disclaimers are noted, as are disclaimers and dedications of a patent to the public that are registered after publication of the patent. When a patent has been the subject of a request for re-examination or of litigation in a federal court, the filing is noted in the record and the result of the proceeding is reported. Re-issue patents and re-examination certificates are in separate records and their issuance is noted in the record of the original patent.

5,046,659

Sep. 10, 1991

Latching structure for food container
LIT-REEX: NOTICE OF LITIGATION

 Inline Plastics Corp. v. Mobil Oil Corp., Filed Feb. 1, 1995, D.C. (Bridgeport)
Connecticut, Doc. No. 3:95CV200(AVC)

 Reexamination requested Mar. 22, 1993 by Inline Plastics, Corp.,
Reexamination No. 90/003,016 (O.G. Jun. 1, 1993) Ex. Gp.: 2401

INVENTOR: Warburton, Richard T., Canandaigua, New York

ASSIGNEE-AT-ISSUE: Mobil Oil Corporation, Fairfax, Virginia (02)

ASSIGNEE-AFTER-ISSUE: Date Transaction Recorded: Dec. 26, 1995 ASSIGNMENT OF
ASSIGNOR'S INTEREST (SEE DOCUMENT FOR DETAILS). TENNECO PLASTICS COMPANY 1603
ORRINGTON AVENUE EVANSTON, ILLINOIS 60204 Reel & Frame Number: 7881/0871

APPL-N0: 611,576

FILED: Nov. 13, 1990

INT-CL: [5] B65D 1#22

US-CL: 220#4.22; 24#662; 220#4.21; 220#4.23; 220#4.24; 220#339;

CL: 220;24;

SEARCH-FLD: 229#2.5R, 2.5EC; 220#4.1, 4.2, 4.3, 4.21, 4.22, 4.23, 4.24, 306,
339, 315, 352

REF–CITED:

	U.S. PATENT DOCUMENTS		
2,706,065	4/1955	* Stone	220#4.21
3,149,747	9/1964	* Burgess	220#4.21
3,234,077	2/1966	* Reifers et al.	229#2.5EC
3,565,146	2/1971	* Arnolds	220#4.23
3,771,712	11/1973	* Richards	229#2.5EC
4,030,850	6/1977	* Hyde	220#306
4,193,496	3/1980	* Barratt	206#380
4,333,580	6/1982	* Sweigart, Jr.	220#4.21
4,512,474	4/1985	* Harding	220#4.23
4,576,330	3/1986	* Schepp	229#44

	FOREIGN PATENT DOCUMENTS	
1117491	2/1982	* Canada
1418897	12/1974	* United Kingdom

Figure 2.7   LEXPAT: LEXIS-NEXIS

    1602694   11/1981   * United Kingdom   220#4.24
    2118142   10/1983   * United Kingdom   229#2.5R
PRIM-EXMR: Garbe, Stephen P.

ASST-EXMR: McDonald, Christopher

LEGAL-REP: McKillop; Alexander J.
Speciale; Charles J.

ABST:
  Latching structure for thermoformed plastic containers for food and the like
wherein the lid and base of the containers are each provided with mating male
and female elongated elements where the locking takes place at the end of the
elongated elements rather than along the sides of these elements.

NO-OF-CLAIMS: 12

EXMPL-CLAIM: <=13> 1

NO-OF-FIGURES: 17

NO-DRWNG-PP: 7

SUM:

BACKGROUND OF THE INVENTION

   The present invention relates to improvements in thermoformed plastic
containers for food or other articles and particularly to latching structure for
holding the lid and base of the container in closed condition.

   Containers for food or other articles thermoformed from plastic material
normally comprise a lid and base which may be hinged to each other or may be
separate parts. In order to hold the lid and base of the container in closed
condition, it is necessary that the lid and base have latching structure which
can be manually opened and closed with relative ease. However, the structure
should be capable of locking the container in closed condition to avoid
accidental opening.

   Various types of latching or locking structures have been proposed in the
past. For example, cylindrical male and female locking elements have been
proposed as disclosed in U.S. Pat. No. 4,576,330. Elongated rib structures
comprising cooperating male and female elements have been proposed as disclosed
in British Patent Specification 1,418,897 and in Canadian Patent 1,117,491. In
the prior elongated rib structure locking elements the locking action has taken
place on the long sides of the ribs. This required that the ribs be located in
such a position on the container that both sides of the ribs are engageable by
the cooperating male and female elements to provide the locking action.

   It would be desirable to provide mating male and female rib elements where
the locking takes place at the end of the ribs rather than along the sides of
the ribs. This permits the latching structure to be located at various locations

Figure 2.7   cont'd

on the container and also provides for a more positive latching action while permitting ease of manual operation in opening and closing the latching structure on the container.

SUMMARY OF THE INVENTION

It is an object of the present invention to overcome the deficiencies of the prior art in providing a latching structure for a container which is easy to operate in opening and closing the latching structure of the container.

In accordance with the present invention there is provided a container for food or other articles comprising a lid having a horizontal flange extending around the periphery thereof and a base having a horizontal flange extending around the periphery thereof adapted for engagement with the horizontal flange of the lid when the container is in closed condition. Latching structure is provided for latching the lid to the base. The latching structure includes at
***

Figure 2.7   concluded

US PATENTS FULLTEXT

US PATENTS FULLTEXT is produced by The Dialog Corporation and mounted on DIALOG. It contains the full text of US patents since 1974, with partial coverage of selected technologies from 1971 through 1973. It is subdivided into file 652, with patents published from 1971 to 1979, file 653, with patents published from 1980 to 1989, and file 654, with patents from 1990 to the present, and can be searched in full under the OneSearch acronym PATFULL. File 654 is updated weekly with the current week's patents. Figure 2.8 illustrates excerpts from the full citation for US 5,046,659 showing the bibliographic and examination information from the first page of the patent, post-issuance status change information, the 'Brief Description of the Drawing' section, and a short passage from the Background of the Invention and Summary of the Invention sections of the disclosure.

All the bibliographic information shown in the patent is searchable and displayable. Bibliographic information is displayed in the form shown in the patent document, but bibliographic data are indexed in standard DIALOG format and are searchable with standard DIALOG field codes. In addition to the data that appear on the face of the patent, the IFI CLAIMS assignee code is provided.

Although the full text of the patent is provided in the database, the subdivisions of the patent are presented in a specific order, with the description of the drawings immediately following the abstract and preceding the remainder of the patent specification text.

Post-issuance actions, reassignments and re-examination information from the CLAIMS CURRENT PATENT LEGAL STATUS database (DIALOG file 124) are integrated into the patent record.

1/9/1 (Item 1 from file: 654)
02005401
Utility

LATCHING STRUCTURE FOR FOOD CONTAINER

PATENT NO.: 5,046,659
ISSUED: September 10, 1991 (19910910)
INVENTOR(s): Warburton, Richard T., Canandaigua, NY (New York), US (United
States of America)
ASSIGNEE(s): Mobil Oil Corporation, (A U.S. Company or Corporation),
Fairfax, VA (Virginia), US (United States of America)
[Assignee Code(s): 56432]
EXTRA INFO: Reexamined, certified February 22, 1994 (19940222)
Assignment transaction [Reassigned], recorded December 26, 1995 (19951226)

POST-ISSUANCE ASSIGNMENTS

ASSIGNEE(s): TENNECO PLASTICS COMPANY 1603 ORRINGTON AVENUE EVANSTON,
ILLINOIS 60204
Assignor(s): MOBIL OIL CORPORATION -- signed: 11/17/1995
Recorded: December 26, 1995 (19951226)
Reel/Frame: 7881/0871
Brief: ASSIGNMENT OF ASSIGNOR'S INTEREST
Rep.: ARNOLD, WHITE & DURKEE RONALD B. COOLLEY P.O. BOX 4433 HOUSTON, TX
77210

APPL. NO.: 7-611,576
FILED: November 13, 1990 (19901113)
U.S. CLASS: 220-4.22 cross ref: 24-662; 220-4.21; 220-4.23; 220-4.24;
220-339
INTL CLASS: [5] B65D 1-22
FIELD OF SEARCH: 229-002.5R; 229-002.5EC; 220-4.1; 220-4.2; 220-4.3;
220-4.21; 220-4.22; 220-4.23; 220-4.24; 220-306; 220-339; 220-315; 220-352

References Cited

U.S. PATENT DOCUMENTS

2,706,065 4/1955 Stone 220-4.21
  3,149,747 9/1964 Burgess 220-4.21
  3,234,077 2/1966 Reifers et al. 229-2.5EC
  3,565,146 2/1971 Arnolds 220-4.23
  3,771,712 11/1973 Richards 229-2.5EC
  4,030,850 6/1977 Hyde 220-306
  4,193,496 3/1980 Barratt 206-380
  4,333,580 6/1982 Sweigart, Jr. 220-4.21
  4,512,474 4/1985 Harding 220-4.23
  4,576,330 3/1986 Schepp 229-44

Figure 2.8   US PATENTS FULLTEXT: DIALOG file 654

NON-U.S. PATENT DOCUMENTS

1117491 2/1982 CA (Canada)
  1418897 12/1974 GB (United Kingdom)
  1602694 11/1981 GB (United Kingdom) 220-4.24
  2118142 10/1983 GB (United Kingdom) 229-2.5R

PRIMARY EXAMINER: Garbe, Stephen P.
ASST. EXAMINER: McDonald, Christopher
ATTORNEY, AGENT, OR FIRM: McKillop, Alexander J.; Speciale, Charles J.
CLAIMS: 12
EXEMPLARY CLAIM: 1
DRAWING PAGES: 7
DRAWING FIGURES: 17
ART UNIT: 241
FULL TEXT: 429 lines

REEXAMINATION

CERTIFICATE: B15046659
Certified: February 22, 1994 (19940222)
Sequence: 2232
Request No.: 90-003016
Requested: March 22, 1993 (19930322)
Requestor: Inline Plastics Corp, Milford CT US,AS A RESULT OF
REEXAMINATION, IT HAS BEEN DETERMINED THAT: The patentability of claims
1-12 is confirmed. new claims 13-19 are added and determined to be
patentable. 14. A container for food or other articles comprising: a lid
having a horizontal flange extended around the periphery thereof, a base
having a horizontal flange extended around the periphery thereof and
adapted for engagement with the horizontal flange of said lid when said
container is in closed condition, means for latching said lid to said base,
said latching means including; at least one substantially rectangular male
rib depending from said horizontal flange of said lid, the opposite ends of
the said rib having outwardly extending shoulder structure, the sides of
said rib being substantially straight. at least one substantially
rectangular female recess in said flange of said base dimensioned to
receive a cooperating said male rib in said led, the opposite ends of said
female recess having inwardly extending shoulder structure adapted to mate
with said outwardly extending shoulder structure of said male rib in said
female recess being substantially straight, said ends of said male rib and
said ends of said female recess being constructed and arranged to deflect
with respect to each other so that when said male rib is pressed into said
female recess said shoulder structure on said male rib will snap into
position beneath said shoulder structure in said female recess and
interlock therewith to latch said lid to said base, said cooperating male
rib and female recess being in isolation from any other male rib or female
recess of said latching means.

ABSTRACT

Latching structure for thermoformed plastic containers for food and the

Figure 2.8   cont'd

like wherein the lid and base of the containers are each provided with mating male and female elongated elements where the locking takes place at the end of the elongated elements rather than along the sides of these elements.

For further objects and advantages of the present invention reference may be had to the following description and claims and from the accompanying drawing.

BRIEF DESCRIPTION OF THE DRAWING

FIG. 1 is a perspective view of a container for food or other articles embodying the present invention showing a lid hinged to a base and latching structure for latching the lid to the base in closed position.

FIG. 2 is a fractional plan view of one corner of the container shown in FIG. 1 with the container in closed condition.

FIG. 3 is a sectional view taken along the lines 3--3 in FIG. 2 showing the container and latch in closed condition.

FIG. 3A is a sectional view similar to FIG. 3 showing the container and latch in open condition.

FIG. 4 is a sectional view taken along the lines 4--4 in FIG. 2 showing the latch in closed condition.

FIG. 4A is a sectional view similar to FIG. 4 showing the latch in partially open condition.

FIG. 5 is an exploded perspective view of another embodiment of the container of the present invention where the lid and base of the container are identical.

FIG. 6 is a sectional view taken along the lines 6--6 in FIG. 5.

FIG. 7 is a sectional view taken along the lines 7--7 in FIG. 5 showing the container and latch in open condition.

FIG. 7A is a sectional view similar to FIG. 7 showing the latch and container in closed condition.

FIG. 8 is a sectional view taken along the lines 8--8 in FIG. 5 showing the container and latch in open condition.

FIG. 8A is a sectional view similar to FIG. 8 showing the container and latch in closed condition.

FIG. 9 is a fractional plan view of a modification of the invention similar to FIG. 2 showing the latching structure in a different location.

FIG. 10 is a sectional view taken along the lines 10--10 in FIG. 9 showing the container and latch in closed condition.

FIG. 10A is a sectional view similar to FIG. 10 showing the container and latch in open condition.

FIG. 11 is a sectional view taken along the lines 11--11 in FIG. 9 showing the container and latch in closed condition.

FIG. 11A is a sectional view similar to FIG. 11 showing the container and latch in open condition.

BACKGROUND OF THE INVENTION

The present invention relates to improvements in thermoformed plastic containers for food or other articles and particularly to latching structure for holding the lid and base of the container in closed condition.

Containers for food or other articles thermoformed from plastic material normally comprise a lid and base which may be hinged to each other or may

Figure 2.8   cont'd

be separate parts. In order to hold the lid and base of the container in closed condition, it is necessary that the lid and base have latching structure which can be manually opened and closed with relative ease. However, the structure should be capable of locking the container in closed condition to avoid accidental opening.

Various types of latching or locking structures have been proposed in the past. For example, cylindrical male and female locking elements have been proposed as disclosed in U.S. Pat. No. 4,576,330. Elongated rib structures comprising cooperating male and female elements have been proposed as disclosed in British Patent Specification 1,418,897 and in Canadian Patent 1,117,491. In the prior elongated rib structure locking elements the locking action has taken place on the long sides of the ribs. This required that the ribs be located in such a position on the container that both sides of the ribs are engageable by the cooperating male and female elements to provide the locking action.

It would be desirable to provide mating male and female rib elements where the locking takes place at the end of the ribs rather than along the sides of the ribs. This permits the latching structure to be located at various locations on the container and also provides for a more positive latching action while permitting ease of manual operation in opening and closing the latching structure on the container.

SUMMARY OF THE INVENTION

It is an object of the present invention to overcome the deficiencies of the prior art in providing a latching structure for a container which is easy to operate in opening and closing the latching structure of the container.

In accordance with the present invention there is provided a container for food or other articles comprising a lid having a horizontal flange extending around the periphery thereof and a base having a horizontal flange extending around the periphery thereof adapted for engagement with the horizontal flange of the lid when the container is in closed condition. Latching structure is provided for latching the lid to the base. The latching structure includes ***

Figure 2.8   concluded

USPATFULL

USPATFULL is produced by Chemical Abstracts Service and is mounted on STN. The same data are available in CHEMICAL PATENTS PLUS on the World Wide Web at <URL http://casweb.cas.org/chempatplus/>. USPATFULL contains the full text of US patents since 1974, with partial coverage of selected technologies from 1971 through 1973, and graphic images of patents published from 1994 to the present. It is updated weekly, two days after issuance of the patents, with CAS indexing for patents indexed in *Chemical Abstracts* up to the current week. Figure 2.9 illustrates excerpts from the full citation of US 5,661,172, showing the bibliographic and examination information from the first page of the patent, a short passage from the Background and Summary of the Invention sections of the disclosure, the claims and the CAS indexing.

All the bibliographic information in the patent is searchable and displayable in STN and Derwent formats. For patents filed under the PCT, the number and date of the corresponding published PCT application is shown in the Patent Information field [PI]. The full text of the patent is searchable and displayable, and the available page images are downloadable both in the STN file and in CHEMICAL PATENTS PLUS. Searching and display of titles and abstracts are free in CHEMICAL PATENTS PLUS.

USPATFULL has thesauri of the US *Manual of Classification* and the International Patent Classification code, allowing searchers to find appropriate classification codes, create strategies using the codes, and find the definitions of codes in patents retrieved in this file and other patent databases. Both the US Patent Classification codes assigned at the time of issue [INCL] and the updated codes [NCL] are searchable and displayable.

For patents indexed in *Chemical Abstracts* and for US patents that are equivalent to non-US patents previously indexed in *Chemical Abstracts*, the CAS indexing is searchable. The record includes the *Chemical Abstracts* accession number and the patent number and date of the indexed patent [OS], CA classification codes [CC], CA supplementary terms [ST] and CA indexing terms [RN]. CAS registry numbers may be searched with the RN qualifier. Although the file status banner indicates that the CAS indexing is updated to the current week, searchers should be aware that indexing for patents in the CAPLUS database is not instantaneous, but lags several weeks behind the issue date of the patents.

QPAT-WW

QPAT-WW is produced by Questel-Orbit and mounted on the World Wide Web at <URL http://www.qpat.com/>. It contains US patents published from 1974 to the present and all European patents and applications. It is updated weekly with the current week's patents. The database contains the front-page bibliographic and patent examination fields, the abstract and the full text of the patents. An annual or one-day subscription to the database permits unlimited searching, display, and downloading of the ASCII text of the patent documents and display of patent images. European patent applications and granted patents (A and B documents) are merged into a single ASCII file. As of early 2000, the text of only English-language, European patent documents could be searched. The addition of PCT applications and PATENT ABSTRACTS OF JAPAN is promised later in 2000.

QPAT provides for multi-step searches using both the free text of the entire record and search terms limited by a field qualifier. Unqualified terms are searched in the patent number, assignee, inventor and text fields; other fields are searched using a field tag selected from the database reference guide linked through the Help button. Patent document numbers, application numbers and priority numbers are shown in Derwent format rather than the format printed in the patent, and may be searched in Derwent format, as unpunctuated strings of numerals or with commas. Parent application numbers mentioned in the patent specification are

```
L1        ANSWER 1 OF 1  USPATFULL
AN        97:76154  USPATFULL
TI        Use of efaroxan and derivatives thereof for the treatment of
          Alzheimer's disease
IN        Colpaert, Francis, Castres, France
          Briley, Michael, Gaillac, France
          Imbert, Thierry, Viviers-les-Montagnes, France
PA        Pierre Fabre Medicament, Boulonge, France (non-U.S. corporation)
PI        US 5661172  19970826                                    <--
          WO 9501791  19950119
AI        US 1996-581516  19960111 (8)
          WO 1994-FR841  940707
                  19960111  PCT 371 date
                  19960111  PCT 102(e) date
PRAI      FR 1993-8497  19930709
DT        Utility
REP       US 4855385  Aug 1989  514/332.000   Kester et al.
EXNAM     Primary Examiner: Criares, Theodore J.
LREP      The Firm of Gordon W. Hueschen
CLMN      Number of Claims: 5
ECL       Exemplary Claim: 1
DRWN      No Drawings
AB        The present invention relates to the use of efaroxan and
          derivatives for the treatment of Alzheimer's disease.

SUMM      This application is filed under 35 U.S.C. 371 of PCT/FR94/00841,
          filed 07 Jul. 1994, which claims priority of application 93/08497
          filed in France 09 Jul. 1993.

          The present invention relates to the use of efaroxan and
          derivatives for the treatment of Alzheimer-like senile dementia,
          pre-Alzheimer's syndrome, progressive supranuclear palsy and other
          neurodegenerative diseases.

          Alzheimer's disease is a progressive neurodegenerative disease
          particularly, but not exclusively, affecting the central
          cholinergic system (Meynert's nucleus basalis) manifested by a
          loss of cognitive faculties, a loss of intellectual capacities,
          and behavioral and personality disorders.
*
*
*
CLM       What is claimed is:
          1. Method for the treatment of Alzheimer-like senile dementia,
          pre-Alzheimer's syndrome, and progressive supranuclear palsy, in a
          mammal suffering therefrom, comprising the step of administering
          to the said mammal an amount of a compound selected from those of
          formula I ##STR2## in which R.sub.1 represents hydrogen or linear
          or branched C.sub.1 -C.sub.6 alkyl, R.sub.2 represents hydrogen or
          methyl, chloro, bromo, or fluoro, and R.sub.3 represents hydrogen
          or methyl, hydroxyl, methoxy, fluoro, chloro, or bromo, and a
```

Figure 2.9   USPATFULL: STN

therapeutically-acceptable salt thereof, a racemic mixture thereof, and an optically-active isomer thereof, which is effective for said purpose.

2. Method of claim 1, wherein R.sub.2 and R.sub.3 represent a hydrogen atom.

3. Method of claim 1, wherein R.sub.1 represents an ethyl, n-propyl, or i-propyl group.

4. Method of claim 2, wherein R.sub.1 represents an ethyl, n-propyl, or i-propyl group.

5. Method of claim 1, wherein the compound is selected from the group consisting of: 2-(2-ethyl-2,3-dihydrobenzofuranyl)-2-imidazoline, 2-(2-n-propyl-2,3-dihydrobenzofuranyl)-2-imidazoline, and 2-(2-i-propyl-2,3-dihydrobenzofuranyl)-2-imidazoline.

```
INCL     INCLM: 514/402.000
NCL      NCLM:  514/402.000
IC       [6]
         ICM: A61K031-415
EXF      514/402
ARTU     125
CAS INDEXING IS AVAILABLE FOR THIS PATENT.

CHEMICAL ABSTRACTS INDEXING    COPYRIGHT 1998 ACS
---------------------------
                PATENT   KIND  DATE
             ------------- ---- -------
OS       CA 122:151400 * WO  9501791  A2  19950119
* CA Indexing for this record included
CC       1-11 (Pharmacology)
             Section cross-reference(s): 63
ST       efaroxan deriv neurodegenerative disease treatment; cerebral palsy
         treatment efaroxan deriv
IT       Amnesia
             (efaroxan and its derivs. for the treatment of neurodegenerative
             diseases)
IT       Cerebral palsy
             (progressive supranuclear; efaroxan and its derivs. for the
             treatment of neurodegenerative diseases)
IT       Mental disorder
             (Alzheimer's disease, efaroxan and its derivs. for the treatment
             of neurodegenerative diseases)
IT       Pharmaceutical dosage forms
             (capsules, efaroxan and its derivs. for the treatment of
             neurodegenerative diseases)
IT       Nervous system
             (disease, degeneration, efaroxan and its derivs. for the
             treatment of neurodegenerative diseases)
IT       Pharmaceutical dosage forms
```

Figure 2.9   **cont'd**

	(injections, i.v., efaroxan and its derivs. for the treatment of neurodegenerative diseases)
IT	Pharmaceutical dosage forms (oral, efarxoxan and its derivs. for the treatment of neurodegenerative diseases)
IT	Pharmaceutical dosage forms (tablets, efaroxan and its derivs. for the treatment of neurodegenerative diseases)
IT	89197-32-0, Efaroxan 89197-33-1 143249-90-5 (efaroxan and its derivs. for the treatment of neurodegenerative diseases)

Figure 2.9   concluded

shown in the format printed on the patent, but may be searched in any format when qualified as related application numbers. The default operator for QPAT searches is OR, but nested Boolean queries are supported. Search terms can be restricted to any of the front-page bibliographic fields, the abstract, and the claims. Extensive help pages are available through links. Search terms are automatically stemmed: standard English word endings are stripped off and all words beginning with the same root are searched. At the option of the searcher, searches can be expanded by reviewing related terms in the index and modifying the search, using 'fuzzy logic' to generate phonetically related terms, or generating a set of statistically related terms that occur together with the search term. Answer sets can be combined with Boolean logic, and all sets are retained and are available for re-use in further searching and for viewing answers for the duration of the search session. Answers can be ranked by relevance.

Figure 2.10 shows the QPAT search page with a search in the combined US and EP database for patents assigned to Abbott or Syntex containing the name of the drug 'deslorelin'. The answer set is shown in Figure 2.11, where the full-text search retrieved five patents. The default is of a listing of the relevance ranking, the patent number, and the title of the patent, and searchers have the option of changing the view to a listing of abstracts or keywords in context and of sorting the patents in chronological order. The first page and text can be viewed by clicking on the appropriate patent. US patents cited on the front page of the patent can be viewed by clicking hyperlinks. The image of the patent document can also be displayed or downloaded; clicking the Image button creates an automatic secure connection to the DELPHION INTELLECTUAL PROPERTY NETWORK.

DELPHION INTELLECTUAL PROPERTY NETWORK

The DELPHION INTELLECTUAL PROPERTY NETWORK is mounted on the World Wide Web at <http://patents.ibm.com/> by IBM Corporation, and runs on the VERITY search engine. It contains searchable databases of the full text, basic

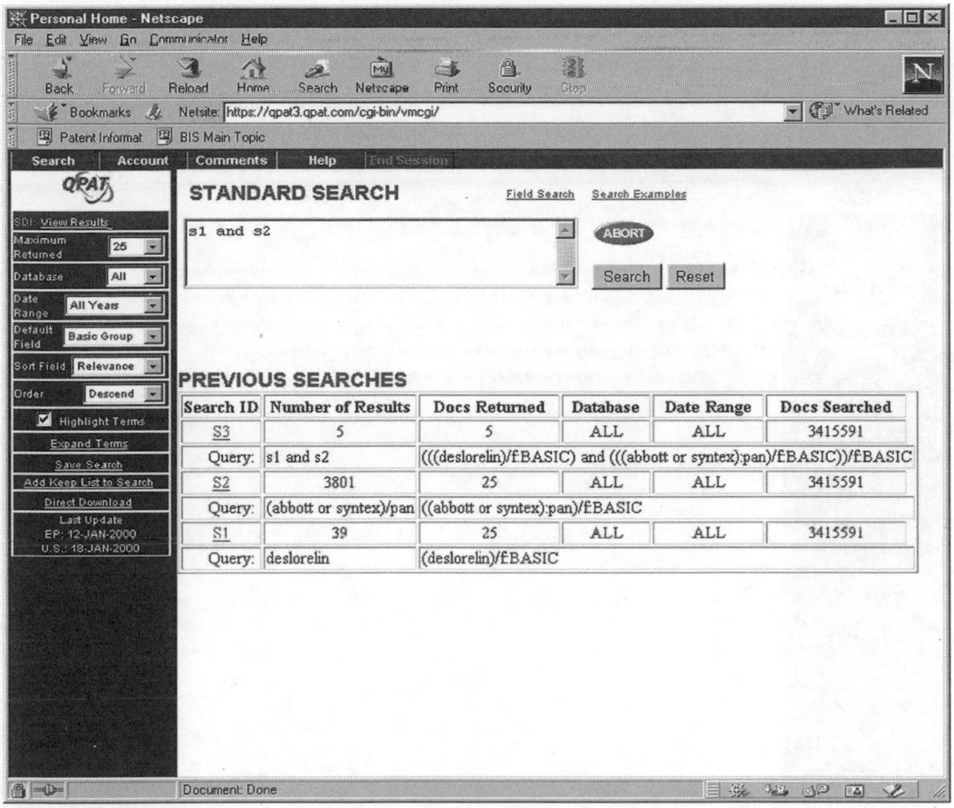

Figure 2.10   QPAT search screen

bibliographic information, abstracts and claims from US patents published since 1971 and images of US patents published since 1974. Other files contain the bibliographic records and images of European patent applications, granted European patents, PCT applications from 1990 to the present and PATENT ABSTRACTS OF JAPAN. The searcher can select US first page, US first page and claims, US full text, EP-A, EP-B, PAJ, or any combination, to be searched. As of early 2000, IBM is planning to add a file based on the DERWENT WORLD PATENTS INDEX. The database is updated weekly, with the images lagging a week behind the searchable data. US patent classification codes can be browsed by class number or title. Searches can be undertaken via a simple search page with a single search box allowing: unqualified searching for a word, phrase or inventor name; a patent number search page; or a Boolean text search with two search boxes allowing qualification to most fields; and an Advanced Text Search page with individual boxes for each of the indexed fields (the various fields are combined with the AND operator, and ranked with the VERITY ACCRUE operation). A maximum of 200 patents can be retrieved and displayed. Patent classification codes are not directly searchable, but hyperlinks in the front-page

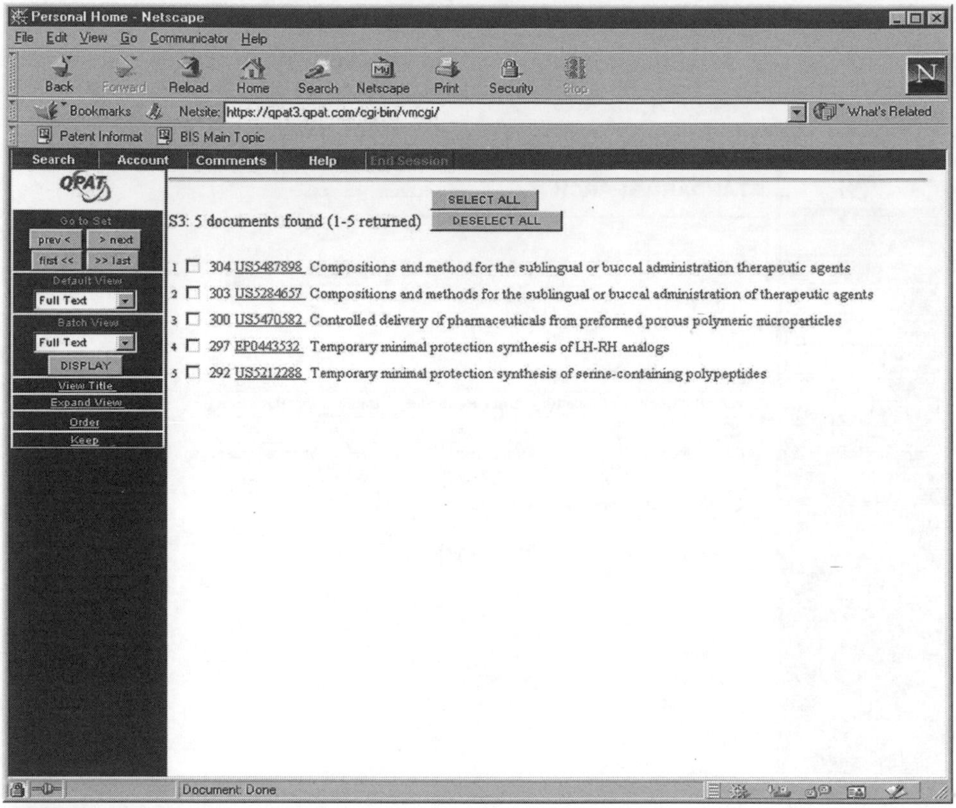

Figure 2.11   QPAT search results

display of a patent retrieved by other means can be clicked to generate a listing of other patents with the same IPC or US Patent Classification code.

Figures 2.12 and 2.13 show the DELPHION INTELLECTUAL PROPERTY NETWORK Boolean Search and Search Results screens for the same search shown in Figures 2.10 and 2.11. It should be noted that only four patents were retrieved because the search was limited to the Title and Abstract fields of European patents. The search results are provided as a list of patent numbers with titles. Clicking on a patent number displays the first page information and the first claim; hyperlinks to the rest of the claims and the full text are available. Links are provided for US patents cited by the patent examiner and for the claim text. In addition, there are links to later patents citing this patent in their examiner's searches and to later continuing patents identifying this patent as related. The front-page display of US patents includes some post-issuance patent status information: whether the patent has lapsed, been reinstated, withdrawn or re-examined, and whether a Certificate of Correction has been issued. For IBM patents, and for other companies' patents that have been registered, a link is

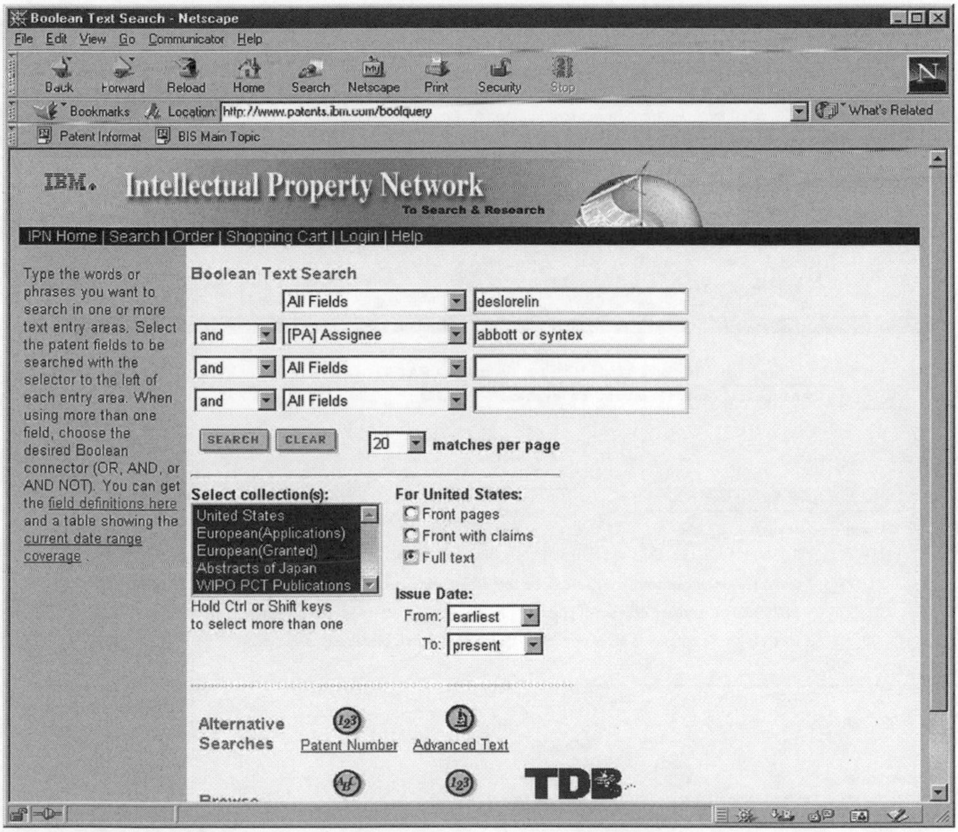

Figure 2.12   INTELLECTUAL PROPERTY NETWORK Boolean Search screen

provided to information about licensing the patent. Patents can be clustered automatically on the basis of text term analysis. The image of the patent can be displayed and printed, or a box can be checked to download or order a copy of the patents from Optipat Inc. The same pull-down box can be used to order Smart Patents from the Aurigin Workbench. Both searching and displaying images are free and do not require the searcher to register as a user. There is a charge for downloading or ordering patent copies. In addition to the free file, the INTELLECTUAL PROPERTY NETWORK FOR BUSINESS is available with an SSL connection and group billing.

USPTO patent databases

The US Patent and Trademark Office (USPTO) Web site <URL http://uspto.gov/> provides access to full-text and bibliographic databases of US patents issued since 1971. The US patent database is updated weekly on Tuesday, the day of issue of

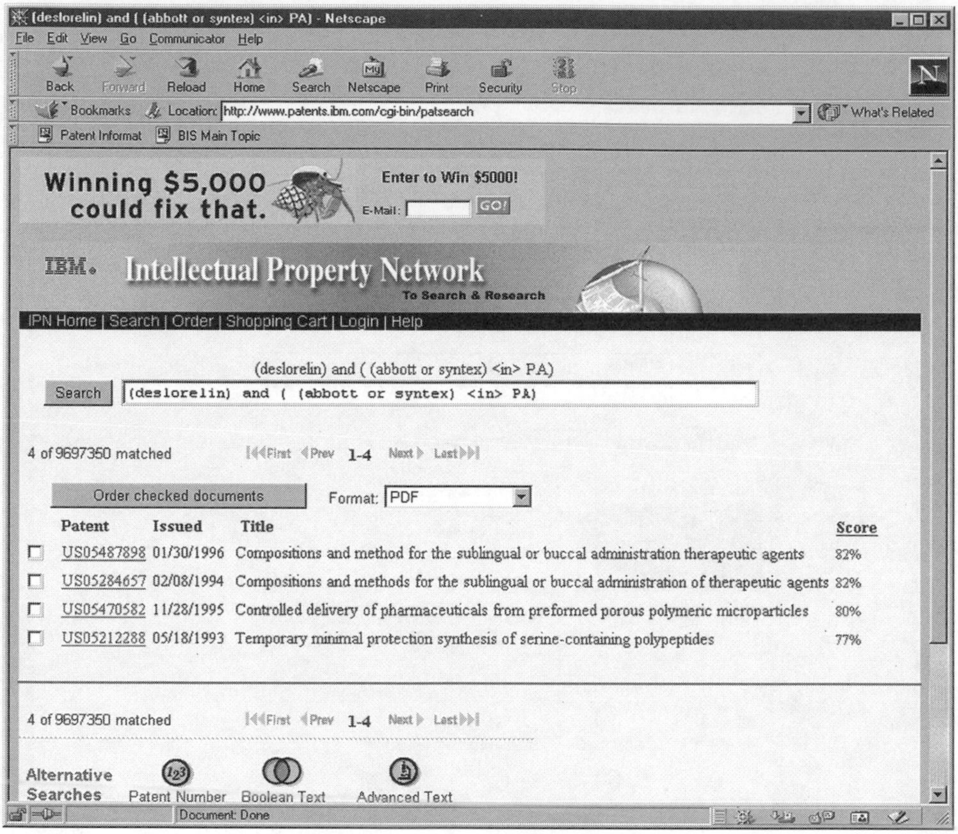

Figure 2.13   INTELLECTUAL PROPERTY NETWORK Search Results screen

new US patents. The Web site also has browsable files of the *Manual of Classification*, the Index and the class definitions for the current US patent classes.

Patent images can be displayed, but the quality of the TIFF images discourages printing or downloading. All bibliographic data can be searched with a field qualifier. Updated US classification codes are provided in the bibliographic file, but the full-text file has only the classification originally printed on the patent. In the bibliographic database a Boolean search page allows two-term searching with the AND, OR, ANDNOT and XOR operators. The Advanced Search page allows the searcher to create a single, complex, multi-form query. Results can be ranked chronologically or by relevance at the searcher's option. The full-text database does not support the XOR operator or relevance ranking; in place of the Advanced Search page, the full-text file has a Manual Search page.

Figures 2.14 and 2.15 show the USPTO Manual Advanced Search and Search Results screens for the same search shown in Figures 2.10 and 2.11 and Figures 2.12 and 2.13. If the search is performed in the bibliographic database rather than the full-text file no patents are retrieved because the search is limited to the Title

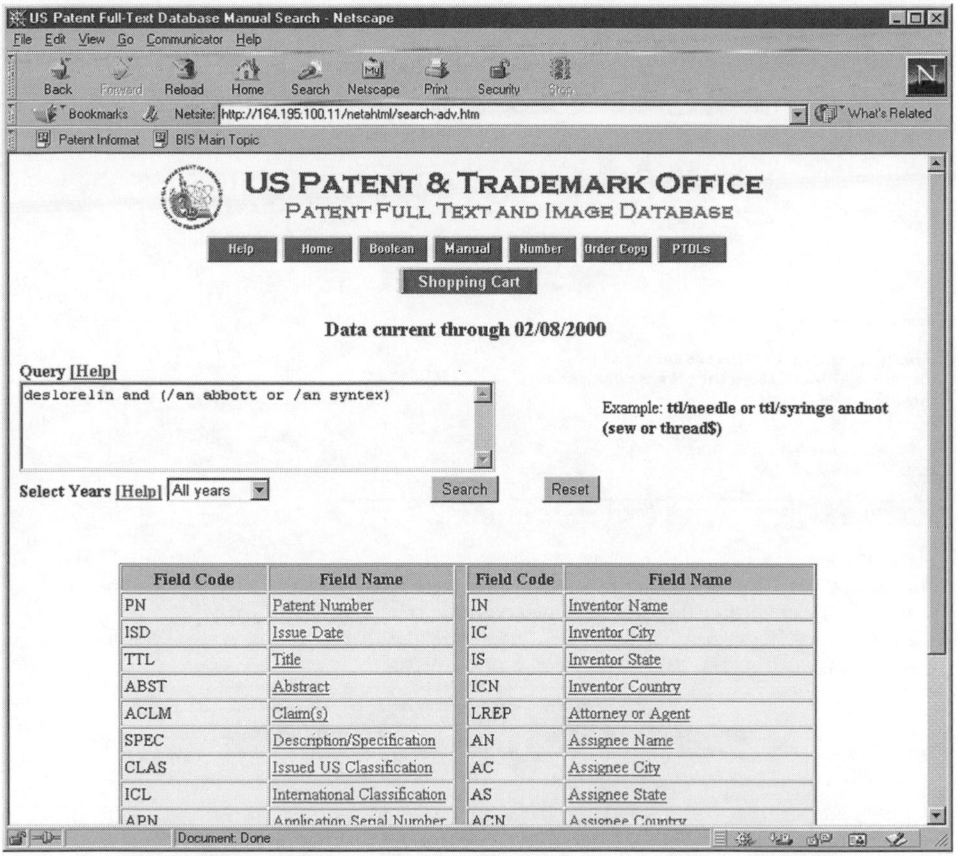

Figure 2.14   USPTO Manual Advanced Search screen

and Abstract fields. The search results are provided as a list of patent numbers with titles. Clicking on a patent number displays the first page information. Links are provided for US patents cited by the patent examiner. In addition, there are links to later patents citing this patent in their examiner's searches and to later continuing patents identifying this patent as related. Clicking on the US Patent Classification code link displays the definition of the class code from the *Manual of Classification*. Both searching and displaying records are free and do not require the searcher to register as a user.

MicroPatent WORLDWIDE PATSEARCH

The MicroPatent Patent and Trademark Information Web site, <URL http://www.micropatent.com/>, includes a searchable database of US patents, European and PCT patent applications and abstracts of Japanese patent

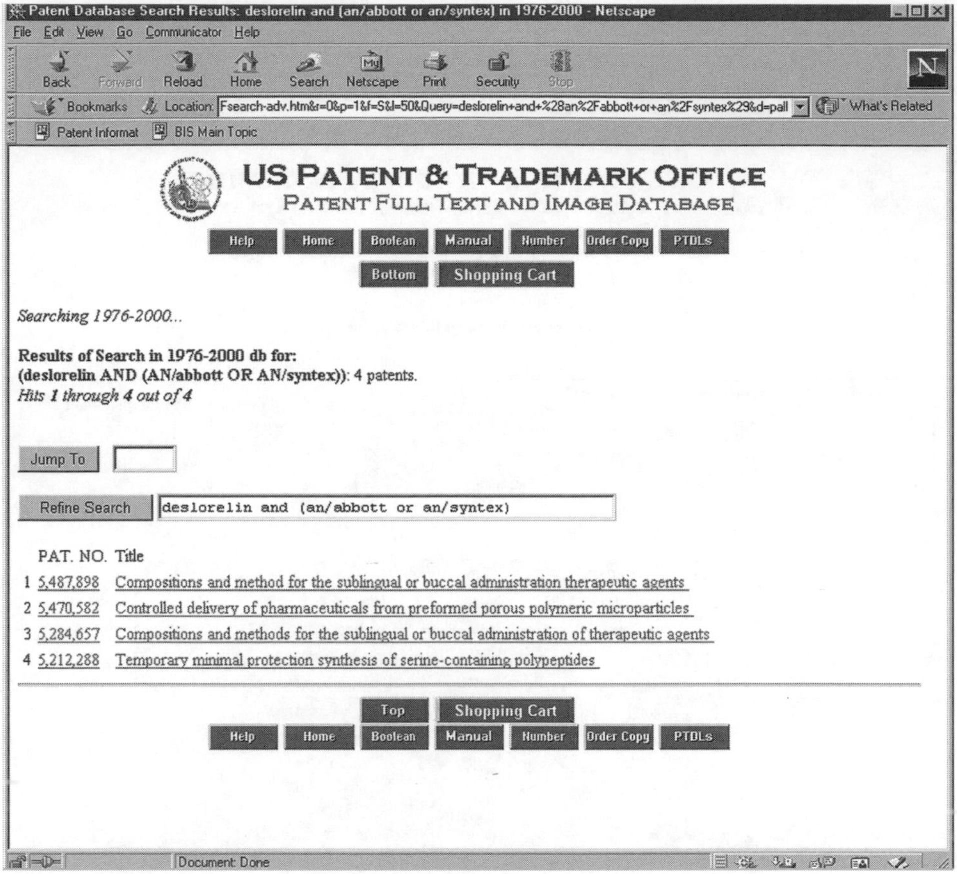

Figure 2.15   USPTO Manual Search Results screen

applications. The complete image of these documents and of European-granted patents and US patents issued since 1964 can be downloaded to the user's computer; patent copies can also be ordered for delivery by mail or fax, and full text can be delivered by e-mail. For a higher price it is possible to download or order any US patent issued since 1790 or any patent from a large collection of international patents. When a copy of a European patent application based on a published English-, French- or German-language PCT application is ordered, the corresponding WO document is delivered automatically. The US patents are searchable in full text, and the text of the specifications retrieved can be displayed. PCT applications published since 1983 have been scanned, and searchable copies of the full text have been generated by optical character recognition. The *US Official Gazette* Notices section from 1997 through the current week can be displayed at no charge. For subscribers, or for a daily access fee, WORLDWIDE PATSEARCH provides searching of the full-text data, bibliographic data and abstracts of European and PCT applications published from 1978 to the present, US patents from 1976 to the present, and the JAPIO abstracts of Japanese patent applications published since 1995. In addition to a single-query Boolean search, it is possible to perform multi-step searches with the Search History interface which also permits sorting search results by IPC or patentee name.

MicroPatent's file of scanned PCT applications represented a breakthrough: PCT applications are filed on paper, and WIPO does not record the text of the applications in electronic format. WO documents consist of copies of the application as filed, with only the first page generated from a digital file. To make these documents available, MicroPatent scanned the paper copies of English-, French-, German- and Spanish-language patent applications published since 1983, and submitted them to optical character recognition. Approximately 8.5 per cent of the PCT applications published during that period are in Japanese, Russian or Chinese and were not amenable to this treatment. The file has been loaded on DIALOG as File 349, WIPO/PCT PATENTS FULLTEXT.

European Patent Office databases

The European Patent Office (EPO) began producing patent databases for the use of its patent examiners and those of the member states of the European Patent Convention; in the early 1990s EPO took over the INPADOC database and organized the EPO Information and Documentation Service, EPIDOS, which introduced a series of CD-ROM databases and patent image products under the name ESPACE. Due to a major policy change in 1987, EPIDOS has reduced the cost of licensing data to search services and has begun distributing data to the general public over the Internet at little or no cost, revolutionizing access to patent information. The INPADOC database, discussed above, has been distributed more widely, and search services are now permitted to merge additional data into the files. Full-text European patent databases and patent images from the ESPACE collections are now available through many search services and Web sites, and the search files used by the EPO examiners are being distributed over the Internet.

In 1988 EPO introduced its Distributed Internet Patent Services, providing ESP@CENET links from the patent offices of each of the EPO member states. The EPO ESP@CENET server provides searchable front-page databases of published European patent applications, PCT applications, and a file of worldwide patents with links to the patent images. ESP@CENET also has the English-language PATENT ABSTRACTS OF JAPAN. Each of the 19 member states has a file of the latest two years or more of patents published through its national patenting systems, searchable in the national language. The national patent office search pages can also be used to search the files on the EPO server. Search and display of patent images on ESP@CENET is free of charge, and users are not required to register. No provision is made for direct downloading of the patent images, which display as single pages. ESP@CENET's worldwide patent database contains the front-page patent documents collected in the GLOBALPAT database, which is published on CD-ROM. GLOBALPAT has the patents required for the PCT Minimum Documentation: US, EP, PCT, British, French, German and Swiss patent documents going back to 1920 for national patents, and additional patents from countries around the world. An English-language abstract is provided for one member of each patent family, and searching for a patent number retrieves the bibliographic record for the abstracted patent, and links to the image of that patent and the image of the requested patent when it is present in the file. Patent families are taken from the EPO family database that was formerly searchable as EDOC on Questel and is now merged into the Questel-Orbit PLUSPAT file. The GLOBALPAT CD-ROM database is also mounted independently by the Technical University Ilmenau in Germany and is available free of charge.

Complete and up-to-date patent status information for European patent applications is provided through the European Patent Register. Formerly available only through a dial-up connection for a modest fee, the Register was moved to a free Internet site in 2000. The status data include all actions in the EPO, including all fee payments, mailing dates for official actions and responses, and hearing dates for appeals and opposition proceedings. Because the authority of the EPO ceases when the patent is granted and registered with the patent offices of the designated state, only a limited amount of post-grant status information is provided.

EUROPEAN PATENTS FULLTEXT

The EUROPEAN FULLTEXT PATENTS file on DIALOG, file 354, is produced by The Dialog Corporation from data provided by the European Patent Office. It contains the full text of European A documents (the published applications) from 1986 and the full text of B documents (the granted patents) from 1991. For patents dating back to 1983 there is selective full-text coverage, although no selection criteria have been made public by the EPO. The file has bibliographic coverage of all European patent documents since the EPO's inception in 1978. It is updated weekly with the current week's patents. Figure 2.16 shows the bibliographic data and excerpts from the legal status, specification text, and English, German and French claims of EP 557,436.

Patents are in English, French or German, with titles and the claims of granted patents in all three languages. English-language abstracts are added to the records of French- and German-language patents a few weeks after they are added to the database. In addition to the text of the patents, EUROPEAN PATENTS FULLTEXT includes patent status information published in the *European Patent Bulletin*. Although DIALOG intends the database to include all text of both published patent applications (A documents) and granted patents (B documents), text for some of the patents is missing, including the text of Euro-PCT applications in English, French or German which are not published by the EPO. DIALOG provides information about the number of words in the specifications and translated granted claims in both free formats as well as full formats. All bibliographic information is searchable, including the addresses of the applicant

DIALOG (R) File 348: European Patents
(c) 2000 European Patent Office. All rts. reserv.

00554360
ORDER fax of complete patent from DIALOG SourceOne. See HELP ORDER348
LATCHING STRUCTURE FOR CONTAINER FOR FOOD OR OTHER ARTICLES
VERSIEGELUNG AN BEHALTERN FUR LEBENSMITTEL ODER ANDERES
STRUCTURE DE FERMETURE POUR DES RECIPIENTS DESTINES A CONTENIR DES
ALIMENTS OU D'AUTRES OBJETS
PATENT ASSIGNEE:
  VISKASE CORPORATION, (786690), 6855 West 65th Street, Chicago, Illinois
    60638, (US), (applicant designated states: BE;DE;FR;GB;IT;NL)
INVENTOR:
  WARBURTON, Richard, Thomas, 4519 Emerson Road, Canandaigua, NY 14425,
    (US)
LEGAL REPRESENTATIVE:
  Ackroyd, Robert et al (52395), W.P. THOMPSON & CO. Eastcheap House
    Central Approach, Letchworth, Hertfordshire SG6 3DS, (GB)
PATENT (CC, No, Kind, Date): EP 557436 A1 930901 (Basic)
                              EP 557436 A1 950412
                              EP 557436 B1 970409
                              WO 9208649 920529
APPLICATION (CC, No, Date):   EP 92900796 911112; WO 91US8437 911112
PRIORITY (CC, No, Date): US 611576 901113
DESIGNATED STATES: BE; DE; FR; GB; IT; NL
INTERNATIONAL PATENT CLASS: B65D-043/16; B65D-021/02;
CITED PATENTS (WO A): US 2706065 A; US 3149747 A; US 4193496 A; US 4333580
  A; US 4512474 A; US 4576330 A
LEGAL STATUS (Type, Pub Date, Kind, Text):
Application: 930901 A1 Published application (A1with Search Report
                          ;A2without Search Report)
Examination: 930901 A1 Date of filing of request for examination:
                          930511
Change: 941130 A1 Representative (change)
*
*
*Assignee: 950830 A1 Applicant (transfer of rights) (change):
                          VISKASE CORPORATION (786690) 6855 West 65th
                          Street Chicago, Illinois 60638 (US) (applicant
                          designated states: BE;DE;FR;GB;IT;NL)
*Assignee: 950830 A1 Previous applicant in case of transfer of
                          rights (change): MOBIL OIL CORPORATION (202672)
                          3225 Gallows Road Fairfax, Virginia 22037-0001
                          (US) (applicant designated states:
                          BE;DE;FR;GB;IT;NL)

Examination: 951220 A1 Date of despatch of first examination report:
                          951106

 Grant: 970409 B1 Granted patent
*
*

Figure 2.16   EUROPEAN PATENTS FULLTEXT: DIALOG file 348

*Assignee: 970709 B1 Proprietor of the patent (transfer of rights):
               Kama Europe Limited (2283160) Columbus House,
               30 Manchester Road Northwich, Cheshire CW9 5ND
               (GB) (applicant designated states:
               BE;DE;FR;GB;IT;NL)
*Assignee: 970709 B1 Previous applicant in case of transfer of
               rights (change): VISKASE CORPORATION (786690)
               6855 West 65th Street Chicago, Illinois 60638
               (US) (applicant designated states:
               BE;DE;FR;GB;IT;NL)
Oppn None: 980401 B1 No opposition filed
LANGUAGE (Publication,Procedural,Application): English; English; English
FULLTEXT AVAILABILITY:

Available Text	Language	Update	Word Count
CLAIMS B	(English)	EPAB97	804
CLAIMS B	(German)	EPAB97	844
CLAIMS B	(French)	EPAB97	933
SPEC B	(English)	EPAB97	3341

Total word count - document A   0
Total word count - document B   5922
Total word count - documents A + B 5922

SPECIFICATION The present invention relates to a container according to the
  preamble of claim 1 for food or other articles, and is particularly
  concerned with a latching structure for holding a lid and a base of the
  container in a closed condition.
    Containers for food or other articles thermoformed from plastic ...
  *
  *

CLAIMS 1. A container (10;30;50) for food or other articles comprising: a
  lid (11;31;51) having a horizontal flange (14; 34; 54) extending
  around the periphery thereof, a base (12; 31'; 51') having a
  horizontal flange (16; 34'; 54') extending around the periphery ...
  *
  *

CLAIMS 1. Behalter (10; 30; 50) fur Nahrungsmittel oder andere Artikel mit:
  einen, Deckel (11; 31; 51) mit einem sich um dessen Umfang
  erstreckenden horizontalen Flansch (14; 34; 54), einer Basis (12;
  31'; 51') mit einem horizontalen Flansch (16; 34' 54'), der sich um
  deren Umfang herum erstreckt und fur einen Eingriff mit dem ...
  *
  *

CLAIMS 1. Recipient (10; 30; 50) pour aliments ou autres articles,
  comprenant: un couvercle (11; 31; 51) ayant un rebord horizontal (14;
  34; 54) s'etendant autour de la peripherie de celui-ci, une base (12;
  31'; 51') ayant un rebord horizontal (16; 34'; 54') s'etendant autour
  de la peripherie de celle-ci et etant adapte pour entrer en...

Figure 2.16   concluded

and agent. Patent document, application, and priority numbers are shown in standard DIALOG format. The Basic Index includes the inventor, patentee and patent number, as well as words from patent status actions. PCT document numbers are listed in the patent number field of Euro-PCT records. Patentees (which are not technically assignees in European patent law) are indexed under a Company field as well as the Patentee fields. Patentee codes, assigned by the EPO, are also searchable.

Changes in the status of the European patent application and details of patent prosecution are provided within the patent's record. These data include all changes of registered patent agent, reassignments and oppositions, complete with mailing addresses. More up-to-date patent status information can be obtained from the EUROPEAN PATENT REGISTER database, accessible directly from the European Patent Office.

EUROPATFULL

The EUROPATFULL file on STN also contains full text and complete bibliographic information from European patent applications. EUROPATFULL was originally loaded with patents published since the beginning of 1996, but the backfile is gradually being increased. The STN ChemPort link enables searchers to display patent images directly from the ESP@CENET site.

INPI databases

L'Institut National de Propriété Industrielle (INPI), the French Patent Office, produces the EPAT and PCTPAT databases, mounted on Questel-Orbit, the FPAT database on Questel-Orbit and DIALOG, and the ECLATX database on Questel-Orbit, as well as the PHARMSEARCH database (discussed below).

EPAT is an enhanced version of the European Patent Office first-page database. It contains the EPO's record for all European patents, and patent applications and all PCT applications designating the EPO published since the EPO's establishment in 1978. The file is updated weekly, one or two days after the publication, with current patent publications and updates of the existing records.

The document, application and priority numbers and dates of the patent are recorded, as are the country codes of the designated states. Records for European patents originating from PCT applications carry the document and application numbers of the PCT application. Patent document and priority numbers are indexed in their original format in the /PN and /PR fields and in updated Derwent format in the /XPN and /XPR fields, which do not print in any of the standard formats. The patent kind code indicates the current status of the indexed patent. Inventor and patentee names and addresses are given. The issue of the *EPO Bulletin* and of the *PCT Gazette* in which the publication was announced is also indicated.

The original title of the patent in English, French and German is given, as are the International Patent Classification codes assigned by the EPO. All but one language may be suppressed by displaying answers in a format specifying the preferred language. Abstracts are provided for all applications, and the English and French text of the first claim of granted patents is added to the record within one month of the grant date. The language of the application, the published document and the proceedings in the EPO are indicated.

The current status of the patent or application is indicated by the patent kind code and by entries in fields that give the date of publication of the search report and supplementary search reports, the date the applicant requested examination of the application, and other events in the prosecution of the application. The references cited in the search report or a cross-reference to the PCT search report are provided along with the corresponding *Bulletin* issue. The filing of an opposition to the grant of the patent is indicated by the name of the opposer and the filing date. The date of the grant of the patent or the abandonment of the application is provided when applicable. The name and address of the patent agent, but not those of an examiner, are given. Subsequent to patent grant, information about transfer of rights or licences recorded by the EPO is added to the record. If the patent lapses for failure to pay maintenance fees, the lapse date is recorded. In addition to the status of the European patent itself, EPAT contains information about the French legal status of granted European patents. For patents covering approved drugs, the file also provides the name and registration number of the approved drug and information about any Supplementary Protection Certificate applications or grants.

Although the full text of European patents is not present in the EPAT file, Questel-Orbit has made the text of the specification and claims available in the EPTEXT file. This file contains the text of European patent applications published since 1983, when the EPO began storing patents in electronic form; and earlier patent applications that were scanned by the EPO were converted to electronic form by optical character recognition. The patent number is the only bibliographic information in the record and serves as a link for cross-file searching.

PCTPAT has records for all patent applications published under the Patent Cooperation Treaty. All the bibliographic information in the published application is provided, including the complete names and addresses of applicants and patent agents for patents published in the PCT *Gazette* since 1982. For patent applications published from 1978 to 1982, only limited data are provided. The database is updated weekly with the current week's publications. Because PCT applications are forwarded to national and regional patent offices after preliminary examination and subjected to substantive examination, grant and opposition proceedings at each patent office, there is little patent status information in the records of the WO documents. The text and claims of PCT applications have been scanned and converted to electronic form by optical character recognition by the EPO, and may be searched and displayed in the WOTEXT file.

Figure 2.17 shows the full record for WO 95/01791. The document [PN], application [AP] and priority [PR] numbers and dates of the patent are recorded, as are the country codes of the designated states [DS], with countries designated for a regional patent identified by the regional patent office code in parentheses. Patent document and priority numbers are indexed in their original format in the /PN and /PR fields and in Derwent format in the /XPN and /XPR fields, which do not print in any of the standard formats. The patent kind code indicates the current status of the indexed patent. Inventor [IN] and patentee [PA] names and addresses are given.

The original title of the patent in English [ET] and French [FT] is given, as are the International Patent Classification codes [IC1] assigned by WIPO and the European Patent Classification code [EC]. Records can be printed in either English or French. Abstracts are provided in English [EAB] and French [FAB]. Records can be restricted to English or French versions of bilingual fields. The language of the published document is provided [APL].

The current status of the application is indicated only by the patent kind code and a non-searchable field noting whether the application was published with or without a search report [EREM, FREM]; post-issuance actions are not provided. The cited references in the Search Report are provided in full [RR]. The name and address of the patent agent [RP], but not those of an examiner, are given.

FPAT is INPI's French national patent database. It contains records for all French patents and patent applications published since 1966, and is updated every Friday with the current week's patent publications and updates of the existing records. Records are additionally present for medicinal patents published from 1961 to 1965.

The document, application and priority numbers and dates of the patent and its current status, are recorded. Patent document and priority numbers are indexed in their original format in the /PUB and /PR fields and in Derwent format in the /XPN and /XPR fields, which do not print in any of the standard formats. Inventor and patentee names and the country of origin of the patentee are provided.

The original French title of the patent is given, as are the International Patent Classification codes assigned by INPI and the corresponding ECLA codes. FPAT has French-language abstracts for patents published since 1981, but does not contain the text of the claims. English and French keywords are provided for patents published since 1987. Selected drawings are provided from documents published since 1989.

The current status of the patent or application is indicated as the legal nature of the document. The date of grant of the patent and date of publication of the examination search report are given, as are the corresponding issue numbers of the *Bulletin Officiel de Propriété Industrielle*. The patents and literature citations in the search report are in the online record. The name of the applicant's agent is listed. If the patent lapses due to failure to pay maintenance fees, the lapse date is recorded. For patents on approved drugs, information is provided about Supplemental Protection Certificate applications and grants.

```
1/3 PCTPAT - (C) INPI/WIPO- image
PN    - WO9501791 A2 19950119 [1994WO-FR00841]
AP    - (PCT)WOFR9400841 19940707 [1994WO-FR00841]
PR    - FR9308497 - 19930709 [1993FR-0008497]
ET    - USE OF EFAXORAN AND ITS DERIVATIVES FOR THE PRODUCTION OF DRUGS FOR
        TREATING NEURODEGENERATIVE DISEASES
FT    - UTILISATION DE L'EFAROXAN ET DE SES DERIVES POUR LA FABRICATION DE
        MEDICAMENTS DESTINES AU TRAITEMENT DES MALADIES NEURODEGENERATIVES
PA    - PIERRE FABRE MEDICAMENT [FR / FR]  45, place Abel-Gance F-92100
        Boulogne (FR) (except US)
      - COLPAERT, Francis [FR / FR]  33, boulevard Sizaire F-81100 Castres
        (FR) (only US)
      - BRILEY, Michael [FR / FR]  Baradou F-81650 Gaillac (FR) (only US)
      - IMBERT, Thierry [FR / FR]  16, route de Saix F-81290
        Viviers-les-Montagnes (FR) (only US)
IN    - COLPAERT, Francis [FR / FR]  33, boulevard Sizaire F-81100 Castres (FR)
      - BRILEY, Michael [FR / FR]  Baradou F-81650 Gaillac (FR)
      - IMBERT, Thierry [FR / FR]  16, route de Saix F-81290
        Viviers-les-Montagnes (FR)
EAB   - Use of a compound of general formula (I) wherein R1  is a hydrogen
        atom, a linear or branched C1 -C6  alkyl radical, R2  is a hydrogen
        atom, a methyl, chloro, bromo or fluoro group, and R3  is a hydrogen
        atom, a methyl, hydroxy, methoxy, fluoro, chloro or bromo group, and
        its therapeutically acceptable salts, its racemic or optically active
        isomers, for the preparation of a drug for treating Alzheimer-like
        senile dementia, pre-Alzheimer syndrome, progressive supranuclear
        palsy and other neurodegenerative diseases.
FAB   - La presente invention concerne l'utilisation d'un compose de formule
        generale (I) dans laquelle R1  represente un atome d'hydrogene, un
        radical alkyle lineaire ou ramifie en C1 -C6 , R2  represente un atome
        d'hydrogene, un groupe methyle, chloro, bromo ou fluoro, et R3
        represente un atome d'hydrogene, un groupe methyle, hydroxy, methoxy,
        fluoro, chloro ou bromo, ses sels therapeutiquement acceptables, son
        racemique ou ses isomeres optiquement actifs, pour la preparation d'un
        medicament destine au traitement de la demence senile du type
        Alzheimer, du syndrome pre-Alzheimer, de la paralysie supra nucleaire
        progressive et d'autres maladies neurodegeneratives.
IC1   - IPC[6 ]
      - A61K-031/415
EC    - A61K-031/415
DS    - AU; CA; JP; NZ; US; AT (EP); BE (EP); CH (EP); DE (EP); DK (EP); ES
        (EP); FR (EP); GB (EP); GR (EP); IE (EP); IT (EP); LU (EP); MC (EP);
        NL (EP); PT (EP); SE (EP)
RP    - AHNER, Francis /  Cabinet Regimbeau 26, avenue Kleber F-75116 Paris
        (FR)
EREM - Published:
        Without international search report and to be republished upon receipt
        of that report
FREM - Publie:
        Sans rapport de recherche internationale, sera republie des reception
        de ce rapport.
```

Figure 2.17   PCTPAT citation: Questel-Orbit file PCTPAT

```
RR    - Cited in the search report
      - EP71368 (A) (Cat. Y, D); EP486385 (A) (Cat. A); US4855308 (A) (Cat. A)
      - J. MED. CHEM., vol. 27, no.5, 1984 pages 570 - 576 C.B. CHAPLEO ET AL.
        'Alpha-Adrenoreceptor Reagents. 2. Effects of Modification of the
        1, 4-Benzodioxan Ring System on alpha-Adrenoreceptor Activity' (Cat. Y)
      - ARCH. INT. PHARMACODYN. THER., vol.277, no.2, 1985 pages 180 - 191 G. JOLY
        ET AL. 'Antagonistic Effects of S9871 or (imidazolinyl-2)-2-dihydro
        2,3 benzofurane and its Stereoisomers on Some Central and Peripheral
        Actions of alpha2-Agonists' (Cat. X)
      - PSYCHOPHARMACOLOGY, vol.89, no.4, 1986 page S31 S.J. SARA ET AL.
        'ENHANCEMENT OF COGNITIVE FUNCTION IN THE RAT BY ALPHA2 ANTAGONISTS OR
        ELECTRICAL STIMULATION OF THE LOCUS COERULEUS' (Cat. Y)
      - BEHAV. NEURAL BIOL., vol.51, no.3, Mai 1989 pages 401 - 411 S.J. SARA ET
        AL. 'Idazoxan, an alpha2-Antagonist, Facilitates Memory Retrieval in
        the Rat' (Cat. Y)
      - J. PSYCHOPHARMACOL., vol.4, no.2, 1990 pages 90 - 99 S.L. DICKINSON ET
        AL. 'Specific alpha2-adrenoceptor antagonists induce behavioural
        activation in the rat' (Cat. X)
      - NEUROCHEM.INT., vol.18, no.1, 1991 pages 137 - 140 H.DE VOS ET AL.
        'EFAROXAN (RX 821037) IS A POTENT AND SELECTIVE alpha2-ADRENOCEPTOR
        ANTAGONIST IN HUMAN FRONTAL CORTEX MEMBRANES' (Cat. X)
APL   - FR
```

Figure 2.17   concluded

Wila Verlag/Bertelsmann databases

Wila Verlag/Bertelsmann Informations-Service produces the PATOS series of patent databases mounted on STN, the EUROPATFULL database on STN, and the PATE and PADE databases mounted on FIZ Technik. PATOSEP and PATE cover European patent publications, PATOSWO covers PCT applications, PATOSDE and PATDE cover German patent publications, and EUROPATFULL is a full-text European patent file with published applications and granted patents from 1996 to the present. The files are updated weekly.

PATOSEP has bibliographic and status information for European patents and published applications from the beginning of the European patent system in 1978. Although each patent number is represented by a single record, the file is divided into segments for Offenlegungsschriften (published specifications), Patentschriften (granted patents), and Rechtsstand (legal status data), which may be searched separately. Figure 2.18 shows the PATOSEP record for EP 687807. The title of the patent is given in English [TIEN], French [TIFR] and German [TIDE]. Inventor names and full addresses [IN], patentee names and addresses [PA] and a numeric patentee code [PAN] are provided, as are patent agent names and addresses [AG] and patent agent code numbers [AGN]. Cross-references to the Wila Verlag/Bertelsmann print abstract publications [OS, SO] are provided. The record includes the language of the application and publication [LA], and the patent kind code and its German definition [PIT]. The type of document [DT] is

```
L1    ANSWER 1 OF 1  PATOSEP  COPYRIGHT  2000WILA

PATENT APPLICATION

AN    1995:1582789 PATOSEP   ED 19960103  EW 199551   FS OS
TIEN  Heater unit and catalytic converter.
TIDE  Heizungseinheit und katalytischer Umwandler.
TIFR  Unite de chauffage et convertisseur catalytique.
IN    Abe, Fumio, 1-29, Souga-cho, Handa-city, Aichi-prefecture, 475,
      JP;
      Hashimoto, Shigeharu, 29-1, Mukaiyama, Wakamatsu-cho,
      Okazaki-city, Aichi-pref. 444, JP;
      Kondo, Tomoharu, 43, Izuminishikama-cho 4-chome, Toki-city,
      Gifu-pref. 509-51, JP
PA    NGK INSULATORS, LTD., 2-56, Suda-cho, Mizuho-ku, Nagoya City Aichi
      Pref., JP
PAN   302181
AG    Paget, Hugh Charles Edward et al, MEWBURN ELLIS York House 23
      Kingsway, London WC2B 6HP, GB
AGN   34621
OS    ESP1995080 EP 0687807 A1 0046
SO    Wila-EPZ-1995-H51-T3b
DT    Patent
LA    Anmeldung in Englisch; Veroeffentlichung in Englisch
DS    R DE; R FR; R GB
PIT   EPA1 EUROPAEISCHE PATENTANMELDUNG
PI    EP 687807      A1 951220
OD                   951220
AI    EP 95-302043   950327
PRAI  JP 94-134701   940616
IC    ICM  F01N003-28
      ICS  F01N003-20
MCLMEN 1. A heater unit comprising:
        a honeycomb heater comprising a metallic honeycomb structure
      having a large number of parallel passages extending along an
      axial direction, and at least one electrode for electrification of
      the honeycomb structure, attached to the honeycomb structure;
        a metallic casing for holding the honeycomb heater;
        supporting means for supporting the honeycomb heater in the
      casing, absorbing displacement of the honeycomb heater with
****  flowing outside the honeycomb heater is controlled at 20% or less
      of the total flow amount of exhaust gas.
ABEN A heater unit has a honeycomb heater comprising (a) a metallic
      honeycomb structure having a large number of passages parallel to
      the direction of an exhaust gas flowing through the heater unit
      and (b) at least one electrode for electrification of the
      honeycomb structure, attached to the honeycomb structure, and a
****  flow direction. A gas flow-controlling means is provided at the
      inlet and/or side of the honeycomb heater so that the amount of
      the exhaust gas flowing outside the honeycomb heater is controlled
      at 20% or less of the total flow amount of exhaust gas. The heater
```

Figure 2.18   **PATOS: STN file PATOSEP**

unit, when exposed to severe driving conditions of automobiles, etc. and subjected to vibration and the expansion and contraction caused by thermal shock, gives rise to neither breakage of honeycomb heater nor peeling and can maintain the purification ability for exhaust gases of automobiles, etc.

FA   A1; PRAI; ICS; AG; INA; PAA; AGA; AGN; PAN; MCLMEN; ABEN

GRANTED PATENT
AN   1995: 1582789 PATOSEP UP 19980802 EW 199830 FS PS
TIEN   Heater unit and catalytic converter.
IN   Abe, Fumio, 1-29, Souga-cho, Handa-city, Aichi-prefecture, 475, JP;
       Hashimoto, Shigeharu, 29-1, Mukaiyama, Wakamatsu-cho, Okazaki-city, Aichi-pref. 444, JP;
       Kondo, Tomoharu, 43, Izuminishikama-cho 4-chome, Toki-city, Gifu-pref. 509-51, JP
PA   NGK INSULATORS, LTD., 2-56, Suda-cho, Mizuho-ku, Nagoya City Aichi Pref., JP
PAN   302181
AG   Paget, Hugh Charles Edward et al, MEWBURN ELLIS York House 23 Kingsway, London WC2B 6HP, GB
AGN 34621
OS   EPB1998037 EP 0687807 B1 980722
SO   Wila-EPS-1998-H30-T3
DT   Patent
LA   Anmeldung in Englisch; Veroeffentlichung in Englisch
DS   R DE; R FR; R GB
PIT   EPB1 EUROPAEISCHE PATENTSCHRIFT
PI   **EP 687807**   **B1 19980722**
OD   19951220
AI   EP 1995-302043   19950327
PRAI JP 1994-13401   19940616
REP   EP 618353 A   WO 92-02714 A
       US 5177961 A   US 5202548 A
IC   ICM F01N003-28
       ICS F01N003-20
MCLMEN 1. A heater unit comprising:
      a honeycomb heater comprising a metallic honeycomb structure (1, 10, 12) having a large number of parallel passages extending along an axial direction, and at least one electrode (22) for passing electric current through the honeycomb structure, attached to the honeycomb structure;
         a metallic casing (3, 19) for holding the honeycomb heater; and
         one of the following (a), (b) and (c):
           (a) supporting means (6, 16) for supporting the honeycomb heater in the casing, absorbing displacement of the honeycomb heater with respect
****
           (c) buffer means (27) for securing the electrode, which is connected directly to the honeycomb structure and has an insulating member (26) secured thereto, to the casing and absorbing displacement of the honeycomb heater with respect to the casing in a direction substantially perpendicular to the axial direction, said buffer means (27) comprising a buffer member provided between the insulating member

Figure 2.18   **cont'd**

```
        (26) and the casing;
           said heater unit further having gas flow-controlling means (7)
        provided at the inlet and/or at the side of the honeycomb heater so that
        an amount of the exhaust gas flows outside the honeycomb heater, which
        amount is in the range 2 to 20% of the total flow amount of exhaust gas.
   FA   B1; PRAI; ICS; AG; INA; PAA; AGA; AGN; PAN; MCLMDE; REP; MCLMEN

   LEGAL STATUS

   AN   1995:1582789 PATOSEP UPLS 19990715  EW 199924   FS RS
   SO   WILA-Agg.-incl.-1999-H26
   DT   Historie
   PIT  EPLS LEGAL STATUS
   PI   EP 687807        BL 19990616
   LSEN EP-Bul Code       Text
        951220 AD         Application date . . . . . . . . . . . 950327
        951220 OD         Laid open date (publication) of A-Doc.
        960327 EX-RQ      Examination requested  . . . . . . . 960126
        970521 EX-OffAct  First office action . . . . . . . . . . . 970407
        980722 PD-B1      Publication date of B1 document
        990616 OP         Opposition
   OP   (990616) 990422 OP-01: Emitec Gesellschaft fuer Emissionstechnologie mbH,
        Hauptstrasse 150, D-53797 Lohmar, DE;
        AG-OP: Kahlhoefer, Hermann, Dipl.-Phys., Patent- und Rechtsanwaelte Bardehle,
        Pagenberg, Dost, Altenburg, Geissler, Isenbruck Uerdinger Str. 5, 40474
        Duesseldorf, DE.
   FA   OP; LS
```

Figure 2.18   concluded

provided for each sector of the database. Patent document number [PI],
application number [AI], and priority number [PRAI] and the associated dates are
in STN or Derwent format, at the searcher's option. The first publication date is
also given in the OD field. Each designated state [DS] is associated with a code
for regional filing – a distinction that has greater meaning in the PATOSWO file,
where national filings are also designated. The main claim [MCLMEN] of patents
published since 1992 and the abstract [ABEN] are shown in the language of filing.
For patents granted since 1990, the main claim is also given in German. Citations
printed in the STN ALL format give multilingual fields only in English; to see the
German and/or French text the appropriate display formats are ALLDE, ALLFR,
and MAX. PATOSWO has bibliographic information from PCT applications
published since 1983. Abstracts are in English and, since 1992, German-language
abstracts are available for patent applications filed in German.

PATOSDE covers German national patent publications. It includes patent
applications and examined patent applications published since October 1968,
granted patents published since 1980, and utility models published since 1983.
Bibliographic information and the main claim are present in all records, and
abstracts are available for patents published between 1991 and 1994. All text is in
German.

PATDPA

The PATDPA database is produced by the Deutsches Patentamt, the Patent Office of the Federal Republic of Germany, and supplied on STN by FIZ Karlsruhe. The database covers German patents and European and PCT patent documents designating Germany. It includes full bibliographic information, abstract text and status information for all published applications, granted patents and utility models reported in the *Patentblatt* since 1968. Patent applications pending in the former East German patent office at the time of reunification are included. The drawings from the first page abstract of Offenlegungsschriften (published patent applications) published from 1983 to the present are printable. Figure 2.19 illustrates the PATDPA record for EP 687,807.

PATDPA has a single record based on the serial number of each patent application [SN]. The original publication number [AN] and the German registration number of European patents [PSR] are provided. The Family Information [FI] field records the document number and a description of each level of publication of the German patent document and the corresponding European and PCT applications; it does not include family members from other countries. The patent application number and date [AI] and document numbers and publication dates are given [PI, FI]. Records for European and PCT applications include a list of the ISO country codes of designated states [DS]. Priority application numbers and dates [PRAI] are reported, the German national application being used when foreign priority is not claimed. When a related German patent application exists, it is identified in the record. The patent assignee [PA] field includes the name of the assignee and its address [PAC], a numerical patentee code [PAN] and an indication of the type of organization to which the patent is assigned [PAT]. All the inventors and their addresses [IN] are listed. Where a change of inventors or assignee is recorded, both old and new names are indexed. The *Patentblatt* date and week and a full citation to each edition of the *Patentblatt* reporting on the cited patent [SO] are given. The CAS accession number is given in the records of patents that appeared in *Chemical Abstracts* prior to the last update of the record.

The original title [TI] and, for German patents, the author abstract of the patent application are given in German. Index terms consisting of the uninflected forms of the terms in the abstract [PST] are given as an aid to searching. The IPC codes [ICM, ICS] are identified. Patent and literature citations made by the examiner are indexed, and the examiner's field of search is identified [RE, REP]. The language of the published document is given [LA].

All the patent status information on file with the patent office is reported in the database [NTE]. This includes the publication of the examined application corresponding to a published patent application, changes in ownership, licensing agreements, patent lapse dates and each step in the prosecution of a patent application. The name and full address of the German patent agent representing the applicant [AG] is given. When a change in the status of the patent application

```
L1    ANSWER 1 OF 1  COPYRIGHT 2000 DPA/FIZ KA
AN    EP687807 PATDPA    ED  19960201    EW  199605
SN    EP95302043.5          DED 19960201    DEW 199605
UPS   19990617              weitere UP-Felder: HELP UPD
PSR   DE69503574
TI    (B1) (A ) Heizungseinheit und katalytischer Umwandler
IN
INC   Abe, Fumio (*JP Aichi-prefecture, Handa-city, 475)
      Hashimoto, Shigeharu (*JP Okazaki-city, Aichi-pref. 444)
      Kondo, Tomoharu (*JP Toki-city, Gifu-pref. 509-51)
INO   Abe, Fumio (*JP Aichi-prefecture, Handa-city, 475)
PA    NGK Insulators Ltd. (*JP Nagoya, Aichi)
PAO   NGK Insulators Ltd. (*JP Nagoya, Aichi)
PAN   1017713 JP
PAT   (CORP) Juristische Person
AG    derzeit kein Vertreter bestellt
SO    DE-Patentblatt 118 (1998) Heft 35, EP B1 EP-Patentschrift
DT    Patent
LA    Englisch
NTE   19940616: FPRD (32) Erstes Prioritaetsdatum
      19950327: ADR  (86) Anmeldetag d. EP-Anm. m. DE-Benennung
      19951220: AOR  (87) EP-Publ. der EP-Anmeldung mit DE-Benennung
      19960126: EXR   Eingangstag des Pruefungsantrages in EPA
      19980722: PGR   (87) EP-Patent mit DE-Wirk.
      19990422: PGEIR Einspruch 01 erhoben - Einspruch erhoben
PIT   EP AR Europaeische Patentschrift, Einspr-.-Frist 9 Mon.
PI    EP 687807      B1 19980722 PGR OP9 (87) letzte Publ./
                 EP-Schrift
DS    R: DE FR GB DE; R FR; R GB
AI    EP 1995-302043 A 19950327 ADR     (86) EP-Anm. mit DE-Ben.
      DE 1995-69503574 E 19950327 ADRN   (22) DE-AKZ fuer EP-Patent
PRAI  JP 1994-134701 A 19940616 CP      (32) Unionsprioritaet
FI
FIA   EP 1995-302043 A  19950327 ADR     (86) EP687807
FIP   EP 687807      A1 19951220 AOR LEN (87) EP-Publik. mit DE-Ben. :
             R: DE FR GB
      EP 687807      B1 19980722 PGR     (87) EP-Patent mit DE-Wirk. :
             R: DE FR GB
RE
REP   EP 618353       A    SRE  (56) Aus nation. Recherchenber.
      WO 92/02714     A    SRE  (56) Aus nation. Recherchenber.
      US 5177961      A    SRE  (56) Aus nation. Recherchenber.
      US 5202548      A    SRE  (56) Aus nation. Recherchenber.
IC
ICM   F01N003-28                  (511) IPC-Hauptklasse
ICS   F01N003-20                  (512) IPC-Nebenklasse
PST   EINHEIT; HEIZUNG; HEIZUNGSEINHEIT; KATALYTISCH; UMWANDLER
FA    AG; DS; ICS; INC; OP; PSR; PST; REP
OP    Emitec Gesellschaft fuer Emissionstechnologie mbH (*DE 53797 Lohmar)
```

Figure 2.19   PATDPA: STN

is reported in the *Patentblatt*, the record is amended and all new data are added to the existing record. More up-to-date patent status information can be obtained from the GERMAN PATENT REGISTER database, accessible directly from the Deutsches Patentamt.

Chinese patents abstracts in English

The online version of *Patent Abstracts of China*, produced by INPADOC, is mounted as CHINAPATS on Questel-Orbit and as file 344 on DIALOG. It covers all patent applications published by the People's Republic of China, the first of which appeared in September 1985. The database is updated monthly with bibliographic data for patents published about eight months earlier.

All patent document, application and priority numbers and dates are indexed in the original published format. All patent assignee and inventor names are indexed with their countries of residence; when no corporate or governmental assignee is present, the Assignee field contains the names of the inventors in uninverted form. For patent applications claiming the same priority as other patent publications indexed in the INPADOC database, the record includes the document number, patent kind code and publication date of all equivalent patents indexed before the Chinese patent was added to the INPADOC file. For patents equivalent to those whose INPADOC record contains a cross-referenced *Chemical Abstracts* or Derwent accession number at the time of indexing the Chinese patent, the cross-reference accession numbers are provided in the CHINESE PATENTS ABSTRACTS record.

The original title is translated into English and the International Patent Classification codes assigned by the Chinese Patent Office are given. English-language abstracts produced by the Patent Documentation Service Centre of the Chinese Patent Office are prepared for all patents issued to Chinese inventors; only the bibliographic record is available online for patents issued to non-Chinese applicants, which are presumed to be equivalent to patents indexed in other databases.

JAPIO

JAPIO covers published Japanese patent applications, '*kokai*', issued from October 1976 to the present. It is produced by the Japanese Patent Information Organization (JAPIO), an agency of the Japanese Patent Office, and mounted on Questel-Orbit, DIALOG, LEXIS-NEXIS, STN and through several Internet patent search services. The database contains abstracts published in the CD-ROM publication PATENT ABSTRACTS OF JAPAN and bibliographic citations for all *kokai* not selected for abstracting. It is updated monthly with data from the printed abstracts, which are published about five months after the issue date of the patents. Figure 2.20 shows the full JAPIO citation for JP 08-004521.

05049021   ** Image available**
HEATER UNIT AND CATALYTIC CONVERTER

PUB. NO.:   08-004521 [JP 8004521 A]
PUBLISHED: January 09, 1996 (19960109)
INVENTOR(s):   ABE FUMIO
                HASHIMOTO SHIGEHARU
                KONDO TOMOHARU
APPLICANT(s): NGK INSULATORS LTD [000406] (A Japanese Company or
                Corporation), JP (Japan)
APPL. NO.:   06-134701 [JP 94134701]
FILED: June 16, 1994 (19940616)
INTL CLASS: [6] F01N-003/20; F01N-003/24; F01N-003/28; F01N-003/28
JAPIO CLASS: 21.2 (ENGINES & TURBINES, PRIME MOVERS -- Internal
                Combustion); 32.1 (POLLUTION CONTROL -- Exhaust Disposal)

ABSTRACT
PURPOSE: To prevent a honeycomb heater from being damaged and peeled off by
the expansion and contraction due to vibration and thermal shock while the
purification capacity of exhaust gas is maintained under the severe
conditions of automobile and the like by properly controlling the bypass
flow of exhaust gas to the outer periphery of the honeycomb heater.

CONSTITUTION: A gas flow adjusting means to control the bypass flow amount
of exhaust gas to the outer periphery side of a honeycomb heater (1) to 20%
or less of the total exhaust gas amount is provided in the upstream and/or
side part of the honeycomb heater 1. Also an ignition catalyst 8 comprising
a honeycomb structural body with many through-holes in gas flow direction
is arranged closely to the honeycomb heater 1, and held in a metallic can
body 3 to form a catalytic converter. Thus, when the ignition catalyst 8 is
moved closely to the honeycomb heater 1, a bypass flow is reduced by a back
pressure of the ignition catalyst 8 in the downstream and, because the
honeycomb heater 1 is close to the ignition catalyst 8, a purification
capacity obtained becomes large.

Figure 2.20   JAPIO: DIALOG file 347

JAPIO indexes all patent, application and priority numbers and dates in the
original published format and in the host search service's standard format, and
both formats print in the record. For documents published before 2000 and
applications filed before 2000, document and application numbers incorporate the
Japanese Imperial year, the current Western year minus 1988 and, for dates before
8 January 1989, the current Western year minus 1925. All patent applicant and
inventor names are indexed. JAPIO has standard seven-digit patentee codes for
companies with many patents, and the names of the companies that have codes are
printed in a standardized format. Because the names are transliterated from the
Japanese alphabet, company and inventor names – especially those of non-

Japanese origin – are often spelt in unfamiliar ways. Searches in JAPIO for non-Japanese names should rely on the printed company code manual, liberal use of the **Expand** command, and an open, imaginative mind. The record also includes a citation to the PATENT ABSTRACTS OF JAPAN.

JAPIO includes an English translation of the original title of all patents. An abstract, written in English as a summary of the complete specification and claims, is provided for patents applied for by Japanese nationals in selected chemical, mechanical, electrical and physics technologies. Approximately 60 per cent of the records in the database have abstracts. As of 2000, additional abstracts and records for non-Japanese inventors were being added to the backfile and were available on some, but not all, search services and Web sites.

All records include the International Patent Classification codes assigned by the Japanese Patent Office. Patents published from 1976 to 1979 also have Japanese national patent classification codes. JAPIO classification codes are given to each record and alphanumeric fixed keyword codes are applied by JAPIO to some records.

In contrast to the limited information available in the English-language JAPIO database, the Japanese-language PATOLIS database contains bibliographic and status information for all levels and types of Japanese patent documents, with abstracts and drawings.

PATENT ABSTRACTS OF JAPAN is also searchable on the Internet at the Japanese Patent Office site, <URL http://210.141.236.195/index_e.html>, or as a link from the ISTA Inc. site, <URL http://www.intlscience.com/ > and the Trilateral Agreement site of the US, European and Japanese Patent Offices. This version of the database contains published applications from January 1993, with a four-month delay in posting. The records contain drawings and are supplemented with patent status information. Search and display of records is free. Free search and display of records is also available from the European Patent Office's ESP@CENET site, the DELPHION INTELLECTUAL PROPERTY NETWORK and the PATON/PAJ site of the Universitäat Ilmenau at <http://atlas.patent-inf.tu-ilmenau.de/brs/paj_eng.html>. PATENT ABSTRACTS OF JAPAN is searchable on the Internet as part of the MicroPatent WORLDWIDE PATSEARCH service, which is available through subscription or for a daily search fee.

APIPAT

APIPAT is a database of patents relating to all aspects of petroleum technology, produced by API EnCompass, formerly known as the Central Abstracting and Indexing Service of the American Petroleum Institute (API) and now owned by Engineering Information, Inc. The database is mounted on DIALOG and STN. APIPAT was founded in 1964 and, in its early years, API screened patent specifications and prepared abstracts for indexing. Since 1972 most of the records have been derived from the DERWENT WORLD PATENTS INDEX or from *Chemical Abstracts*. APIPAT is the online version of the printed API *EnCompass*

```
DIALOG(R)File 353:APIPAT
(c) 1998 American Petroleum Institute. All rts. reserv.

0253391  API Document No.: 9640424  Derwent WPI Accession No.: 96-031832
Honeycomb heater for catalytic converter purifying automobile engine
    exhaust gases - has gas flow controller at inlet and/or side of heater
    ensuring no more than 20 per cent of total exhaust gas flows outside
    heater
Patent Assignee: NGK INSULATORS LTD
Priority (CC,No,Date): JP 94134701 940616
Patent (CC,No,Date):  EP 687807 951220
Designated States: DE; FR; GB
Int Pat Class: F01N-003/20; F01N-003/28
API Bulletin Headings: AIR POLLUTION CONTROL; CATALYSTS/ZEOLITES;
    ENVIRONMENT, TRANSPORT & STORAGE; HEALTH & ENVIRONMENT;
    POLLUTION-CONTROL CATALYSTS
Index Terms: ABSORPTION; AIR POLLUTANT; ALLOY; AUTOMOBILE; AUTOMOTIVE
    EMISSION CONTROL; *AUTOMOTIVE EMISSION CONTROL EQUIP; AUTOMOTIVE ENGINE
    ; AUTOMOTIVE EXHAUST GAS; AXIAL; CASING; *CATALYTIC MUFFLER; CELLULAR;
    CHANNEL; CONTROL EQUIPMENT; ELECTRODE; ENGINE; EXHAUST GAS; FAILURE;
    FLUID FLOW; FORCE; GAS; HEATING EQUIPMENT; INLET; INSULATING MATERIAL;
    LIGHTOFF TEMPERATURE; MOTION; MOTOR VEHICLE; MOUNTING; *MUFFLER;
    ORIFICE; OUTLET; PARALLEL; PHYSICAL PROPERTY; PHYSICAL SEPARATION;
    POLLUTANT; POLLUTION CONTROL; *POLLUTION CONTROL EQUIPMENT;
    PREVENTION; PURIFYING; SORPTION; STRESS; THERMAL INSULATION; THERMAL
    STRESS; USE; VIBRATION; WASTE GAS; WASTE MATERIAL
Sets of Linked Terms: 0002
Linked Terms:
    CELLULAR; HEATING EQUIPMENT
    AXIAL; CATALYTIC MUFFLER; CHANNEL; MUFFLER; PARALLEL; POLLUTION CONTROL
      EQUIPMENT
Template: NOT AVAILABLE
```

Figure 2.21 APIPAT: DIALOG file 353

Industry Alert Bulletins; it may be searched by non-subscribers for a maximum of three hours per year. The database is updated monthly; records are necessarily delayed several months after the publication of the patents, as the patents are indexed by API only after the original delay for processing by Derwent or CAS. Figure 2.21 illustrates the APIPAT record for EP 687,807.

Patent and priority numbers and dates are provided for the indexed patent. Records of patents indexed before 1978 include equivalent patent numbers. The records of European patents and PCT applications carry the ISO country codes of designated states in a separate field. Patent assignee names [OS] are provided for all records, and inventor names are in the records of patents indexed before 1972.

Cross-reference accession numbers from WORLD PATENTS INDEX are present in records from 1972 to date, and may be used for cross-file searching. Cross-reference accession numbers for *Chemical Abstracts* and *Petroleum*

Abstracts are included in the Source field.

The title is taken from the source abstract, and the abstract is reproduced in the subscriber files for records indexed from 1980 to the present. International Patent Classification codes present in the source record are indexed. API Bulletin Headings are searchable. APIPAT references are intensively indexed by API, using the Derwent or CA abstract as a basis for indexing. Controlled index terms from the API Thesaurus are searchable alone, linked in groups of related concepts, and with the role qualifiers /A for reactants, /P for products and /N for substances that are neither reactant nor product. A system of templates allows for coordination of index terms to define features of the invention. For index terms of narrow scope, broader index terms are automatically posted to the record. Individual words from multi-word index terms may be searched. The API-controlled vocabulary includes terms for the advantages expected from an invention, for processes, apparatus and chemical substances taking part in the invention, and for structural features of chemical substances. Generic chemical structures are indexed by linked structural fragment codes. When appropriate, supplementary index terms that are not in the API Thesaurus are applied to the record. Category codes, headings from the API Thesaurus and printed abstract publications may be searched to limit searches to major fields. Specific compounds may be searched using CAS registry numbers, and role qualifiers may be applied to the registry numbers.

WORLD PATENTS INDEX/APIPAT

Questel-Orbit has merged the WORLD PATENTS INDEX files with APIPAT to form the combined file WPAM and the non-subscriber file WPAMNS, in which the indexing applied by both Derwent and API is searchable in the records of patents covered by both services. Records carry the Derwent primary [AN] and secondary [XRAM, XRPX] accession numbers and contain the API accession number in the XR field. Records that were not indexed by Derwent are included in the database, and these carry a Derwent accession number beginning with '1965'. Abstracts provided to API by *Chemical Abstracts* are omitted from these files, but all other data present in the DWPI files or APIPAT are included. Figure 2.22 shows the WPAM citation for EP-687,807, which corresponds to the APIPAT citation in Figure 2.21. Non-subscribers may search only those fields available to non-subscribers in the WPI and APIPAT databases.

The bibliographic data in the merged file are taken from DWPI, thus enhancing the APIPAT record with equivalent patent data [PN, NP, NC, AP], inventor names [IN], and Derwent company codes [PA]. Cited patents from EP and WO documents prior to 1998 are also included.

Because the title and abstract in most APIPAT records were provided by Derwent, it is not surprising that these are identical in the merged file. Unlike APIPAT records, WPAM records are updated with abstracts of the granted equivalent patents [USAB] from major countries prior to 1998. Derwent's collected IPC codes [IC] are searchable. In addition to the controlled indexing applied by API, WPAM records contain Derwent's controlled indexing [DC, MC, M3].

```
1/1      (WPAM) - (C) Derwent- image
AN   -   1996-031832 [04]
XA   -   C1996-011006
XP   -   N1996-026849
TI   -   Honeycomb heater for catalytic converter purifying automobile engine
         exhaust gases - has gas flow controller at inlet and/or side of heater
         ensuring no more than 20 per cent of total exhaust gas flows outside
         heater
DC   -   H06 J04 Q51
PA   -   (NIGA ) NGK INSULATORS LTD
IN   -   ABE F, HASHIMOTO S, KONDO T
NP   -   5
NC   -   5
PN   -   EP-687807 A1 19951220 DW1996-04 F01N-003/28 Eng 46p *
         AP: 1995EP-0302043 19950327
         DSR: DE FR GB
     -   JP08004521 A 19960109 DW1996-10 F01N-003/20 17p
         AP 1994JP-0134701 19940616
     -   US5614155 A 19970325 DW997-18 F01N-003/10 40p
         AP: 1995US-0412279 19950328
     -   EP-687807 B1 19980722 DW1998-33 F01N-003/28 Eng
         AP: 1995EP-0302043 19950327
         DSR: DE FR GB
     -   DE69503574 E 19980827 DW1998-40 F01N-003/28
         FD:      Based on EP-687807
         AP: 1995DE-6003574 19950327; 1995EP-0302043 19950327
PR   -   1994JP-0134701 19940616
CT   -   EP-618353 US5177961 US5202548 WO9202714
IC   -   F01N-003/10 F01N-003/20 F01N-003/28 F01N-003/24
AB   -   EP-687807-A
         A heater unit has metallic honeycomb heater (1) with many parallel axial
         passages and at least one electrode for electrifying the honeycomb. The
         electrode is secured to a casing (3) for the heater via an insulating
         support (6). At least one member absorbs movement of the heater relative
         to the casing and perpendicular to its axis. A gas flow controller at the
         inlet and/or side of the heater ensures that no more than 20% of total
         exhaust gas flows outside the honeycomb. In some aspects the member(s)
         is/are specified as being of metal and/or preventing axial movement of
         the heater relative to the cover.
         USE - Heaters in and for a catalytic converter purifying automobile
         engine exhaust gases.
         ADVANTAGE - The heater does not break due vibration and/or thermal strain
         while maintaining purification of exhaust gas. (Dwg.1/46)
USAB -   US5614155-A
         A heater unit, comprising: a honeycomb heater comprising (i) a metallic
         honeycomb structure having an inlet, an outlet, an outer peripheral wall
         and a number of parallel passages extending along an axial direction, and
         (ii) at least one electrode attached to the honeycomb structure for
         electrification of the honeycomb structure; a metallic casing for holding
         the honeycomb heater; and a gas flow-controlling device for controlling
```

Figure 2.22   WORLD PATENTS INDEX/APIPAT: Questel-Orbit file WPAM

flow of exhaust gas through the heater unit, such that about 2 to 20% of the exhaust gas flows outside the honeycomb heater, between the honeycomb heater and the metallic casing. (Dwg.0/46)

MC - CPI: H06-C03 J04-E02 N06-D
M3 - *01* M411 M424 M730 M740 M903 Q421 Q508
BH - AIR POLLUTION CONTROL
BH - CATALYSTS/ZEOLITES
   - ENVIRONMENT, TRANSPORT & STORAGE
   - HEALTH & ENVIRONMENT
   - POLLUTION-CONTROL CATALYSTS
IT - ABSORPTION-N; AIR POLLUTANT-N; ALLOY-N; AUTOMOBILE-N; AUTOMOTIVE EMISSION CONTROL-N; *AUTOMOTIVE EMISSION CONTROL EQUIP-N; AUTOMOTIVE ENGINE-N; AUTOMOTIVE EXHAUST GAS-N; AXIAL-N; CASING-N; *CATALYTIC MUFFLER-N; CELLULAR-N; CHANNEL-N; CONTROL EQUIPMENT-N; ELECTRODE-N; ENGINE-N; EXHAUST GAS-N; FAILURE-N; FLUID FLOW-N; FORCE-N; GAS-N; HEATING EQUIPMENT-N; INLET-N; INSULATING MATERIAL-N; LIGHTOFF TEMPERATURE-N; MOTION-N; MOTOR VEHICLE-N; MOUNTING-N; *MUFFLER-N; ORIFICE-N; OUTLET-N; PARALLEL-N; PHYSICAL PROPERTY-N; PHYSICAL SEPARATION-N; POLLUTANT-N; POLLUTION CONTROL-N; *POLLUTION CONTROL EQUIPMENT-N; PREVENTION-N; PURIFYING-N; SORPTION-N; STRESS-N; THERMAL INSULATION-N; THERMAL STRESS-N; USE-N; VIBRATION-N; WASTE GAS-N; WASTE MATERIAL-N
LT - CELLULAR-N; HEATING EQUIPMENT-N
LT - AXIAL-N; CATALYTIC MUFFLER-N; CHANNEL-N; MUFFLER-N; PARALLEL-N; POLLUTION CONTROL EQUIPMENT-N
UP - 1996-04
UE - 1996-10; 1997-18; 1998-33; 1998-40
UAPI - 1996-03

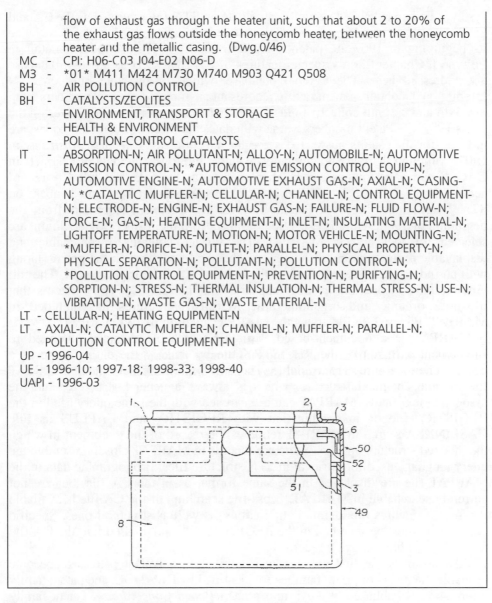

Figure 2.22   concluded

Chemical Abstracts Service (CAS)

CA SEARCH, the online version of *Chemical Abstracts*, produced by the Chemical Abstracts Service (CAS) is available on most of the major online systems, and an enhanced version is available on STN International as the CA and CAPLUS files. Over 15 per cent of the references included in the database since its beginning in 1967 are patents. As CA SEARCH is described in detail in Volume I, Chapter 2, only special features of CA SEARCH as a patent database are addressed here. The CAOLD database, which is available only on STN International, contains patent family records and associated registry numbers from the sixth and seventh collective index period of *Chemical Abstracts*, covering the years 1957–66. Patent numbers, some with dates and kind of document codes, are indexed for all patents abstracted since the inception of *Chemical Abstracts* in 1907. Although there are no computer-readable bibliographic data or abstracts in CAOLD, the page images can be displayed so as to make the full CA record accessible online. CAS introduced MARPAT as an enhanced patents database on STN International in 1990. Patents indexed by *Chemical Abstracts* from the beginning of 1988, with the exception of those from the former Soviet Union, are selected for inclusion in MARPAT. The service contains a searchable and displayable representation of the generic chemical structures in the patent, along with an indication of the location of the indexed structure in the patent. The full bibliographic record and abstract appear as in the CA file. Only patents that illustrate organic and organometallic Markush structures are included in MARPAT. Figure 2.23 illustrates the MARPAT citation for WO 9501791.

MARPAT is a document-based, structure-searchable database intended to supplement a search of the REGISTRY file by making the entire scope of a generic chemical structure available. The only searchable data in the MARPAT file are the chemical structure, which is always a generic structure, and the associated text fields. MARPAT can be searched with the same query used in the REGISTRY file or in combination with REGISTRY and CAPLUS as File CASLINK. A search in MARPAT retrieves the record of the document in which the indexed structure appears. Structure records in MARPAT closely resemble the query language used for retrieval in STN structure files. Bibliographic data in the MARPAT file are displayed in the same format as in the CA file, but are not currently searchable in MARPAT. Cross-file searching of the CA file is available if a search requires bibliographic limitations, as well as structural ones. Specific compounds must be searched in the REGISTRY file and crossed into the CA file to display the bibliographic record.

CAS abstracts the first member of a family of equivalent patents to become available. Members of patent families are identified by INPADOC, and patent family information is published by CAS in a printed *Patent Concordance*. Patent family information is searchable in CA and CAOLD, and is displayable in MARPAT, but is not online on search services other than STN. The patent number and date [PI] are indexed, and the publication year is searchable. Basic patent countries are represented as both the country name [SO] and the ISO code. Designated states for European and PCT patent applications and patent kind codes have been indexed only since 1982. The application number and/or a priority number [AI] and the corresponding date are present in the record of most patents. For patents indexed from 1967 to 1981, only the earliest priority or the national application number is indexed; multiple priorities

```
L6    ANSWER 1 OF 1  MARPAT  COPYRIGHT 2000 ACS
AN    122:151400  MARPAT
TI    Use of efaroxan and its derivatives for the treatment of
      neurodegenerative diseases
IN    Colpaert, Francis; Briley, Michael; Imbert, Thierry
PA    Pierre Fabre Medicament, Fr.
SO    PCT Int. Appl., 6 pp.
      CODEN: PIXXD2
DT    Patent
LA    French
IC    ICM A61K031-415
CC    1-11 (Pharmacology)
      Section cross-reference(s): 63
FAN.CNT 1
      PATENT NO.    KIND  DATE          APPLICATION NO.   DATE
      ------------  ----  --------      ---------------   --------
PI    WO 9501791    A2    19950119      WO 1994-FR841     19940707
      WO 9501791    A3    19950309
           W:  AU, CA, JP, NZ, US
           RW: AT, BE, CH, DE, DK, ES, FR, GB, GR, IE, IT, LU, MC, NL, PT, SE
      FR 2707166    A1    19950113      FR 1993-8497      19930709
      FR 2707166    B1    19950929
      AU 9472308    A1    19950206      AU 1994-72308     19940707
      AU 688346     B2    19980312
      EP 707477     A1    19960424      EP 1994-921698    19940707
      EP 707477     B1    19991117
           R:  AT, BE, CH, DE, DK, ES, FR, GB, GR, IE, IT, LI, LU, MC, NL, PT, SE
      JP 08512305   T2    19961224      JP 1994-503865    19940707
      AT 186640     E     19991215      AT 1994-921698    19940707
      US 5661172    A     19970826      US 1996-581516    19960111
PRAI  FR 93-8497           930709
AB    Efaroxan and its therapeutically acceptable salts, its racemic or
      optically active isomers (Markush structure given), are used for the
      treatment of Alzheimer-like senile dementia, pre-Alzheimer syndrome,
      progressive supranuclear palsy and other neurodegenerative diseases.
      The efficacy of 2-3 mg of efaroxan 4 times/day after 4 wk treatment
      of patients affected with progressive supranuclear palsy are
      reported.

MSTR 1
```

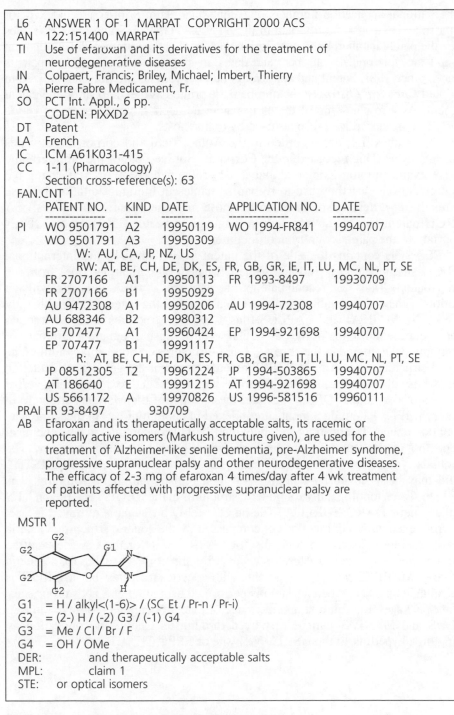

```
G1    = H / alkyl<(1-6)> / (SC Et / Pr-n / Pr-i)
G2    = (2-) H / (-2) G3 / (-1) G4
G3    = Me / Cl / Br / F
G4    = OH / OMe
DER:        and therapeutically acceptable salts
MPL:        claim 1
STE:  or optical isomers
```

Figure 2.23   MARPAT citation: STN file MARPAT

and the national application numbers of patents that claim priority are indexed for later patents. The patent family data in the STN CA, CAPLUS and MARPAT files include the patent number, kind, publication date, application number and application date, and multiple priority numbers and dates are present in the records of patents published since 1981. Patent and application number formats are not standardized in the printed *Chemical Abstracts*; the numbers are printed as they appear on the patent document. As a result, some of the early patent numbers have not been converted properly to the standardized formats used by online hosts.

Inventor names [IN] are recorded in the Author field and corporate patentees and assignees [PA] are recorded in the Corporate Source field of the bibliographic database. Names in non-Roman alphabets are romanized by CAS staff using the same conventions that they use to romanize names in literature citations. These may result in different spellings from those in other patent databases. CA SEARCH patent records also include a language indicator [LA] and a CODEN appropriate to the patent country and document type.

CA SEARCH contains the title of the patent in English [TI], the International Patent Classification codes [IC] and some US patent classification codes from the indexed patent. Titles for recent patents are enhanced by CA indexers with an indication of the claimed subject matter. The abstract of the patent is available only in STN's CA, MARPAT and CAPLUS files. Chemical structures in the abstract do not represent the full scope of the patent claims or disclosure, but are a summary of the compounds discussed in the abstract. Large structures do not display online. The chemical structures shown in MARPAT records represent the generic structures in patents whose claims are in Markush format, with associated text indicating verbal limitations of the claims [DER, STE] and the location of the Markush structure in the patent [MPL]. Patent documents are indexed in depth by CAS in the same way as other documents. The abstract and indexing [ST, IT] concentrate on new chemical concepts, not on the aspects of the disclosed invention that are claimed as new. The compounds synthesized in the patent's examples are indexed in the CA REGISTRY file and may be retrieved by searching on their registry numbers. Although it is possible to search topologically for generic structures in the REGISTRY file on STN or in the generic DARC EURECAS file on Questel-Orbit, what is retrieved is a set of specific, exemplified compounds encompassed by the generic structure. Generic structures are not indexed topologically for CA SEARCH or the CA file, and the verbal indexing of generic structures is necessarily imprecise. A search for a generic structure in MARPAT can retrieve patents with generic structures, but MARPAT is only available on STN. When a search is performed using one of STN's proprietary software packages, the full text and/or image of patent documents retrieved in CA, CAPLUS and MARPAT can be displayed through its ChemPort connection by clicking on a hyperlink to the USPTO Web site or ESP@CENET.

PHARMSEARCH

PHARMSEARCH is a database of French, British, German, European and US pharmaceutical patents produced by the French Patent Office, L'Institut National de Propriété Industrielle (INPI), and is mounted on Questel-Orbit. A companion file of chemical structure records is searchable in the MERGED MARKUSH SERVICE (MMS) on the Markush DARC system. Bibliographic records are searchable and displayable through enhancements to the Markush DARC system or may be crossed into the bibliographic file. When released in 1989, the database contained patents published since the beginning of 1987, but the coverage of the database is being extended retrospectively and now covers PCT applications published since 1989, British and German patent applications published since 1992, French, US and European Patent Office documents published since 1983 and the series of French medicinal patents that began in 1961. Patents found to be equivalent to previously indexed patents did not originally appear in the database, but are now listed as related patents [RL]. When a patent claiming the same priority as a previously indexed document has a different claim scope , the 'equivalent' patent is indexed. The database is updated every two weeks. Figure 2.24 illustrates the citation for FR 2,707,166.

The document [PN], application [AP], and priority [PR] numbers and dates of the patent are recorded. Patent document and priority numbers are indexed for cross-file searching in Derwent format in the /XPN and /XPR fields. Patentee names and addresses [PA], the names of inventors and their country of origin [IN] are provided.

Patent titles are given in French [FT] and English [ET]. Each record has a short English-language abstract [EAB], and patent documents in French also have a French-language abstract [FAB]. An image from the patent document is provided when appropriate. International Patent Classification codes are searchable [IC]. INPI's indexers assign index terms for chemical structures, process steps and pharmaceutical components, posting the terms to separate fields identifying the role of compounds in the patent, including new uses for known drugs [NUS], therapeutic effects [THEF] and processes. Numeric PHARMSEARCH classification codes [PHCN] are assigned. Compound numbers [CN] correspond to structure records in the MERGED MARKUSH SERVICE (MMS) companion file. Specific compounds and generic structures from the claims, together with examples, are indexed topologically, and the structure records are searchable and displayable in the MMS file. In Markush DARC, the parent structure is displayed, and each variable group for a Markush structure is shown as a separate screen along with the molecular substructure to which it is attached.

CURRENT DRUGS

CURRENT DRUGS FAST-ALERT, produced by Current Patents Ltd and mounted on DataStar and Questel-Orbit, is a database of 'informed summaries'

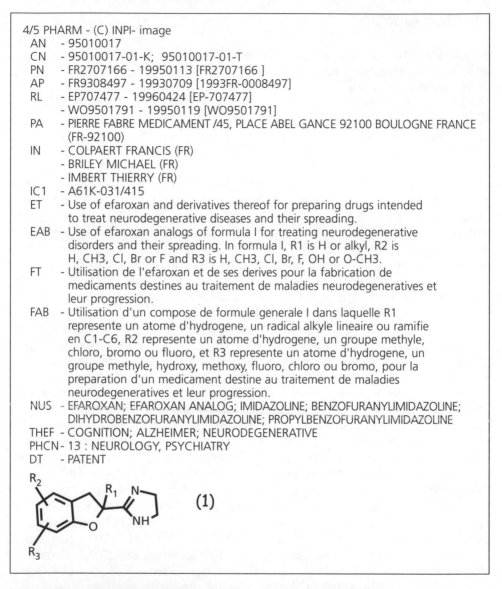

```
4/5 PHARM - (C) INPI- image
 AN   - 95010017
 CN   - 95010017-01-K;  95010017-01-T
 PN   - FR2707166 - 19950113 [FR2707166 ]
 AP   - FR9308497 - 19930709 [1993FR-0008497]
 RL   - EP707477 - 19960424 [EP-707477]
      - WO9501791 - 19950119 [WO9501791]
 PA   - PIERRE FABRE MEDICAMENT /45, PLACE ABEL GANCE 92100 BOULOGNE FRANCE
        (FR-92100)
 IN   - COLPAERT FRANCIS (FR)
      - BRILEY MICHAEL (FR)
      - IMBERT THIERRY (FR)
 IC1  - A61K-031/415
 ET   - Use of efaroxan and derivatives thereof for preparing drugs intended
        to treat neurodegenerative diseases and their spreading.
 EAB  - Use of efaroxan analogs of formula I for treating neurodegenerative
        disorders and their spreading. In formula I, R1 is H or alkyl, R2 is
        H, CH3, Cl, Br or F and R3 is H, CH3, Cl, Br, F, OH or O-CH3.
 FT   - Utilisation de l'efaroxan et de ses derives pour la fabrication de
        medicaments destines au traitement de maladies neurodegeneratives et
        leur progression.
 FAB  - Utilisation d'un compose de formule generale I dans laquelle R1
        represente un atome d'hydrogene, un radical alkyle lineaire ou ramifie
        en C1-C6, R2 represente un atome d'hydrogene, un groupe methyle,
        chloro, bromo ou fluoro, et R3 represente un atome d'hydrogene, un
        groupe methyle, hydroxy, methoxy, fluoro, chloro ou bromo, pour la
        preparation d'un medicament destine au traitement de maladies
        neurodegeneratives et leur progression.
 NUS  - EFAROXAN; EFAROXAN ANALOG; IMIDAZOLINE; BENZOFURANYLIMIDAZOLINE;
        DIHYDROBENZOFURANYLIMIDAZOLINE; PROPYLBENZOFURANYLIMIDAZOLINE
 THEF - COGNITION; ALZHEIMER; NEURODEGENERATIVE
 PHCN - 13 : NEUROLOGY, PSYCHIATRY
 DT   - PATENT
```

(1)

Figure 2.24   PHARMSEARCH record: Questel-Orbit file PHARM

and bibliographic data for agrochemical and pharmaceutical patents in selected therapeutic areas. Anti-microbial, cardiovascular, central nervous system, anti-cancer, metabolic disease, biotechnology and immunology patent documents from the UK, USA, Japan and the European Patent Office, as well as PCT applications, are included, with coverage of the various therapeutic categories beginning at various times since July 1989. The latest six weeks are provided in a current file and older patents are in an archive file. Discounts are available online to subscribers to print the ID Patent Fast-Alert bulletins in two or more therapeutic areas. Summaries of patents in the bulletins and the online database are provided less than ten days after the patents are available to the database producer, and the database is updated weekly. The focus of these services is to inform the scientific community of advances in drug development, rather than to provide access to patents as legal documents or prior art.

The patent number, designated states and priority country and number are searchable, with the number and ISO country code searchable separately. The patent assignee or, for unassigned patents, the inventor, appears in the Patent Assignee field, and up to three inventors are listed as the surname followed by a maximum of two initials. The Priority Data field includes the date, country and serial number of the first priority of the patent, with each being searchable independently. The priority date, the filing date of the application and the publication date of the patent document are searchable. The original titles, with an English-language abstract for all patents except Japanese-language PCT applications, are provided. The emphasis in CURRENT DRUGS abstracts is on the pharmaceutical utility disclosed in the patent and on the specific compounds exemplified in the patent; although the abstract identifies the novel features of the claims in a general sense there is no attempt to define the generic scope of the claims. CURRENT DRUGS section codes and descriptors are provided, as are IPC codes.

DRUG PATENTS INTERNATIONAL

DRUG PATENTS INTERNATIONAL, produced by IMSworld Publications Ltd and mounted on Questel-Orbit, STN and DataStar, is a database of patents covering marketed drugs. IMSworld provides pharmaceutical business information to subscribers, with emphasis on the marketing aspects of the industry, rather than the scientific aspects addressed by CURRENT DRUGS. This database has been designed to provide pharmaceutical executives with information about the patents that cover marketed single-entity drugs. There were only about 1050 drugs in the database as of 1997, with individual records for each indexed patent. Data are derived from searches in other databases to identify patents claiming a drug, the patent specification is 'evaluated' to determine the scope of its claims, and equivalent patents are found by consulting INPADOC and/or Derwent's patent family databases. The expiry date of the patent, with information about the availability of patent term extensions, is calculated for each patent, and the data are published in the printed *Patents International*. Although the database is updated monthly, most drugs have already been patented by the time they are eligible for coverage by this database, and therefore it is not necessarily very current. It does not purport to provide the drug's entire patent status; comments on additional patent families are provided only as Notes and Comments in the record for the original patent on the drug. Since most marketed drugs are eventually covered by numerous patents on pharmaceutical compositions and production processes, DRUG PATENTS INTERNATIONAL does not provide the entire answer for most questions, but it does have the information deemed most important by senior managers.

Figure 2.25 illustrates the record for US patent 4,071,622, which claims a new method of use for the compound deslorelin, as it appears in Questel-Orbit file DPINNS. Although a record in DRUG PATENTS INTERNATIONAL relates to a patent, the title of the record is the generic name of the compound the patent covers [NA], provided in several official versions if they exist. The patent [PN] number can be searched in the host's standard format or as the publication number independent of the ISO country code. For countries that grant patents after unexamined publication, both numbers are provided, but dates may not be provided for unexamined publications. The patent country [PC] can be searched by name or ISO code. Application dates are searchable, but the application serial number is not provided. Priority numbers and dates [PR] are included, with the priority number searchable in the host's standard format or as the serial number recorded from the patent. The name of the assignee [PA] and its country of residence [AR] can be searched, and the corporate producer of the marketed drug is indexed. It should be noted that the database producer does not identify producers other than the original marketer of the drug except when a licence agreement is noted in the Country Comments field [CM] or when patents belonging to other companies are discussed in the Notes field [NO].

Technical information about the patent is sparse but the type of patent claim [PT] – such as product, process or product-by-process – is reported. 'Method of use; equivalent to product' is inserted when no product patent is found, but this is not necessarily true in cases where other methods of use for the title drug are known. The CAS registry number [RN] of the compound is provided along with synonyms for its generic name [SY], trade names, descriptors for the drug's activity [DE], and IMSworld's therapeutic class codes [TC]. There is no title, abstract or claim text.

The expected expiry date is given in the text fields. For most patents, it has been estimated, but some extended terms are noted. The availability of patent term extensions or imposition of licences of right are indicated where the patent law provides for them. IMSworld does not promise that the expiry data reflect the actual status of the patent, and more detailed information about patent expiry dates may be provided in the Country Comments field. In the STN version of the database the chemical structure of the drug molecule can also be displayed.

Since the fee for displaying a single record in DRUG PATENTS INTERNATIONAL is as high as the fee for a patent family search in INPADOC, it is extremely expensive to display all the records for a given drug, especially as marketed drugs have usually been patented worldwide. Unless the information in the [CM] field of each country is of special value, it would be wise to display only one patent record in DRUG PATENTS INTERNATIONAL and to search for equivalent patents and expiry information elsewhere.

```
1/1 DPINNS - (C) DPIN
AN  - 011630
NA  - DESLORELIN
PN  - US4071622 - 19780131 [US4071622]
PC  - USA [US]
APD - 1976-02-11
PR  - USA NO 657344 19760211 [1976US-0657344]
    - USA NO 662759 19760301 [1976US-0662759]
PT  - METHOD OF USE; EQUIVALENT TO PRODUCT
CM  - US 4071622 CLAIMS METHODS OF USE OF DESLORELIN AS AN ANTICANCER AGENT.
      SCHERING PLOUGH HAS SEVERAL US PATENTS RELATING TO THE ANTICANCER
      PROPERTIES OF DESLORELIN. US 4659695, NORMAL EXPIRY 21 APRIL 2004 CLAIMS
      METHODS OF USE FOR THE TREATMENT OF PROSTATE CANCER. ON 8 JUNE 1995 THE
      AMENDMENTS TO THE US PATENT LAW UNDER THE GENERAL AGREEMENT ON TARIFFS
      AND TRADE (GATT) CAME INTO FORCE. AS A RESULT THE ESTIMATED EXPIRY DATE
      OF US 4659695 HAS BEEN RESET TO 8 FEBRUARY 2005 FROM 21 APRIL 2004. US
      4666885 NORMAL EXPIRY 19 MAY 2004, TERM RESET TO 2 AUGUST 2004, AND US
      4775660, NORMAL EXPIRY 4 OCTOBER 2005, TERM UNAFFECTED, BOTH CLAIM
      METHODS OF USE FOR THE TREATMENT OF BREAST CANCER; US 4760053, NORMAL
      EXPIRY 26 JULY 2005, TERM RESET TO 2 AUGUST 2005, CLAIMS METHODS OF USE
      FOR THE TREATMENT OF SEX STEROID DEPENDENT CANCERS; AND US 4775661 NORMAL
      EXPIRY 4 OCTOBER 2005, TERM UNAFFECTED, IS A COMPOSITION PATENT CLAIMING
      KITS FOR THE TREATMENT OF BREAST CANCER.
PA  - ABBOTT
AR  - USA
SY  - SOMAGARD; BACHEM 9022
DE  - CYTOSTATIC GONADORELIN RELEASING HORMONE ANALOGUES
TC  - L2A3; G03H
RN  - 57773-65-6 CMPD
NO  - THE ONLY PRODUCT PATENTS IDENTIFIED FOR DESLORELIN ARE THE UK, FRENCH AND
      BELGIAN PATENTS LISTED HERE. THE OTHER PATENTS LISTED IN THIS FAMILY
      CLAIM METHODS OF USE OR COMPOSITIONS OF DESLORELIN. SCHERING CORP HAS A
      WIDELY FILED PATENT FAMILY CLAIMING COMPOSITIONS FOR THE TREATMENT OF SEX
      STEROID DEPENDENT CANCERS. THESE PATENTS RELATE TO US PRIORITY NO 636883
      OF 2 AUGUST 1984, GIVING NORMAL EXPIRIES FOR MOST EQUIVALENTS OF AROUND
      AUGUST 2005. THE REGENTS OF THE UNIVERSITY OF CALIFORNIA HAVE A CANADIAN
      PATENT CLAIMING COMPOSITIONS OF DESLORELIN AS FEMALE CONTRACEPTIVES.
      CANADIAN PATENT 1195617 SHOULD NORMALLY EXPIRE ON 22 OCTOBER 2002. THE
      ONLY EQUIVALENT IDENTIFIED, JAPANESE PATENT 87/41648 SHOULD NORMALLY
      EXPIRE IN JULY 2002. THE SALK INSTITUTE FOR BIOLOGICAL STUDIES HAS A
      PATENT FAMILY CLAIMING A METHOD OF TREATMENT OF MALE MAMMALS TO PREVENT
      REPRODUCTION. THESE PATENTS RELATE TO US PRIORITY NO 815590 OF 14 JULY
      1977, GIVING A NORMAL EXPIRY DATE FOR MOST EQUIVALENTS OF AROUND JULY
      1988. THE US EQUIVALENT, US 4218439, SHOULD NORMALLY EXPIRE ON 19 AUGUST
      1997. ON 8 JUNE 1995 THE AMENDMENTS TO THE US PATENT LAW UNDER THE
      GENERAL AGREEMENT ON TARIFFS AND TRADE (GATT) CAME INTO FORCE. THE
      ESTIMATED EXPIRY DATE OF US 4218439 IS NOT AFFECTED. THE SALK INSTITUTE
      HAS TWO LATER US PATENTS, US 4569967, NORMAL EXPIRY 11 FEBRUARY 2003,
      TERM RESET TO 24 OCTOBER 2003, AND US 4701499, NORMAL EXPIRY 20 OCTOBER
      2004, TERM UNAFFECTED, CLAIMING A PROCESS AND POLYMER SUPPORT USED FOR
      THE PREPARATION OF DESLORELIN. THERE ARE SEVERAL PATENT FAMILIES COVERING
      VETERINARY USES OF DESLORELIN, SUCH AS FOR THE PREVENTION OF
      REPRODUCTION, TREATMENT OF ENDOMETRIOSIS AND FOR INDUCING BIRDS TO MOULT.
```

Figure 2.25   DRUG PATENTS INTERNATIONAL: Questel-Orbit file DPINNS

GENESEQ

Biopolymers from patents in the DERWENT WORLD PATENTS INDEX database are indexed structurally in the GENESEQ database, produced by Derwent Information Ltd and available through Oxford Molecular and DoubleTwist.com and as the DGENE database on STN. Polypeptide sequences with four or more amino acid residues, polynucleotides of ten or more bases, and all probes and primers of any length whose sequence is disclosed in a patent specification, are indexed; the backfile was constructed to include all sequences in patents back to 1980. Unlike other protein and nucleotide sequence databases, GENESEQ indexes generically describe sequences as well as fully defined sequences.

   Figure 2.26 illustrates the record for US 5,487,898, corresponding to the sequence of deslorelin as it appears in STN file DGENE. The record includes the expanded title from DERWENT WORLD PATENTS INDEX [TI], a description of the compound whose sequence is described [DESC], keywords [KW] and an abstract [AB] directed to the sequence rather than to the full scope of the patent. The organism from which the biopolymer was derived [ORGN] is indexed. The amino acids [AA] present in a polypeptide, sequence length [SQL], and actual sequence [SEQ] are given, and a feature table describes modifications and structural variations on any of the amino acids or base residues. The location of the sequence in the patent document is provided [PSL]. The patent number [PI], application number [AI] and priority numbers [PRAI] and dates are indexed, as is the date of entry of the data [DED]. The patentee and Derwent patentee code [PA], and the names of the inventors are given. The GENESEQ accession number [AN] corresponds to the sequence, with the DERWENT WORLD PATENTS INDEX accession number in the OS field. Cross-references to related GENESEQ sequence records are provided.

Other databases that include patents

The databases summarized above are not the only ones that provide patent information online. The availability of patent information has, in fact, exploded during the 1990s. Patent office online databases exist for limited searching in many countries, some of them available to the public by direct modem connections or on the World Wide Web and others on major search services. Complete Japanese patent data are available in Japanese on PATOLIS. A registry of Canadian patents and patent applications published since 1978, with images of patents published since 1920, is online on the World Wide Web at <URL http://cipo.gc.ca/>. Italian patents since 1983 can be searched in the ITALPAT database, produced by JUSTINFO Ltd, and mounted on Questel-Orbit, and recent Italian patents can be searched on the FILDATA S.r.l. World Wide Web site at <URL http://www.fildata.it>. US patents databases are available from a number of

```
L1      ANSWER 1 OF 2  DGENE COPYRIGHT 2000 DERWENT INFORMATION LTD
AN      1996P R89934  peptide     DGENE
TI      Compositions for oral administration of therapeutic peptide(s)
        - comprise a solvent and oral mucosal membrane transport
        enhancing agent to increase bio:availability of peptide(s)
IN      Lu M F; Reiland T L
PA      (ABBO)    ABBOTT LAB
PI      US5487898 A  19960130            18 pp
AI      91US-0750843  19910826
PRAI    94US-0193374  19940207
        91US-0750843  19910826
        92US-0983111  19921130
PSL     Claim 4; Column 5
DED     18 JUL 1996  (first entry)
DT      Patent
LA      English
OS      1996-105191 [11]
DESC    Luteinising hormone releasing hormone active peptide
        **Deslorelin**
KW      Luteinising hormone releasing hormone; active peptide;
        **Deslorelin**; sublingual; buccal; oral; administration;
        composition; solvent; mucosal membrane transport; enhancer;
        LHRH
ORGN    Synthetic
AB      The present peptide is the LHRH active peptide
        **Deslorelin**, the prepn. of which is disclosed in US pat.
        no. 4071622. A pharmaceutical compsn., comprising 100 mg/ml of
        the peptide, and a carrier comprisng a solvent system of 20-95%
        w/v of a non-toxic alcohol and 0.5-50% w/v of an oral mucosal
        membrane transport enhancing agent, can be used for the
        sublingual or buccal admin. of the peptide. The compsn. allows
        the oral admin. of the peptide, which would otherwise have to
        be given intravenously, subcutaneously or intraperitoneally,
        due to low absorption efficiency
AA      0 A; 1 R; 0 N; 0 D; 0 B; 0 C; 0 Q; 0 E; 0 Z; 0 G; 1
        H; 0 I; 1 L; 0 K; 0 M; 0 F; 1 P; 1 S; 0 T; 2 W; 1 Y;
        0 V; 1 Others;
SQL     9
SEQ
        1 xhwsywlrp


FEATURE TABLE:
Key             |Location|Qualifier|
===========+======+======+=================
Modified_site  |1       |label    |OTHER
               |        |note     |"5-oxoprolyl"
Misc_difference|6       |note     |"D-form residue"
Modified_site  |9       |note     |"prolyl-N-ethylamide"
```

Figure 2.26   GENESEQ citation: STN file DGENE

worldwide sites in addition to those discussed above.

Many databases available through the major host systems treat patents as technical literature. As a rule, such databases index patents in the same way that they index journal articles, making little distinction between background disclosures and claims. Many of these databases omit most of the special bibliographic fields in patents, making it difficult to obtain a copy of the abstracted patent or to identify an equivalent patent. Some of the databases obtain patent information from the patent office *Gazette* or from another abstracting service and identify the secondary source as the abstracted publication. In addition to databases that make patents or their surrogates the subject of individual records, many databases index articles that discuss patents or report on patents as news.

Patent numbers are reported as references in many technical publications. Although SciSearch does not index patents, it is an excellent source of patents related to scientific research reported in the journal literature, as the reference citations indexed from the literature by SciSearch include many patents. Full-text databases include patents as cited references and sometimes discuss the content of the patents in the text.

The monographs reproduced in such databases as the MERCK INDEX, BEILSTEIN and the COMBINED CHEMICAL DICTIONARY from CRC Press, which describe the synthesis and properties of chemical compounds, refer the reader to patents as the source of much of the information in the database. The PHARMAPROJECTS database, which describes pharmaceutical products under development, and DRUG DATA REPORT, DRUGS OF THE FUTURE and NME EXPRESS, produced by Prous Science, include patent numbers supplied by the developers of the new drugs in some monographs. One is often asked to find the patent that claims a particular product. Patents cited in PHARMAPROJECTS and the Prous databases are likely to be the actual patent relied upon for protection. A patent cited in the MERCK INDEX, on the other hand, usually represents the earliest publication describing the synthesis of the compound. Citations in these databases should never be accepted without verification that the compound or its synthesis is actually claimed in that patent.

Databases offering information about patents

In addition to the many databases that index patents as legal and technical documents, a number of databases serve as sources of information about patents or as aids to the use of other patent databases. Such databases include thesauri to the patent classification systems and legal databases that document the fate of patents that have been involved in litigation.

INTERNATIONAL PATENT CLASSIFICATION (IPC)

The INTERNATIONAL PATENT CLASSIFICATION is published in French and English by WIPO, and is available on CD-ROM (as well as in print) in the original languages and in translation. The IPC:CLASS CD-ROM contains seven IPC editions in English and French, the fourth to seventh editions in German, the fifth and sixth editions in Hungarian, and the fifth, sixth and seventh editions in Russian and Spanish, catchword indexes in English, French, German, Russian and Spanish, revision concordance data and IPC symbols data. The IPC classification system is mounted on STN as a thesaurus file in English and as the PATIPC database. The text of the sixth edition of the *International Patent Classification* definitions, as well as a keyword index, is online in the CIB database on Questel-Orbit. The database may be searched using text terms from the definitions, to determine what class code covers a particular subject, and also using IPC codes to determine their definitions. The definitions are written in generic language. Consequently, it is not always possible to retrieve a class code by searching with the term that appears to describe the subject matter of interest.

European Patent Classification: ECLATX

The full text of the *European Patent Classification (ECLA) Manual* in English is online in the ECLATX database mounted by INPI on Questel-Orbit and as a text file on LEXIS-NEXIS. The classification scheme is based on the hierarchical structure of the IPC and has additional subdivisions for the convenience of European Patent Office search staff, with monthly updates to adapt the classification to technological evolution. The ECLATX database may be searched by text terms to determine what class code covers a particular subject, and by IPC codes or European Patent Classification codes to find definitions. The definitions are written in the same generic language as the IPC code definitions in CIB, but the text in this file is in English. The file may be used to find current IPC codes by determining the ECLA class and ignoring final characters designating the subdivisions. ECLATX is most useful when searched for code definitions, which may be viewed in their full context. The definitions for classification codes in Questel-Orbit's PLUSPAT and EPAT records can easily be found by transferring them into ECLATX with the ..**MEM** command. The reverse procedure is not possible as classification codes are indexed in the basic index and every level of the code is indexed in the /TF field; the full codes do not have a unique field identifier.

United States Patent Classification

The full text of the *Manual of Classification* and the *Index to the Manual of Classification* of the US Patent Classification system are searchable in LEXIS-

NEXIS's LEXPAT library. The text of the class definitions for the US patent classification system and the *Index to the Manual of Classification* are incorporated into the CLAIMS REFERENCE database on DIALOG and the IFIREF database on STN, which also contain the thesaurus to the CLAIMS UNITERM and COMPREHENSIVE databases. These files can be searched by text terms from the definitions to determine what classification code covers a particular subject or by classification codes to find their definitions. Searching with free text is unrewarding, as the definitions are written in generic language and anticipating the terms associated with a concept within the hierarchy of the classification definitions is often impossible. The US patent classification definition databases are reloaded with revised class definitions when these are announced by the USPTO. Obsolete class definitions are removed from the databases and their definitions cannot be retrieved online. The US patent classification code is also mounted as a thesaurus on STN and is on the World Wide Web sites of the US Patent and Trademark Office, PATENTAC <URL http://www. patentec.com> and COMMUNITY OF SCIENCE <URL http://cos.gdb.org/repos/ pat/>.

The USCLASS database on Questel-Orbit and LEXIS-NEXIS contains the patent numbers of all US patents published since 1790 with their US Patent Classification codes. The codes are current with the latest reload of the database. The files may be searched by the classification code or patent number, yielding either a list of all patents that have been assigned the code or of all classification codes that have been assigned to the particular patent.

Patent litigation databases

Patents exist in order to protect inventions from exploitation by infringers. They are enforced by filing civil suits in the national court systems. Infringers typically defend themselves by countersuing on the grounds that the patents are not valid or that the owners of the patents have lost the right to enforce them. Legal battles also occur before the grant of a patent in interferences and oppositions to patent grant. Such legal duels often involve high stakes: the life or death of a company may even depend on the outcome of a patent suit. For anyone involved in the practice of patent law, the outcome of patent litigation is a most important aspect of patent information. Oppositions to the grant of patents and patent interferences, although equally important, are handled within the patent offices, rather than the courts, and sometimes also result in published decisions included in the litigation databases.

The most complete sources of legal information are full-text legal databases, such as WESTLAW and LEXIS-NEXIS, which contain statutes, court decisions, and the full text of the *BNA's Patent, Trademark & Copyright Journal*, which covers US intellectual property law. CANADIAN PATENT REPORTER, produced by Canada Law Book, Inc. and available on QL Systems' Quicklaw service, contains decisions rendered in intellectual property cases litigated in the

Canadian courts. JURINPI, produced by INPI and mounted on Questel-Orbit, contains published and unpublished French jurisprudence concerning patents and trade marks, with coverage beginning in 1823. European Patent Office jurisprudence is covered in the JUREP file, and the JURGE database covers German patent and trade mark jurisprudence from 1961. In addition, the text of decisions in intellectual property cases rendered by some courts is available on the Internet.

PATENT STATUS FILE (PAST) and LITALERT, produced by Derwent Information Inc., contain records of post-issuance activity related to US patents. The *Patent Status File* on Questel-Orbit reports all post-issue status changes to US patents reported in LITALERT or in the USPTO *Official Gazette* from 1973 to the present. Changes include: dedications; disclaimers; patent term lapses and extensions; the filing of re-issue applications and requests for examination; the issuance of re-issue patents; re-examination certificates and Certificates of Correction; the filing of patent suits; and adverse decisions in patent litigation. LITALERT, available on Questel-Orbit and DIALOG, contains records of patent and trade mark suits filed in US federal district courts. LITALERT reports the details of pending cases on file with the Office of the Solicitor of the United States Patent and Trademark Office. LITALERT records include the patent numbers and other bibliographic data of the patents in suit, as well as the names of the litigants. However, as the Solicitor's records of pending cases are not complete, failure to retrieve a record of a pending suit from LITALERT cannot be taken as evidence that no suit has been filed. The PATENT STATUS FILE is essentially a cumulative index to LITALERT and the US *Official Gazette*. Backlog information from PATENT STATUS FILE and LITALERT are available on CD-ROM and are incorporated in Derwent's CD-ROM subscription service, OG PLUS, along with searchable bibliographic data and images of the full text of the *Official Gazette* of the USPTO. The information in PAST overlaps heavily with that provided in the CLAIMS CURRENT PATENT LEGAL STATUS database, which is discussed earlier, but PAST contains less detail.

Selecting a database

Patents cover every aspect of applied art, science and technology, so patent databases can be used to answer questions that arise in almost any field of knowledge. The best retrieval is obtained from databases that provide deep indexing and/or abstracts that summarize the factual content of the patent without the awkward generic language of the claims or the verbosity of full text. Databases that write their own patent abstracts do not cover every patent issued in the countries they index; most such databases are devoted to a restricted field of knowledge. The least selective source of comprehensive abstracts, DERWENT WORLD PATENTS INDEX, has been providing abstracts in an increasing number of technologies for one member of each patent family and some equivalent granted patents since 1963. JAPIO provides descriptive English-language abstracts for Japanese patent applications published in most technologies since 1980, but only for patents belonging to Japanese nationals. Patent databases such as DERWENT WORLD PATENTS INDEX, APIPAT and the CLAIMS UNITERM and COMPREHENSIVE databases that supply controlled indexing can be extremely powerful for searching the technologies they cover in depth.

Because patents are so complex and current information is so important, it is unlikely that online searching of patent databases will be replaced by CD-ROM patent databases. The CD-ROM databases available as of 2000 are valuable chiefly as current awareness tools for bibliographic searches and for high-quality document delivery. ASSIST, which includes the US *Manual of Classification*, the Index and Classification Definitions to the *Manual of Classification*, a concordance of US patent classes to the seventh edition of the IPC code, an index of classification changes, an index of original patent assignees, an index of US patents with their current classification code, the text of the *Manual of Patent Examining Procedures*, the roster of registered patent attorneys and agents, and the USPTO examiners directory, is available from USPTO. Bibliographic information from current US patents is available on CD-ROM on Derwent's OG 125 PLUS service, which also provides patent status and litigation data. Both MicroPatent and Derwent produce CD-ROMs containing US patent images. Other MicroPatent databases contain the front-page information from US patents, the full text of the patents without images, and the PATENTBIBLE – a product that provides tools for searching patents. Images of European, PCT and many national patents are distributed on CD-ROM by the European Patent Office in the ESPACE product line, which allows searching only of bibliographic data. The first-page information from European and PCT patent specifications is available in the ESPACE FIRST CD-ROM series, which is fully searchable. First-page information from US, European, PCT, British, German, French and Swiss patents from 1971 to the present are cumulated in the ESPACE GLOBALPAT CD-ROM collection. CD-ROM databases of German patents are produced by Wila Verlag/Bertelsmann and by the Deutsches Patentamt, and CD-ROM databases of French patents are produced by INPI. Derwent publishes the PATENTS OF RUSSIA CD-ROM with English-language information about Russian and Soviet patents and copies of the specifications. JAPIO distributes Japanese patent specifications on CD-ROM. For searches in large databases or for the technological information retrievable from text terms or indexing, it is necessary to search online.

For online searches in any field, searchers may employ the free text and patent classification codes provided in the databases that document all of the patents issued in one or more countries. For free-text searching, the more text the database provides, the more likely the search will be to retrieve every relevant patent. Searching both the main claim and the abstract, however, does not always double the chance of retrieving a particular patent. In many patents the abstract is simply a summary of the main claim, written in the same generic language, and provides little additional information. Dependent claims, on the other hand, often contain specific language that is missing from the main claim. Full-text searching, while it gives access to all the details in the patent disclosure, retrieves irrelevant details as readily as important ones. Free-text searching gives good results only when the terms in the query include all possible synonyms for the concept being searched and when all the terms are unambiguous.

Most versions of INPADOC have only titles and IPC codes as guides to the subject matter disclosed in patents, while USCLASS has only current patent classification codes, so they are of little use in searches for technical content. Most patent titles are too short to yield reliable search terms. Although patent classification codes are sufficiently precise for manual searching, they are too highly posted to use alone for online retrieval. Subject searches in these databases should be attempted only when no other database covers the appropriate country and time range. However, INPADOC is a valuable source of updated patent family and legal status information, and many patents are indexed sooner in INPADOC than in databases that prepare abstracts and indexing.

If both technical and legal status information is needed, it is usually advisable to search a combination of databases, using a database with enough searchable text or indexing to retrieve patents covering a particular technical subject, and a database with full bibliographic citations and/or legal status information to determine the claim scope and status of equivalent patents issued in the countries of interest. It is also advisable to search more than one database whenever comprehensive retrieval is needed. Many patents are long and complex; patents of over 100 pages are not uncommon. It is difficult to index such long documents comprehensively, and the indexing policies of patent databases are so diverse that a search of any one database may fail to retrieve vital references that can be retrieved elsewhere. Searches for technical information, even when only patent references are desired, ought not to be restricted to patent databases. Many of the databases discussed in other chapters of these three volumes contain patents, and normal search strategies will retrieve any pertinent patent references that are present in the database.

The number of databases to be searched, and the time range to be searched for the answer to a particular question, depends on the use that is to be made of the information. In searches directed to the technical information in the patent disclosure, patent databases merely supplement databases that index the journal literature. In searches intended to discover whether an invention is patentable, both patent and literature databases should be searched exhaustively, for no published information is too old or too obscure to prevent a patent from issuing. When the objective of the search is to discover whether a product or process is covered by one or more patents, the search must focus on the patent claims. Only unexpired patents are relevant to such searches; older patents are of interest only when it is possible that an equivalent patent in another country may still be in force. When a patent that seems to cover the product or process is found, a supplementary search should be made to determine that patent's current legal status.

The most common patent question, 'What patent covers this product?', is unfortunately the most difficult to answer. Patents do not customarily name the commercial product they protect, and it may be very difficult to determine whether a specific product is actually covered by the claims of a patent written in generic terms. IMSworld's DRUG PATENTS INTERNATIONAL database provides the results of searches in other databases for the patent, claiming about 1000 marketed drugs, and the databases produced by Prous Science include patent data on marketed drugs and drugs in development; such databases are, however, unavailable for other industries. The most convenient way to find the patent that claims a product is often the most obvious way – obtain a sample of the product and look for a patent number stamped on the product or printed on its packaging. It should never be forgotten that many products are marketed without patent protection, and that other products are protected by more than one patent. Even when a patent covering a product in one country has been identified, it is not safe to assume that the product is covered in all countries where equivalent patents are in force.

In addition to the databases that provide full coverage of the publications of a national or international patent office, there are databases that are especially suited to individual disciplines or fields.

Citation indexes

Cited references appear on the front page of many patent publications – for example, US patents – and on search reports attached to European patent applications and PCT applications. The cited references can be patents, journal references, grey literature, mail order catalogues, or any other publications deemed relevant to the patentability of the claimed invention. The references can be provided by the applicant or identified during a search of the prior art at the patent office, but they are always selected by a patent examiner. There are two schools of thought about the meaning and value of patent citation analysis. One school equates patent citations with literature citations. According to proponents of that theory – notably, Francis Narin and his colleagues at CHI Research, Inc. – patents cited in many later patent publications relate to more important inventions, companies whose patents are cited frequently are doing more significant research than companies whose patents are cited less frequently, and the research done by companies whose patent applications contain citations to the scientific literature is more scientific than that of companies whose patents carry citations to other patents. According to this theory, statistical manipulations of citation data can identify technological trends and evaluate research programmes. The other school of thought is that cited references in patents are merely the results of searches for references that teach or suggest the invention claimed in that patent application. The references are cited only because they disclose closely-related technology, not because the inventor has acknowledged a contribution by the cited publication. The examiner has neither the time nor incentive to evaluate the references for their intrinsic value, and patents claiming scientifically or commercially important inventions are no more likely to be cited than less valuable patents with more detailed summaries of the prior art. According to this theory, references cited in patents are useful because they summarize the results of an expert search. The examiner's search is an invaluable starting-point for a search to determine the patentability or validity of a patent or published application.

All the front-page and full-text patent databases include cited references. Citing references for US patents can be found in the CLAIMS/CITATION database, and in most of the US patent databases on the World Wide Web. The usefulness of the citations is rather limited in single-country database. Many inventions are filed in several patent offices, each office does an independent search, and an examiner cites only one member of a family of equivalent patents. Only the DERWENT PATENT CITATION INDEX cumulates all of the patent families cited in any of a family of patent applications.

Physical sciences

Roughly one-third of all patents are classified as 'chemical'. Most new chemical compounds and chemical process technology are reported in patents, usually long before they are reported in chemical journals, but retrieving chemical information from patents presents special problems. Searching for all references to a compound by using free text is bound to fail: a single compound can be named a great many ways, Markush structures in patents include vast numbers of compounds which are never named at all, and most chemical structures are represented in patents only as diagrams. Only controlled indexing of the structural features of a compound can guarantee that all documents that describe it will be retrieved.

Because patents are so important to the chemical industry, the first patent databases were developed specifically to provide access to chemical patents. DERWENT WORLD PATENTS INDEX provides English-language titles and abstracts that summarize the novel aspects of patents published in 40 countries. For *Chemical Patents Index* subscribers, DERWENT WORLD PATENTS INDEX provides controlled indexing of products and processes, including fragmentation code indexing or topological structure indexing of the broadest generic chemical structure in the patent. The CLAIMS UNITERM and COMPREHENSIVE databases provide controlled indexing of the claims and examples of US chemical patents. There are terms for specific chemical substances, fragmentation codes for generic chemical structures, and *Chemical Abstracts* registry numbers for specific compounds in some of the records. There are also terms for aspects of chemical and chemical engineering processes and for all kinds of chemically-related product, as well as property descriptors for chemically-related products and processes. The CLAIMS COMPREHENSIVE database, accessible only to subscribers, is particularly good for identifying polymers. Chemical aspects of pharmaceutical patents can be retrieved using both topological structure indexing and keywords in PHARMSEARCH. Patents related to the petroleum industry are deeply indexed in APIPAT, using a controlled thesaurus of product, process and compound terms tailored for petroleum patents. The WORLD PATENTS INDEX/APIPAT files on Questel-Orbit combine the strengths of both files. Most chemical *kokai* belonging to Japanese persons and organizations are abstracted in JAPIO.

Chemical patents can also be retrieved from databases that are not limited to patents. *Chemical Abstracts* provides structural indexing of chemical compounds in its REGISTRY file, and the registry numbers retrieved there can be used to retrieve patents indexed in CA SEARCH, CAOLD, CASREACT, CLAIMS, APIPAT and the MERCK INDEX. *Chemical Abstracts* patent citations can be retrieved directly by searching the generic structure records in MARPAT. DERWENT REACTION DOCUMENTATION SERVICE (DJSM on STN) includes reactions reported in patents since 1975 and allows searching for products, reactants and transformations with structural fragment codes and reaction codes.

Other aspects of physical science are disclosed in patents in all areas of the mechanical, electrical and chemical arts. The inventions claimed in patents can seldom be classified as theoretical physics or mathematics because natural laws and mathematical algorithms are not patentable subject matter, but practical applications of mathematics and physics are patentable. One of the subjects abstracted for JAPIO is physics. In the DERWENT WORLD PATENTS INDEX, physics is relegated to the Genera/Mechanical Patents Index, which is not coded systematically, and the Electrical Patents Index, which is indexed in less depth than is the Chemical Patents Index. A number of databases that are not limited to patents, including PHYSICS BRIEFS, INIS, PASCAL and INSPEC include patents in the area of physics. US patents on electronic data processing published since 1984 are abstracted in INFORMATION SCIENCE ABSTRACTS. In addition, patents on computer science and information technology are included in other databases that index electrical patents, including the Electrical Patents Index sections of DERWENT WORLD PATENTS INDEX.

Earth sciences

Patents on geology and environmental sciences are classified as chemical or general/mechanical, depending on the focus of their claims. DERWENT WORLD PATENTS INDEX Section H, devoted to petroleum, was established in 1971 and is indexed with Manual Codes. Geological and environmental aspects of the petroleum industry are covered in depth in APIPAT and TULSA.

Biological and health sciences

Increasing numbers of patents classified as 'chemical' actually concern biology, biotechnology, pharmacology and medical technology. PHARMSEARCH, DRUG

PATENTS INTERNATIONAL and CURRENT DRUGS are devoted entirely to pharmaceutical patents. DRUG DATA REPORTS, DRUGS OF THE FUTURE and NME EXPRESS, produced by Prous Science, and PHARMAPROJECTS, produced by PJB Publications, include patent numbers in records describing drugs in development. Biopolymers from patents in the DERWENT WORLD PATENTS INDEX database are indexed structurally in the GENESEQ database. Polypeptide structures have been added to the CAS REGISTRY file on STN, and are directly searchable for transfer to the CA file. Patent references are included in many of the biosciences databases, including BIOTECHNOLOGY ABSTRACTS, CURRENT BIOTECHNOLOGY ABSTRACTS, SUPERTECH, IRL LIFE SCIENCES COLLECTION, PASCAL, TOXLINE and BIOBUSINESS. Most bioscience-related *kokai* belonging to Japanese persons and organizations are abstracted in JAPIO, but those relating to medical devices were, until recently, represented by only titles and a few index terms. There are also references to bioscience patents in many databases that index chemical patents. The guidelines for selecting chemical patents for deep indexing in the CLAIMS UNITERM and COMPREHENSIVE databases and in the *Chemical Patents Index* sections of DERWENT WORLD PATENTS INDEX include most patents in bioscience fields. Pharmaceutical patents are included in DERWENT WORLD PATENTS INDEX's FARMDOC section and are searchable by subscribers with a special Galenic code that was introduced in 1976 and with the other retrieval codes that have been available since 1963. Microbiology and biotechnology patents and patents relating to foods and nutrition published since 1970 are classified in DWPI's section D. Patents on medical devices are included in the non-chemical sections of DWPI that have been available since 1974.

Agricultural science

Agricultural patents are indexed by many of the agriculture databases, including CAB ABSTRACTS and AGRIS. Most agricultural *kokai* belonging to Japanese persons and organizations are abstracted in JAPIO. Patents relating to agricultural chemicals and veterinary science are included in CURRENT DRUGS FAST-ALERT and in databases that index chemical patents, including the CLAIMS UNITERM and COMPREHENSIVE databases and the Chemical Patents Index sections of DERWENT WORLD PATENTS INDEX. The DERWENT CROP PROTECTION FILE, formerly known as PESTDOC, includes patent records. Agriculture patents with chemical or veterinary medical features have been included in DERWENT WORLD PATENTS INDEX's AGDOC section since 1965, and are searchable by subscriber coding. Other agricultural patents have been included in the non-chemical sections since 1974.

Engineering and energy

Patents relating to engineering are found in a great variety of databases that index patents, including INIS, PHYSICS BRIEFS, PASCAL, INSPEC, ISMEC, FLUIDEX, CHEMICAL ENGINEERING ABSTRACTS and CA SEARCH. *Kokai* in the field of physics and most engineering fields are abstracted by JAPIO. Chemical engineering patents are included in the guidelines for selecting patents for deep indexing in the CLAIMS UNITERM and COMPREHENSIVE database, and other engineering patents have been included without indexing in CLAIMS since 1963. Chemical engineering patents have been indexed in the Chemical Patents Index of DERWENT WORLD PATENTS INDEX since 1970, and other engineering patents have been included in it since 1974. Electrical engineering patents have been indexed for subscribers to the Electrical Patents Index sections of DERWENT WORLD PATENTS INDEX since 1982. DOE ENERGY, INIS, and TULSA feature patents on energy. Patents relating to the petroleum industry are indexed in depth in APIPAT and the combined WORLD PATENTS INDEX/APIPAT files.

Social and behavioural sciences

Patents relevant to the social and behavioural sciences include those claiming psychological testing methods and devices, educational aids, behaviour modification programmes, toys and games. In addition to patents that claim inventions such as these, there are a great many patents in areas, such as pharmacy and medicine, that disclose the results of experiments that test the behavioural responses of animals to various stimuli. The results of behavioural tests are usually presented as examples in patents, and are best located by searching full-text databases.

Humanities

Patentable subject matter includes new art forms and techniques for their application, musical instruments, games, toys, clothing and furnishings. In addition to patents that claim new apparatus or new methods for using or producing them, there are design patents that claim actual decorative designs. Design patents are indexed in CLAIMS and LEXIS-NEXIS, but the claimed subject matter in the patents is defined by the drawings which are not searchable in the online records. Although LEXIS-NEXIS and the enhanced records in CLAIMS have brief descriptions of the drawings, searching for design patents is more efficient if done manually.

Business

Methods of managing assets can be patented, but the most important uses for patent information in business are as guides for business development and as sources of competitive intelligence. Monitoring the expiry dates of patents that protect competitive products allows a company to enter the market as soon as the patents expire. A company can identify sources of equipment or raw materials by discovering which companies own patents on the equipment or materials, and it can identify customers for its products by discovering which companies have patented technology that uses the products. By studying the patent portfolio of a competitor or a potential acquisition, one can learn what kind or research it has been pursuing and what kind of products it can sell exclusively.

Statistical manipulation of patent assignee data and patent classification codes can be used to create summaries of industrial trends. Information can be downloaded from patent databases for manipulation with statistical software programs. The host systems provide statistical software online. STN's **Select** command automatically ranks the terms it extracts from a set of records, and the **Analyze** command facilitates tabulation of the records. Data from the databases mounted on Questel-Orbit can be manipulated online with the ..**MEMSORT** command; the **Get** command performs multi-step analyses similar to those formerly available on the ORBIT service. DIALOG allows the user to do statistical analyses with the **Rank** command.

Statistical manipulation of patent data can be misleading. Because patent publications from different countries vary in their significance, the results are meaningless if all patent documents in a multinational file are given equal weight. A granted patent may be the first publication in the USA, for example, while a granted German patent may be the third publication covering the invention; if each Questel-Orbit INPADOC record is treated equally, a granted German patent will be given three times as much weight as a granted American patent. A company that begins filing European patent applications in place of national patent applications appears to be filing fewer equivalent patent applications if only the number of eventual publications is counted without factoring in the number of designated states. If the number of designated states is counted, a company that files patent applications through the Patent Cooperation Treaty and routinely designates all member states will appear to have broadened its filing strategy as the number of PCT member states has grown. The 'number of patents' data in patent family records is particularly misleading in such cases. Differences among the various editions of the *International Patent Classification Manual* can lead to apparent discontinuities in statistical trends when one IPC is replaced by a number of more precise codes. Statistics derived from a database that covers only one country or that represents an entire family of equivalent patents in a single record, while they are based upon more uniform units of intellectual property, still fail to distinguish between patents that protect valuable products and those that are filed defensively.

Selecting a host system

Cross-file searching is particularly useful in patent searches. Full bibliographic and legal status information is not available in the databases that provide deep indexing. Most databases index only one member of a patent family and others cover only selected patents. After a relevant patent has been found, a supplementary search is often needed in order to determine whether there is an equivalent or related patent in another country or to locate a readable copy of the patent disclosure. The ease with which one may complete a patent search online varies from host to host, depending on the databases that are available on the system, the extent to which the databases have been harmonized for cross-file searching, and the software provided for cross-file searching. Most of the patent databases discussed in this chapter are mounted on Questel-Orbit, STN and/or DIALOG. The availability of patent databases on the various hosts has been changing at an enormous rate: new files are being introduced and old ones are being reloaded, existing databases have been loaded by new vendors, and search software is being modified.

Questel-Orbit

At the time this chapter was written in 2000, Questel-Orbit had recently been created from two separate search services, each with an emphasis on intellectual property databases and with software designed to handle searches for patent information. Most of the databases unique to ORBIT had been transferred to Questel and the Questel search software was being enhanced so as to reproduce the patent data handling features not already available on Questel.

Questel-Orbit has nearly all of the deeply indexed patent databases. DERWENT WORLD PATENTS INDEX, CLAIMS, CHINAPATS and JAPIO are mounted on Questel-Orbit, as well as many chemistry, energy, and engineering databases that contain substantial numbers of patents, including CA SEARCH, BIOTECHNOLOGY ABSTRACTS, INSPEC, TULSA, and PASCAL. ORBIT has combined DERWENT WORLD PATENTS INDEX with the APIPAT database, merging the API records with the Derwent records so that the indexing can be used in a single search rather than a sequential cross-file search.

Questel-Orbit carries PHARMSEARCH and INPI's French, Patent Cooperation Treaty and European Patent Office patent documentation files, as well as the IPC and European patent classification definitions in CIB and ECLATX. The Questel-Orbit PLUSPAT database is enhanced with ECLA codes, additional patent family members and abstracts from the Minimum Documentation collection. A US full-text patents database, USPAT FULLTEXT, and EPTEXT and WOTEXT – databases containing the text, but not the bibliographic records of European and PCT patent applications – were mounted in early 2000. Markush structures can be retrieved from DERWENT WORLD

PATENTS INDEX by searching the MERGED MARKUSH SERVICE database and crossing answers into the bibliographic DWPI database. Markush structure and specific compounds can be searched in MERGED MARKUSH SERVICE and crossed into the bibliographic PHARMSEARCH database, or the structures and bibliographic records can be displayed directly in MPHARM. CA SEARCH is loaded on Questel-Orbit in the CAS file and may be searched with CAS registry numbers transferred from topological searches of the CAS REGISTRY in the generic DARC EURECAS database. The generic DARC and Questel-Orbit cross-file searching capabilities can be used to retrieve patent families from the DERWENT WORLD PATENTS INDEX by retrieving CAS registry numbers in the EURECAS file, crossing to CA SEARCH to retrieve patent references, and crossing the patent document and application numbers into DWPI. Multi-file searching and duplicate identification and removal can be performed with the help of the **Cluster** command. Questel-Orbit has adopted the Derwent formats for cross-file searching of patent and priority numbers and has additional XPN and XPR fields in all patent database records for the cross-reference formats. Data are indexed in the format provided by the database producer and in the original Derwent format, as well as in the expanded year-2000 compatible Derwent format used for standard cross-file searching. Cross-file searches employ the ..**MEM** and *MEM commands to 'memorize' a list of search terms and search the terms. MEM lists can be created from any field in the record; the list can be edited by deleting items and terms can be truncated, limited, requalified and searched selectively. With the ..**MEMSORT** and **Get** commands, it is possible to perform statistical analyses of any data in records obtained from a search.

STN International

The STN computer in Columbus, Ohio, is the home of the CA and CAPLUS files – the exclusive version of the CA SEARCH database enhanced with abstracts – and of the CAOLD file with references to chemical compounds indexed in *Chemical Abstracts* prior to 1965. The MARPAT database, available only on STN, contains topological indexing for generic structures in patents in the CA file. Only STN has CAS registry numbers in CLAIMS records indexed since 1980. STN has combined the CLAIMS Thesaurus and Compound Registry with the US *Manual of Classification* in a single IFIREF file. Chemical patents in STN's USPATFULL file can be searched with all of the indexing applied to the US patent or its equivalent in the CAPLUS database, and TIFF images can be downloaded. In addition, when searching is done with STN Express or one of the STN Internet interfaces, original patent images can be displayed by linking to EXP@CENET or the USPTO Web site. The STN computer in Karlsruhe, Germany, has INPADOC, JAPIO, the PATDPA German patents database, the DERWENT WORLD PATENTS INDEX file, the DERWENT PATENT CITATION INDEX, the PATOS EPO, PCT and German patent files and EUROPATFULL. Although some of the STN databases are physically located in Germany and others are in the USA, databases can be searched in clusters without regard to their origin. STN has most of the major scientific, technical and medical databases. The DERWENT JOURNAL OF SYNTHETIC METHODS and CASREACT can be searched for chemical reactions by means of the chemical structures of reactants and structures. On STN, the registry numbers of chemical substances retrieved from the REGISTRY file through both topological and text searches are automatically placed in cross-file searchable answer sets. The Chemical Abstracts Service has provided many of the databases on STN with registry numbers that were not present in the records supplied by the database producers, so that direct cross-file searching with registry numbers can be done in these databases only on STN and not on other host systems. CAS has identified corresponding CAS registry numbers for most of the compounds in the CLAIMS COMPOUND REGISTRY and posted them in the IFICDB and IFIUDB files with the qualifier URN. These converted registry numbers are automatically retrieved when a list of registry numbers is crossed over from the REGISTRY file.

STN allows searching and display of patent document and application numbers in either the standard STN format or in Derwent format at the searcher's option. A search for a number in any recognized format is performed regardless of the format set for the searcher's account. Duplicate identification and grouping of patent records is provided for multifile searches by the **FSORT** command. Cross-file searching is greatly facilitated by the continuous assignment of search statement numbers during a session. Terms can be extracted from records in STN databases with the **Select** command, and the list of terms can be edited to change their qualifiers before they are searched in another database. The **SmartSelect** command was created to facilitate economical extraction of patent and application numbers for cross-file searching. A simplified version of **SmartSelect**, the **Transfer** command, can be used after searching one or more databases for records for the same patent or patent family members. When the **Transfer** command is used for cross-file searching, STN automatically returns to the original database, extracts the appropriate terms, returns to the target database, and performs the search.

DIALOG

DIALOG carries the DERWENT WORLD PATENTS INDEX, the DERWENT PATENT CITATION INDEX, INPADOC, CLAIMS, JAPIO and CHINESE PATENTS ABSTRACTS databases along with a great many patent-containing technical databases. The US PATENTS FULLTEXT database merges IFI/Plenum's patentee codes and post-issuance status actions with fully searchable text. EUROPEAN PATENTS FULLTEXT has all the European patent text available electronically and has a full-text searchable file of PCT applications. Only DIALOG has the CLAIMS CITATION databases. It is possible to transfer back and forth between databases with the **File** command without erasing the previous search strategy. A search in DERWENT WORLD PATENTS INDEX can be done using either Derwent's format or DIALOG's. Most bibliographic patent data fields can be converted to search terms using the **MAP** command to create saved searches to be executed in other databases. Priority, application and publication numbers will **MAP** in DIALOG format. Since the DIALOG format in the DERWENT WORLD PATENTS INDEX files is derived from Derwent's modified numbers, some patents cannot be transferred successfully from other files. DIALOG has modified the **MAP** protocol for Japanese patent numbers so that all possible versions of the number are searched, often retrieving entirely unrelated patents as false drops. Because DIALOG's format for application and priority numbers does not integrate the year of filing as Derwent's format does, searches for patents based on US applications (which are assigned in series of 100 000 that restart every ten years or so) have always retrieved patents from every series in the database – another source of unrelated false drops. As part of the 'Year 2000' adjustment to the DIALOG software, however, it has become possible to include the four-digit application year to application numbers. Related and duplicate patents retrieved in a multifile search can be grouped with the **IDPAT** command, but duplicate records identified by the command include all records with overlapping priority information.

Acknowledgements

The author wishes to express thanks to STN International, The Dialog Corporation and Questel-Orbit Inc. for providing computer access, and to the producers of the databases discussed in this chapter for permitting the publication of exemplary records.

Further reading

For further information on patents, patent law, and some of the more esoteric aspects of patent searching, the following list of books, manuals and journal articles may be helpful.

Barnard, J. M. (1991), 'A Comparison of Different Approaches to Markush Structure Handling', *Journal of Chemical Information and Computer Science*, **31** (1), 64–68.
Global Patent Sources (1996), London: Derwent Information Ltd.
Gordon, T. T. and Cookfair, A. S. (1995), *Patent Fundamentals for Scientists and Engineers*, London: CRC Press.
Guide to Patent Expiries (4th edn) (1999), London: Derwent Information Ltd.
Maynard, J. and Peters, H. (1991), *Understanding Chemical Patents*, (2nd edn), Washington DC: American Chemical Society.
Simmons, E. S. and Kaback, S. M. (1996), 'Patents, Literature' in *Kirk-Othmer Encyclopedia of Chemical Technology*, (4th edn), New York: Wiley, 102–156.

Vacek, G. (1994), 'Japanese Patent Information', *World Patent Information*, **16** (1), 41–45.
Van Dulken. S. (ed.) (1992), *Introduction to Patents Information*, (2nd edn), London: British Library, Science and Information Service.

For information about patents and patent searching the Internet has replaced the library as the best source. Patent offices, database producers and host search services have World Wide Web sites with the text of patent law and patenting procedures manuals, database descriptions, code manuals and links to other sites with additional information. Possibly the best place to begin searching for patent information is the European Patent Office's Web site at <URL http://www.european-patent-office.org/>. The link to 'Patent Info Products' leads to descriptions of the products made and distributed by EPIDOS and comprehensive lists of the countries, types of patents and types of patent status actions in the INPADOC databases. Another link leads to a description of the European Patent Organization and its patenting procedures. The link to 'Patent Information' on the Internet is to a comprehensive listing of other sources of patent information on the Internet, including links to patent offices, database producers, search services that carry patent databases, patent information providers of all kinds and law firms that specialize in patent law. Among the useful and informative Web sites are those of the World Intellectual Property Organization at <URL http://www.wipo.org/>, and the US Patent and Trademark Office at <URL http://www.uspto.gov/>. The Derwent World Wide Web site at <URL http://www.derwent.co.uk/> includes update information for DERWENT WORLD PATENTS INDEX, a patentee code dictionary, a listing of patenting countries, types of documents and time ranges, and a searchable database of patents added to the database in the latest three weeks. Web sites directed to the needs of patent searchers are hosted by the Patent Information Users Group (PIUG) in America at <URL http://www.piug.org/> and the Patent and Trade Mark Group (PATMG) of the Institute of Information Scientists in the UK at <URL http://www.luna.co.uk/~patmg/>. Both sites contain news, answers to frequently asked questions, and links to sites useful for patent searching. PIUG and PATMG share an Internet discussion list, PIUG-L, where patent information specialists from around the world share information about databases, patent law, search techniques and even job opportunities.

Addendum

While this chapter was in press, some changes in patent database availability took place. The IBM INTELLECTUAL PROPERTY NETWORK was transferred to a joint venture and renamed the DELPHION INTELLECTUAL PROPERTY NETWORK. Substantial changes to the site have already been made and modifications are continuing. MicroPatent has licensed its PCT full-text database to both DIALOG and STN. Rather than replacing the INPADOC database with an enhanced INPADOC PLUS database as previously announced, Questal-Orbit has named the enhanced database PLUSPAT and continues to offers its version of the INPADOC database as well.

Chapter 3

Business and economics

Jacqueline Cropley and Gwenda Sippings

Expansion of the market

The availability of business information has grown steadily, in terms of both sources and delivery mechanisms. As products come closer to the real requirements of business customers, the number of people accessing electronic business information directly is increasing dramatically. Now that a wider market has finally been reached, and so-called end users are seeing the volume of electronic information for themselves, it is likely that demands on the producers will also increase.

If vendors respond to these requirements, there is great potential for this online sector. As so many users are coming new to online information, the requirements being articulated are broadening. At this stage it is difficult to predict exactly where business databases will be going. Everything depends on vendor willingness and ability to meet new demands. Innovation and responsiveness should be rewarded.

This chapter reviews some of the main products in the market and indicates probable directions. The emphasis is on services which are in common use or readily accessible – but, even here, it is impossible to be comprehensive. There are many different products. Vendors offer popular services in many formats. Product development is now continuous. Services are offered and withdrawn from the market much more frequently than before. Examples here are representative of what is available on the market at the time of writing, but there will be many new developments. Users have many opportunities to select services and suppliers that meet their needs precisely, either choosing comprehensive, all-purpose, standard systems or highly customizable, specialized services. Purchasers are recommended to discuss options in detail with the vendors so that they will be confident that the chosen services will give them what they require.

A number of issues face the business consumer of online services. How databases meet the needs of the business community, as well as its practical requirements and restrictions, has a distinct bearing on their use. Customer behaviour, research purposes, and business constraints and imperatives have created a recognizable pattern in strategies for researching electronic information. A balance must be struck between the benefits derived from the data, the cost, the convenience and compatibility of the products, evolution of the market and integration with working practices.

This chapter considers context first and follows up with examples of the key types of data. Finally, it touches on future developments and their significance for the business user.

New product development

The degree to which traditional vendors will be able to continue to produce new products remains to be seen. Currently it seems that it is niche players and new entrants to the electronic market who are making the greatest innovations. Without the weight of historical legacy to restrict them they are able to produce showy products using modern technology which gives them a short time to market. These products capture the imagination of the business user in a way that some of the older ones have never managed. Vendors who can combine a modern, business-oriented approach with sound, comprehensive data have the opportunity to make strong inroads into the online market. The process has already begun, and some interesting products are starting to emerge from traditional vendors, too.

Presentation

There is a dangerous divide opening up in the business information sector. On one side are services which offer high-quality, consistently presented, long backfiles of data, delivered in the traditional manner. These services were originally designed for use by information intermediaries who have had to learn a range of information retrieval skills to get the best out of the systems, and even to find information at all.

Some of these services are still command-driven, so users need to know the precise commands and syntax to be able to find the material they want. To make searching easier, and thereby to attract more direct use by business people, menu-driven structures have been commonly introduced. These have particularly been used on CD-ROMs where the menu presentation does not slow down the search, as it does with those online services which still follow the original teletype process in which each line of the menu has to be printed so that the user can select from it. Again, bypassing the menu requires a knowledge of syntax, or at least a knowledge of the correct order of commands. LEXIS-NEXIS's <URL http://www.lexis-nexis.com> Short Cut feature is an example of this:

BUSFIN;HBR;imitation w/15 speed w/10 innovation;.kw

Here, the search is to be conducted within the HARVARD BUSINESS REVIEW file in the Business and Finance library, and the results list is displayed in Key Words in Context (KWIC) format, showing the text surrounding the search terms in the retrieved items.

Menu structures make it clear to the user what options are available at each stage of the search. They may suggest ideas that help the user find the information wanted, for example, to show headline or contextual information to verify the search strategy. In presenting the options, however, the menus can restrict search options and may lead the user in directions which he or she may not want to go. For example, a commonly found tree structure in company databases forces an initial selection of country. The user may not know the country of origin of the desired company, or it may be a multinational organization where segmentation by location is unhelpful. Alternatively, menus may take the user through a number of stages before reaching the next, desired step – for example, logical search development options may be offered, when all that is needed is a jump straight from the initial retrieved list to a printing-out of the results.

Hence menu-driven systems have met with a mixed response both from experienced researchers and from the occasional or unskilled user whom they were meant to help. The professional searcher might be happier dropping back into command mode that offers greater flexibility and speed. Unskilled users become frustrated and lost because they cannot find their way to the right part of the menu tree, or cannot step back a stage, or simply because they are not offered a selection that they require.

The approach favoured by Internet browsers differs from both syntax searching and menus. A number of search engines are offered, usually with a standard default. Once the search engine is chosen, the underlying principle is because the Internet is widely used, people will quickly find out how to enter the search details. Little information is given on-screen, but it is clear enough where to enter the search terms. People who are sufficiently curious to follow the Options links can find out how to enter more complex searches than basic free text. The idea of modifying the search is introduced gently. Once the first few results are displayed, the option to refine the search may be suggested if the initial results are unsatisfactory or too many items are retrieved to be manageable.

Each search engine works differently. The major ones link to one another, so that the user can switch easily between them. One of the strongest links currently is between YAHOO! and ALTAVISTA: YAHOO! works best at the directory level, selecting sites by category and ALTAVISTA retrieves items by free text. Distinctions are developing between the major engines according to how far down into Web sites they index and the degree to which they use metadata. As few Web site creators understand the options, the effectiveness of these features is currently unclear. Commercial sites will probably take advantage of all the index features, but most other useful sites will be best retrieved at the free-text level.

The most useful feature of Internet interfaces for personal customization is the ability within browser software to bookmark sites and pages. Users can set up their own virtual data collections by storing links to the material they find useful while they are viewing the page of interest, and organizing these into groups if desired.

These presentation concerns lead to the other side of the information divide. Here, assessment of product value is based more on ease of access and use and attractiveness of interface than on pure quality of product.

Users of business information have been bombarded with new office software in their working environment. Software houses have invested heavily in the development of products that appeal to the average businessperson and encourage people to use a computer. The most successful movement in this area has been the take-up of Windows systems and graphical user interfaces (GUIs). Although companies have offered multifunctional GUIs for a number of years, it is only recently that these systems are finding their way into near universal access, mainly through Windows installations.

People are exposed to Windows-style technology at home, in educational establishments and at work. In the past, front-line businesspeople had limited reason to use computers and it was the specialist back-office people who were able to spend time and effort learning specific systems, commands and menus. Front-office staff have limited appetite for this. Unless a system is essential for their work – for example, an internal accounting system – they have no time to spend learning how to use computer software, since they have more pressing tasks to concentrate on. Consequently, with the older-style electronic database systems, few people were encouraged to explore in order to find new uses for their machines. Now there is a steady movement by companies to put computers on everyone's desks, and there is a place for online systems which take full advantage of the technology trend. That the door is open is shown by the fact that people are now experimenting with Internet browsers, where they are packaged with other software. A number of information providers now offer their data with a Web browser-style interface, even where there is no Internet connection.

These considerations mean that many new products are gaining ground in the market. They may have no defined future. They may have little track record. They may have no historical information. Yet what they currently offer seems to excite and meet the requirements of many business users.

Changing working methods

GUI-based systems represent much more than the simple adoption of new hardware and software; they are changing business working habits and offering people new ways of carrying out their business. As a result, working methods are changing. People who have never used computers are finding uses for them. Many companies make it their policy to have all their staff work with computers, for a number of corporate benefits, especially improved communication. Other people start to use them by choice, because they see applications which are useful and, more importantly, can learn them very quickly.

There is also a benefit of psychological timing. Because GUIs are still relatively new, everyone has to learn how to work with them. Even people with years of computer experience have had to invest a little time in learning how to get the best out of the new software. A situation in which everyone has something to learn creates an easier environment for senior businesspeople to build up a new skill since loss of face is minimized. This is a major factor in the traditional, hierarchical business environment in which senior personnel are reluctant to admit that they might have something to learn or, worse, that junior staff may be more knowledgeable than they are.

Graphical user interfaces make people comfortable with computer systems. The other feature which helps the electronic information world is that, with GUIs, it is possible to present the user with many different kinds of software, with all the access points on-screen simultaneously, in the metaphor of the desktop. Companies are taking advantage of this. They may offer core applications to their staff, such as e-mail, word processing, spreadsheets and internal databases, and any other information that is desired alongside these. Database services that can be accessed through a Windows interface can appear beside all the other software; all the user has to do is click on the appropriate icon. By adapting the skills learnt to operate the other in-house software, such as the software's menus, icons and choices, the user can get into external database software and carry out searches.

Internet access is growing because modern office software offers it as an easy option. The Internet browser software encourages people to try out research by making the process technically straightforward. Likewise, links from intranets to external databases make online data even more accessible. As yet, many traditional vendors have found it difficult to produce effective Windows-based interfaces, but as expertise and competition grows the trend will become established.

As an example of a simple-to-use GUI system, REUTERS BUSINESS BRIEFING product <URL http://www.factiva.com> enables the end user to point and click to select news items, rather than enter text. The screen gives guidance to predefined options and user choices (Figure 3.1). Once headline results are returned, the user is guided to double-click on items to retrieve in full text, or to modify the search further (Figure 3.2). The screen is simply and clearly arranged.

Suddenly, online searching has become a task similar to other activities that the businessperson carries out regularly. It is no longer a question of moving to another desk to find an online terminal, or using a computer when all the individual's other day-to-day work is carried out manually. Nor does it involve using software that is very different in presentation from familiar internal systems. The means of conducting research is on the desk, and he or she is therefore encouraged to do just that. Searching online can become a readily available method of quickly checking facts or of obtaining preliminary information, as well as the essential research exercises which might previously have been all that were done. Once the opportunity and the means are there, the whole area of electronic information research has the opportunity to expand.

Notably, this has not been driven by developments in online information.

Figure 3.1   REUTERS BUSINESS BRIEFING search

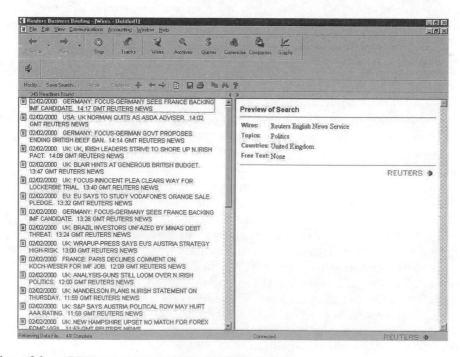

Figure 3.2   REUTERS BUSINESS BRIEFING results

Attaching easier-to-use front ends to online information retrieval and introducing CD-ROMs expanded the market a little, but the breakthrough was achieved by the universal access to computers and a widely available commercial product, Microsoft Windows, which has aimed to emulate the way businesspeople work and which emphasizes this in its advertising. Access to the Internet is establishing the research habit and familiarizing people with techniques in a manner which they can absorb with apparently little effort.

Ironically, information vendors had been going in the opposite direction. While trying to make access to their systems easier in order to attract end users, information providers still stressed the differentiation of their systems, rather than their universal ease of use. Before GUIs, with their common look and feel, products were very different from one another, sometimes deliberately so. For the would-be user, involved in broad-ranging business information research, this was a major obstacle.

The need for multiple systems

For most business users, there is no single business information database that meets all requirements. Most companies have to access a wide range, in order to obtain all the information they require. This is reinforced by the need to have an information advantage over the competition. To know about issues which competitors do not, and to find out more quickly than others do, are imperatives for most businesses. Alongside this is the need to be able to take advantage of the information discovered.

This creates several objectives. First, it is important to have the best-quality sources and those that are most comprehensive for the purpose. This can entail establishing access to as many sources as the company's staff can cope with. Second, skilled researchers must be employed to make the most of the systems and the information that they contain. These people may be information intermediaries or the end users, all of whom have to be properly trained. As access to the systems is becoming easier, the number of end users is growing rapidly. Third, information should be easily integrated with the main work which is carried out by the end user, and the ability to do this is becoming increasingly significant for companies, if they are to take full advantage of their research.

If there is just one key information source, fulfilling all these aims is relatively easy. People can be trained on the one system, and the technical requirements for passing information directly from the data source into the user's work product can be dealt with fairly straightforwardly. Difficulties mount as the number of systems which need to be dealt with increases. Even if just six databases are required, this may be more than can easily be handled, and many businesses need many more than this to cover the different types of information which they require. Furthermore, even experienced researchers forget systems they use only occasionally. No-one is able to search everything with equal efficiency or effectiveness, even if this is performed as a full-time job. Additionally, different databases offered by the same host often contain variations in presentation, causing problems, delays, missed information and wasted time. The more new databases that become available, the more the problem grows.

On top of this are technical issues, where hardware and software requirements for different database services can be in conflict. This complexity has taken on a new dimension now that some systems run in Windows and others in DOS, and different versions of each operating system are required.

Costs

Cost is a major issue for businesses: few have the financial resources to spend as much as they might like on database searching, even if their staff have the time to carry out the research. There are definite spending limitations and, for small companies in particular, this can be a very serious obstacle. The more databases that are required, the more difficult it becomes for companies to manage their online budget. The money must be divided so that all the core systems are accessible, and this can leave very little for supplementary, unallocated searching.

Business information is highly priced. Corporate researchers rarely benefit from educational and other discounts. A few suppliers offer volume discounts but, given the fact that companies need so many different services, the volume of discount is unlikely to match the scale of their research, spread, as it is, over systems from a number of different suppliers. One system may answer only a small proportion of the overall searching task, so any discount is likely to be correspondingly minor.

The principle of expensive business information is well established. Vendors not only consider that companies are able to profit highly from the information that they retrieve, but also perceive that commercial companies have plenty of money and can afford costly data. The more expensive the information, the greater the potential for competitive advantage, for lesser organizations are not able to expend comparable amounts on their research. While this may sometimes be true, in that some companies are resigned to the high costs as a necessary part of their business overheads, most companies nowadays have been through several recessionary periods and are constantly seeking to reduce costs. All expenditure is under scrutiny.

Research can be difficult to justify, because so much is conducted as a precaution, in case information exists which changes their situation. As more data become available electronically, computer research bills inevitably rise. Year-on-year price increases often exceed the rate of inflation. As online business information is global, companies are also vulnerable to exchange rate volatility which can place great pressure on costs. Conversely, if exchange rates change in the purchaser's favour, overseas online vendors may be forced to raise their prices to protect their profits. Once this is done, prices do not drop if the exchange rate swings back.

Further problems are caused by upper usage limits and retrospective pricing. Companies agree a commitment level and, if this is exceeded, additional fees have to be paid or the following year's usage is charged at a more expensive rate. This might work if usage always increases. If it does not, either because need reduces, or a competitor provides a more attractive product, the user is likely to become uncomfortable with the costs of using that particular service.

Truly invaluable information is paid for, correctly reinforcing the vendors' view of the market, that companies can afford to pay a good price for the material they require. However, other information needs may not be met. Either the research is too expensive in itself, or there is no further room in the overall information research budget. Companies pay a finite price for their information. Any vendor that wants to add its product to the services that are used by a company must fight for market share within the budget.

Business databases are offered with various payment schemes. Pay-as-you-go still exists, but many vendors now protect their revenue streams with upfront commitments, mainly on an annual basis, but sometimes covering two or three years. In itself, this arrangement is out of line with the frequently changing requirements of modern businesses.

There is also the problem that the commitment cycle for the information provider may not fit the budget cycle of the purchasing company. It is impossible to make adjustments if, part-way through the committed period, budgeting allowances and constraints change from those anticipated. The vendor business aims can prevent it from offering a commitment period to suit the buyer. Vendors need to forecast their revenue accurately, so it is the purchaser who is forced to take the risk. Needless to say, this can make prudent buyers underestimate their needs in order to avoid overcommitment, so that they may subsequently find it difficult to keep their research on that provider's database within the prescribed limits.

The need for advance commitments can price vendors out of consideration, if they are not core services. The more competition there is among suppliers offering similar products, the more selection may be governed by cost rather than quality. One service per category of information may be all that can be bought upfront. Conversely, if suppliers offer pay-as-you-go access, their usage may still be squeezed out by expenditure on other services. This constitutes a problem not only for the researcher when trying to decide what service to use for an enquiry, but also for the vendor trying to sell the product.

These concerns might be minor if research was low-cost, but the high pricing of business information makes costs significant. Business researchers have to use a range of resources. With only so much money to spend on research, they have to make careful judgements both about what services to make available and which to use for a given enquiry. In most cases, cost will govern their decision more than, ideally, it should.

People who use electronic business information in educational environments are surprised by the extent of behavioural differences brought about solely by the high cost of commercial access to business information services. Interest in

Internet sources often begins because of the perception that the information provided is cheaper than that obtained by other methods.

As pressures on information users continue and the costs rise, there is only one way the market can go. Companies will need to curtail their expenditure, either through spending less with a wide range of suppliers or by reducing the number of suppliers and placing all their research with a few. While the latter option might be preferred by many vendors, it is clearly only to their advantage if theirs is the chosen product. Who remains viable in the online business market depends on how well vendors meet the challenges now offered. It is not necessarily the case that the best information products will prevail: the services which survive will be those which sell the best. As users make their selection, there will be a market for information brokers to provide the missing sources.

Cost-effective information research

Traditional advice for online research is to do one's thinking offline. Searchers are encouraged to plan their strategy in depth before logging on to an online service. This is particularly important given the expense of business databases: with time-based charging, any pause for thought can rack costs up appreciably. Search-based charging or injudicious selection of display options can be excessively expensive if an inappropriate strategy or method is used.

Even CD-ROM services have pricing constraints, although time charge pressures are removed. Business CD-ROM software sometimes comes with a finite limitation on the number of searches that can be conducted using the disc, governed by the price paid. Once exceeded, the practice is to top up the service with more credit, for a supplementary payment. The vendor limits how much research can be done to maintain the high cost of the information. Different operations using the disc may be charged at separate rates.

Similarly, with online research, costs vary depending on what the user wishes to do. For example, pricing differs according to type of display or for activities deemed of greatest value by the vendor, such as a per label printout charge for mailing label formats on marketing databases. Amending search strategies attracts varied charges, according to how it is done. Quite simply, experienced users with sound knowledge of the data, their presentation, the vendor's pricing strategy and search techniques can conduct a piece of research more cheaply than users who are feeling their way. This means that expertise still features strongly. Knowing how to search remains more important for traditional electronic research than the intuitive strategies favoured by modern software suppliers trying to draw new customers into the marketplace.

Because of the high take-up of end-user searching, and the increasing numbers of alternative services, these factors are becoming less easy to control than previously. Even professional online researchers use so many different services, depending on need, that no-one can be fully efficient on all of them. End users may have an eye on costs, for it is they who ultimately have to pay for the information. Nevertheless, their prime aim is to obtain the results they want, and they have much less sympathy than information professionals for vagaries of pricing (however market-led) which make one method of conducting the research more costly than another. They use the method that best serves their purpose and evolve their own style. This is reinforced by the fact that they have little time for training, updates or reading tips and hints.

Far more important than cost and search structure is the fact that business information research is highly interactive. It is still sound advice to know the basic commands before logging on, and in particular how to pause a search or save it and log off to allow time for reflection. Boolean logic seems to be surviving even the Internet age, perhaps because it is offered as a search option in a way that does not intimidate the user. As Internet search engines feature Boolean search capabilities, this suggests that people do use them, although it is unlikely that this often happens at a conscious level.

Much of the value of business databases is that they contain unexpected material and information on topics beyond the searcher's specialist knowledge. Business research is frequently speculative. Questions stem from the desire to know what is going on more than to track reports of a known event. The enquirer wants to know what has been happening in an industry or to a company in recent weeks. What are the forecasts? What factors will affect the future?

As the results of the initial query appear on screen, the searcher devises supplementary searches as a reaction to the material retrieved. This is not the straightforward process of amending the search because the results are insufficient, too vague or too overwhelming. It is responding to leads given in the retrieved data set, which point to other lines of enquiry. A surprise announcement of a new product from a company competing with the company which formed the subject of the search may lead to an investigation of that product and its market and the market shares of other organizations in that industrial sector. A board appointment may prompt an investigation of the background of the new director and this, in itself, may lead to further study of other companies in which that person has worked. Business enquiries are not static. Where all this research is at a cost, in terms of time or search charges, and not fixed-price, some thought must be given to the best way to go about it. As the search evolves, consideration to mounting expense has to feature somewhere.

Database structure

Knowing the coverage of the database and using the structure effectively are important. Most databases have some level of field structure for key fields, even if they also contain large amounts of free-text material. Graphical interfaces frequently offer form-based searching, where the different parts of the form map against the database fields. Depending on the database's syntax requirements, command-based searching either requires field restrictions or is made more specific by their use.

Structured databases have a lengthy history. Many of the longstanding services have a strict infrastructure. Data are posted in fields, supplemented by coding and indexes. Views of the indexes or thesaurus displays help the user determine useful search terms. Relevance of search results is greatly improved by using the structure to define the search. Business information is riddled with soft, imprecise terminology. The use of codes, or the restriction of a search term to a particular field or part of a field, helps the searcher home in on relevant material.

Often the problem for a researcher is a surfeit of information. This may occur because the initial search is too general, or it may simply be that there is a mass of information published on the topic, which the search properly retrieves. This is very visible where business activity receives extensive media attention. For example, a takeover bid may go through numerous phases, each attracting a series of stories and commentaries. A significant economic event, such as a stock market crash, is reported and analysed repeatedly. Many business databases cover these issues, but they have different content. Without searching all, it is hard for even an experienced researcher to know which would give the best results on that particular occasion.

For example, the most useful article for the user may be a summary article that highlights all the significant stages of the story, rather than going through each aspect as the matter unfolds. Which database would be better? A news service such as REUTERS BUSINESS BRIEFING or WALL STREET JOURNAL <URL http://www.wsj.com> picks up all the interim steps, but would also include detailed analysis. A magazine database might concentrate on analysis, but possibly omit some of the detail which may be significant for the searcher's purposes (for example, *The Economist* ECON or *Fortune* FORTUN on LEXIS-NEXIS <URL http://www.lexis-nexis.com>).

Services that allow the user to interrogate the index before searching do not necessarily help here, since they can be misleading. A search term may appear much more frequently in one database than another – for example, the word 'merger' features more often in the FINANCIAL TIMES <URL http://www.ft.com> than in IAC MANAGEMENT CONTENTS (Information Access Company) <URL http://www.iacnet.com>. Yet the latter may hold a good summary article which covers all the searcher's needs. Many of the hits in the newspaper database may just be minor references, not helpful to the search. The divergence between frequency of hits and relevance to the enquiry can be even greater with full-text databases. Even a superficially specific search term, such as a company name, may generate a results list full of passing references, as well as material of direct relevance, particularly if the company is a market leader.

Databases offering relevance ranking can improve the management of results lists by relegating material of lesser apparent interest to lower positions on the list. This technique is gaining in popularity because it is frequently used by Internet search engines. As it becomes more familiar, people are beginning to understand its utility and cope with the sometimes seemingly idiosyncratic positioning of entries on the list caused by the statistical algorithms used. Professionally managed databases tend to provide reasonably consistent and comprehensible results lists. Relevance ranking is less predictable in wide-ranging Internet searches, where many sites have packed their pages with certain words designed to raise their positions in the rankings above what might normally be warranted. Although this practice often discourages end users, its occurrence is tolerated to a surprising degree because people perceive that the Internet gives them access to material that they cannot easily find elsewhere.

Terms which are ambiguous can lead to high irrelevance. For example, the word 'shipping' refers generally to distribution and specifically to maritime activity. Words such as 'bond', 'lead' or 'spring' mean completely different things, according to context. There are many words to describe motor vehicles of various types, and the same terms are used in conjunction with components ('truck tires', 'car windscreens') as well as the finished product ('truck market', 'car sales').

Using field structures and coding help focus the search. However, since there are many different coding systems, the researcher has to understand what is required in which field – particularly for those services offering several choices of search codes. Some databases have their own coding systems, particularly for industry sectors. Well developed is the IAC Predicasts classification, which cascades from four to seven levels, allowing for general and specific searching. Standard systems include: SIC Standard Industrial Classifications for the United Kingdom, the United States and Canada (all different); NAICS (North American Industry Classification System) codes replacing the US SIC codes; the United Nations' SITC Standard Industrial Trade Classification; and the European Communities NIMEXE classification (nomenclature of goods for the external trade statistics of the Community and statistics of trade between member states).

Companies may be identified by the DUNS number from Dun & Bradstreet, CUSIP numbers from the Committee on Uniform Securities Identification Procedures or registered numbers such as CRO numbers from the Companies Registration Office for the United Kingdom. Real-time systems use a variety of specialist company codes. There are many other vendor-specific coding systems in operation, such as the widely used Kompass classification, covering 45 000 categories in the business-to-business market. Industry classifications are particularly difficult in terms of consistency over time. Some suppliers set great store by their industry and product classifications, and are assiduous in being as predictable as possible. For other databases, the product suppliers select their preferred classifications, with perhaps the most divergent examples of this being in the various Yellow Pages services. Sometimes just one classification is allowed; sometimes many. Diversified service companies consequently may be found by up to 20 or more individual sector classification codes, or just one, under diversified or general services.

Particularly for high-tech sectors, all the available classification systems rapidly become outdated, and application of codes for new technologies – often precisely the ones that attract most research interest – can be very inconsistent. The classifications are revised occasionally, but not frequently enough to keep pace with product development and sectoral crossovers. Additionally, once a classification changes, historical searches have to be treated with great care, as results can be misleading where products are classified differently over time. For example, much concern has been voiced in the USA about the substantial differences in breakdown between NAICS and US SIC.

There is no doubt, though, that industry, product and company searches using the appropriate code are much more effective than words, even if limited by field name – for example, 'CO=' in DIALOG databases, indicating the company name field, or '@start' for FT Profile for the title or headline and the first two paragraphs. The form-filling layouts in graphical interfaces make these distinctions more straightforward, as the user just has to enter the search term in the appropriate box or select it from a list.

The one prime danger with field searching is that a negative result will be obtained if that field is not completed for the required record, or if the field contains a different value – for example, a different product classification from the one expected. A free-text search might pull up the record anyway, because there is a chance that the chosen search term appears elsewhere. A product classification number not appearing in the product field is unlikely to occur elsewhere in the record, so the record is not retrieved, even if there is no limitation by field. This can be especially dangerous where the number of records retrieved is high, as the volume of hits may conceal the fact that a key document is missing, and the actual documents retrieved may be of lesser significance.

Although most data vendors supply products of good quality, all suffer occasionally from mistakes. These are highly prevalent in full-text databases, where words are misspelt in the text. This can cause the search to miss the record. Less forgiveable are abstracted databases where misspellings also occur. Checking the inverted index of a database is always revealing – for example, by using DIALOG's **Expand** command – as it is very clear that words are regularly spelt incorrectly. Checking the index can also help with another level of unpredictability, where alternative spellings are used, particularly for names and product information. Business is international. Relevant commentary may come from anywhere. There are many national and regional variations in terminology, even within a single database. Suppliers of numeric data are particularly assiduous in checking data validity, as wrongly entered figures can dramatically change results.

The Centre for Information Quality Management (CIQM) works actively with database vendors to maintain high quality standards. Database labelling can help regular users be sure of what they are getting. Quality assurance policy statements cover accuracy, spell-checking and correction policy and other important quality matters. The database labels cover many other issues on coverage and structure. Dun & Bradstreet has led the business information field in publishing sample labels.

Purpose and timing

With so many business databases on the market, differentiation is not just by subject area but also by purpose. Some databases are packaged in such a way that they meet the needs of a particular customer base specifically, although their content may be of interest to others. Real-time, marketing and economic analysis services are good examples of this. Nevertheless, a researcher from one of these market sectors may sometimes find that another service is more appropriate for a slightly different type of enquiry.

End users need data which can slot into whatever they are working on, whether it is research, report production, a publication or analysis. The ultimate purpose is not always articulated at the time of the search, even if they are carrying it out directly themselves. They may think first of getting the data, and only later realize that these are available in another form more suited to their purpose. In addition, enquirers frame their requests for information on the basis of various assumptions they make about the data. They may guess how the data are presented, or ask for material in a particular form with which they are already familiar. It is very common to make a broad-based general request, when actually the real need is for a piece of very specific information.

If the correct purpose is not determined one of three things may happen:

1. The results disappoint, because they are too broad, too narrow, or miss the real issue at the heart of the enquiry.
2. Unnecessary work is carried out manually, when the system could have output the results in a more appropriate format.
3. The true value of the database is not realized, and a high price is paid for a service not properly used. The service may have been costed at a particular rate, and even purchased for a specific purpose because it offers certain key facilities, but instead it is used as a general information retrieval tool.

Examples of problems that arise include obtaining a full set of financial figures for a company, when all information is discarded except for a few lines which could have been precisely specified. The user may not be able to understand the figures in detail, and may have preferred commentary and analysis in which the company's performance is analysed by an expert. Figures may be output in graphical format, forcing the user to calculate the underlying figures, when the latter is what is actually required.

Conversely, time may be spent on converting detailed figures into graphics when the software is able to do this directly. Financial ratios may be available on the database, avoiding the need to calculate them. What sounds like a simple, specific request, such as a series of currency rates, can disguise the fact that the user plans to convert various economic data into a common currency to produce comparisons or rankings, which may be available for output directly from the database.

Another issue to review is the currency of the information, which can be critical for business analysis. Are forecasts or history required? Does all the information have to relate to a particular year? If a comparison is required, it may be better to produce comparative figures all relating to a defined period – the latest for which data are consistently available – rather than to produce the latest data on each individual component of the search. For example, all companies in a ranking using 1998 financial results, where only a few have reported for 1999, may be adequate, since like is being compared with like. Conversely, another enquirer who wants the latest position for each company, regardless of date, is not going to be satisfied with the harmonized, common denominator search. Real-time news may be imperative if the business issue is highly current and changeable. A general background request for information may be adequate if the enquirer knows the matter well, and merely wants to recapitulate on a few points. The most recent economic statistics often appear in news reports months before databases of economic time series are updated.

Answering these questions before going online helps determine which database should be used, with the most appropriate data and software. Once the type of database has been decided, there are other features which can be used to save money by avoiding fruitless searching. For example, a company's most recent financial return may be too out-of-date for the defined purpose. Checking the last date the accounts were filed saves wasting time and money retrieving the older material. Checking indexes individually or across several files can give an indication of whether further investigation on a given database is worthwhile. Searching multiple files simultaneously and deduplicating can gather widely scattered material effectively. Libraries, cross-file searches and data collections bring together related material to search together. For other research, it can be more effective to select a single file, or manually to select two or three to search together. Some sources are abstracted in one database and full text in another. Which is better for the research question in hand?

Sometimes, even the most current online information is not the answer. Knowing the real deadline is important. Businesspeople work under a great deal of pressure and demand everything immediately. Apart from the practicality for busy researchers in determining the priorities of their work, fast and immediate may not produce the best result for the user. Lengthy searches or comprehensive reports may be useless if the user does not have time to digest the results. An analysis may be essential if individual detail is longwinded and scattered.

Some database vendors offer an electronic service that presents commonly required information on demand. Other information can be produced as an independent research enquiry on request, such as an update to a credit report, or supplied from manual files – for example, by facsimile transmission in response to an online request or telephone call. Where the instant online search produces negative or inadequate results, a delay of a few hours or days may give the user exactly what is required. All depends on urgency.

Lastly, a balance has to be drawn between the iterative nature of searching business information databases and the cost. It is possible to conduct broad-ranging research more cheaply if some thought is given to possible directions beforehand, even if the ultimate detail is not clear until the initial research results come out. The initial search may spark off new lines of enquiry. Discovering that an individual is a director of a given company can lead to a request for that person's other directorships. A reference to a company's growing interest in a particular sector may provoke a search for the major companies involved in that industry and their market share. Pursuing the enquiry while online, or saving the search so that it can be retrieved and expanded later can reduce the overall cost.

These strategies can be particularly effective with business news databases where initial search results often list a number of routine details, such as quarterly financial statements, share movements, funding issues and appointments, as well as significant news stories. Knowing which the user wants to focus on makes the search more cost-effective, as well as providing a better end product. If it is the substantive news, this can be printed out in fuller detail than the routine information, which can be suppressed entirely if necessary. Conversely, it may be the routine reports which are of interest. Iterative and spontaneous though business research may need to be, many search results are predictable.

Saved searches, offline input and push technology

Repeated searching, or core repeated searching with minor modifications, can be carried out on many databases by creating and storing the searches and running them regularly by calling them up by name. This is still the basis for SDI (selective dissemination of information), current awareness work and regular screening. Business information searches may be less static than in other disciplines because of business changes, such as change of company name or sector developments. Equally, the business interest of the enquirer may change, so care must be taken to ensure the profiles are up-to-date.

Some databases allow the user to create the search offline, using the software interface, then dial up and upload the search to run on the online system. This feature is also found in CD-ROM/online database combinations in which the historical search is carried out on the CD-ROM and the details are automatically forwarded to the online search to retrieve the latest updates.

In conjunction with Internet technology and e-mail, new services are appearing in which the profiles run automatically at regular intervals, so that no intervention is required. Results are posted to a file, for later consultation, or to an electronic mail box. These may appear on-screen automatically as alerts or ticker messages, or the user's attention may be drawn to the new information immediately – for example, by a beep sound from the computer or a flashing icon.

Besides the search and display approach, filters may be used to operate on data feeds. These select relevant information according to the criteria defined, either pre-set as options from the supplier or customized, and deliver it immediately to the user. As this is a new method of working for many people, take-up is currently slow, but it can be expected to increase rapidly as more people understand its utility.

Types of business information and sources

In the past, business information has been categorized by type. Most online and CD-ROM services have segmented the different types of data and offered them as separate products. Sometimes, the same core data are used, but it is enhanced by being offered alongside complementary information for a particular purpose. Users are led to a particular source because of this orientation by type of business. It serves the very practical purpose of concentrating on the issues which are significant for a commercial activity or task. This principle has also made it straightforward for vendors to target a particular customer base. Researchers interested in the core data may find that various sources with different orientations suit their needs, but should be wary if the product direction creates a bias.

The following sections outline and illustrate the main categories which remain recognizable even where vendors draw together the different types of information and package them as a whole.

Company information

This includes static information about companies, such as date of incorporation and significant history. Databases give directory details, including name, registered address, type of company and business, directors' names and similar details based frequently on information from materials lodged at the Companies Registration Office (CRO), the Stock Exchange or the American Securities and Exchange Commission (SEC). Other details include ownership and related companies, including parent and subsidiary information, share structures, trading addresses and product details.

Directory and product information is provided by many sources, usually with a particular orientation. Directory databases include Dun & Bradstreet's WHO OWNS WHOM, available from DIALOG <URL http://www.dialog.com>, which details corporate relationships and can be searched by parent or subsidiary, and Dun & Bradstreet's KEY BRITISH ENTERPRISES CD-ROM <URL http://www.uk.dub.com>, combining directory information with three years' financial information on the 50 000 largest UK companies. KOMPASS <URL http://www.kompass.com> offers extensive details of companies' products and services, export information, and directorships.

Figures 3.3, 3.4 and 3.5 show a search on WHO OWNS WHOM. The user can search by a number of categories as indicated on the heading tabs. The search options are clearly indicated and, where appropriate, there are pick lists to aid selections – for example, under the Industry tab, those for SIC codes. These examples show options on the Company Information tab, showing a company search and the family tree retrieved for that organization. The user can then click on the required company to retrieve the full record.

Basic information is provided for registered companies, such as the 1.4 million

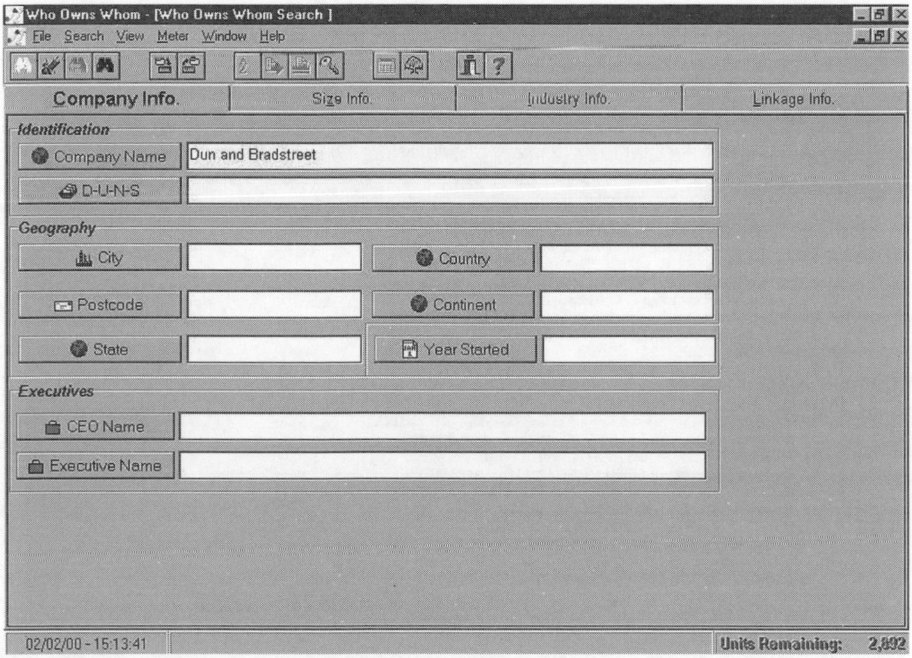

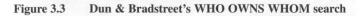

Figure 3.3   Dun & Bradstreet's WHO OWNS WHOM search

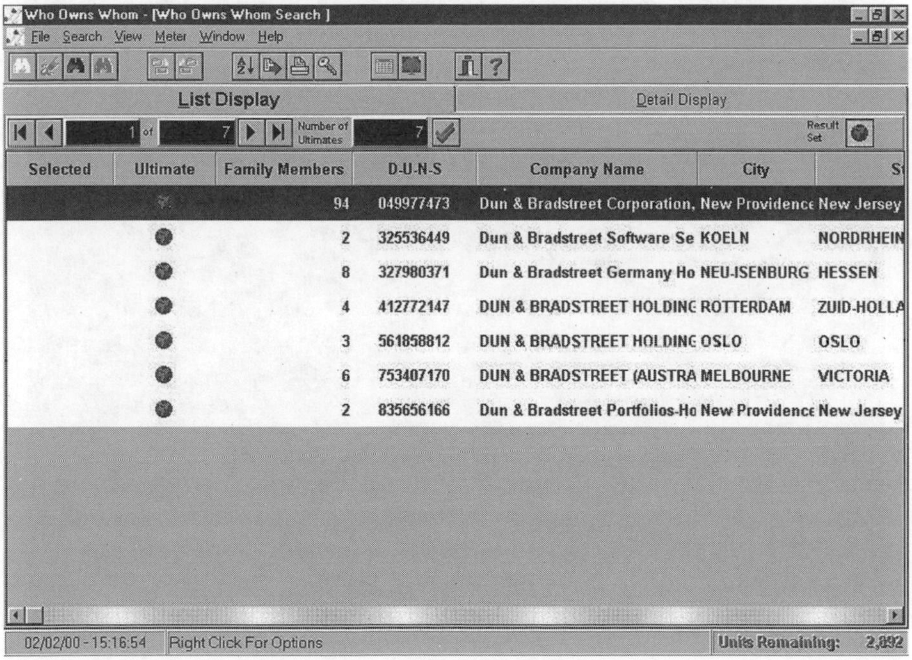

Figure 3.4   Dun & Bradstreet's WHO OWNS WHOM results

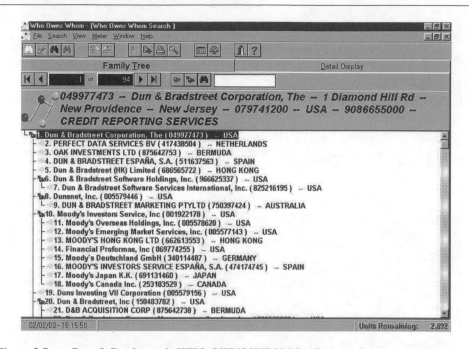

Figure 3.5   Dun & Bradstreet's WHO OWNS WHOM family tree view

Figure 3.6   COMPANIES HOUSE DIRECT

companies registered at the CRO. This is supplied by COMPANIES HOUSE DIRECT <URL http://www.companies-house.gov.uk>, and by JORDANS <URL http://www.jordans.co.uk>, ICC <URL http://www.icc.co.uk>, Dun & Bradstreet <URL http://www.uk.dub.com> and EQUIFAX INFOCHECK <URL http://www.infocheck.co.uk>, along with other data. The base information includes company name, registered address, registered number and date of latest accounts filed.

The COMPANIES HOUSE DIRECT service, relaunched in September 1997, adopts a Web browser style for a more user-friendly approach. From the Company Enquiries and Orders screen, users can select company details, filing history, mortgage index, appointments, previous names, and request a microfiche search. Some options incur a charge to view. Users can also retrieve information about directors and secretaries (see Figure 3.6).

Company financial information

Company performance is probably the greatest concern for business research. It is corporate information which drives the business-critical real-time markets. Interest permeates all commercial sectors from large-scale companies wishing to identify new business opportunities and threats, to small and medium-size enterprises (SMEs) checking fundamental issues, such as credit information and activities of their competitors and suppliers. Financial information includes the company's capital structure, its accounting periods, the dates of accounts filed, and full balance sheet and profit and loss information.

Interest in company performance is exactly reflected by the amount of corporate information that is available, in online and CD-ROM products and extensively on the Internet. There are a number of sources to choose from. Services are provided using official information, such as the financial reports submitted to the SEC in the USA and the CRO in the UK. Particularly in the USA the officially reported information is closely specified and subject to intense scrutiny. Information from these sources is highly reliable and holds much internal consistency. It rarely contains more than what is required by statute or regulation. Straightforward systems such as the SEC ONLINE database <URL http://www.sec.gov> present the data exactly as filed, with no further attempt to standardize records or add value. NAARS LEXIS-NEXIS on <URL http://www.lexis-nexis.com> contains complete financial statements for 4000 publicly traded American companies, accompanied by relevant accounting literature. The service is produced in conjunction with the American Institute of Certified Public Accountants (AICPA).

Commercial sources either repackage the official information or they obtain their data by alternative means, usually directly from the companies themselves but sometimes from third parties. Repackaging includes offering analytic software to facilitate comparisons, trend and performance analysis, and market rankings. Such repackaging helps researchers make their own evaluations. Data may be exactly as reported or harmonized to ensure that each line of a financial report for one company is directly comparable with the same line for another.

Financial details on major English companies come through such services as ICC; The Dialog Corporation <URL http://www.dialog.com>; EXPERIAN <URL http://www.experian.com>; DATASTREAM/ICV <URL http://www.datastream. com>; ONESOURCE <URL http://www.onesource.com>; JORDANS; FAME CD-ROM (Financial Analysis Made Easy) <URL http://www.bvdep. com>; EXTEL <URL http://www.ft.com>; EQUIFAX INFOCHECK; PERFECT INFORMATION <URL http://www.perfectinfo.co.uk> and PRIMARK <URL http://www.primark.com>. American data are on SEC ONLINE; EDGARPLUS <URL http://www.sec.gov>; PRIMARK; MEDIA GENERAL PLUS <URL http://www.mgfs.com>; ONESOURCE; STANDARD AND POOR'S (S & P) <URL http://www.mcgraw-hill.com>; and IAC COMPANY INTELLIGENCE <URL http://www.iacnet.com>, which combines public record information with material obtained from questionnaires and interviews.

Figures 3.7 to 3.10 illustrate the use of PRIMARK GLOBAL ACCESS which enables users to retrieve a variety of data products. In the example, the familiar Extel Company Report is retrieved.

Information is readily retrievable by searching on company name. Online services usually show the highest frequency of update. However, since much of the data online can also be obtained readily in hard copy – often free of charge or at nominal cost – choosing to use the electronic information can increase expenditure noticeably, with little consequential cost savings. If regular review of certain companies is needed, the hard copy route may be best, particularly where information direct from the companies themselves contains supplementary material, commentary, tabulations, graphics and pictures, none of which are offered by the database vendors.

The CAROL service (Company Annual Reports On-Line) <URL http://www. carol.co.uk> on the Internet gives free access to annual reports and links to company Web sites. The service is supported by the company's other fee-earning activities. It has a simple search screen, inviting users to select by first letter of company name or by work category.

The following example from CAROL (Figure 3.11) shows the Welcome screen with the Reports button selected. The user asks for an annual report in the Telecommunications category. A list of companies whose reports are accessible appears, and the required one is selected. The annual report and accounts are retrieved, and an index to its sections appears on the left of the screen. The user can easily jump to the Profit and Loss or other section of the report.

Of course, online access allows for unpredicted enquiries. Use of electronic information may be justifiable on space-saving grounds, but a key use may be for screening purposes, compiling lists of companies conforming to specific criteria. These can be used for sales and marketing purposes and competitive analysis. In the active mergers and acquisitions market screening can be used to identify potential acquisition and divestment candidates. Online data may be more up to date than hard-copy material, particularly for those companies which do not

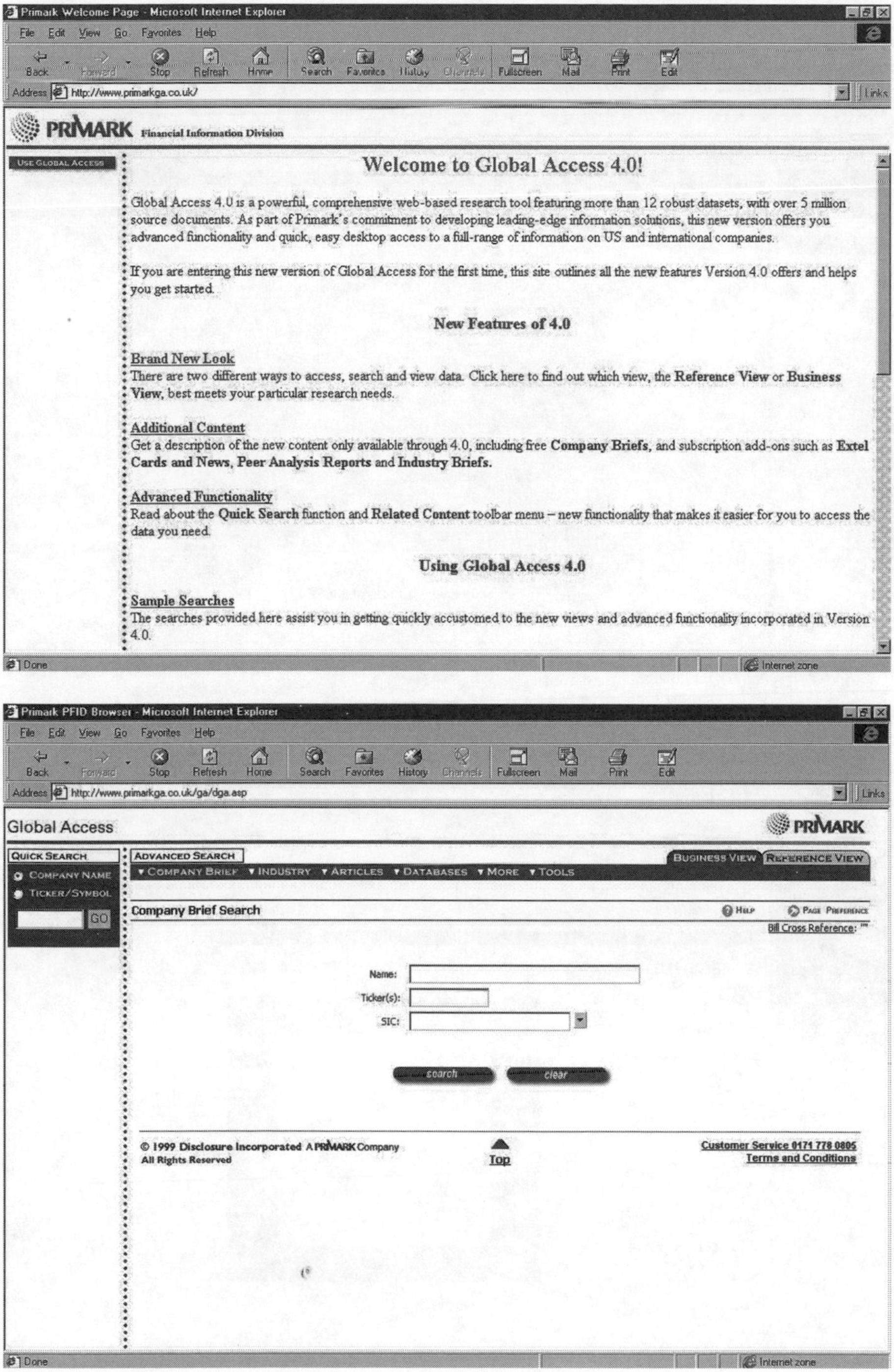

Figure 3.7   **PRIMARK GLOBAL ACCESS search**

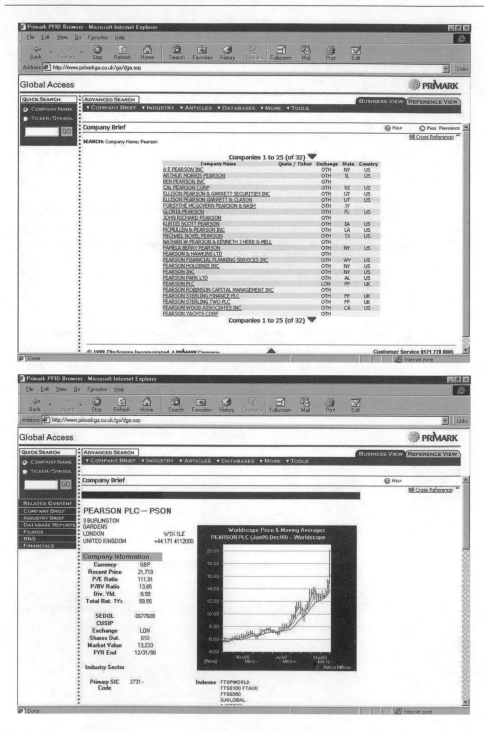

Figure 3.7   concluded

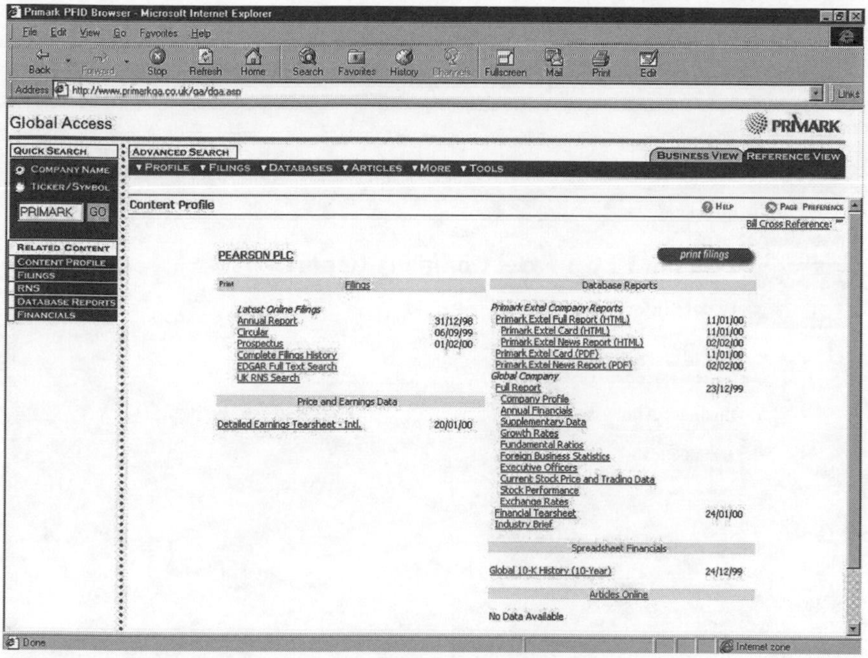

Figure 3.8   **PRIMARK GLOBAL ACCESS search results**

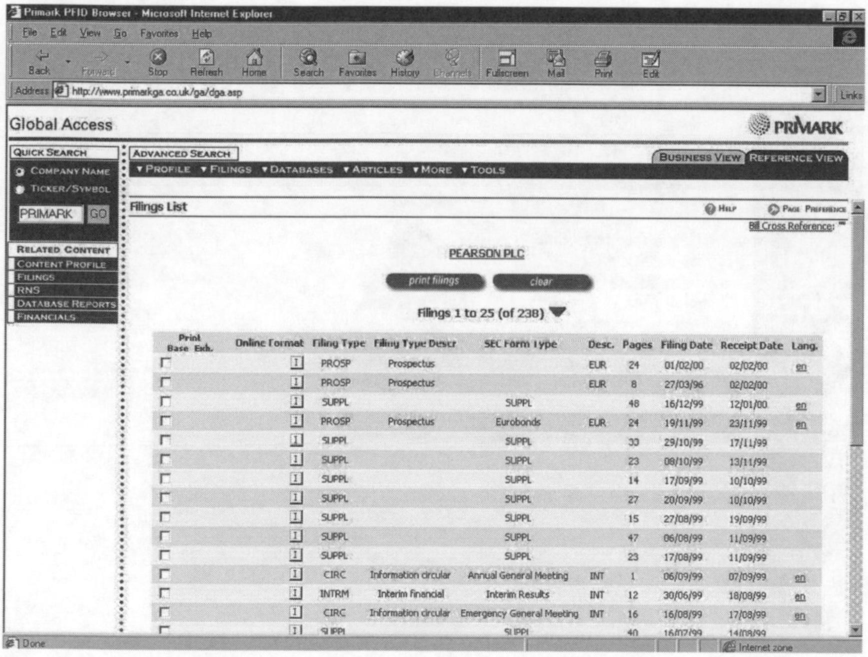

Figure 3.9   **PRIMARK GLOBAL ACCESS search results filings**

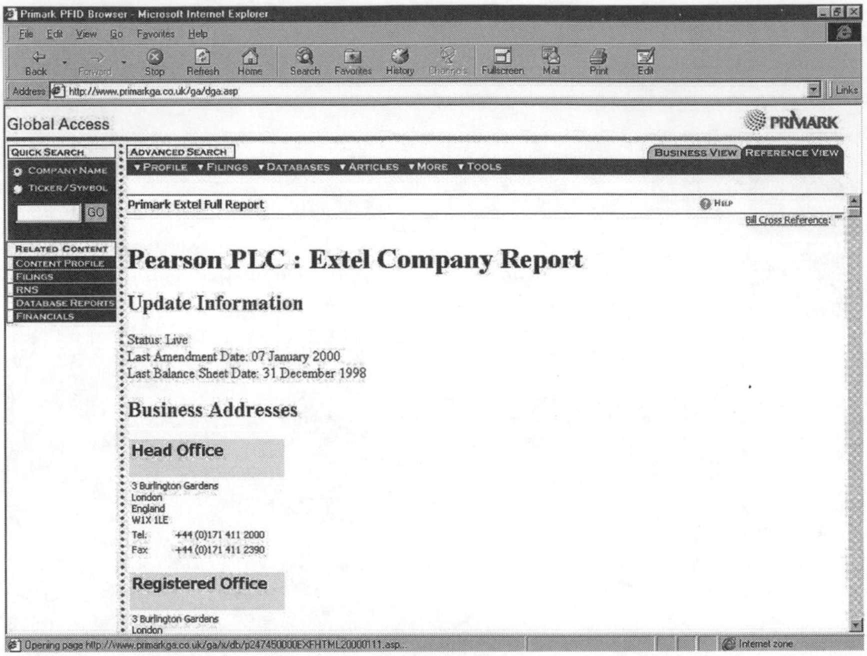

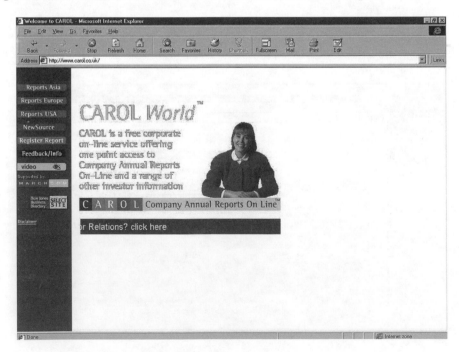

Figure 3.10   PRIMARK GLOBAL ACCESS search results Extel Report

Figure 3.11   CAROL company report selection

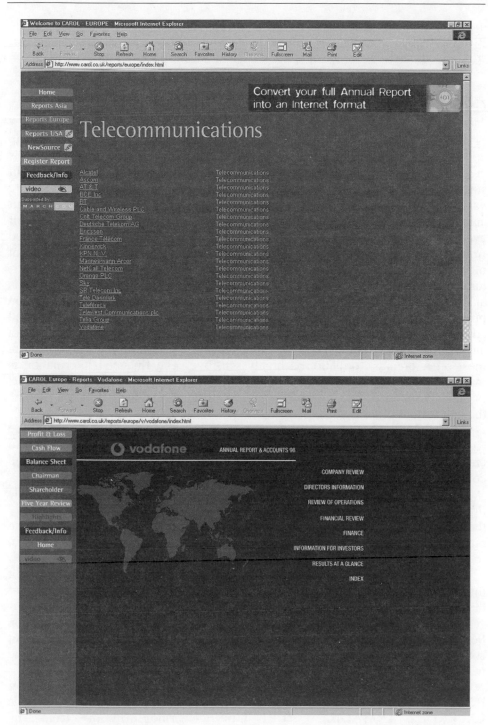

Figure 3.11 concluded

maintain extensive mailing lists for interim reports and specialized information. Electronic data can also be output in different formats and manipulated for specialized needs, using the supplier's software or third party products.

Credit status information

A company's financial information, from the same sources as before, is given in conjunction with other details that have a bearing on the company's creditworthiness. Most of these systems offer an opinion on the company's credit status. Analytical software may be provided to facilitate comparisons which are valid within the limitations of the information provided. Advanced services permit calculations so that users can create their own credit scores, based on their evaluation of the relative merits of the data supplied. Credit data are compiled from official records and reports of a company's trading history, including relevant other information such as directors' outside or previous interests. Court judgements and all legal charges are recorded. The company's payment record is analysed, based on reports from representative suppliers. The information provider suggests recommended credit limits, based on the information given, and advises whether guarantees should be sought. Although the financial data from annual reports and details such as judgements are public domain information, most other credit information is highly sensitive. The financial information is mainly offered to provide back-up evidence to support the strong opinion elements of the data supplied. The information provider's views and the stated opinions are the key feature of the service.

The opinions of credit-scoring companies are closely guarded, as they can have significant impact on a company's conditions of trade. Consequently, access to credit databases is restricted to *bona fide* users – namely, organizations with a commercial need to evaluate companies' trading abilities on a regular basis.

Before the databases were offered online, enquiries mainly had to be made through recognized financial institutions with the expertise to interpret correctly the often cryptic comments in credit reports, and understand the scoring mechanisms and implications. The same care must be taken by any researcher in order to make sensible use of the information obtained.

Occasional enquirers may be better served by direct query to the credit information company for individual replies, rather than trying to obtain access to the complete database. The complete report is the same; it is just that the search is carried out by the information provider, and faxed or mailed to the researcher. Some services also offer the option to discuss the report further. The credit company can often check for supplementary, more up-to-date information if time permits.

The most well known international supplier of credit information is Dun & Bradstreet <URL http://www.dub.com>. Other services in the UK include EXPERIAN, ARMADILLO <URL http://www.rmonline.com> from The Raymond Morris Group Limited, and INFOLINK, which uses information from the United Association for the Protection of Trade (UAPT). UAPT was established so that companies can share financial experience, to help them with their commercial activity. As a consequence, trade references and reports of payment behaviour are a particular strength of the data. Payment analysis records are compiled from reports from trading partners. Although not entirely objective, they do offer a completely different view of a company from conventional financial data taken from the financial returns which that company's own staff have created, and which reflect the company's own perspective of its activity, albeit in a regulated format.

The other information offered by credit databases can be equally illuminating. The existence of court judgements and charges are indicators of a company's trading record and ability to pay. Credit scoring weights a number of factors relevant to a company's creditworthiness and ability to trade. Where the database records the number of credit checks which have been made on a given company, this can also be significant. Clearly, particular care is required here. A high number of credit checks may merely indicate that the company's trading partners are all reputable companies with strict policies of checking business activity on a regular basis: it may indicate a high volume of business activity, or expansion involving large amounts of new business. Alternatively, it may be a negative sign, indicating that companies feel the need to be cautious before conducting business with the organization. The data should be taken as indicators to investigate further. Commentary and opinion offered as part of the report by the information provider can help.

Credit status reports are standardized because it is important to look at all the relevant matters and judge the company's activities as a whole, rather than look at just a few elements which may not be illuminating in isolation. This is especially important because of the close link between a credit enquiry and a proposed business transaction, which is usually the reason for requesting a credit check. Examining just one or two items can be misleading and damaging. The whole value of the credit status process is that a rounded, all-encompassing view is taken. This may be unfamiliar territory for researchers used to searching other databases which carry material on an as-available basis, with no attempt to take the overview, or explain incidents and gaps.

Charging is on a per report basis, with different categories of report being offered, depending on the type of information required. For example, the researcher may already have the company's annual report, so the financial accounts information is unnecessary, but the opinion can be vital. Because, historically, credit status information suppliers worked regularly with a small number of high-volume clients, their pricing strategy offers reports at a lower unit cost the more that are requested. This has carried across into online searching, now that access is more widely available.

Credit information has a completely different provenance from directory and regulated information, where companies are selected because they fit certain categories of size or business activity. Credit reports can be created on any company. The credit databases regularly cover major companies, but they also contain data on other organizations simply because a credit check has been made and the data now exist on their files as a consequence of this. For this reason, there are often data online for very small companies which do not feature in databases of financial account information or even in news databases.

If there are no publicly available data – for example, if the organization is private or too small to have to report financial information – the credit information provider tries to build a picture by contacting the company itself or by direct observation. In the latter case this may be carried out by sending investigators to the company's trading or registered address and finding out as much as possible about the organization's activities.

Credit information is time-sensitive. Business changes, in particular, can cause it to become out-of-date quickly. Requests for updates should always be ordered if data are old, and the researcher must check the date of compilation. Reports on major businesses undergo constant renewal. Older reports on other companies may be removed as a matter of policy – for example, as is done by Dun & Bradstreet – or left as an indication that the company is known to the information provider.

Because of the strong opinion element of credit information, it is a matter of business preference which data supplier to choose. Evaluations by the different information providers can be surprisingly divergent, because of the different weight they give to the various elements of credit evaluation. A company can be considered a credit risk by one credit information provider, while another shows no cause for concern. It is hard to compare a credit report from one supplier with a report on the same company from another. It is certainly dangerous to compare a report on one company from one supplier directly with a report on another company from a different supplier because the basis of the evaluations is likely to be significantly different.

The EXPERIAN LINK online service gives access to credit and financial information on companies, businesses and directors. From a password entry screen, users reach a clear menu of information. Their choice leads to a search screen, and the data matching their entry are retrieved. Once the material appears, sections of it can be viewed, on a varying scale of charges. The Risk Narrative choice gives a brief company profile, notes on trading performance and balance sheet strength, productivity and other business, such as registration of mortgages, a credit evaluation and risk analysis. Figures and directors' details are also included. Figure 3.12 illustrates this.

Because of the report orientation of the data and the cautions on comparisons, it is not practical to use credit data for automated screening unless the database is structured for this purpose. The raw data do not lend themselves to this kind of processing. Researchers accustomed to screening by using accounts data may be tempted to export credit data into spreadsheets for similar activity, but this is not advised.

MOODY'S <URL http://www.moodys.com> and STANDARD AND POOR'S offer American credit information and some international information which is slightly different from the UK system. Their evaluations concentrate on the upper

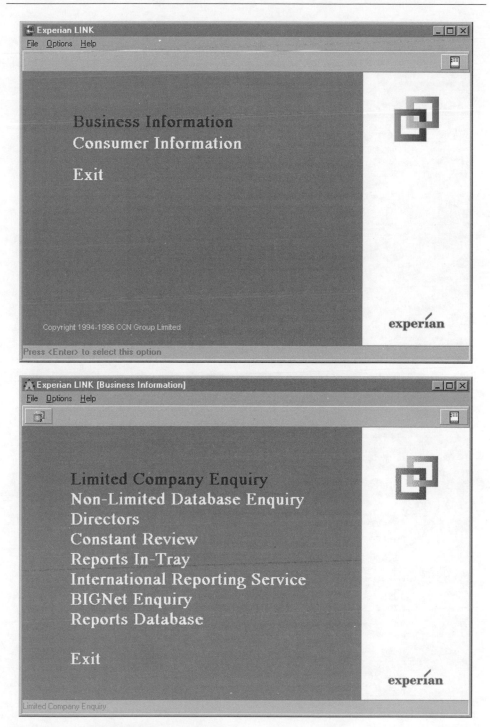

Figure 3.12   EXPERIAN LINK screens

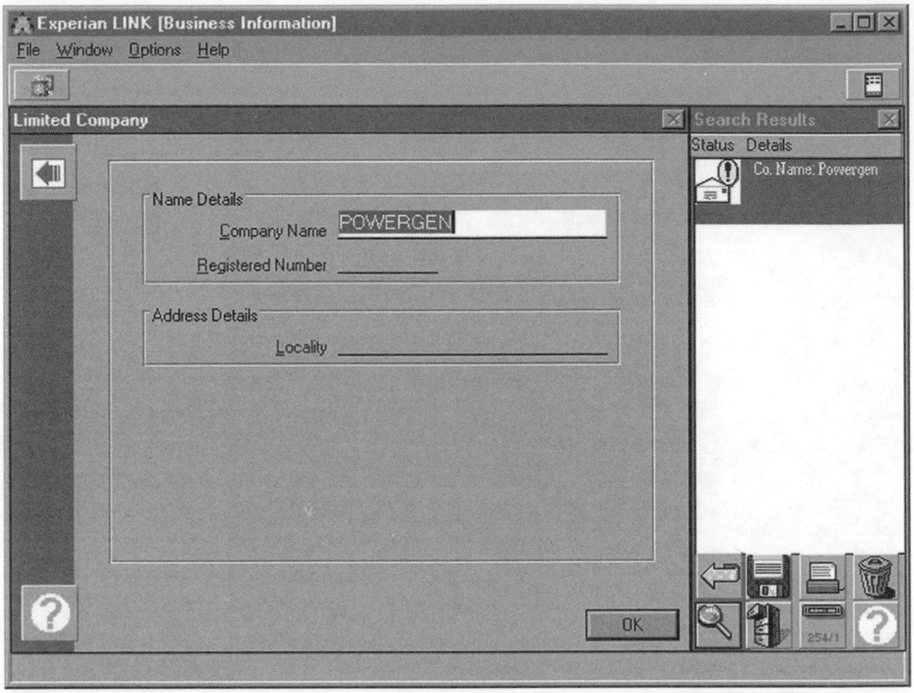

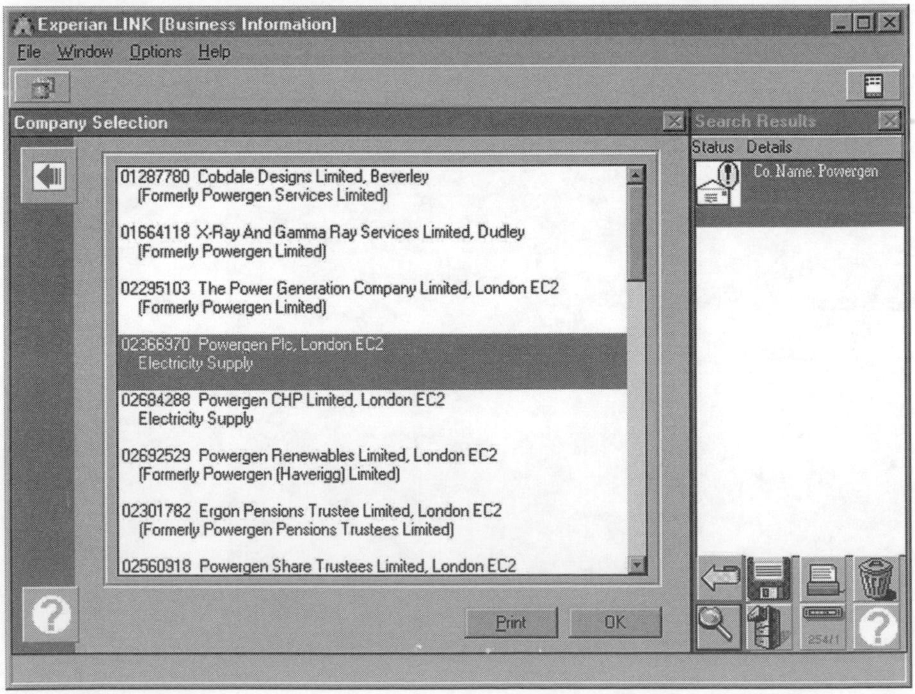

Figure 3.12 cont'd

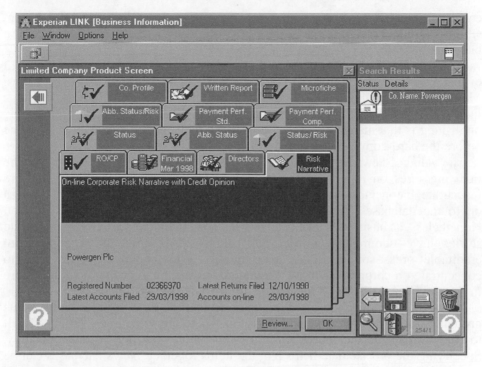

Figure 3.12   concluded

end of the market and have a strong investment element. MOODY's and STANDARD AND POOR's provide ratings showing their opinions on a company's standing. Ratings are jealously guarded by the companies themselves, and much heralded if they are favourable. This is because they have an absolute relationship both to the cost of finance for that company and its opportunities for conducting business. Many companies work specifically with businesses with particular Moody's or S & P ratings. A downgrading – for example, from AAA to AA – can make a big difference to that company's future. These ratings are therefore used regularly for screening, which is acceptable because of the universal familiarity with what the ratings indicate. Although these two operators are highly influential, particularly in the USA, they too can rate companies differently from each other.

Business news information

Business news is reported widely in the British and American press, as well as in major international newspapers and magazines. There are many news databases, some of which offer individual titles and others a range which can be searched together. National and regional newspapers are included, although some databases are visibly more assiduous in including national news than local detail. The latter can be particularly important for product, plant and employment information, which may have a significant bearing on a company's trading performance at a later date.

News databases offer snapshots of company activity. They report significant events over time, and regulated matters such as annual meetings and share issues. Major surveys, analyses and reviews also feature, covering countries, markets, industries, government and economic matters. One advantage of electronic publishing is that many newspapers now make their information available online before the hard-copy versions are on sale.

The value of news reporting is as good as the stories included. Because of the time pressures on reporters, stories sometimes appear in the press which are inaccurate, inconclusive or inadequately followed up. Many of these carry through on to the databases, so all stories cannot be accepted as statements of fact. Nonetheless, as businesses take heed of what appears in the press, even inaccurate stories have commercial impact. Of course, most news information from creditable press sources is of good quality. Newspaper databases tend to concentrate on corporate activity, leaving government and economic issues more to the news magazines with their more discursive, analytical approach.

Newspaper readers are familiar with the many surveys and supplements grouping stories by topic, industry or region. These are sometimes a little difficult to trace online, as the individual stories in the review are posted separately. Specifying the precise date helps pull the items together. News databases can be searched for most topics of business interest.

The first major company databases providing historical business information online were news services and, because of the original lack of competition, they have built up a great following. There are many such services on offer, with software features designed to facilitate company searching. In particular, specifying that the search term is a company name or is to be found in the company field avoids retrieving irrelevant material, as might occur when the company name includes a place name or common words, such as US Steel.

Businesspeople have become accustomed to asking loosely for anything available on a company and expecting to be provided with a news history. Commonly found services include several on FT PROFILE <URL http://www.ft.com>, including the formerly independent MCCARTHY PRESS CUTTINGS SERVICE, REUTERS BUSINESS BRIEFING, replacing the older TEXTLINE <URL http://www.dialog.com> service, and LEXIS-NEXIS. There are also numerous CD-ROM databases covering individual newspapers. In practice all the major business press can be searched electronically, either separately or in conjunction with other products. Many services are available in full text, such as THE FINANCIAL TIMES <URL http://www.ft.com>, THE TIMES AND THE SUNDAY TIMES <URL http://www.the-times.co.uk>, THE GUARDIAN <URL http://www.guardian.co.uk>, THE NEW YORK TIMES ONDISC <URL http://www.nytimes.com>, WALL STREET JOURNAL ONDISC <URL http://www.wsj.com> and WALL STREET JOURNAL EUROPE. Others are merely abstracted.

FT PROFILE's Windows interface leads users through options to select their search strategy (Figure 3.13) and then goes online to retrieve results (Figure 3.14). The user is given the option to view headlines, and to highlight and retrieve the full article, with a price warning displayed first.

Both the full-text approach and abstracting are useful. Full text gives the complete story as published, although if the database is an online one, pictures, graphics and tabular data are excluded. On the other hand, abstracts reveal the key issues to the researcher more quickly than full text. This is because news is essentially a moment-by-moment information source, and using it for historical research is adapting it to a different purpose. First, material is repeated from article to article, or gaps are left in a story because those elements were not considered by the news editor to be newsworthy. Second, when a newspaper is published, the news it contains may also be the subject of radio and television coverage, and news editors can assume knowledge in the reader because of other press activity at the time of publication. This cross-fertilization of news dissemination is often lacking in a historical search. The publisher's aims are focused on a very different consideration from what may be necessary for the historical record or to understand a situation from start to finish. An abstracter can help alleviate this in his or her presentation. Also graphics, tables and other data present on the printed page can be alluded to. With full text, these issues are not dealt with.

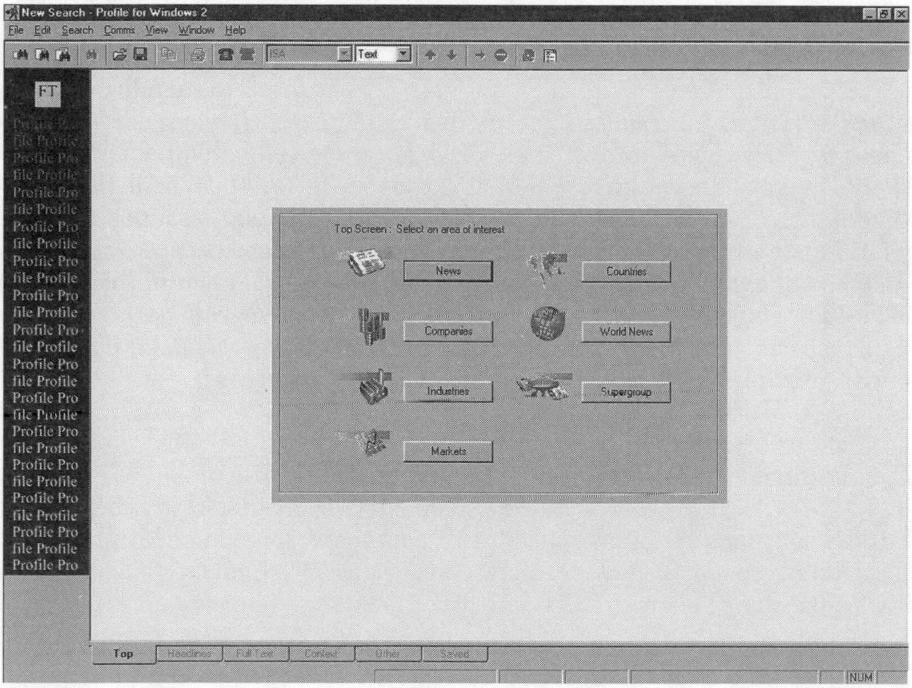

Figure 3.13   FT PROFILE search

Figure 3.13   concluded

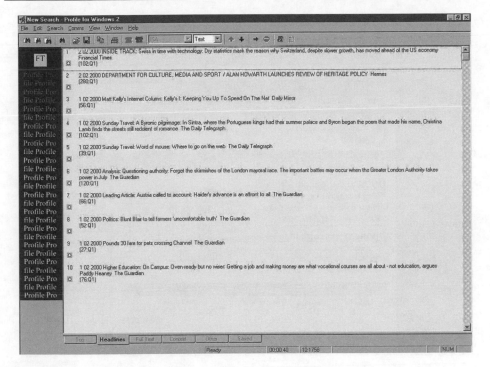

Figure 3.14   FT PROFILE search results

Business news databases do not hold all the news printed on business topics in the press; they do not even cover all stories featured in the business pages. In particular, commentary and editorial are often omitted. The type of business news most often picked for inclusion is company information. Key stories are usually selected, particularly if there are financial or competition implications. Other corporate information such as appointments or production difficulties may be excluded. Sometimes, the significance of a minor reference in a newspaper does not emerge until later, so these omissions can be troublesome. All this means that news data should not be relied on exclusively. Regrettably, this is often forgotten, because of the early history of news databases, when there were few alternative sources.

Several newspaper services have established Web sites on the Internet. Some just offer the news of the day, while others provide access to their archive services, and can be used for historical business information searching. As these sites are usually produced by the newspapers themselves, they reflect the structure of the printed copy of the newspaper, and it is more easily possible to search by newspaper section than on most of the online newspaper databases.

The Internet sites tend to contain material omitted from the databases. There is more on appointments, professional and academic examinations, and similar information that is a matter of report rather than news. The heavily used Internet-based newspaper services are better for checking current news than for substantial

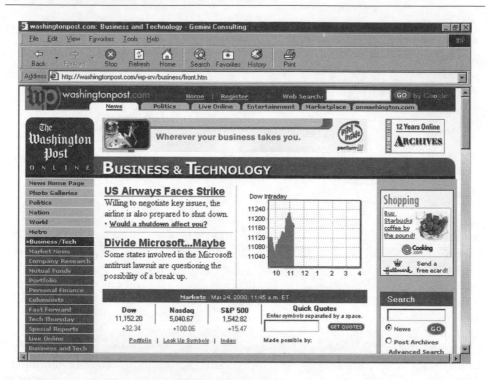

Figure 3.15   WASHINGTON POST business screen

historical research, as some sites run slowly because the volume of use is too great for the power of the sites' servers. Thus, following hypertext links one-by-one can be prohibitively slow. Examples of newspaper Web sites include THE TIMES AND THE SUNDAY TIMES, THE DAILY TELEGRAPH <URL http://www. telegraph.co.uk>, THE WALL STREET JOURNAL, and THE LOS ANGELES TIMES <URL http://www.latimes.com>. Figure 3.15 shows how the business sections of the current issue of the WASHINGTON POST <URL http://www. washingtonpost.com> can be selected from a pull-down menu. This site concentrates on the day's news. *The Washington Post's* historical information can be found online through hosts such as DIALOG and LEXIS-NEXIS.

Marketing information

Marketing databases fall into two categories. The first kind is mainly product-oriented, giving extensive detail on product launches, branding, market share and media activity. Corporate details of the producer may be sublimated to advertising and creative information – for example, the news that an advertising agency has obtained a new account. The advertising and marketing professions are seen as key consumers of these databases, so orientation is closely to their requirements.

The other style of marketing data is market research. These services offer detailed reports on sectors and products and may contain comparisons between different companies and product categories, and comprehensive statistics.

Long popular with market information researchers are the IAC PREDICASTS databases. IAC PROMT encompasses a number of originally separate files covering all aspects of market, product and sector information, including MARS (Marketing and Advertising Reference Service), Aerospace/Defense Markets and Technology, New Product Announcements Plus and several others. The database can be found widely – for example, on DIALOG, LEXIS-NEXIS, Questel-Orbit, FT PROFILE and REUTERS BUSINESS BRIEFING and on the Internet through Insite <URL http://www.iac-insite.com> and Insite Pro <URL http://www.insitepro.com>, designed for end-user and professional research respectively. IAC PROMT holds full-text and abstract information from articles from newsletters, newspapers, press releases, reports and magazines, as well as annual report information. Although in its early years it focused on US information, for some time now it has been equally strong on European material, and has managed this expansion more effectively than many other services. It is one of the best sources of tabular information, presenting key data in simple tables which can be easily retrieved because of the detailed Predicasts coding allocated to each record.

In a database sector where detailed product segmentation is critical in order to make sense of marketing data, the IAC PREDICASTS files are distinguished by detailed product, event and country classifications which permit precise identification and which also cascade from the general to the specific. Event codes specify particular activities, such as advertising or research and development, as well as corporate events such as name changes. Using these codes provides a very high level of retrieval accuracy. This makes the database a favourite for serious business research, particularly on account of its widespread coverage.

There are a number of databases of market research reports, which analyse market sectors and provide detailed information on the companies involved and the factors acting on the markets. Databases include EUROMONITOR MARKET RESEARCH <URL http://www.euromonitor.com>; EIU MARKET RESEARCH <URL http://www.eiu.com>; MINTEL MARKET RESEARCH REPORTS <URL http://www.mintel.co.uk>; FIND/SVP MARKET RESEARCH <URL http://www.findsvp.com>; Euromoney's WORLD MARKETING DATA AND STATISTICS CD-ROM; FINDEX <URL http://www.dialog.com>; MARKINTEL <URL http://www.investext.com>; DATAMONITOR MARKETLINE UK SNAPSHOTS <URL http://www.datamonitor.com> and MARKET AND BUSINESS DEVELOPMENT <URL http://www.profound.com>, concentrating more on British markets; FREEDONIA MARKET RESEARCH <URL http://www.dialog.com> and BCC MARKET RESEARCH (Business Communications Company) <URL http://www.dialog.com/>, concentrating mainly on American sectors. ICC KEY NOTE CD-ROM and the online equivalent ICC KEY NOTE MARKET RESEARCH <URL http://www.icc.co.uk>, supplied through several hosts, offers full-text reports on 220 consumer and industry markets. Euromoney produces WORLD CONSUMER MARKETS ON CD-ROM

<URL http://www.euromoney.com>, covering a similar number of markets worldwide. CONSUMER REPORTS <URL http://www.dialog.com> from the Consumers Union covers US consumer markets. Euromonitor's THE WORLD DATABASE OF CONSUMER BRANDS AND THEIR OWNERS 1997 ON CD-ROM <URL http:www.euromonitor.com> provides worldwide information on the manufacturers of consumer goods and their brands.

More specific information can be found in services such as FROST AND SULLIVAN MARKET INTELLIGENCE <URL http://www.frost.com>, focusing on technical and specialist industries; JUPITER MARKET RESEARCH <URL http://www.dialog.com> looking at online developments and their effects on consumer behaviour; and BEVERAGE MARKETING RESEARCH REPORTS <URL http://www.dialog.com>.

In the area of market research data, the most steady development of services has been undertaken by The Dialog Corporation which originally sold its specialized market research information service, the PROFOUND database, to the marketing and advertising sectors in the UK. The database was carefully structured to meet the specific requirements of this sector. In particular there has been a strong emphasis on detailed full-text information, from major surveys and reports, with the material combined for searching consistently through a single interface. This allows marketing companies to find all the material they require online. Figures 3.16 to 3.20 show The Dialog Corporation's Internet-based PROFOUND service (now accessed at <URL http://www.profound.co.uk>). From the main PROFOUND search menu, Market Research is chosen from the Research Reports options, and a company and industry search entered (Figure 3.16). This produces 139 records. The second page of the results list is displayed here with hypertext links to documents matching the query (Figure 3.17). Item 6 is then selected from the list, and the contents page is displayed, extracts of which are shown in Figure 3.18. For any item which is selected for display of the full text, the cost of the display is shown first, and the researcher is given the option of accepting the charge or changing the selection. If the search is for a topic of regular interest, alerts can be set up from the results page. The search data are carried over to the Alert Manager feature, and can be modified if needed, and saved (Figure 3.19). By returning to the initial search menu and selecting Stock quotes, share price information for the company can also be displayed (Figure 3.20).

Another example of a specialized approach is the production of mailing lists. Dun & Bradstreet DIRECT MARKETING SERVICE <URL http://www.dub.com> permits researchers to construct target lists online, using Dun & Bradstreet's UK MARKETING DATABASE. Output lists and labels are ordered online and despatched by post. EMMA <URL http://www.bvdep.com>, Easy Mailing and Marketing Applications, is a CD-ROM service which offers information on 650 000 limited liability British companies for marketing purposes on a menu-driven system. EMMA uses ICC data. The prime aim of the database is to facilitate production of mailing labels and customized lists and reports. Data may be output directly or downloaded into spreadsheets, word-processing or database software.

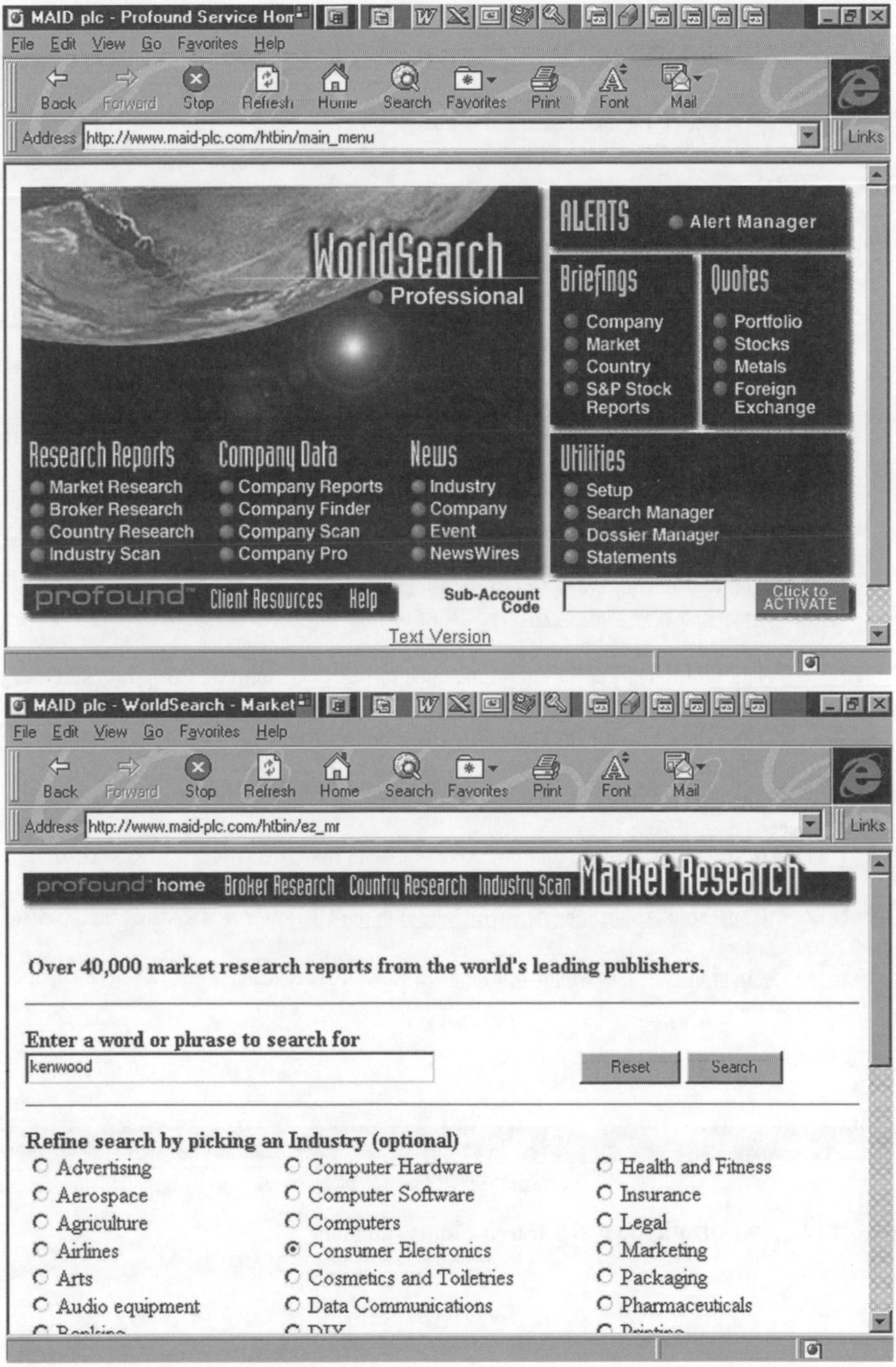

Figure 3.16   MAID PROFOUND search

profound home   WorldSearch

Save Search   Create Alert

GET   ● **Selected** ○ **Table of contents** ○ **Context** ○ **Price**

Researchline

Displaying titles 11 to 20 of at least 139 records

1. ☐ U.S. Home Audio Equipment Markets - Market Overview, Total Market, Analog Players, Analog Recorders, Digital Players and... - FROST AND SULLIVAN - February, 1997 (76 pages)

2. ☐ U.S. Home Audio Equipment Markets - Speaker Systems, Add-On Equipment, Strategic Analysis and Distribution Channel Marke... - FROST AND SULLIVAN - February, 1997 (99 pages)

3. ☐ U.S. Home Audio Equipment Markets - Strategies for Success, Company Profiles and Database of Industry Participants Profi... - FROST AND SULLIVAN - February, 1997 (96 pages)

4. ☐ The World Market for Consumer Electronics - Market Overview, New Product Development and Key Market Drivers - EUROMONITOR/STRATEGY 2000 - January, 1997 (62 pages)

5. ☐ The World Market for Consumer Electronics - Distribution, Corporate and Production Strategies - EUROMONITOR/STRATEGY 2000 - January, 1997 (47 pages)

6. ☐ The World Market for Consumer Electronics - Company Profiles and Future Outlook - EUROMONITOR/STRATEGY 2000 - January, 1997 (103 pages)

7. ☐ The German In Car Entertainment Market - EUROMONITOR, Market Research Europe - November, 1996 (30 pages)

8. ☐ In Car Entertainment and Car Accessories in the UK - MARKET ASSESSMENT - August, 1996 (57 pages)

9. ☐ Household Appliances (Brown Goods) in the UK - KEY NOTE, Market Report - May, 1996 (99 pages)

10. ☐ Audio in Europe's Major Markets - EUROMONITOR, Market Research Europe - April, 1996 (18 pages)

Next 10

profound home   Dossier · Portfolio · Alert Manager · Utilities · Client Resources   Help?

Figure 3.17   MAID PROFOUND search results summary

WorldSearch

profound home

Get   ⦿ **Selected Sections** ◯ **Price Selected Sections**

The World Market for Consumer Electronics - Company Profiles and Future Outlook

From **EUROMONITOR/STRATEGY 2000** - January 1997

This document is one of a series of four which form the original full report.

☐❧ *Download the Full REPORT*

☐❧ *Download the Full Document*

☐▤   1 Key Company Profiles

  ☐▤   1.1 Akai

      ☐   Table 1 Akai: Breakdown Of Sales By Business Activity 1996*

      ☐   Table 2 Akai: Turnover And Sales 1995-1996

  ☐▤   1.2 Alpine Electronics

      ☐   Table 3 Alpine: Breakdown Of Sales By Business Activity 1996

      ☐   Table 4 Alpine: Principal Subsidiaries 1996

  ☐▤   1.3 Clarion Co Ltd

      ☐   Table 5 Clarion: Breakdown Of Sales By Business Activity 1996

  ☐▤   1.4 Daewoo Electronics Co Ltd

      ☐   Table 6 Daewoo Electronics Co Ltd: Trading Divisions 1996

      ☐   Table 7 Daewoo Electronics Co Ltd: Breakdown Of Sales By Activity 1994

      ☐   Table 8 Daewoo Electronics Co Ltd: Key Strategic Areas Of Operation 1996

Figure 3.18   MAID PROFOUND selected search results

☐ ▦ Table 9 Daewoo Electronics Co Ltd: Breakdown Of Sales By Geographic Area 1993-1996

☐ ▦ Table 10 Daewoo Electronics Co Ltd: Overseas Video Production Capacity 1996

☐ ▦ Table 11 Daewoo: Key Financial Data 1992-1995

☐ ▦ Table 12 Daewoo: R&D Expenditure 1993-1995

☐ ▦ Table 13 Daewoo Electronics Co Ltd: Production Portfolios By Geographic Area 1996

☐▣ 1.5 Hitachi Ltd

☐ ▦ Table 14 Hitachi Breakdown Of Sales By Business Activity 1993-1996

☐ ▦ Table 15 Hitachi: Principal Major Subsidiaries 1996

☐ ▦ Table 16 Hitachi: Breakdown Of Sales By Production Base 1993-1996

☐ ▦ Table 17 Hitachi: Consumer Product Sales 1993-1996

☐ ▦ Table 18 Hitachi: Key Financial Data 1992-1996

☐ ▦ Table 19 Hitachi: R&D Expenditure 1992-1996

☐▣ 1.6 Kenwood Corp

☐ ▦ Table 20 Kenwood: Breakdown Of Sales By Business Area 1996

☐▣ 1.7 Lg Electronics

☐ ▦ Table 21 Lg: Breakdown Of Sales By Business Activity 1992-1995

☐ ▦ Table 22 Lg: Breakdown Of Sales By Geographic Area 1993-1995

☐ ▦ Table 23 Lg Breakdown Of Overseas Sales By Region 1994-1995

Figure 3.18   cont'd

☐ ▦ Table 80 The World's Top Ten Markets For Consumer
Electronics 2000

☐ ▦ Table 81 Forecast Sales Of Consumer Electronics In The World's
Major Markets 1996-2000

☐▣ 2.5 Growth In The Major Markets

☐ ▦ Table 82 The World's Twenty Fastest Growing Consumer
Electronics Markets 1996-2000

☐ ▦ Table 83 Forecast Growth In The World's Major Consumer
Electronics Markets 1996-2000

☐▣ 2.6 Forecast Breakdown By Audio/Visual

☐ ▦ Table 84 The Forecast Consumer Electronics Market By
Audio/Visual Sales 1996-2000

☐ ▦ Table 85 The Forecast Consumer Electronics Market By
Audio/Visual Sales - Percentage Analysis 1996-2000

☐▣ 2.7 Detailed Sector Breakdown

☐ ▦ Table 86 Forecast Sales Of Consumer Electronics By Sector By
Value 1996-2000

☐ ▦ Table 87 Forecast Sales Of Consumer Electronics By Sector By
Value - Percentage Analysis 1996-2000

☐▣ 2.8 Sector Growth Rates

☐ ▦ Table 88 Growth In The Consumer Electronics Market By Sector
By Value 1996-2000

☐▣ 2.9 Segmentation By Area Of Usage

☐ ▦ Table 89 Forecast Sales Of Consumer Electronics By Area Of
Usage 1996-2000

☐ ▦ Table 90 Forecast Sales Of Consumer Electronics By Area Of
Usage - Percentage Analysis 1996-2000

☐▣ 2.10 Visual Products

Figure 3.18   concluded

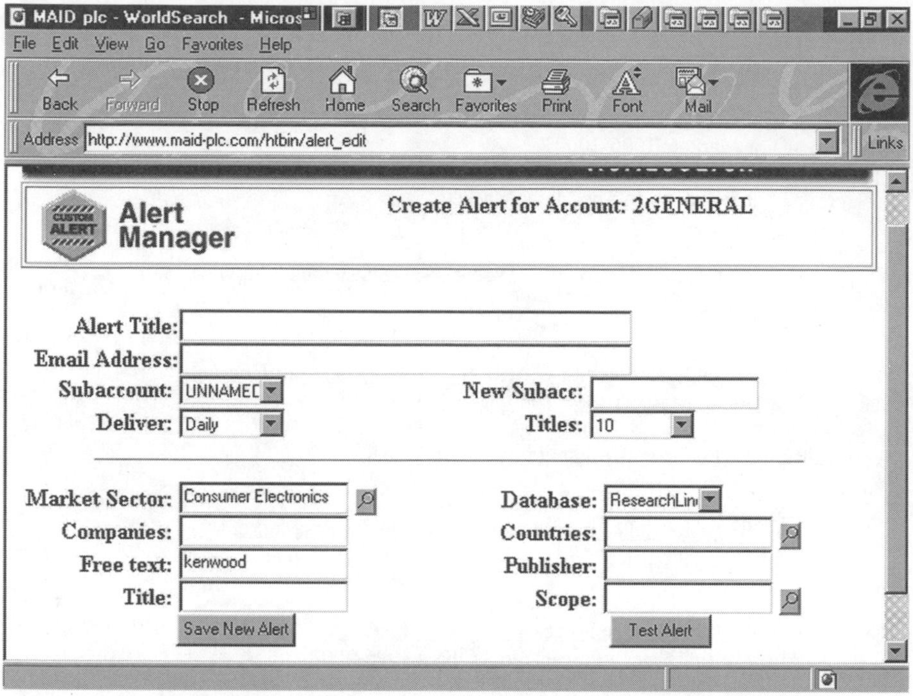

Figure 3.19   MAID PROFOUND Alert Manager

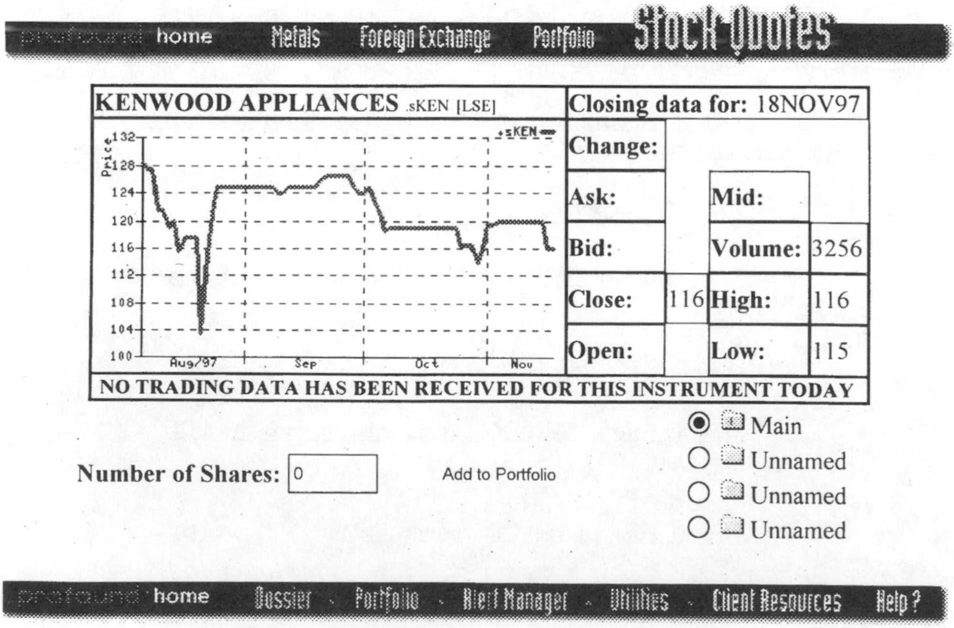

Figure 3.20   MAID PROFOUND stock quotes

Figures 3.21 to 3.23 show the production of mailing labels. The selection of companies is made by specifying the industry from EMMA's activity definitions (Figure 3.21). Data can be sorted as required. The printout shown gives details of the companies' activities in display format 2, listed in company name order. A mailing list is created by sorting the retrieved data into postcode order, and tagging the records relating to the required geographic areas. The mailing list template is selected to fit the paper labels to be used for output. This example prints details for just the tagged companies (Figure 3.22), and it is possible to print out the details for all the companies on the retrieved list. Particularly helpful is the option to create labels for just the companies that have not been marked. This feature allows for rapid negative selection where the majority of the items on the list are required for output. The mailing list produced here is addressed to the sales director for each company. EMMA provides a pick list of common functions, and there is also the option to input other functions in free text. Finally, as an example, the company record for one of the chosen companies is printed out, using the Company Report button (Figure 3.23).

Industry information

This covers reviews, analyses and news on industrial sectors, outlining principal companies, sector activity and developments. Trade, production and import/export statistics are complemented by analytical breakdowns. Industry information can be found in specialized databases – for example, covering all aspects of a commodity or product. It may appear alongside corporate information in news, research and analytical databases.

Industry information can also be derived from financial databases where data on companies can be analysed and aggregated to create sectoral views of the industries within which they operate. This can be particularly helpful for sectors which are not treated independently. As these reports are artificially derived by back construction from corporate data, some care has to be taken. Key players in the market may be omitted, and other companies' positions may be overstated. This may particularly be the case if this method picks up a number of large diversified services companies, whose actual impact on the market in question may be small.

REUTERS BUSINESS BRIEFING and IAC PROMT are popular services, with the latter being particularly strong in trade journal coverage. It has backfiles from 1972, so is invaluable for tracking cyclical developments. There are numerous files giving industry information on LEXIS-NEXIS and The Dialog Corporation. These include IAC TRADE AND INDUSTRY DATABASE, BUSINESS AND INDUSTRY <URL http://www. dialog.com>, and IAC F & S INDEX (Funk and Scott). IAC MAGAZINE DATABASE specializes in popular and consumer magazines, giving good coverage of consumer issues. IAC INDUSTRY EXPRESS specializes in presenting the latest industry news from high-value trade journals and newsletters, updated daily. ABI/INFORM

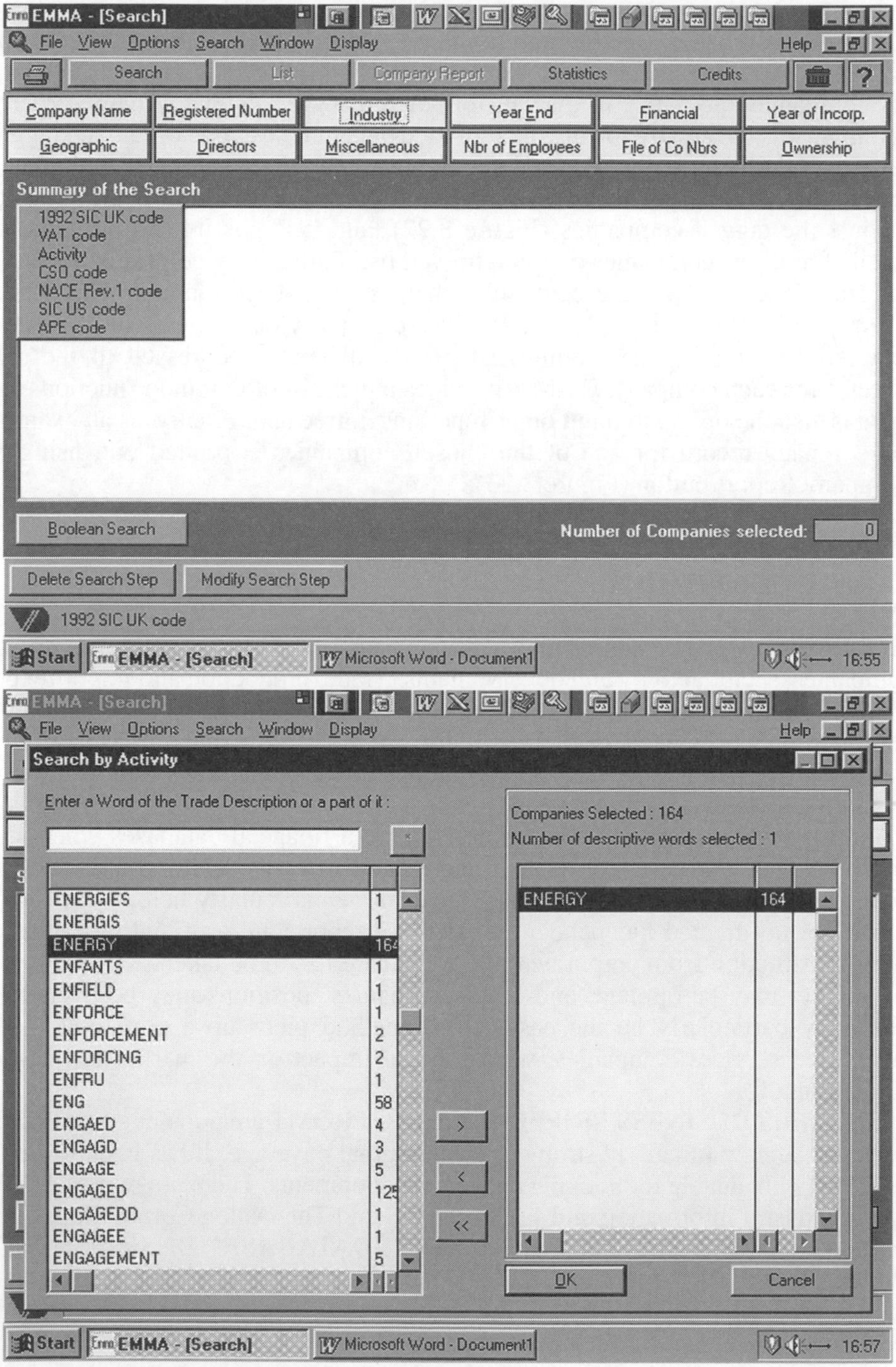

Figure 3.21   EMMA initial search specification

Figure 3.21   concluded

List   Page 1

164 Companies
Sort by Company Name, Ascending

Mark	Company Name	Activity
1	A.E. SILVER LIMITED	The installation of energy monitoring computer systems. Trading as 'Energy Technique Developments'.
2	ABB METERING INTERNATIONAL LIMITED	The sale and distribution of electricity meters, energy monitoring equipment and budget payment sytems for water
3	ABB METERING SYSTEMS LIMITED	The design, manufacture and sale of electricity meters, energy monitoring equipment and budget payment systems
4	ACOUSTIC ENERGY LIMITED	The development, manufacture and marketing of Acoustic Energy loudspeakers.
5	ADVENTEC LIMITED	The manufacture of radiant heating equipment and energy management systems.
6	AEG ANGLO BATTERIES (UK) LIMITED	The research and development of high energy density batteries and the development of peripheral equipment.
7	AHS EMSTAR PLC	A group engaged in contract energy management, comprising the design, installation, finance, operation and
8	AMEC P L C	A group engaged in building, civil, mechanical and electrical engineering, offshore and onshore process and energy
9	AMEC PROCESS AND ENERGY LIMITED	Engineering, construction and fabrication in the energy industries, both offshore and onshore, and environmental
10	ANIXTER INTERNATIONAL LIMITED	A group engaged in the provision of products for voice, data, multimedia and energy networks.
11	AQUA CONTROL SERVICES LIMITED	The manufacture and assembly of boiler house control panels and the installation of energy saving controls.
12	ASSOCIATED CONTRACT ENERGY LIMITED	The provision of contract energy management to manufacturing industries and the NHS, also heating design,
13	ASSOCIATED ENERGY PROJECTS PLC	The provision of waste management and renewable energies, including energy from waste.
14	BASPET ENERGY SERVICES (U.K.) LIMITED	The collection and transmission of information for BB Energy (UK) Ltd and Baspet Energy Services SA of Panama
15	BEAVER VALLEY SYSTEMS LIMITED	Computer consultancy and the distribution, installation and support of control systems for the energy, defence and
16	BERKELEY ENVIRONMENTAL SYSTEMS PLC	The manufacture, installation and maintenance of building and energy management systems.
17	BESTOBELL VALVES LIMITED	The manufacture of stop flow control and relief valves, steam system and energy management controls.
18	BG PUBLIC LIMITED COMPANY	A group engaged in the purchase, transportation and supply of gas, supported by a broad range of services to
19	BP ENERGY LIMITED	The provision of management services, specifically in the production and use of energy.
20	BRECKS HEATING SERVICES LIMITED	Industrial energy engineering and hot dip galvanising.
21	BRITISH NUCLEAR INDUSTRY FORUM	The provision of services for the sound economic development of nuclear energy in the UK and globally.
22	BS & B SAFETY SYSTEMS LIMITED	The manufacture and sale of mechanical pressure relief devices and safety systems for process & energy facilities.
23	G L REALIZATIONS LIMITED	A group engaged in the assembly and supply of high performance fire prevention equipment for petro-chemical,
24	C M L REALIZATIONS LIMITED	The assembly and supply of high performance fire prevention equipment for the petrochemical, energy and building
25	CHEM SYSTEMS (UK) LIMITED	A group engaged in the provision of management consultancy services to the energy, hydrocarbon and chemical
26	CHEM SYSTEMS LIMITED	Consultants, offering comprehensive services to the energy, hydrocarbon and chemical industries.
27	CLUGSTON GROUP LIMITED	A group engaged in civil engineering, building contracting, plant and tool hire, distribution and warehousing, energy
28	CLUGSTON LIMITED	The provision of civil engineering and building contracting services, plant and tool hire, distribution and warehousing
29	COMPACT LIGHTING LIMITED	The manufacture and distribution of low energy lighting equipment.
30	CONNECT LIGHTING SYSTEMS (UK) LIMITED	The manufacture and supply of low energy lighting systems.
31	CORNELIUS PARISH,LIMITED	A group engaged in the research for and the development and management of energy related projects, the
32	CORNWALL COLLEGE MANAGEMENT SERVICES L	The provision of conferencing, training, recruitment and energy services.
33	COUNTRYWIDE SURVEYORS (1994)	The provision of survey & valuation work for residential & commercial properties, surveying, planning &
34	CRE GROUP LIMITED	The provision of consultancy and environmental services to the energy industry world-wide. Commenced trading
35	CROWN INSULATION (BRISTOL) LIMITED	The supply and fitting of insulating material and other energy saving products.
36	CUMBRIA ENERGY LIMITED	The supply of energy, primarily gas.
37	DAIICHI JITSUGYO CO. LIMITED	The wholesale of machinery & equipment for the electronics, engineering, plastics, pharmaceuticals, energy, steel,
38	DELTA TECHNICAL SERVICES LIMITED	The design and manufacture of telemetry and energy saving microelectronic modular systems.
39	DRESSER (HOLDINGS) LIMITED	A group engaged in the design and construction of petrochemical plants, and the provision of products and services
40	DRESSER U.K. LIMITED	A group engaged in the provision of products and services to energy, natural resource and industrial markets.
41	DULAS LTD	Electronic engineering with particular emphasis on the provision of renewable energy services.
42	DURABLE BERKELEY COMPANY LIMITED	The marketing and supply of energy control, security and bomb blast films for glass in industry, commerce and local
43	ECOLITE LIMITED	The manufacture, conversion and installation of low energy lighting systems.
44	EDISON MISSION ENERGY LIMITED	The provision of marketing and development services on behalf of Edison Mission Energy Company.
45	EMERALD FIELD CONTRACTING LIMITED	The operation of the Emerald Field, Midland & Scottish Energy Ltd, on behalf of the field partners and the provision
46	ENERGY AND TECHNICAL SERVICES GROUP PLC	The provision of energy and technical services, including contract energy management, gas and electricity
47	ENERGY COST ADVISORS LIMITED	The provision of advisory services on energy costs in indust industry and commerce.
48	ENERGY INDUSTRIES COUNCIL	A group engd in the promotion and representation of the interests of members in marketing equipment and services

30/10/97

Figure 3.22   **EMMA search results**

Figure 3.22   cont'd

Figure 3.22   concluded

Company Report   Page 1

POWERGEN PLC	Independent company
Trading address :	**Registered Number** : 02366970
53 New Broad Street,	**Phone** : 0171 638 5742
London	**Fax** : 0171 826 2890
Central London	**Postcode** : EC2M 1JJ
	Date of Incorporation : 01/04/89

Activity	: A group engaged in the generation and sale of electricity.
Latest Accounts	: 31/03/96 (Consolidated)
Turnover	: Above £100 million
Pre-tax Profit	: Above £100 million
Net Assets	: Above £100 million
Total Assets	: Above £100 million
Nbr of Employees	: 2,001 to 5,000 employees
Audit Fee	: £ 300,000
Non-audit Fee	: £ 700,000

Figure 3.23   EMMA company record printout

<URL http://www.umi.com> (Abstracted Business Information), available online
since 1971 and also on CD-ROM, has added Internet access. The earlier material
is in bibliographic citation and abstract form. Since 1987 the data include
substantial full-text and image material from business journals. The INDUSTRIES
file on Citicorp's ADP GLOBAL REPORT <URL http://www.eiu.com> pulls
together information on 30 industry groups from STANDARD AND POOR's, The
Dialog Corporation and EXTEL. Responsive Database Services' (RDS)

BUSINESS AND INDUSTRY ON THE WEB <URL http://www.bidb.com> covers US and international information equally, with 60 per cent in full text.

There are numerous specialized industry databases, produced by sectors specialists and trade associations. Databases include COMPUTER NEWS FULL TEXT <URL http://www.dialog.com>; BANKING INFORMATION SOURCE <URL http://www.umi.com>; CONSUMER REPORTS specializing in product testing; IMSWORLD DRUG MARKET – COMPANIES and IMSWORLD DRUG MARKET – COUNTRIES <URL http://www.ims-international.com> specializing in company and sales data and health-care environments; PHIND: PHARMACEUTICAL AND HEALTHCARE INDUSTRY NEWS <URL http://www.pjbpubs.co.uk>; MATERIALS BUSINESS FILE <URL http://www.dialog.com>; PIRA – PACKAGING, PAPER, PRINTING AND PUBLISHING, AND NONWOVENS ABSTRACTS <URL http://www.pira.co.uk>; IAC PHARMA-BIOMED BUSINESS JOURNALS; and several FT REPORTS databases (*Financial Times*) <URL http://www.ft.com> – for example, ENERGY AND ENVIRONMENT and TECHNOLOGY.

Because of the high value of business information, there are two special categories which are of particular value in electronic form – namely, newsletter and broker research databases. Both provide the latest information on prospects for industry sectors and markets. Research reports issued by stockbrokers and investment houses form part of these organizations' investment advisory services to their clients. Their analysis and advice comes from intimate knowledge of the companies and markets covered, and evidences a high degree of personal expertise. The hard-copy reports are designed to support investment advice and circulation is strictly controlled among clients of the investment organization and a few subscribers at high cost. Newsletter services offer similar expert opinion on a highly priced commercial basis. Newsletters are published by prominent sector and financial experts and research bodies.

ICC INTERNATIONAL BUSINESS RESEARCH <URL http://www.icc.co.uk> and INVESTEXT <URL http://www.investext.com> are frequently encountered investment research services. Both offer the text of the reports from the brokers and investment advisers with a delay after publication, when the information has ceased to be market-sensitive. Any investment advice contained in the reports should be ignored, as the reports are essentially written for immediate consumption, and the opinions may have been superseded by the time the reports appear online. By enforcing the delay, this information becomes accessible in the public domain, since the cost of subscribing to the hard-copy recommendations is too high for most businesspeople requiring the information just for research purposes. The strength of the information for this marketplace lies in its analytical content and in the depth of expertise on the organizations and issues covered.

One of the most easily accessible newsletter databases is IAC NEWSLETTER DATABASE which covers well over 100 titles in full text. Many individual newsletters can be found in NEXIS's Markets and Industry Library <URL http://www.lexis-nexis.com>. FINANCE AND BANKING NEWSLETTERS

<URL http://www.dialog.com> covers publications from Euromoney, Securities Data Publishing, Investment Dealers Digest (IDD) and Phillips Business Information. TELECOMMUNICATIONS NEWSLETTERS <URL http://www. dialog.com> is another example of an industry-specific newsletter database. Newsletters often feature alongside other publications in the specialized industry databases. EIU VIEWSWIRE <URL http://www.eiu.com> issues up to 100 daily business briefings on market and business developments.

Business opportunities

This is a growing segment of the market. Business opportunity databases fall into different categories, addressing various commercial needs. There are services covering invitations to tender and project details, with the relevant conditions and contact details. Databases of regulatory changes, timetables and operating environments highlight implications and opportunities for businesses. Also falling into this category are databases covering exhibitions, trade and marketing events, and forthcoming activities of interest to commercial sectors.

The business opportunity databases improve companies' ability to compete. They allow businesspeople to discover openings through research without prior contact or knowledge; and this is especially helpful for SMEs. There is often just a small window of opportunity to tender for a project, respond to a proposal or obtain funding, and regular checks on the opportunities databases allow companies to keep pace. Most of the opportunities databases are aimed specifically at the business end user, and are simple in structure and search capability.

The huge volume of information on LEXIS-NEXIS has been made more accessible by a Windows interface. However, users still need to have a fair command of search strategy because of the costs of using the online help facilities. This service hosts a vast amount of information, but significant investment in training is needed to use it competently. This makes it more popular with regular users than occasional ones. Figure 3.24 uses the LEXIS-NEXIS BBC WORLDWIDE MONITORING FILE. The results are shown in reverse chronological order by date (Figure 3.25), and the user marks one for selection and display (Figure 3.26).

TENDERS ELECTRONIC DAILY and TENDERS ON THE WEB <URL http://www2.echo.lu/echo/databases/ted/en/tedhome.html> list opportunities in the European Community, Community funded-projects worldwide and Japanese tenders. The file corresponds to *Supplement S of the Official Journal of the European Communities*. Worldwide export opportunities for British companies appear on the Department of Trade and Industry's EXPORT INTELLIGENCE SERVICE <URL http://www.ft.com>. INTERNATIONAL BUSINESS OPPORTUNITIES SERVICE <URL http://www.dialog.com>, produced by leading European banks, uses Predicasts coding to identify countries and products.

Trade fair and conference details appear on EVENTLINE <URL http://www.dialog.com> and MEETING AGENDA <brothier@surcouf.scalay.

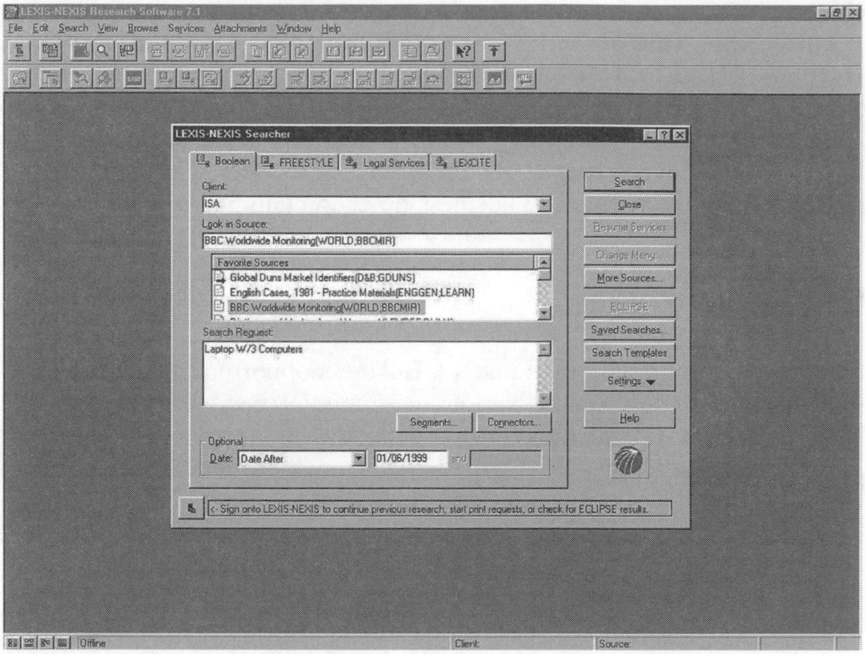

Figure 3.24   LEXIS-NEXIS search

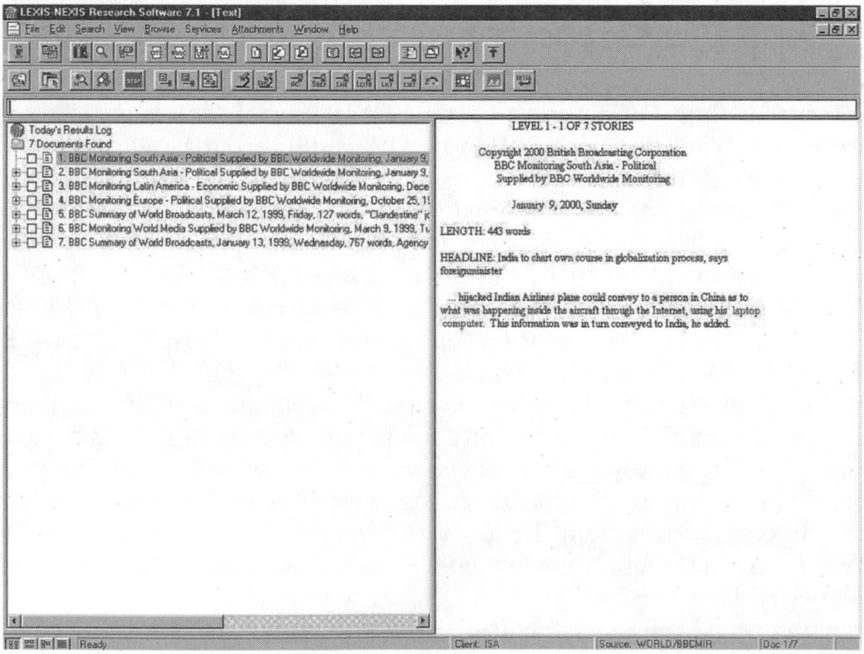

Figure 3.25   LEXIS-NEXIS KWIC view results

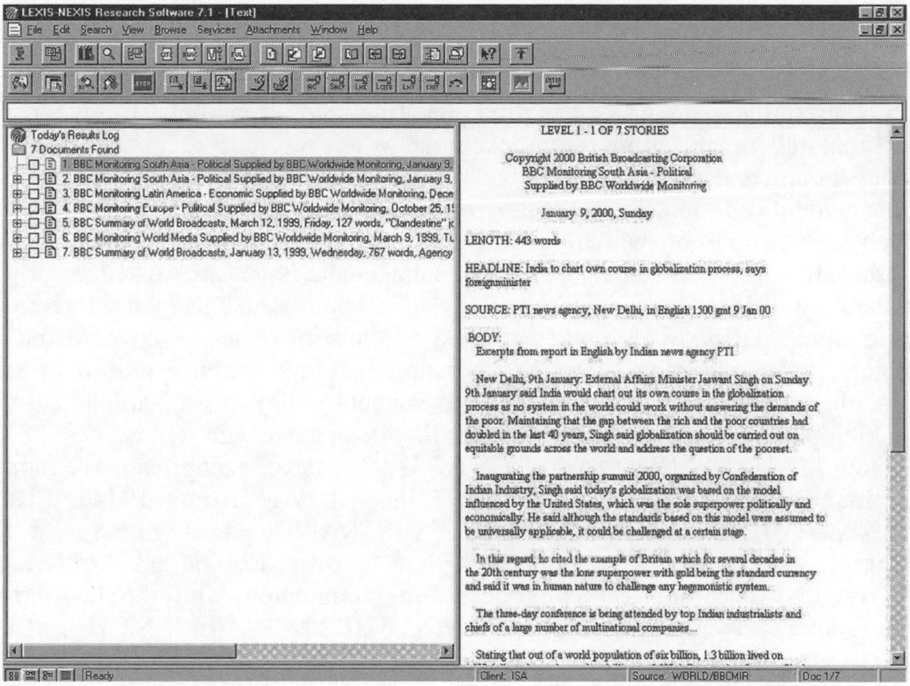

Figure 3.26   LEXIS-NEXIS full view results

cea.fr>. Euromoney's WORLD DATABASE OF BUSINESS INFORMATION SOURCES ON CD-ROM <URL http://www.euromoney.com> includes trade fairs, as well as information on organizations, publications and databases. The British Library Document Supply Centre's (BLDSC) INSIDE CONFERENCES database <URL http://www.dialog.com> covers conference papers which often give valuable insight into future developments. Financial assistance appears on EPRC Ltd's EUROLOC <URL http://www.eprc.strath.ac.uk/EPRC> for Europe (European Policies Research Centre), and AIMS which details funds and assistance for British businesses and matches company profiles with the eligibility requirements. EPRC Ltd also produces STARS covering advisory services and regulatory issues. WORLD BANK BUSINESS OPPORTUNITIES SERVICE <URL http://www.worldbank.org> offers World Bank IBRD funding opportunities. SUMMARY OF PROPOSED PROJECTS <URL http://www. dialog.com> and SCAN-A-BID <URL http://www.dialog.com> are sister databases covering information from the United Nations' hard-copy publication *Development Business* and inviting bids. COMMERCE BUSINESS DAILY <URL http://www.govcon.com> gives information on goods and services required by the US government. ENTREPRENEUR'S GUIDE TO FRANCHISE AND BUSINESS OPPORTUNITIES covers investment opportunities in the USA. BUSINESS INTELLIGENCE PROGRAM RESEARCH CATALOG provides early warnings of trends and changes affecting business.

Management databases

Management databases contain items of management theory and practice. They can be used to explore principles, find operating methods and also to give insight into featured organizations – for example, where a chief executive expounds policy or an operating manager explains how a project has been carried out. Management information features frequently in news, sector and marketing databases, several of which include key management journals among their sources. In the specialized databases the management issues are treated as subjects in their own right. Management activity also features in the focused sector or professional databases. Management and administrative issues covered include strategy and planning, finance, personnel, employment, administration, technology, legislation, corporate and government policy, organizational activity, working patterns and practices, research, theory, analysis and trends.

IAC MANAGEMENT CONTENTS is the most comprehensive source of management information, with files dating from 1974. PIRA's MANAGEMENT AND MARKETING ABSTRACTS <URL http://www.pira. co.uk> has back coverage of similar length, and covers 175 journals, conferences and reports. The database is produced in conjunction with the Institute of Management which also has its own service, THE MANAGEMENT HELPLINE <URL http://www.inst-mgt.org.uk>. RDS's BUSINESS AND MANAGEMENT PRACTICES <URL http://www.rdsinc. com> on DIALOG also has wide coverage, with 250 sources. ANBAR MANAGEMENT INTELLIGENCE <URL http://www.anbar.co.uk/anbar.htm> has a CD-ROM and an Internet service, backed up by a faxed full-text facility by arrangement with the British Library Document Supply Centre. SCIMA <URL http://helecon.hkkk.fi/library/> and HELECON ON CD-ROM include material from the hard-copy *SCIMP European Index of Management Periodicals*, (Selective Cooperative Indexing of Management Periodicals), created from material selected by the European business schools. IAC BUSINESS ARTS (Applied Research, Theory, and Scholarship) <URL http://www.iacnet.com> covers research and academic material in business and management science. ABI/INFORM and ASAP PUBLICATIONS online and on CD-ROM contain much management information. ABI/INFORM's precise subject classifications help specific recall from a database of wide business and geographic coverage. This is particularly useful for management research, as the terminology is often soft and ambiguous: management literature is notorious for eyecatching article titles, especially in combination with a dramatic photograph or picture, but which in isolation give no clue whatsoever to the content.

There are many individual files of management material, such as FORTUNE <URL http://www.pathfinder.com.fortune> and MANAGEMENT TODAY <URL http://www.managementtoday.haynet.com/magazines/mantod/>. The seminal HARVARD BUSINESS REVIEW ONLINE <URL http://www.hbsp.harvard. edu> is the most prominent. This contains full-text articles from 1976, abstracts from 1967 and, in keeping with the publication's prominence in management publishing, also offers 700 classic management articles published between 1925 and 1970, making it the business database with the greatest potential for historical research. Many of the older subjects are still influential today.

There is a substantial crossover of interest in management topics between the UK and the USA, so it is particularly productive, in this category of information, to search both American and European sources. Key trends are picked up in the literature on both sides of the Atlantic, although there are differences in approach which can be identified by restricting the search to sources from one country or the other. Even so, influences continue to appear, and checking more widely helps to illuminate the issue. There is a perceived lag in popular management theory and practice, with the UK slightly behind the USA, although this does not necessarily carry through to the business research community or to ideas emanating from elsewhere in the world. These days, as business gurus confess to mistakes, delayed uptake can be helpful, and seeing the commercial consequences of theories and activities can save money and time.

People

Information on individuals ranges from listings of directorships for executives through to profiles, appointments and reviews of business involvement. Snippets can be obtained from news items which are usually corporate-based. Derived data on individuals are found in company databases where the names of executives feature as post-holders or as participants in significant events.

Executive profiles in business and management journals can be a productive information source, but some care has to be taken as, sometimes, relevant personal details may be relegated to a side-bar in the hard-copy publication, and some databases omit anything which does not appear in the body text. This kind of detail survives better on Internet-based services where the presence of photographs also helps considerably.

The most frequently found information is on corporate executives. One of the largest, most reliable files is TECHNIMETRICS EXECUTIVE DIRECTORY <URL http://www.technimetrics.com> on DIALOG, which covers more than 340 000 senior executives from the largest 57 000 companies worldwide. Information is obtained directly and regularly from the companies, and updated in between by anything relevant that appears in the press. Some 2000 updates are made weekly, demonstrating how quickly directory information becomes out-of-date. The TECHNIMETRICS approach is more consistent and systematic than the executive directory method in which information on individuals and their roles is derived mainly from publicly filed documents. EXECUTIVES on ONESOURCE uses Hemmington Scott information, also found in HEMMINGTON SCOTT PEOPLE DATABASE <URL http://hemscott.co.uk> on FT Profile. DUN & BRADSTREET EXECUTIVES REPORT <URL http://www.dub.com> is an online report service covering personal data and company responsibilities. DUNS ELECTRONIC BUSINESS DIRECTORY (ELECTRONIC YELLOW PAGES)

<URL http://www.dialog.com> can be used to identify US professionals and businesspeople. THE BUSINESS CENSUS <URL http://www.marketinguk.co. uk> from TDS Inform details British business decision-makers. STANDARD AND POOR'S REGISTER OF DIRECTORS AND EXECUTIVES <URL http://www.mcgraw-hill.com> covers the USA.

For a wider coverage of individuals, LEXIS-NEXIS's PEOPLE library <URL http://www.lexis-nexis.com> contains a range of directories and biographical information including GALE BIOGRAPHICS <URL http://www.gale.com> and MARTINDALE-HUBBELL LAW DIRECTORY <URL http://www.martindale. com>, as well as selecting material from the news databases by topic, with EXECHG and OBITS focusing on executive changes and obituaries. MARQUIS WHO'S WHO <URL http://www.bowker-saur.co.uk>, online on DIALOG, for example, and the CD-ROM MARQUIS WHO'S WHO PLUS, provide biographical information on more than 82 000 prominent Americans in business, industry, finance and other walks of life. Sector files such as Gale Research, Inc.'s WHO'S WHO IN TECHNOLOGY <URL http://www.gale.com> focus on specific groups.

A database which is becoming popular with marketing and service companies is PROSPECT LOCATOR <URL http://www.experian.com>, a CD-ROM product containing names and addresses of 20 million UK households, classified by Experian's MOSAIC system, and packaged with mapping software for precise market segmentation.

Personal credit information

Credit information on individuals is available to companies with a legitimate business interest. Following the principles for corporate credit information, it offers basic details such as address, age and status, and also covers court judgements and similar items which impact on an individual's credit standing. Information on an individual can be drawn together with that on other members of the person's household, and even previous occupants of the residence. Credit scoring includes assessments of property value through postcode information. All this information is extremely sensitive and open to misinterpretation, so access is strictly limited – even more so than for the corporate equivalents.

Databases include AUTOMATED CREDIT ENQUIRY (ACE), and EQUIFAX INFOCHECK <URL http://www.infocheck.co uk>, covering 45 million British consumers. US businesses can obtain standard Insta-Vu consumer credit reports through CDX, Credit Data Exchange Inc <URL http://www.creddata.com>.

Information on consumer credit markets and products is found in the industry files. For example, ABI/INFORM and BIS BANKING INFORMATION SOURCES <URL http://www.umi.com> cover publications such as *Credit Card Management* and *Credit Card News*.

Economic information

This covers the main economic statistics, using both official and analytical sources, sometimes reaching back over 40 years, as well as forecasting services. Textual services give commentary and analysis at both macroeconomic and microeconomic levels. There are databases covering economic theory as well as analyses of politics and policy, sourced mainly from economic magazines.

Most economic research needs raw statistics. Information covers econometric and socio-demographic data, trade statistics and financial markets. Economic data such as industrial production, retail sales and gross domestic product are traditionally used by economists, analysts and planners. While these people still form a significant proportion of users, these data, in addition to interest and exchange rates, equity and commodity prices, are used in other areas such as market-trading research, financial derivatives and treasury risk management. Large users purchase magnetic tapes of numeric data for manipulation on their own computers, but there are several online and PC-based services. The prevalence of high-speed modems and Internet access enables some providers to bulk deliver data throughout the day for loading on the client's network servers or intranets. There has been a major move in this market to make data more accessible, and the prime databases now have Windows interfaces. Where once it was necessary to learn specialized commands to identify, search, manipulate, display and output the data, these tasks have now become much easier. Primark Analytic software <URL http://www.primark.com> makes it easy to produce graphs from DATASTREAM/ICV historical time series, for example. Vendors such as Datastream and DRI (Data Resources, Inc.) can offer their data in such a way that dynamic links can be built, enabling the latest version of a graph or series to be obtained simply by opening the file.

This ease of use has opened up the market for both end-user access and for information professionals who have sometimes found the numeric material daunting, particularly if their training has followed text traditions. Providers of time series information are now able to focus more on key elements of data supply – namely, coverage, consistency, quality, continuity of supply and service.

There have long been menu-driven systems, with DATASTREAM/ICV having been the most prominent. Menus force the researcher to answer a series of questions that define the data precisely, and ensure that the correct figures are retrieved. Standard output formats display the data as required, whether as a single figure, a detailed report or graphics. As with many menu services in the text arena, the amount of data searched and retrieved by this method may be restricted and the options for analysis and manipulation do not offer the full capabilities.

For serious research it is important to understand the data. Economic data are published for use by economists and analysts, so the raw figures can be confusing and misleading for the amateur. Data are provided as time series. They are sometimes referred to as historical data to distinguish them from real-time information, but cover current statistics and forecast data as well as back series.

There are many time series published which seem superficially similar, but which contain differences of statistical importance. Figures are reworked on different bases, and adjusted for seasonal fluctuations and other elements. Most data is supplied with notes which help the user understand the figures, and which explain the specialized purpose of the time series and apparent discrepancies. The data may come with analytical interpretations from the providers. Knowledgeable data support from the vendors can be crucial. Good data organization and series documentation distinguish the high-quality data providers in this market.

For major services such as IMF data (International Monetary Fund) <URL http://www.imf.org>, where hard-copy versions are readily available, it is helpful for the novice user to study the figures on paper first and look at the notes, such as in the monthly publication, *IMF International Financial Statistics*. This helps the user understand how the data are presented, what the variations are, and the significance of the differences. Figures often appear in hard copy long before reaching the databases, because of traditions of paper publishing and some legal requirements. As all data are presented with their dates, it is relatively easy to determine that later data than are shown on the database may be available. Checking the status of the time series before searching it, to see the last date posted, can save time and money. Information commonly in the public domain, such as current inflation and employment rates, can be found in news databases, although care has to be taken to match like with like and to ensure that the latest figures are calculated on the same basis as the historical electronic data in question.

All the economic information vendors have invested heavily in making their products accessible. Even when the technology was able to offer little in the way of user-friendly features, they provided detailed practical training, manuals and comprehensive support and consultancy. Now that it is possible to help users with GUIs and more understandable interfaces, the look and feel of these services has been transformed: much of the mystery has disappeared, and the data are accessible to a wider market.

Leading suppliers of numeric economic data include WEFA <URL http://www.wefa.com> (Wharton Economic Forecasting Associates) and DRI/McGraw-Hill <URL http://dri.mcgraw-hill.com>. Major international services are featured by several information vendors, such as the IMF INTERNATIONAL FINANCIAL STATISTICS DATABASE; IMF DIRECTION OF TRADE DATABASE; OECD MAIN ECONOMIC INDICATORS DATABASE <URL http://www.oecd.org>; OECD NATIONAL ACCOUNTS DATABASE and UN DEMOGRAPHICS <URL http://www.unsystem.org>.

Data series are wide-ranging and cover all areas from macroeconomic to the most specific microeconomic series – for example, in CRONOS <URL http://europa.eu.int/en/comm/eurostat/> or the CSO MACRO-ECONOMIC DATA BANK. Forecast data are offered by WEFA's FINANCIAL FORECAST, covering 250 time series, and DRI WORLD FORECAST DATABASE, covering 46 countries. DRI's COUNTRY DATABASES span major industrial nations and emerging markets, containing, for example, 15 000 key economic indicators on the UK in UNITED KINGDOM, and 23 000 American financial, demographic and economic series in US CENTRAL, dating back to the 1940s. US CENTRAL is sourced from government, federal and official bodies, trades associations and industry representatives, financial institutions and business information providers. Time series include indicators such as 'housing starts and completion', 'plant and equipment expenditures', 'exports and imports by end-use on census basis', 'real earnings', 'commercial banking' and 'consumer credit activity', 'federal finance', 'agricultural pricings' and 'consumer confidence'. WEFA FINANCIAL covers 4000 American financial time series.

DRI has introduced Windows software, DRIpro, which is designed to help researchers find the correct data and consult the relevant documentation and update times. The software permits keyword searching of 65 of the most popular time series databases, and connects through DRIgraph Link to proprietary graphing software. Data can also be readily downloaded into spreadsheets and DRI's database manager, TSL (time series library). Demonstrating how fully data can be integrated into a business's requirements, the DRI RISK MANAGEMENT DATA MODULE tracks key time series on a daily basis and delivers them electronically into users' risk management software. Figure 3.27 shows how catalogue searching is used to navigate through the vast databases. Primary keyword searching includes country, concept or industry, and the search can be further narrowed or combined with keywords. The data can be downloaded in various formats, including into spreadsheets such as Excel or Lotus. The amount of data can be controlled by specifying the interval and frequency, and notes and supporting documentation can be retrieved at the same time, if required. The data can also be downloaded directly into a graph (Figure 3.28) which can be embedded into documents.

Economic literature is covered well in textual databases. Key bibliographic services include ECONOMIC LITERATURE INDEX <URL http://www. vanderbilt.edu/aea> and PAIS INTERNATIONAL (Public Affairs Information Service) <URL http://www.dialog.com>. KEESINGS RECORD OF WORLD EVENTS <URL http://www.ft.com> on FT Profile and KEESINGS ON CD-ROM digest economic and political stories. There are also a number of country report products. ABECOR, The Associated Banks of Europe Corporation Economic Reports <URL http://www.lexis-nexis.com>, on LEXIS-NEXIS, provides concise overviews of economic factors in more than 100 countries. COUNTRY REPORT SERVICES <URL http://www.dialog.com>, from Political Risk Service <URL http://www.prsgroup.com>, provides economic performance profiles on a similar number of countries and reports more widely on political and economic conditions. Other databases include QUEST ECONOMICS ON CD-ROM <URL http://www.dialog.com>, Profound's COUNTRY REPORTS <URL http://www.dialog.com>, and COUNTRY REPORTS on Citicorp's ADP GLOBAL REPORT.

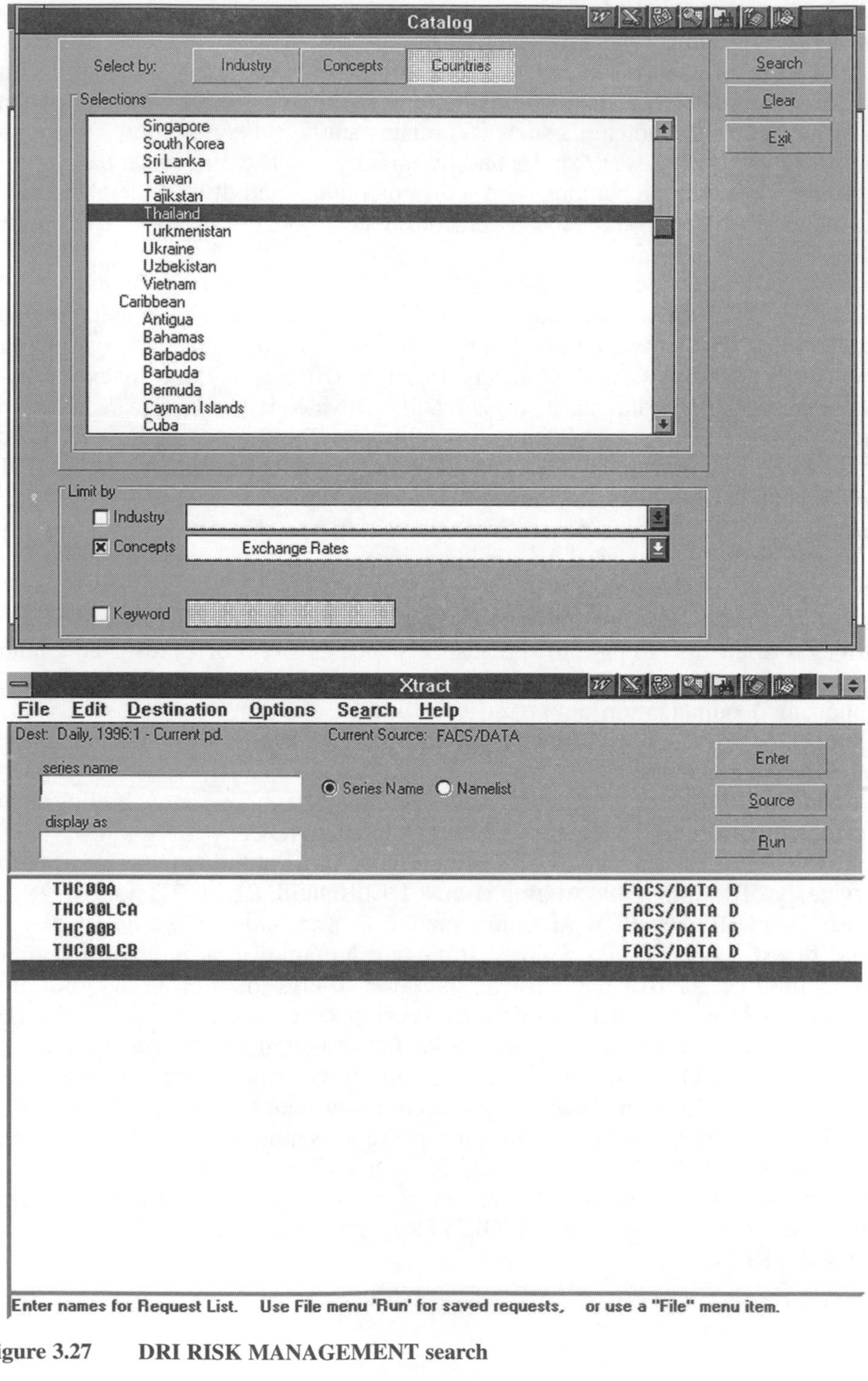

Figure 3.27   DRI RISK MANAGEMENT search

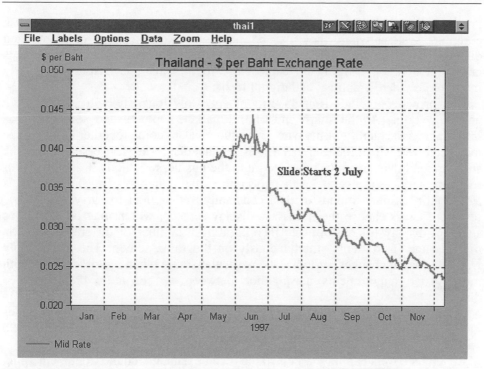

Figure 3.28   DRI RISK MANAGEMENT search results in graphical format

Financial markets

The stock markets, international capital and money markets are covered extensively by means of statistical, real-time, near real-time and news services. The most sophisticated services are heavily customized to meet business requirements. They offer many related types of information on the same screen – for example, news, various market indicators and rates, and graphics. The most time-critical business and market-sensitive services display changing data in coded form, including colour coding. This maximizes the amount of information displayed, yet makes trends and market directions immediately clear. The services which do not operate in real time and the historical services have many more search facilities. Real-time services which offer search capabilities, as well as display, operate more on a drill-down or link basis, where the user indicates the data in question and selects another level of related information, such as history, fundamental data or volume of activity.

Real-time services account for the highest use and value of all online services. Many researchers never see real-time data, concentrating instead on historical research. Real-time users tend to be very specialized and almost invariably end users, for it is important to act immediately on the information supplied to realize its value. Typical users are financial specialists, brokers and traders, research analysts or corporate finance executives. Data feed directly into in-house computer systems where they may be incorporated into a series of customized displays. The data are often a combination of financial and tradable instruments and critical news. Multimedia came early to this market. Displays regularly incorporate video, graphical and digital feeds.

Key providers include Reuters, Bloomberg, Dow Jones Telerate, Bridge Data and NewsEdge. At the sharp end of the market, sophisticated software is as important as the quality of the data. Everything has to come together to maximize the speed with which the user can act on the data displayed. It is essential that the software and data are fully integrated into the business methods. It is normal for real-time services to operate as displays rather than search systems, as the need is to monitor a finite amount of data constantly, rather than to carry out ad hoc research. Users choose the necessary display screens, which may be offered as standard displays or customized, incorporating a number of different views on markets and instruments simultaneously on the same screen. The user simply watches this for changes, or looks at a particular figure when required. Users with more varied requirements may switch between two or more pre-set screen displays.

As an example, BRIDGE EQUITIES <URL http://www.bridge.com> includes global equities, prices, fundamental data and corporate events, covers 280 000 securities and includes 20 years of historical data; BRIDGE CAPITAL MARKETS covers capital markets, fixed income data, G7 country debt, emerging market debt and analytics, money markets and derivatives; BRIDGE COMMODITIES covers energy, soft commodities, grains and metals; and BRIDGE NEWS presents real-time worldwide news. As with many other of the information suppliers, there is an Open Data Gateway allowing the integration of data from other suppliers. Figure 3.29 shows a typical real-time screen using BRIDGE CHANNEL.

For less intensive use, suppliers such as DATASTREAM/ICV present real-time data in a workstation format more familiar in look and feel to information researchers and research analysts who do not work in intensive market and trading environments. Products such as PRIMARK/DOW JONES EQUITIES SERVICE <URL http://www.primark.com> integrate market quotes with fundamental data, breaking news and forecasts, and link with spreadsheet and graphics software. PROFOUND LIVEWIRE <URL http://www.dialog.com> filters 10 000 news stories daily by customized criteria delivering alerts from 20 newswires over a ticker or by flashing an icon. PRESTEL ON-LINE CITIFEED <URL http://www.citifeed.co.uk> on the Internet offers simple Web-based access to the key markets, combined with a share-dealing service. Other news services include REUTERS NEWS EXPLORER <URL http://www.reuters.com>, NEWS ALERT <URL http://www.info.ft.com> through FT DISCOVERY, and BLOOMBERG NEWS <URL http://www.bloomberg.com> on LEXIS-NEXIS.

For historical use FT PRICES ON CD-ROM <URL http://www.ft.com> provides data going back 13 years, such as prices, currencies, interest rates, commodities and managed funds. The DOW JONES ENHANCED CURRENT

Figure 3.29   **BRIDGE CHANNEL real-time screen**

QUOTES <URL http://www.dowjones.com> service provides prices with a 15-minute delay, as a cheaper option than its undelayed DOW JONES REAL-TIME QUOTES. DOW JONES HISTORICAL QUOTES provides the backfiles. One of the most accessible services is DIALOG QUOTES AND TRADING <URL http://www.dialog.com>, from Trade Plus. This provides quotes from the New York stock exchanges, NASDAQ (National Markets System and Over-the-Counter stocks) with a 20-minute delay, and incorporates the facility to buy and sell through participating brokers.

There are several financial instrument and transaction databases, many of which provide fundamental data and enable manipulation and analysis. DATASTREAM/ICV covers equity stocks, global and commodity futures, stock market indices, fixed interest instruments and traded options. TRADELINE AND TRADELINE INTERNATIONAL on DIALOG <URL http://www.dialog.com> accesses IDD Information Services through a gateway, and provides current and historical data on some 175 000 securities, 1600 market indices and exchange rates for 150 currencies. ADP DATA SOURCES <URL http://www.adp.com> covers bonds, deposits, funds, options and stocks in the US market. Citicorp's ADP GLOBAL REPORT's files include FOREIGN EXCHANGE, MONEY MARKETS including real-time rates, and BONDS. Media General Financial

Services has two CD-ROM products, MGFS'S PRICE AND VOLUME DATABASE and MEGAINSIGHT STOCKS AND INDUSTRIES CD-ROM <URL http://www. mgfs.com>. UK services include AFX-UK's COMPANIES and MARKETS files <URL http://www.info.ft. com/afx/> (formerly Extel Examiner).

Mergers and acquisitions information affects so much business activity, from stock market performance to sector activity, market share and competitiveness, that the mergers and acquisitions databases have become very popular. Some concentrate on the financial transaction; others take a market overview. Details of takeovers feature regularly on industry and market research databases. News databases should always be checked to obtain the latest information on merger activity, as situations change rapidly and significantly. The more specialized files tend to concentrate on the whole picture and the end result rather than interim stages, and their records take time to be updated.

Services include ACQUISITIONS MONTHLY INTERNATIONAL <URL http://www.onesource.com>, SDC WORLDWIDE MERGERS AND ACQUISITIONS <URL http://www.securitiesdata.com> (Securities Data Company) and FT MERGERS AND ACQUISITIONS INTERNATIONAL <URL http://www.ft.com>, which combine textual information and commentary with the financial data. LEXIS-NEXIS's MERGERS AND ACQUISITIONS library <URL http://www.lexis-nexis.com> pulls together mergers publications such as IAC MERGERS AND ACQUISITIONS, IDD M & A REPORTS <URL http://www. wsdinc.com>, MERGERS AND ACQUISITIONS and M & A EUROPE, with relevant legislative and regulatory files. Detailed information about transactions appears in ONESOURCE CD/CORPORATE: EUROPEAN MERGERS AND ACQUISITIONS and CD/CORPORATE: US MERGERS AND ACQUISITIONS <URL http://www.onesource.com>, and AMDATA <URL http://www. acquisitions-monthly.co.uk>.

Specialized share services include MOODY'S DIVIDEND ACHIEVERS ON-LINE SERVICE <URL http://www.moodys.com>, reviewing the best dividend performers. TECHNIMETRICS SHARE WORLD <URL http://www. technimetrics.com>, ICC SHAREWATCH <URL http://www.icc.co.uk> and JORDANS SHAREHOLDER SERVICE <URL http://www.jordans.co.uk> provide details of shareholdings, and can be used for tracking changes as well as straightforward enquiries. Jordans also identifies the underlying holders for nominee accounts.

Among the more specialized services for corporate finance work are BONDSPEC, EXBOND <URL http://www.info.ft.com>, CAPITAL DATA BONDWARE <URL http://www.capitaldata.com>, CAPITAL DATA LOANWARE <URL http://www.capitaldata.com> and IDD LOANBASE <URL http://www.wsdinc.com>, which provide core information on capital markets instruments and syndicated loans. These services tend to be used by professionals and research analysts, as a specialized understanding of the different aspects of the data is important for accurate manipulation. Fundamental data can be identified readily. Simpler in approach is PERFECT INFORMATION's ISMA bond service

<URL http://www.perfectinfo.co.uk> which covers 11 000 international bond prospectuses.

Single source information

Although there are many advantages to separating the different types of business information by category, this does not match the way that business users think. People want to know all manner of aspects about a particular issue and are not interested in financial figures, market studies or personnel information in isolation. They want to know, for example, about a company, its performance, its objectives, its market position, its products, its share price, its directors and organizational structure.

Few conventional online databases or CD-ROMs cover all of this. They segment the information according to the sources they obtain it from, and the software. So, for example, a researcher has to look in one database for financial figures, in another for market commentary, in a third for product activity, a fourth for director details and so on. Certainly for online users it has been hard for some categories of information to do much else. The software has not been able to support the different requirements of textual and numeric information, for example. A few CD-ROM products have gone some way to draw the material together, but even here it has often meant switching from one area of the data set into another, so that different software comes into play. There is a trend towards improving the integration of data, but few suppliers have managed it effectively over large volumes of data.

Contrast the separatist, specialized approach with some of the information now going up on the Internet, where companies set up their own sites, giving a detailed view of all their activity in one place. For the purposes of comparison with traditional services, one cannot even be overly concerned here by the obvious issue of bias. Many databases offering financial and product information reflect the same bias in that they take their data directly from the originating company's annual report or press releases. Figure 3.30 shows Citicorp's home page <URL http://www.citibank.com> on the Internet. There are direct links on this page to information on PC banking, credit cards, investment customers, Citibank services and CITIBANK CHANNEL. Using the search facility, financial reports are selected from the list of information categories on the site. Nine items are retrieved. The link to official filings is selected, and the available reports are listed out. These can be downloaded using the hypertext links.

There are a number of Web sites that link to these corporate home pages without creating much database structure at all. They also connect to other sites which give supplementary useful information – for example, trade information and academic research.

No matter what the pedigree of the conventional services, the Internet provision actually mirrors better the way people work. This trend is being reinforced by the new intranet services which many businesses are setting up. One of the first

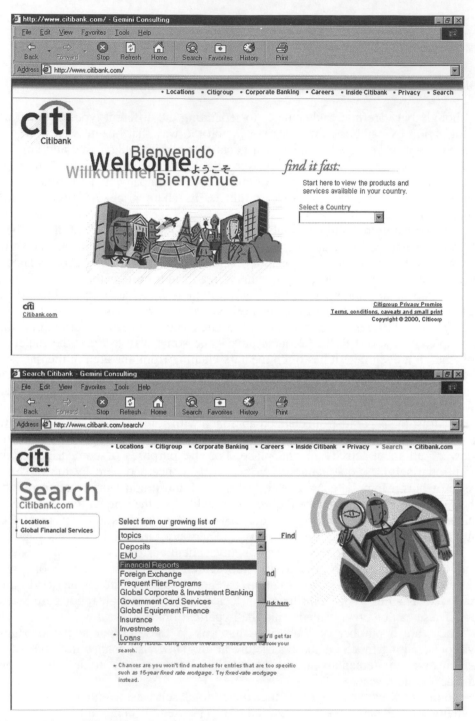

Figure 3.30   Citicorp homepage screens

Figure 3.30 concluded

activities is to offer interface pages linking to key external Internet sites. Of course, intranets can link to external online research or CD-ROM products too, and this facility is an obvious route for these vendors. Nonetheless, linking will fail if the vendor software does not have a familiar look and feel, however good the information content is.

Evolving products

The history of business information has seen the number of products grow from just a few principal services to a huge variety. There has been some rationalization. Some services have merged. Some independent offerings have transferred on to hosts, which either offer a variety of services and hence have widespread appeal, or which specialize in a particular marketplace, so that the product gains penetration by being offered alongside other useful products for that business sector. This much was expected.

However, the forecast fall-out from the market has not happened as anticipated. People thought that major suppliers would win the day, and there would be a small number of superhosts, with a huge client base, offering a substantial number of databases. Small operations and lower-quality services would drop out, as purchasers chose the hosts for convenience and common search strategies, and made quality judgements of one service over another. Instead, it looks now as though the market is taking another direction. Small players are achieving good market penetration with CD-ROM and Internet products. The change from the expected direction is partly because vendors have never quite been able to meet the real needs of the broad market of those businesspeople whom they wanted to reach in order to build their market share. Their products have always required effort to use, so they have remained in the province of professional information researchers and enthusiastic end users prepared to meet them halfway. They have found it hard to produce services that integrate with the user's working environment.

The large hosts have not scooped the market. Indeed, some of those hosts who might most have been expected to do so have found it hard to retain commercial stability. The online market has been full of mergers, takeovers and company failures – much as predicted. Dealing with these internal organizational issues has clearly prevented some vendors from taking advantage of the emerging requirements of the marketplace, and distinctly limited their abilities to respond. The key names among business information vendors today are not always those one might expect, and the process is far from over.

Throughout the history of online information some good products have been lost because of corporate shake-ups and commercial failures. This could happen again, unless some suppliers can align their corporate direction more closely with market demand. For the business market there may be some encouragement, as MAID's crossover with Knight-Ridder in The Dialog Corporation has been in the business field rather than with Knight-Ridder's other databases – for example, in science and technology. At the time of writing (May 2000), it looks as if the information services will survive being sold to The Thompson Corporation.

What will happen to individual services and how they are going to be packaged remains to be seen. Success in these areas will be crucial for the services to retain their market share.

Internet developments

Entirely new services are entering the marketplace. Existing independent services are repositioning. Instead of leading the business end user to the online market, suppliers are going to where the business market actually is. For many businesspeople, business information is on the Internet. It has been the take-up of Internet technology by commercial operators which has created the surge of interest which it now enjoys. Without business demand, services on the Internet would still mainly orientate towards the government and educational issues that built the infrastructure up in the first place.

Although decried for inefficiency, the Internet is something which businesses need. It gives them a marketplace for their products and services. By outlining their wares and prowess in this marketplace they offer information which other businesses can use – and hence its attraction for business researchers. The Internet offers the ideal combination of local information and a global perspective. Businesses need either or both.

Basic access to the Internet is cheap and simple. It offers great potential for information retrieval, advertising, electronic commerce and communication of all kinds. Hence people connect to it. Because the software is universal, cheap, easily kept up-to-date, simple to use and appealing, it creates few barriers for the business user. As there is so much on offer, and exploration is encouraged and facilitated, the user quickly grows confident, interested and even intrepid.

This is a completely different approach from the didactic instruction of the traditional online services, where research had to be conducted on the supplier's terms. Strangely, this success has almost arrived by accident. Vendors have seized on the popularity of the Internet to offer their services in this manner; it has not been a case of a deliberate outside strategy aimed at encouraging business users to use a new delivery mechanism. No single organization is masterminding the Internet, or benefiting wholly from its development and direction; the success is created from the market. Business users like the idea, so access the service. Vendors see the potential, offer products and businesspeople use them. Such simple cause and effect has the disadvantage that it could head off in another direction if other factors come into play, but the current momentum is enough to keep the market moving this way for some time to come, even if other opportunities open up.

The significance for the business information community is substantial – perhaps more than for most other sectors. If mainstream businesspeople use the Internet, that is where they want to conduct their research. Products offered over the Internet have an easy route to their potential market. There is constant development in this market segment at present. New and repackaged services appear all the time. What is less clear is how Internet technology affects traditional online and CD-ROM services without an Internet presence. Many vendors hope that the growing computer habit will encourage businesspeople who become regular computer users to become discerning about where they go to obtain their electronic information. The newly emerging telephony Web access may cream off rapid data access and alerts, but is unlikely to affect detailed research for some time yet.

If there is a direct link to a database from an on-screen icon, the end user will select that as the route to conduct his or her research. That route can be direct to the traditional data server. As the user is now comfortable with operating computers, the old barriers are diminished, and a new customer is drawn in. If this scenario holds, then there is ample room in the market for conventional online access and CD-ROM databases. All that remains is for the vendors to facilitate such matters as pricing and licensing, and to make their front ends easy to use and maintain. Regrettably, these are not easy matters for some suppliers, even if they have the will to facilitate change. In the light of the increasing competition, they will eventually have to resolve these complexities.

Integrated services

A significant obstacle is the overriding issue of integration. Companies are encouraging their staff to communicate by computer, initially through e-mail but also through discussion groups. This leads them again into Internet technology and grouped working and away from single user access and making external enquiries outside the group working environment. It is the opposite approach to the one offered by vendors which restrict information transfer to single user access, storage and printing. The age of walk-up terminals, dedicated to online research, is almost over. The products which are required are those which can easily be accessed, through one familiar interface, and from which information can easily be extracted and used. This means straightforward printing and downloading.

The retrieval method also has to pass the fitness-for-purpose test. If the information cannot be stored for a required period or integrated with other software, because of licensing restrictions, it is unsuited to the businessperson's requirements. Therefore there is no sale. Most business information research has a direct purpose. The online investigation aims to answer a problem for the business worker. The results of the enquiry may need to be incorporated into a report to substantiate the decisions taken as a consequence of the research. Information which is not transferable in this way is useless.

One consequence of the Year 2000 is that some information providers decided to withdraw products which could not be converted economically, or which were nearing the end of their natural life. Reuters, for example, dropped 100 products specifically because of the date issue. Some clear-out is helpful, in that vendors can put effort into new services instead of trying to maintain old ones. Yet it is likely that some people's favourites have been lost, particularly the small, highly specialized services.

It is the idea of integration which opened up the end-user market in the first place. End users can make judgements interactively, in the light of information that they receive online, and can download significant items for further manipulation. Those online suppliers which facilitate this have found that their services have become embedded into the end user's working life and that their invoices are willingly paid. Information from the Internet usually has the same portability. The simple fact is that if it is easier, as it often is, to obtain information from the Internet and integrate it with the internal work product, this is what a pressurized businessperson will do, regardless of other options.

The Internet information navigator sites are technically easy for suppliers to set up. A few pages of hyperlinks create access to a wide range of services, which are maintained by people other than the supplier of the site that links to them. There may be no commercial arrangement between the ultimate information provider and the organization creating the pages that hold the links. All that the navigation providers have to do is ensure that the links remain valid and keep working – although in the fluctuating environment of the World Wide Web this can be a major task in itself. More in-depth products should follow once vendors establish their rights to operate in this way.

The more browser, search and communications technology improves, as it constantly does, the more attractive and useful Internet research becomes. The products will sell because Internet-based providers have such a technical marketing advantage in that as soon as a potential customer learns of the product, they can find the site on the Internet. There is no need to obtain and load special software or be trained in its use. If the demonstration on the site appeals, the user can register for a trial period, or subscribe there and then. Facilitating the investigation and implementation virtually ensures the purchase, provided that the product is right. The competition is simply out of the frame.

New search methods

Key to the integration process is the principle of hyperlinking. Following selected hypertext links emulates the way businesses operate. People draw together material from a variety of sources, and compile it into a report or recommendation. This feels more natural than structured research, which mimics academic disciplines rather than business practice. Hyperlinking is found everywhere on the Internet, and on some CD-ROM and disc-based database products. Although some online databases can produce a similar effect, the principle is rarely found. Online databases work more through indexing and free-text retrieval. These are older technologies, and even with the growing sophistication of search tools, such as using fuzzy logic and relevance ranking (also, of course, used by Internet, CD-ROM and database products), they have never caught the business imagination in the same way that hyperlinking does.

This is ironic in many respects. To construct effective hypertext links, someone (or a computer) has to make a significant connection between related material. In other words, the path has already been trodden, or the association of ideas follows a conventional thought pattern. For originality of thought, old-fashioned indexing and free-text retrieval can produce more surprising results which may create a business breakthrough. Perhaps this is why online products have been popular for so long with pure research workers. For businesses that emphasize communication more than originality, hyperlinking holds a greater appeal. Following a related set of ideas creates the impression of saving time. This is a large part of the appeal of intranets, and it supports the movement towards ever more integration of services into normal business processes.

Market predictions

So, the market for electronic business information is in turmoil – more so than ever before. It is difficult to predict which suppliers will remain in the race or what new products will look like. New interfaces are being offered all the time, although some are inferior to the front ends that they supersede. Because of the short time to market for Internet-based services, no one can be sure what new products are coming through, and which traditional vendors will move across with supplementary or replacement services.

As business users take to the Internet, it remains unclear how much crossover there will be to the more traditional services. This will have a great effect on future market development. Now that intranets hold sway, products must link to these. How far they can then afford to differ in terms of visuals and presentation from standard Internet wares – particularly the highly professional portals – will depend on how valuable they actually are to a commercial concern.

These issues do not create an ideal scenario for the business researcher. As change takes place, familiarity will be an early victim, and some favourite products may not stay the pace. Success is not going to be wholly dependent on quality issues. Rather it will be on matching the developing habits of the end-user market. This chapter has evaluated some of the current products, as they stand today. An enormous range of electronic business information has existed for a long time and is continually evolving, so any exposition has had to be a sampling rather than comprehensive. However – other commercial issues aside – it is easier for services to continue with an existing product and market than to source and create new products from scratch. This means that the core of the databases mentioned here can be expected to continue in some form, although many will change in presentation, and products may be integrated with other services and marketed in a completely different manner. Users should continue to look for the best services for their purposes in terms of data quality, convenience of use and cost, whatever else may also be found.

Further reading

Alampi, M. (ed.), *Gale's Directory of Databases*, 2 vols, Farmington Hills, MI: Gale Research.

Armstrong, C.J. (ed.) (1995), *World Databases in Management*, World Database Series, East Grinstead: Bowker-Saur.

Armstrong, C.J. and Fenton, R.R. (eds) (1996), *World Databases in Company Information*, World Databases Series, East Grinstead: Bowker-Saur.

Buecker, G. (ed.) (1997), *The Multimedia and CD-ROM Directory*, (17th edn), 2 vols, London: TFPL Multimedia Ltd.

Engholm, C. and Grimes, S. (1997), *The Prentice-Hall Directory of Online Business Information*, London: Prentice-Hall.

Online/CD-ROM business information, (monthly), East Grinstead: Headland Business Information.

Webber, S., *Business Sources on the Net*. Available at <URL http://www.dis.Strath.ac.uk/business/index.html>.

What's New in Business Information, (20 per year), East Grinstead: Headland Business Information.

Chapter 4

News and current affairs

Peter Chapman

Introduction

News is all-pervasive, and the appetite for it as a consumer or business product seems to have no limits. In 2000 the death of the printed newspaper is no longer confidently predicted in the UK despite the growth of non-printed, continuously available channels of news through broadcasting, the Internet and real-time online services. It seems as if news is a product to which each medium of transmission brings its own enhancements.

This chapter examines how the computer can keep track of news, both breaking and as a record of events, through traditional online services, CD-ROMs and the Internet.

Definitions

For the purposes of this chapter, news is defined as 'the recording of events in text and still picture formats as, or soon after, these events occur' and current affairs as 'the analysis of events that have taken place or may be about to take place'. As news is all-pervasive, the coverage of sources of news will not be confined by anything other than the availability of these sources in electronic form, accessible by computer.

Background

The recording of events in text and picture formats dates back to ancient times when accounts of military victories and political intrigues were written by commentators and copied by scribes. The advent of printing speeded up the process of creating and distributing such records, especially with the evolution of newspapers and magazines. The development of film and then broadcasting introduced immediacy of record, instant access and the ability to replay the record (although accessing text or still picture versions of the broadcast record could be difficult, if not impossible).

Electronic records can be traced to the decision by newspapers and magazine publishers to adopt computer typesetting. Having created computer-generated text (and subsequently pictures), publishers realized that this resource opened the door to the re-use of material. Allied to the development of effective and efficient full-text retrieval search engines and reliable modems and desktop computers, the first such re-use was the republication of the newspaper or magazine as an online searchable archive.

CD-ROMs proved to be another medium that allowed for re-use of already published material. As a write-once, large-volume storage medium that was easy to distribute, it was ideal for full-text newspaper archives – the content of which did not change after publication in the printed form.

However, the development of the Internet has led not only to the republication of material originally in printed form, but also to the simultaneous and exclusive electronic publication of news alongside the printed format.

Considerations

Before using the computer to find news and current affairs, the following considerations should be taken into account.

- Does the enquirer require breaking news, continuing news stories, news about discrete events, or news during a definable period of time?
- What quantity of coverage does the enquirer require: headlines with dates and sources, abstracts of the stories, the full text alone, or the full text with pictorial coverage?
- What style of writing does the enquirer require: tabloid or broadsheet, reporting of the facts or analytical articles?
- Does the coverage need to be local to the news event, or from a national or international perspective?
- How quickly does the enquirer require the information: immediately, can wait for its arrival on the medium being used by your computer, or can wait for delivery from a non-computer source?
- Does the enquirer need to be sure of the source of the information? Was the original format a printed newspaper or a broadcast programme? If not, does the enquirer need to verify the reliability of the source of the electronic information?
- Does the enquirer need to be able to view the source in its original format?
- Does the enquirer need a variety of sources for the news coverage or will one source do?

- How much is the enquirer prepared to spend in both direct costs and in time to complete the searches?
- Does the enquirer have the time or skill to learn new search commands?

Electronic sources

Traditional online

Traditional online sources are defined here as the large databases of information which are accessed by contacting dedicated computers and which require a log-on and password routine and, probably, a knowledge of the set of search commands specific to the particular databases to be accessed. The strengths of such sources are:

- their validity – the publications covered are respected and trusted
- their coverage – the editorial content of most publications is available in full
- archival sources – many publications have searchable runs covering several years
- breadth of coverage – one search covers many publications
- easy access – the sources are available at defined times and it is rare not to get on to the host computers during these times; speed of download is usually constant
- flexible search commands – many databases have a range of commands which cover different types of user and different search requirements.

Their weaknesses are:

- cost – both in displaying the material in full text and in the set-up charges that can be incurred
- gaps in coverage – early editions of each day's publication, freelance material, and certain editorial sections are often missing; such gaps may not be obvious initially
- timeliness – there can be a gap between publication in print and publication on the database host
- search commands – these are often not intuitive
- lack of pictorial material.

In the UK two longstanding suppliers of news information in traditional online format are FT PROFILE and LEXIS-NEXIS. However, the several other suppliers of online database services also operating in the UK marketplace should not be overlooked. The most aggressive of these in terms of pricing structure, at the time of writing, is the PROFOUND product of The Dialog Corporation. This British database is aimed squarely at end users in the business and specialist professions marketplace. Its strengths are easy-to-use front ends, search support through automatic thesaurus enhancements of search terms, alerting services based on predefined searches, and a wide range of business information sources of which newspapers are a major component.

Against these strengths should be placed the limited number of years covered by the sources carried, the lack of complete coverage in many of the sources carried (as it is business-focused rather than a generalist service) and the simplified search commands which lack the range of many other online services, including its big cousin, DIALOG, which offers all the features of a traditional online database for the newspaper files that it carries. These files cover the world although the core coverage is of the regional and local press in the USA.

Two other US online database hosts carry significant newspaper content:

- DOW JONES NEWS/RETRIEVAL is based around the *Wall Street Journal* and is aimed at the business community which needs current and archival news feeds from the key American financial centres.
- UMI's PROQUEST DIRECT has a wider range of American sources and, at the time of writing, is trying to capture British and European sources with which to expand its coverage. However, it remains a minor player within the UK marketplace for news information.

For the purposes of this chapter, FT PROFILE and LEXIS-NEXIS will be used.

CD-ROM

Large archive databases of print publications were an obvious candidate for publication on CD-ROM as this medium became relatively easy and inexpensive to produce. Most major UK print newspapers boast archive databases on CD-ROM.

The strengths of this medium are:

- one-off cost
- ease of use – search commands can be mastered at the user's leisure
- availability of pictures
- validity of sources
- no online connection required unless the CD-ROM offers a facility to search current material in addition to the material on the disc.

Its weaknesses are:

- a relatively large one-off cost
- usually a single source only per CD-ROM
- differing interfaces between CD-ROMs
- often only available for PCs running Windows
- time lag before CD-ROM version becomes available
- usually covers a discreet period of time and does not cumulate on one disc.

For the purposes of this chapter, CD-ROMs published by Chadwyck-Healey and Televisual Data will be used.

The Internet

Many news publishers have discovered the possibilities which the Internet offers not only to republish archive news information but also to publish current news information, some of which may be exclusive to the electronic medium.

Its strengths are:

- the low cost of both accessing the Internet and accessing most news-related sites
- a standard search interface – the Web browser – and the consequent initial ease of using sites from any news publisher
- the wide range of sources from around the world
- availability on the Internet of publishers whose news sources are not published in other electronic formats – this is especially true of local newspapers within the UK and USA
- material from the printed sources can be enhanced by additional content, links to related sources or through differing styles to suit differing users
- pictures may be available to illustrate the text, and some publishers put up searchable images of the original printed pages
- its rapid rate of development – new sources are constantly being made available
- it is often the best text source for breaking news
- some newspapers may put advertising and 'personals' on the Web, a service not found on other electronic media
- some broadcasters place video and sound archives of their coverage of major news events on their text-based sites.

Its weaknesses are:

- lack of depth – archive runs may not exist, not all the editorial material is on the Web, and content may not stay on for long
- reliability of the information can be called into question – the source of the information may not be clear
- major sources of news are still missing or may be hidden in subscription packages
- access can be difficult at peak times of use, and download times slow
- cannot cross-search many specified sources at one time if these sources are archive databases, as is possible through traditional online databases.

Analysing the available sources

There are three ways of approaching this analysis:

1. taking some sample searches on news and current affairs to see how the differing types of electronic sources would answer them
2. looking at each type of source and analysing how searches are handled

3. looking at the printed newspaper or at the broadcast programme to see how it is handled electronically.

For the purposes of this chapter, the individual components of each type of source will be analysed and sample searches used to highlight the strengths and weaknesses of the various approaches used by each component within the source group.

Traditional online sources

FT PROFILE

For seekers after news and current affairs information in the UK, FT PROFILE is a well-used and trusted online service. It emerged from an early-1980s full-text system called WORLD REPORTER, and has grown steadily since, both in terms of publications available and in the number of interfaces available to the service.
Online access to FT PROFILE services has been provided in three ways:

● through the original command-driven interface, called info, which is no longer available (see Figure 4.1)

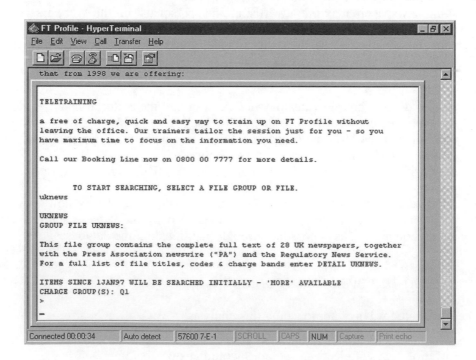

Figure 4.1   UKNEWS: command-driven interface

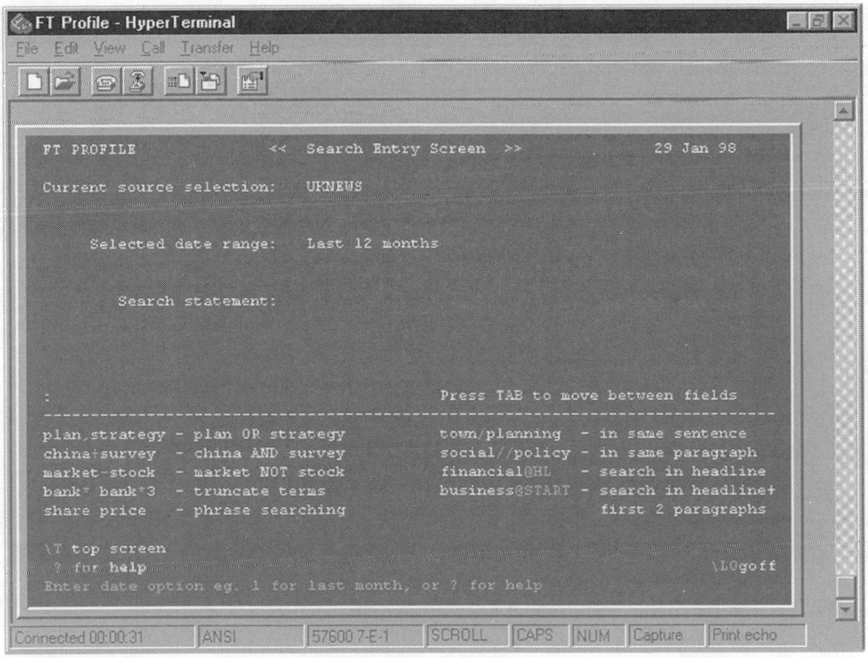

Figure 4.2   FT Profile Infoplus menu-driven interface

● through a menu-driven interface (Infoplus offering on-screen search hints and some guidance on command strategy (see Figure 4.2)
● through a Windows interface (FT Discovery is shown in Figure 4.3).

Most major UK national newspapers, plus several of the UK regional papers, are available in full text, and a wider range of UK newspapers is available in abstract form through the MCCARTHY ONLINE file within the FT PROFILE service. Coverage of international newspapers tends to be focused on those with significant business coverage of their countries.

FT PROFILE is strong on archive files, but does offer a semi-breaking news service through the PA news file. Most files are updated regularly and quickly. It can be a costly service to use full text (charging at several pence per display line) but it is a cost-effective index service for those organizations that can keep significant back runs of the newspapers which it covers. Costs for individual searchers can be identified before a search session begins. As the service relies on the publishers' submitting an electronic file, keyword indexing is patchy, idiosyncratic and not consistent across the files available. The command-driven interface uses a set of basic commands that allow some flexibility and precision in how a search is constructed. Cross-file searching is possible through defined groups or by linking file names. Within the UK, it is the most accessible source for the daily newspaper, the *Financial Times*.

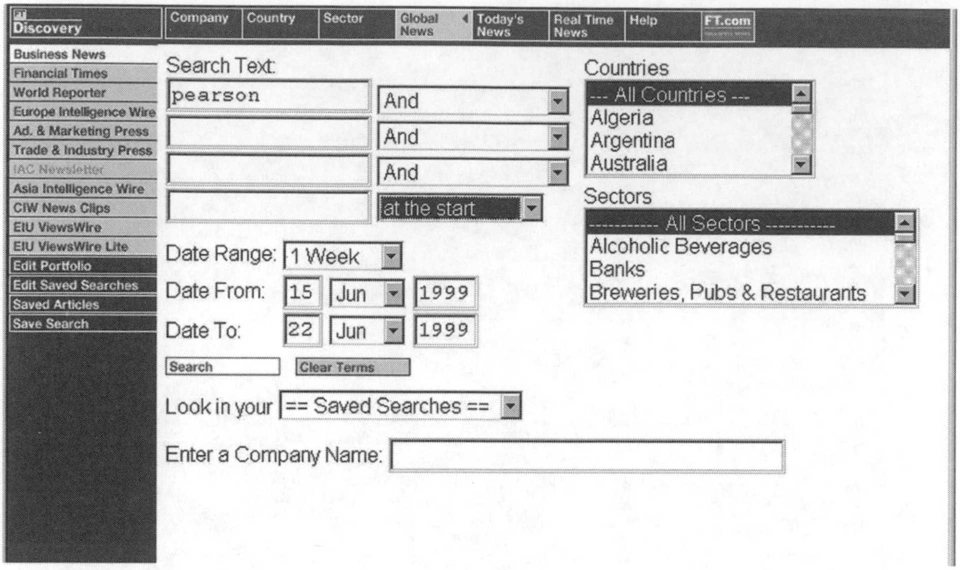

Figure 4.3   FT Discovery Windows-based interface

Internet access, FT PROFILEWEB, was first seen in December 1999, using the existing Discovery interface to link to the entire FT database. Functionality is expected to be increased as the product is taken up by users.

LEXIS-NEXIS

In the past, the NEXIS half of LEXIS-NEXIS might have been considered the US equivalent of FT PROFILE. However, the service has grown at a much more rapid rate than FT PROFILE and now is a truly worldwide source of full-text newspapers and magazines (not to mention broadcast programmes). It is still predominantly American but it rivals FT PROFILE in providing European and world sources. Indeed, by the end of 1998, LEXIS-NEXIS was able to boast an impressive stable of UK regional newspapers. It was announced at the start of 2000 that LEXIS-NEXIS had bought FT Profile. Since the acquisition there has been no change in the way that the two systems operate but it would be logical to expect them to merge – perhaps through a common interface. LEXIS-NEXIS used to suffer from a poor command-driven interface that required specific local software on the user's PC. Although the software is still specific to LEXIS-NEXIS, the interface on Windows is much easier to use, and an end-user interface, Freestyle, that offers slightly more on-screen help to the user has been introduced (see Figures 4.4 and 4.5).

LEXIS-NEXIS has a different charging structure to FT PROFILE, being based on a per article charge. This can be easier to control than the FT PROFILE system of per-line charging.

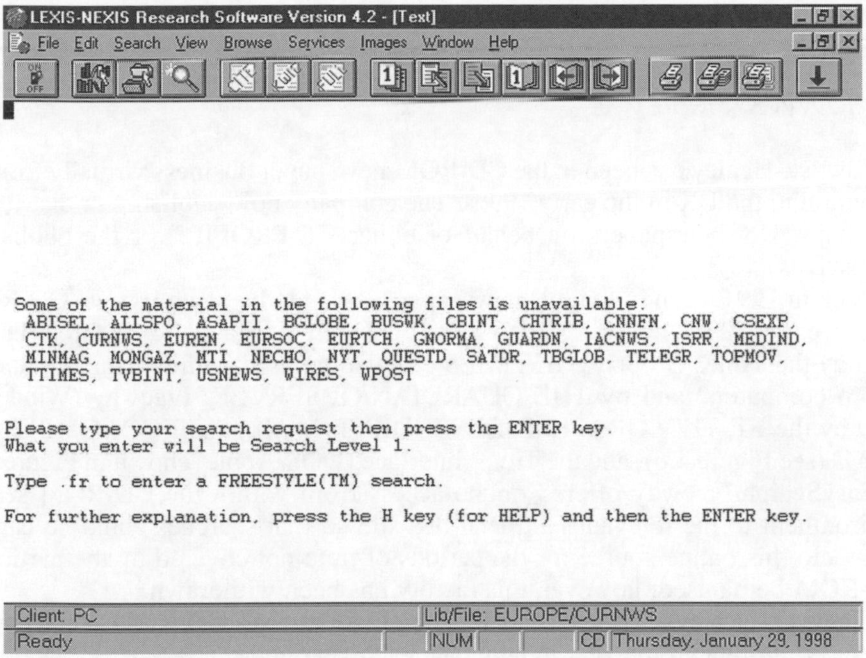

```
LEXIS-NEXIS Research Software Version 4.2 - [Text]                    _  ð  X
File   Edit   Search   View   Browse   Services   Images   Window   Help      _  ð  X
```

```
Some of the material in the following files is unavailable:
ABISEL, ALLSPO, ASAPII, BGLOBE, BUSWK, CBINT, CHTRIB, CNNFN, CNW, CSEXP,
CTK, CURNWS, EUREN, EURSOC, EURTCH, GNORMA, GUARDN, IACNWS, ISRR, MEDIND,
MINMAG, MONGAZ, MTI, NECHO, NYT, QUESTD, SATDR, TBGLOB, TELEGR, TOPMOV,
TTIMES, TVBINT, USNEWS, WIRES, WPOST

Please type your search request then press the ENTER key.
What you enter will be Search Level 1.

Type .fr to enter a FREESTYLE(TM) search.

For further explanation, press the H key (for HELP) and then the ENTER key.
```

```
Client: PC                            Lib/File: EUROPE/CURNWS
Ready                                 NUM            CD  Thursday, January 29, 1998
```

Figure 4.4   NEXIS Windows interface

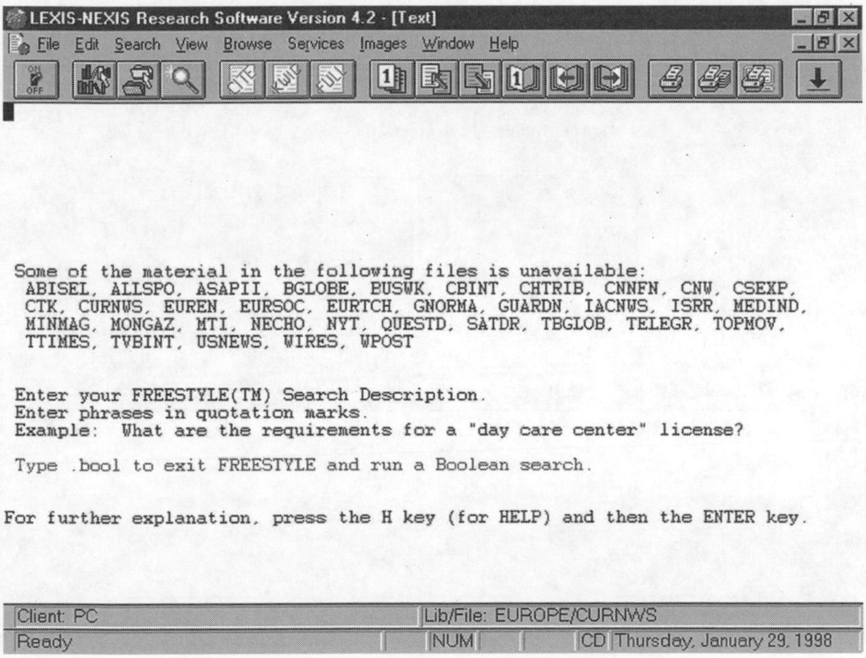

```
LEXIS-NEXIS Research Software Version 4.2 - [Text]                    _  ð  X
File   Edit   Search   View   Browse   Services   Images   Window   Help      _  ð  X
```

```
Some of the material in the following files is unavailable:
ABISEL, ALLSPO, ASAPII, BGLOBE, BUSWK, CBINT, CHTRIB, CNNFN, CNW, CSEXP,
CTK, CURNWS, EUREN, EURSOC, EURTCH, GNORMA, GUARDN, IACNWS, ISRR, MEDIND,
MINMAG, MONGAZ, MTI, NECHO, NYT, QUESTD, SATDR, TBGLOB, TELEGR, TOPMOV,
TTIMES, TVBINT, USNEWS, WIRES, WPOST

Enter your FREESTYLE(TM) Search Description.
Enter phrases in quotation marks.
Example:  What are the requirements for a "day care center" license?

Type .bool to exit FREESTYLE and run a Boolean search.

For further explanation, press the H key (for HELP) and then the ENTER key.
```

```
Client: PC                            Lib/File: EUROPE/CURNWS
Ready                                 NUM            CD  Thursday, January 29, 1998
```

Figure 4.5   NEXIS Freestyle end-user interface

CD-ROMs

Chadwyck-Healey

Chadwyck-Healey has been in the CD-ROM newspaper business virtually from its inception in the UK in the early 1990s. The company now publishes or distributes the major UK newspapers on behalf of either FT PROFILE or the publishers themselves.

Back in 1991, each individual newspaper seemed to be using its own CD-ROM interface. By 1998 there were three styles of search interface: EasySearch (DOS), used by the Times Group (THE TIMES can also be used within Windows and on Acorn computers) and by THE GUARDIAN/OBSERVER, Freeway (Windows) used by the FT, TELEGRAPH, INDEPENDENT, MAIL, and ECONOMIST CD-ROMs (see Figure 4.6), and the Times Interface (DOS/Apple) shown in Figure 4.7.

EasySearch/Freeway offered online access from within the CD-ROM search environment to the relevant FT PROFILE file so that searches could be carried over onto this online source for the periods of time not covered by the particular CD-ROM being used; however, this facility has been withdrawn.

Chawyck-Healey's policy is to issue individual title CD-ROMs that appear regularly throughout the year to cumulate each year end.

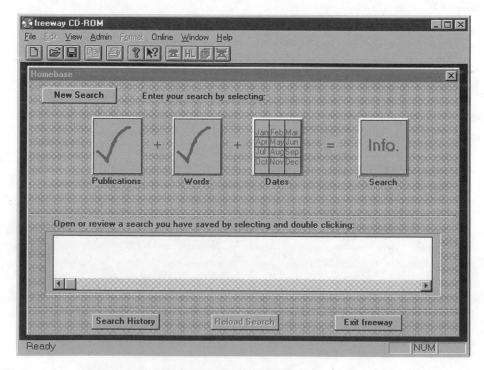

Figure 4.6   Chadwyck-Healey's 'Freeway' interface

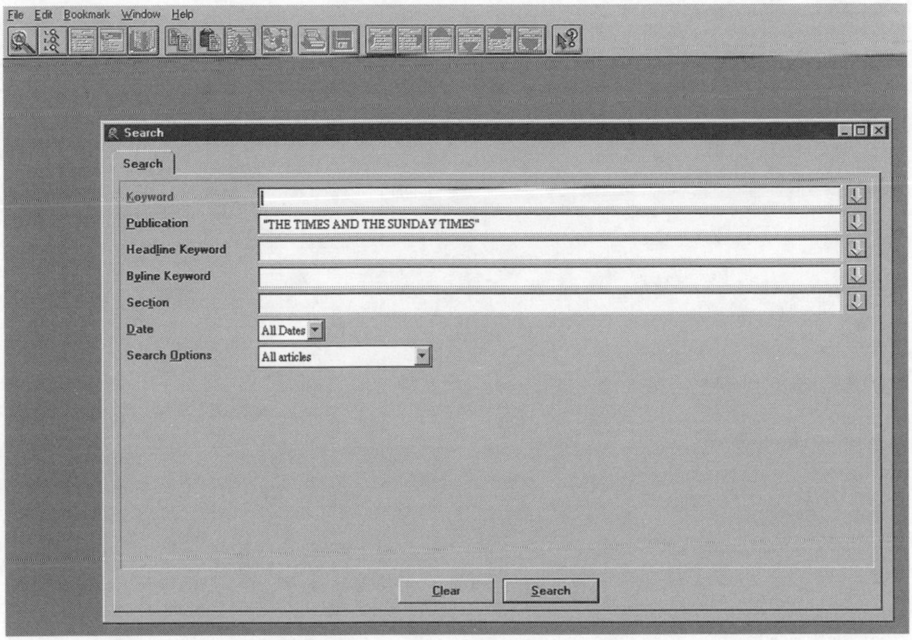

Figure 4.7   Chadwyck-Healey's *Times* interface

Televisual Data

Televisual Data is a small British company based in Scotland. Its original CD-ROM was for THE SCOTSMAN, a daily newspaper published in Edinburgh, and was unique at the time of publication as it was for both the Apple and PC formats and carried pictures directly linked to the text.

Since this first CD-ROM, the company has added several other UK newspapers to its portfolio. The interface is simple and intuitive (see Figure 4.8) and the search engine works in a similar way to that used by the Web version of the titles published on the Internet by the company. However, there is no link between the relevant CD-ROM search interface and the Web service. Users are offered access to I-SEARCH as part of the subscription package.

Like Chadwyck-Healey, Televisual publishes individual title CD-ROMs at intervals over a calendar year, with each title cumulating at the end of the year.

The World Wide Web

News provision on the World Wide Web is still developing. News publishers are scrambling to put their publications or programmes on the Web, whilst search

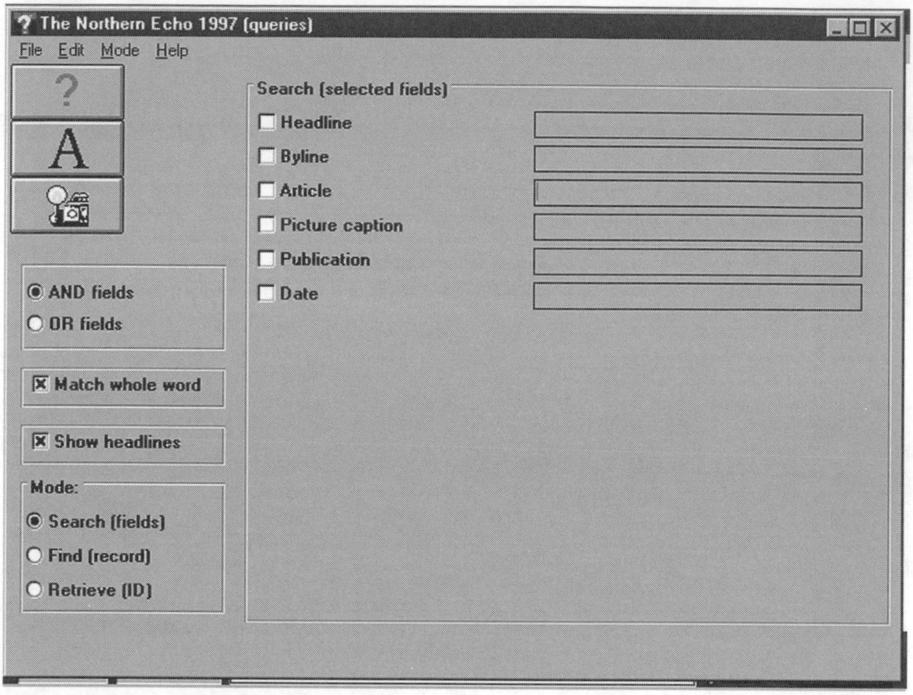

Figure 4.8   Televisual Data interface

engines are turning into news sources, and several companies are promoting the 'Daily Me' through e-mail. Furthermore, traditional online vendors are creating Web interfaces for their databases.

To make sense of this ever-changing scene, one has to examine the strands that are developing. First, there is the never-ending stream of publishers and broadcasters putting a version of their publications and broadcasts on the Web. Figure 4.9 shows an example. Usually these sites are free, but they may require registration, and offer a minimum of the current stories from the relevant print publication. Some offer archives that may be searchable in full-text form as well as by date of publication (see Figure 4.10).

Others offer enhancements to the stories through links to original sources of information (see, for example, Figure 4.11), whilst yet others develop separate areas on their site to go into some depth on the major stories of the moment (Figure 4.12).

The key point for the online searcher looking for news is that a wide range of sources is being made available. However, the downside may be found in the variable quality and lack of depth shown on many news sites.

A second development has been the arrival of the traditional online databases on the Web through a Web-based search interface. DialogWeb from The Dialog Corporation is shown in Figure 4.13.

Charges usually apply but they may be different to those online and, indeed,

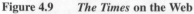

Figure 4.9   *The Times* **on the Web**

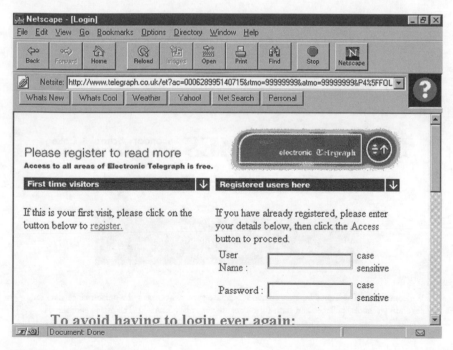

Figure 4.10   *The Telegraph*

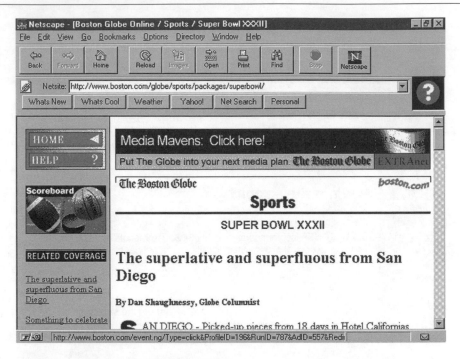

Figure 4.11   Story links on the *Boston Globe*

Figure 4.12   Added value information on *The Times*

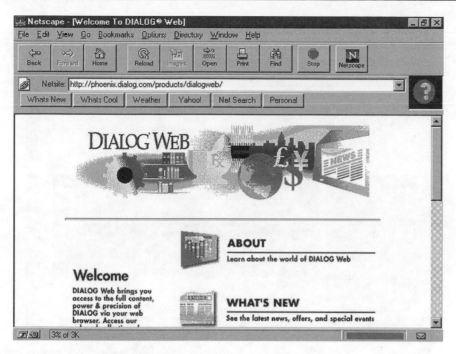

Figure 4.13   DialogWeb entry page

may not be directly comparable. Furthermore, not everything in the traditional online source may be available. The ease of searching traditional command-driven databases through the standard Web browser is the big plus; the downside is the often slow speed of response.

Third, there are companies offering intelligent agents which will track news for clients – the Daily Me that delivers customized news directly to the client via e-mail. Many are free, but may be accompanied by advertising that funds the service. These services can come and go (like many other developments on the Web). Indeed, the original example here – a breakfast briefing through the Kelloggs site – has ceased to exist. However, many search engines (see below) are offering this service, as are certain specialist news services such as the German PAPERBOY shown in Figure 4.14.

On the positive side, these agents will 'learn' from your response to their offerings. Their weakness is that they cannot get everywhere (for example, into searchable archives) and the material that they do find may not be from trustworthy sources.

Finally, the major search engines are moving towards becoming news sources (see Figure 4.15). This is achieved by indexing material into one area and guiding the user into specified sites. However, as with the intelligent agents, search engines are limited by what they can index and often also by what are considered to be major news stories.

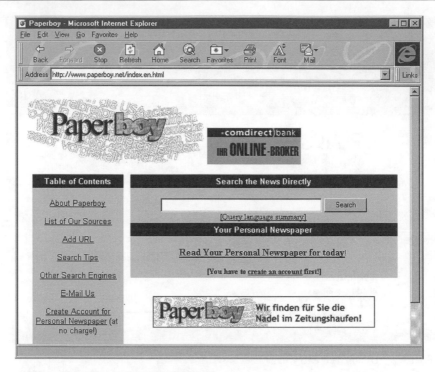

Figure 4.14   Front page of PAPERBOY site

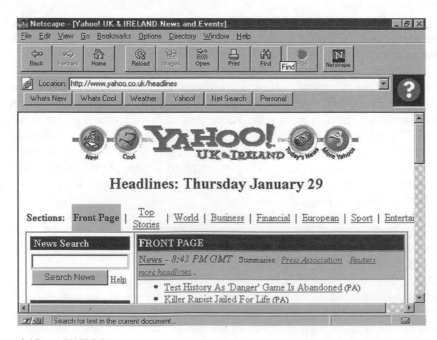

Figure 4.15   YAHOO! news

Search strategies

Most news databases are built upon the principle of free-text searching of the full text of the articles from the news source. Allied to subject indexing by trained indexers, some databases offer the best of all worlds. Those without subject indexing may provide facilities such as thesauri, sounds-like or pattern-matching to enhance the free-text facility. Yet even without these enhancements, free-text searching is a very powerful tool, especially if you are familiar with the original sources from which the database is taken and are used to its style of writing or broadcasting.

Looking for a name

Most news is built around something with a name – be it a person or group of people, an object, a human condition, a locality or an event. Names are very powerful entry points into news databases, but do have to be treated with care as search terms.

People

In the most straightforward situation, the personal name can be searched by entering it in conventional fashion. Thus, if looking for news on Peter Chapman, the name can be entered exactly in this way (in two words). However, there can be pitfalls. The search interface may not support 'adjacency' searching and the search may thus be translated into the imprecise Peter and Chapman, occurrences of which anywhere in the record, whether adjacent or not, will produce a hit. If adjacency searching is supported, this may be foiled by specific kinds of reporting. In a court report, the full name of the defendant will be given. If married with relations, the report might mention the subject in connection with the relation, for example, Peter and Janet Chapman. Thus a simple name search will not suffice. However, most search interfaces allow for searches of words within the sentence or within a certain number of words of each other.

In addition, people's names are prone to alternative spellings, abbreviations, nicknames or the preference of one forename over another. Even if the enquirer is sure of the correct form of name, not all newspapers agree on what is the correct form, and so variant forms of names will occur. This point particularly applies to names translated or transliterated into English from another language. A classic example of this occurred in the early days of FT PROFILE when Colonel Gaddaffi of Libya had many variant spellings across the sources covered, including a version starting with a Q.

Having traced the name, the context in which you want the stories to carry the name becomes important. With people who are constantly in the news, you must use the refinements of the search facility to avoid being overwhelmed with irrelevant material. Thus, names such as Margaret Thatcher, the former British prime minister – who, by the way, was often referred to as Mrs Thatcher – need to be linked closely to an event, locality, another name or a date.

As an alternative, the ability to constrain searches by the presence of the search term in key parts of the article or by the number of times the key term occurs in the article should be used. This latter point is particularly noticeable when looking for profiles (biographies) of a person, as many news sources avoid the use of the word 'profile' to describe biographical or interview articles featuring a particular person.

However, if the name for which you are searching is a person rarely or never likely to be in the news, then care must be taken that any retrieved articles carry the name in the correct context. For example, searches for stories on a British boy called Michael Jackson should be constructed to avoid stories on the American pop singer of the same name. This can be achieved by either including the context with the name or by excluding (with a Boolean NOT) a known descriptor of the name to be avoided (in this case 'singer'). Some online databases offer help here by giving the opportunity to include focus terms on a large result set to ensure that the end results are relevant.

Objects

In theory, specific objects should be retrievable with high precision. Unfortunately, many pitfalls exist to trip the unwary.

Capitalization of proper names helps if recorded by the database source and recognized by the search facility, although not all search interfaces allow for case-specific searches and not all object names are used correctly – for example, the use of the trade name 'Hoover' as a generic term for vacuum cleaners.

The ability of the search interface to find every instance of the search term in whatever context can also cause problems. For example, if searching for articles by motoring correspondents on a popular make of car, such as the Ford Escort, other articles, such as reports of accidents involving Ford Escorts, will also be retrieved. This may help the enquirer but is more likely to be an irritant; thus context or frequency of term within each hit becomes important once again as a method of refining the search results.

Searching sources across more than one country highlights the issue of differing names for the same type of objects (for example, the US 'freeways' and UK 'motorways').

Human conditions

The crucial issue with news stories about human conditions is that different societies and cultures view matters in different ways, and the news media reflect these differences. A simple example is the condition known in the UK as dyslexia whereby pupils have difficulty in reading. This condition has risen to prominence in both the UK and the USA over the last few years but this would not be evident by searching for dyslexia in the US sources as the subject is usually subsumed within the wider term 'learning disorder'.

On emotive subjects such as human sexuality, the media can be split by attitude; some sources may have in-depth coverage of a subject, while others are virtually silent. Yet other databases may contain anti and pro articles from different sources. Thus the context of the request for information becomes important in judging the appropriate news sources from which to draw the information.

Localities

The arrival of the Internet and the parallel rise in local news sources online (particularly within the USA) has revolutionized the retrieval of news emanating from a particular locality. Now it is feasible to go to that locality's local publication to get a truly 'grassroots' feel for what life is like in the area. Nevertheless, searching on locality does need care, particularly in the UK where local papers are not so easily available in searchable form. When coverage is by a national newspaper, beware of the use of the name of a nearby large town in place of the actual minor (in national newspaper terms) locality.

On a related point, getting definitions of wider geographical terms used by papers can be difficult – just what does a UK national newspaper mean by Northern England?

Events

The news media love to give key events snappy names, an example being 'Brown Monday' in the UK. (Brown Monday was the name given by the press to the embarrassment suffered by the UK Chancellor Gordon Brown when, on launching the UK Stock Exchange Electronic Trading System, share prices dived due to uncertainty over his attitude to Britain's membership of the European Monetary System.) Beware of such titles: they may not be used consistently, they may be used only by certain sources, or worst of all, they may be used at different times to describe different events!

Whenever possible, it is advisable to search for events using personal names or places or, if necessary, dates.

Searching by or for dates

As a rule, date searching should be avoided unless there is no other way to restrict a search. This is partly because of the slowness at which the early databases returned a date range search (not such a problem these days), but is mainly to avoid missing good articles summarizing the news sought but written well after the event took place.

Some databases, of course, restrict the search by date automatically. For example, FT PROFILE initially will only search the most recent year, and LEXIS-NEXIS offers the default of the past two years. However, if you are sure that you only want stories written at the time of the subject you are researching, then a date range search around the period can be effective.

For the enquirer genuinely wanting to know what happened on a particular date or range of dates, then traditional online or CD-ROM sources are especially valuable as material can be pinpointed and retrieved by date alone. Don't forget to check the help file to make sure that the format of the date search is correctly entered – it is amazing how many variants there can be in how a date is expressed in an electronic file.

Although specific news sites on the Internet may offer date searching on their archives without a subject being entered, a date search on a search engine not specifically handling news sites would not be a productive way of answering the enquirer's request.

Searching for the date of a news item can be frustrating, especially if it is not recent. Newspapers are good at being the memory of society but, like all memories, they can be infuriatingly imprecise about the actual date on which a news event occurred! It is always wise to check several news sources, and to cross-check against a non-news reference source if there is any doubt about the accuracy of the date given.

Sample search: Louise Woodward

Louise Woodward was a British *au pair* for an American family, who was accused of murdering the baby of her employers. Her case came to trial in the USA in 1997. The sentencing decision of the original trial judge was delivered through an Internet site, so great was the interest that had built up around the case.

This story is a prime example of the strengths and weaknesses of the various online media. As the case caught the public's imagination on both sides of the Atlantic, not only did coverage of the story mushroom – aided by the televising of American courts which allowed the public to follow the case in minute detail – but the issues that the case highlighted were also analysed at great length. Furthermore, as the case raised emotive issues, the media was split between sympathy for either Louise or for the parents of the dead baby. Thus the news researcher would need to be clear about the sort of articles that are required in response to the enquiry on the case and, if seeking a balanced response, would need to be sure to seek a wide range of sources through which to conduct the search.

Turning to traditional online sources first, as we are looking for a specific person, her name can be used. Fortunately, not many prominent persons in the news share this name so an immediate usable result will be obtained from whichever online service is used. However, the articles all describe her as a nanny or an *au pair* (this confusion in job titles in news stories is common) so these terms can be used to qualify the search should exact matches be required.

In addition, the US sources tend to refer to her as British – a term picked up by the British sources as some of the coverage became polarized along national lines. Note, however, that news sources can use varying terms for the same nationality: thus, Louise could as easily have been referred to as English.

The coverage of the case built up slowly from February 1997, then grew rapidly as the trial started. Obviously, date range searches could be used to pinpoint coverage as it was written at key stages in the development of the story. Much background material tends to be written as a story becomes a key ingredient of the day's or week's news, so succinct articles on the start of the story are more likely to be found as backgrounders during each key stage of the story – the trial and the verdict. As an aside, had the case occurred in the UK, the detailed analysis which took place in the USA would have been forbidden until the case had reached a conclusion. Therefore, the background articles would not have been available until Louise's fate was known, rather than as it was being decided.

If using online databases, a range of sources on both sides of the Atlantic can be searched simultaneously. Although this is a strength in terms of recall of relevant articles, it can be a weakness in precision. However, precision can be improved either through the use of ranking of results or through refinements of the original search term. If cost is a factor, then initially selecting certain key news sources before entering the search terms to give what you hope will be representative coverage is one answer. Another saving would be to use the services as an index to key dates and to try to find relevant articles either in hard-copy collections or on the Internet sites of the major newspapers and broadcasters.

Overall, for immediate and comprehensive access, albeit at a cost, traditional online services keep their traditional niche as an immediate source to which to turn.

CD-ROMs

As a story is developing, CD-ROMs are not likely to be an effective search medium unless the enquirer seeks only stories from a specific source – one which is on a CD-ROM with an online agreement for up-to-date material. However, once the story has come to a conclusion (or climax) and the excitement, in newspaper terms, has died down, then CD-ROMs come into their own as a no-cost (to the enquirer) way of sifting through the mountain of articles written and to follow the various strands of the story as they rise and fall in significance. Nevertheless, the enquirer would need access to a range of CD-ROMs from both sides of the Atlantic for a comprehensive and balanced view.

The Internet

Undoubtedly, the Internet has been thrust into the public's consciousness by the US judge's decision to release his verdict using this medium. Even without this dramatic boost, the Internet was showing its strengths as a news medium as the case developed. The availability of the local US town newspaper with its detailed Web site on the case (see Figure 4.16) and of the Web site set up by supporters of Louise Woodward in her home village in the UK (see Figure 4.17), brings a different dimension to the retrieval of stories on the case.

As the screenshot from ALTAVISTA shows, the Internet is gaining a 'memory' even if it is currently only for the more sensational news stories (note in Figure 4.18 the direct link to special reports on 'The British Au Pair Case – 1997'.)

The strengths of the Internet coverage are its diversity, its ability to respond quickly to developments, its ability to carry various media in one package (that is, television, radio, print and animations), and the fact that the wide variety of sources offering information are all accessible through the common Web browser interface.

The weaknesses shown up are the lack of comprehensive search abilities for archive material, the slow speed of access at key times (the verdict Web site crashed because of the heavy use), the lack of depth to some of the sites, and the use of the Internet to put material favouring one viewpoint into the public domain.

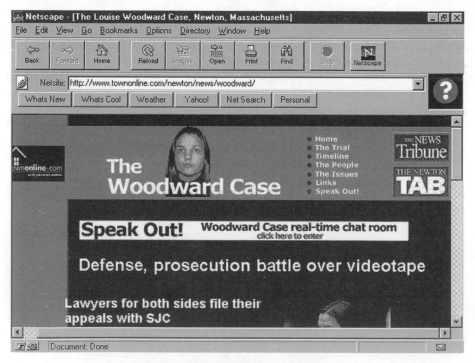

Figure 4.16   *The News Tribune's* **report on the Woodward case**

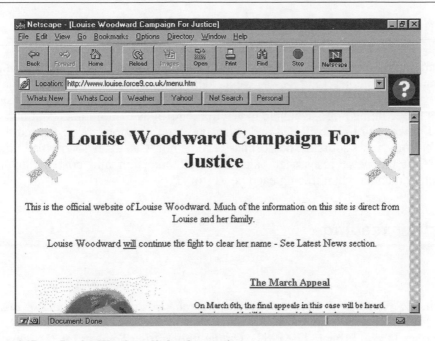

Figure 4.17   Louise Woodward's local news site

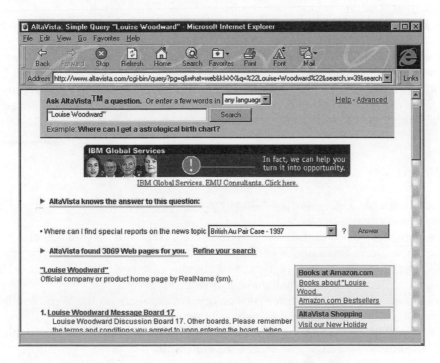

Figure 4.18   Results of an AltaVista search on 'Louise Woodward'

Conclusion

We are moving to a time when news will be constantly available on our PCs either through the Internet (and news agents delivering e-mails) or through online databases that provide real-time, profile-driven search services. Even historic news is becoming more available in electronic form as explorations continue into the digitization of microfilmed and paper-based publications. With the multitude of electronic news sources, the skill has become not 'Can a news story be found?', but 'Can the news researcher balance recall, precision and cost in the most effective manner when tracing each news story?'

Further reading

Books

Adair, S. (1999), *Information Sources for the Press and Broadcast Media*, London: Bowker-Saur.

Nicholas, D. and Erbach, G. (1989), *Online Information Sources for Business and Current Affairs: An evaluation of Textline, Nexis, Profile and DIALOG.* London: Mansell.

Semonche, B. (1993), *News Media Libraries: A Management Handbook*, London: Greenwood.

Spencer, N. (1997), *News Information: Online, CD-ROM and Internet Resources*, London: British Library.

Whatmore, G. (1978), *The Modern News Library: Documentation of Current Affairs in Newspaper and Broadcasting Libraries*. London: Library Association Publishing.

Web sites

Association of UK Media Librarians Web site. Available at <URL http://www.aukml.org.uk/>.

News Division, Special Libraries Association Web site. Available at <URL http://sunsite.unc.edu/slanews/index.html>.

News Division, Special Libraries Association Listserv. Available at <URL http://sunsite.unc.edu/journalism/newslib.html>.

News Division, Special Libraries Association Newspapers on the Web. Available at <URL http://sunsite.unc.edu/slanews/internet/archives.html>.

News Division, Special Libraries Association Online Suppliers. Available at <URL http://sunsite.unc.edu/slanews/online.html>.

University of North Carolina Online Resources for Journalists. Available at <URL http://sunsite.unc.edu/journalism/welcome.html>.

NEWSPAPERS ON THE WEB listing. Available at <URL http://www.newspapers.com/>.

Traditional online news sources

DIALOG and MAID. Available at <URL http://www.dialog.com/>.

DOW JONES. Available at <URL http://www.dowjones.com/>.

FT PROFILE. Available at <URL http://www.ft.com>.

LEXIS-NEXIS. Available at <URL http://www.lexis-nexis.com>

CD-ROMs

Chadwyck-Healey. Available at <URL http://www.chadwyck.co.uk>.

Primary Source Media. Available at <URL http://www.thomson.com/psmedia/>.

Televisual Data Ltd. Available at <URL http://www.televisual.co.uk>.

Chapter 5

Law
John Williams

Introduction

Although a conservative body, there is increasing evidence that the legal profession has embraced new technology and uses it not only at the client–lawyer interface, but throughout the legal process. As an office tool, new technology has revolutionized billing, time management, record-keeping, case management, document assembly packages and file transfers. Computers are also a familiar sight in many courtrooms, especially during the more complex fraud trials. Computer-aided transcription systems have led to the instant availability of transcripts in courts. The potential for e-mail as a means of document transfer and revision has not been fully exploited, but could revolutionize the conduct of litigation. The facsimile machine and the dedicated LEXIS terminal gathering dust in the corner no longer represent technology in the practitioner's office. Issues such as whether or not fee-earners or others are responsible for interrogating databases or entering data have to be resolved. Nevertheless, the idea of modern information technology is accepted and adopted by practitioners, both large and small. Smaller and geographically remote firms can use information technology to supplement law libraries that may be lacking in the more specialized hard-copy material.

In legal education, technology has been introduced as part of degree courses in higher education institutions. The Law Technology Centre, funded by the various bodies responsible for funding higher education throughout the UK, has raised the profile of technology as an integral part of academic teaching and research. Similarly the British and Irish Legal Technology Association (BILETA) and the British and Irish Association of Law Librarians (BIALL) have done much to raise awareness of the implications of technology in legal education. The *Second BILETA Report on IT for UK Law Schools* (1996) stressed the importance of the link between technology and legal education and training. It concluded:

Every law student should have the ability to use information technology to perform specific law-related tasks. These are the ability to produce documentation, the ability to perform legal research, the ability to communicate electronically and the ability to use the major legal Computer Assisted Learning packages.

We believe that the Internet will play an increasing role in legal education in terms of both teaching and research. Therefore, both law students and legal academics must obtain the necessary IT skills to navigate and retrieve electronic information resources of all descriptions from this medium.

Thus we are producing a new generation of lawyers who have undergone integrated information technology training as part of their legal education.

The use of electronic legal databases is a relatively new development for lawyers in the UK. It was not until the late 1970s that two commercial ventures, EUROLEX and LEXIS entered a wary market as competitors. Each offered a differently biased database. EUROLEX contained the full text of materials covering the UK and European case law, legislation and secondary sources. LEXIS originally contained the statute and case law of the USA, the UK and France. The eventual combination of these two databases was, perhaps, the most significant step forward in introducing technology in the practice of law.

Legal material

A look around any law library attached to a law school or a large firm of lawyers will indicate the vast range of legal material available to the profession. This is reflected in the growth of the number of specialist law librarians being recruited within higher education and by private practitioners. Searching for the most appropriate legal authority is no longer the hit-and-miss affair that it once was. It is now an essential skill that the complexity of the law requires all lawyers to possess. The traditional *Law Reports* have been supplemented by reports covering specialist topics such as industrial law, planning law and family law. The flow of legislation from Europe has grown and makes the distinction between 'domestic law' and 'European law' increasingly meaningless. The impact of international law, and also the law of other domestic jurisdictions, has increased the range of material which lawyers must access. A reliance on the *All England Law Reports* plus practitioner textbooks or encyclopaedias is no longer enough to provide the answer to increasingly complex legal problems.

As society becomes more litigious and more aware of rights (especially against the state) lawyers are called upon to research cases in greater depth. The case of Diane Blood, the English woman who successfully claimed her right to use her dead husband's semen to have a baby, illustrates how a case that may once have been considered a matter of domestic law required consideration of European law and also the law of other jurisdictions. The web of law that the lawyer has to untangle is growing more complex and less compartmentalized. In this environment the role of electronic databases becomes all the more crucial in the provision of high-quality legal advice and assistance. Access by non-lawyers is also a key issue as more and more individuals take on the state and big business.

Traditionally lawyers rely on the following primary sources: statutes, case law, statutory instruments and European Law.

Statutes

The cardinal rule of the British Constitution is that parliament is supreme. It can, theoretically, do anything; its actions cannot be constrained by the courts. However, membership of the European Community has imposed some limits on this doctrine as will the Human Rights Act 1998. Nevertheless, the Act of Parliament is an important source of law that can overrule long-established rules of common law. They may also amend, repeal or consolidate earlier legislation. The HMSO hard copy of a statute does not necessarily provide an accurate picture of the law. A good example is the National Assistance Act 1948. The original statute has been amended by later legislation, so that a reading of the original copy would be highly misleading. It is necessary to take account of the many amendments that have taken place. In this respect, electronic databases which update legislation are invaluable in providing the reader with a relatively up-to-date version of the statute.

Similarly, the implementation of a particular piece of legislation may be phased over a period of time or, in some instances, never fully implemented – for example, the Disabled Persons (Services, Consultation and Representation) Act 1986. Again, a reading of the original copy does not reveal this. Publications, such as *Is it in Force?* may be helpful in trying to identify which pieces of legislation are currently in force.

The term 'The Statute Book' is somewhat misleading insofar as it creates the impression of one single reference work whereas, in fact, a variety of different printed sources are available. These range from the official HMSO *Public General Acts* to the *Current Annotated Statutes* series that provides commentary on the legislation as well as the text. *Statutes in Force* endeavours to provide, through the use of a looseleaf format, an official, up-to-date text of statutes currently in force. Unfortunately the series is, in places, out of date.

Secondary legislation

Much of the detail surrounding legislation is to be found in statutory instruments. A complete picture of legislation can only be obtained by referring to the Act of Parliament and also any delegated legislation (statutory instruments) made under its provisions. Statutory instruments are published by HMSO. They may be obtained individually or in the publication *Statutory Instruments*. As with primary legislation, it is essential that reference is made to the amended versions of statutory instruments rather than the original copy.

Recent legislation on devolution for Wales and Scotland set up the Welsh Assembly and the Scottish Parliament with extensive powers to make their own secondary and primary legislation. It will be interesting to see how such legislation is included in electronic databases.

Case law

Case law is an important source of British law. Common law principles still apply, and continue to be developed in many important areas of law. Judges also have responsibility for interpreting Acts of Parliament. The system of judicial precedent places great emphasis on the importance of accurately recording judicial decisions so that they can be cited before later courts.

A wide range of law reports is available in the printed form. The *English Reports* contain most of the cases found in the nominate reports. From 1865 onwards, the Incorporated Council of Law Reporting has produced semi-official reports of cases. These are now known as the *Law Reports*. Courts require citation of the *Law Reports* if a case presented in argument is reported in them. Currently the Council publishes the following reports:

- Appeal Cases
- Queen's Bench Division
- Chancery Division
- Probate and Family Division.

The Council is also responsible for publishing the generic series known as the *Weekly Law Reports*.

Commercial publishers produce a number of law reports. The best known of these is the *All England Law Reports*. This is another generic series covering cases from different courts over a wide range of subject matter. In addition, *The Times*, *The Guardian* and the *Independent* produce daily law reports of what its editors consider to be the most important cases. However, these tend to be shortened versions of the decision and do not, as such, have any authority. They are, nevertheless, often a more immediate means of accessing a judgment as they are invariably published shortly after the decision of the court. Professional journals such as the *Gazette* and the *Solicitors Journal* provide updating services that include summaries of recently decided cases. Specialist reports include *Family Law Reports*, *Medical Law Reports*, *Industrial Relations Law Reports* and the *Housing Law Reports*.

Although having some areas in common with England and Wales, the jurisdictions of Scotland and Northern Ireland have their own specialist law reports. In Scotland these are the *Session Cases* and the *Scots Law Times*. In Northern Ireland cases are reported in the *Northern Ireland Law Reports*.

Some cases never make the law reports, but are available in transcript form. The procedure whereby a case does or does not make the law reports is shrouded in mystery. Indeed, it is a curious feature of the common law system that whether or not a case becomes a precedent will depend on whether cases are included in recognized law reports. Furthermore, the common law presupposes that not every case will be formally reported. If they were, the system would become unmanageable. Ironically, one of the side-effects of greater accessibility to decided cases through electronic databases has been to place a strain on a system that does not really desire long lists of cases which may or may not be relevant. No matter how skilled the database interrogator may be, it is difficult to restrict the number of hits to manageable proportions.

European material

The increasing harmonization of the laws of the member states of the European Union has dramatically increased the need for so-called municipal lawyers to refer to European legal material. The *Official Journal* is the primary source of European Community Law containing directives, legislation, regulation and decisions, in addition to draft regulations and the proceedings of the European Parliament. The *Official Journal* contains an unwieldy collection of information and the only sensible way of interrogating it is by electronic means. European case law is covered by the official series of the *European Court Report* and the *Common Market Law Reports*. In addition to European material there is an increasing need to refer to the municipal law of individual countries both within and outside of the European Union. Electronic databases are responding to this need.

Legal material is becoming increasingly complex and difficult to navigate. The move from the hard copy to the electronic database has gathered pace, as is evidenced by the increasing range of resources available.

The United States

The USA provides a vast array of legal material for the lawyer. The existence of a written constitution plus the division of the government function between the federal and state governments combine with the vastness of the country to create a substantial body of legal material. In many ways, it provides a much more challenging environment than the European Union for the lawyers. The constitutional dimension is ever present, and lawyers need to be constantly aware of its implications at whatever levels of activity. Each state has its own system of government and its own judicial system. The president, Congress and the Supreme Court all participate in the law-making process at national level. This results in a disparate provision of legal material that makes the task of the lawyer particularly daunting. An interesting development in the USA is the availability of a number of comprehensive sites that provide access to legal material at both state and federal level. Two of these sites are mentioned below.

LEXIS

LEXIS's domination of the legal information market has been compromised to some extent by the emergence of many new databases. Nevertheless LEXIS is the system with which most lawyers are familiar. This is due partly to its comprehensive nature and partly because of its high profile in legal education. The introduction of a Windows-based interface has done much to remove some of the irritations in accessing the database and it now provides a reasonably user-friendly environment within which to work. LEXIS-NEXIS Office is an integrated research tool incorporating the LEXIS database within a Windows environment. Searching is made easier by virtue of the availability of a toolbar as opposed to searching using a series of dot commands. The database was introduced in 1973 and was originally accessed via a dedicated terminal and printer. The combined services contain more than 18 300 sources: 13 500 news and business sources, and 4800 legal sources.

LEXIS is organized into Libraries and Files. Its main Libraries are identified on the first three screens that the user encounters when entering the database. For lawyers in England and Wales the Library ENGGEN contains a number of files of immediate value. The files found within this Library are:

- CASES   Cases
- STATIS   Combined STAT and SI files
- STAT   All Public General Acts
- DTAX   Double Tax Instruments
- SI   Statutory Instruments
- LEARN   Cases for Practice Research
- LRNSTA   Acts/SIs for Practice Research

The CASES file contains both reported and unreported cases. Reported cases normally go back to 1936, although the tax cases commence in 1975. The list of law reports is extensive, covering both the specialist and the generalist. Included in the list are:

- *All England Law Reports*
- *Criminal Appeal Reports*
- *Estates Gazette Digest*
- *Family Law Reports*
- *Knight's Industrial Reports*
- *Simon's Tax Cases*
- *Weekly Law Reports.*

Transcripts of unreported cases have been available since 1980. This service is particularly useful as it provides access to the judgments prior to their reaching the hard-copy law reports. The courts covered by the transcript service are:

- All House of Lords cases
- All Privy Council cases
- All Court of Appeal (Civil Division) cases
- All Chancery Revenue List cases
- Selected Queen's Bench Admiralty Court cases
- All Queen's Bench Division (Crown Office List) cases from January 1983
- Land Tribunal cases to December 1993
- Selected Revised Employment Appeal Tribunal cases
- Selected Queen's Bench Commercial Court cases
- Selected VAT Tribunal cases.

In addition to cases, ENGGEN also includes Public and General Acts and statutory instruments of England and Wales. The SI file covers the Statutory Rules, Regulations and Orders of England and Wales that are published in the Statutory Instrument Series. These files may be searched separately (within the STAT or SI files) or together (within the STATIS file). All three files are regularly updated (usually about one month after publication). They are presented in their amended form, thus meeting the demand for a reliable up-to-date version of the legislation or delegated legislation.

The UKTAX Library provides a comprehensive and specialist service for the tax practitioner. The files within this Library are:

- ES   Cases including all cases reported in STC; Tax Cases; VATTR and selected unreported cases from 1980
- STAT   Selected Current Public General Acts published by HMSO
- SI   Selected Current General Statutory Instruments published by HMSO
- STATIS   Combined STAT and SI Files
- DTAX   Current Double Taxation Instruments published by HMSO

Of particular use is the DTAX file that provides a complete and updated text of the double taxation agreements to which the UK is a party.

The UKCURR file in the ENGGEN Library is a general updating file that is updated every Friday. A number of facilities are available within this Library. The WEEKLY file enables the user to browse through summaries of the current week's legal developments in the areas of Civil Litigation, Company/Commercial Law, Criminal, Family/Welfare, Property Law, Public Law and Taxation. Choosing the file 'Public Law' produces a subject heading that can be further interrogated by entering the number associated with an individual title. For example, entering '=4' provides a reference to Alec Samuel's 'Racial Violence and Harassment: Government Proposals for a New Criminal Offence', published in the *Justice of the Peace*.

LEXIS offers a number of different display formats. CITE lists the documents identified in your search. KWIC, VAR KWIC and SUPER KWIC identify those parts of documents that contain the search term. KWIC is the standard setting that displays the search term with 25 words either side. VAR KWIC allows the user to specify the number of words (between 1 and 255) to be displayed either side of the search term. SUPER KWIC is only available when using the LEXIS Freestyle search facility. (This will be considered later.) If the user wishes to read the document in its entirety then the FULL key provides the full text of the document in a format similar to the printed copy. SEGMTS enables the user to search the individual parts of a document. For example, it is possible to view a list of the cases cited, cases referred to, the headnote, the hearing dates, the names of counsel or the solicitors, and any dissenting judgments.

Searching LEXIS may be undertaken in a number of different ways. The traditional Boolean search tool enables you to interrogate the database using the well-tried connectors. Thus searching the ENGGEN library and the CASES file for 'community care AND resources' will identify 48 cases in which both words appear. This can be refined by using the W/n, which finds documents where one word appears within a specified number of another. For example 'community care W/20' reduces the 48 cases identified using AND to 11. These basic connectors may be supplemented by the more specialized ones. Using the ATLEAST connector allows the user to specify the number of times the word should appear within a document before it is retrieved. This reduces the chance of retrieving a rogue case that uses the search term in another context. Entering 'community care AND ATLEAST5 (resources)' produces 20 hits. Naturally, the more specific the search term, the higher the risk of excluding a relevant case. Further variations of the connectors available are PRE/n and NOT W/n.

Freestyle is a new LEXIS feature that allows the user to search the database using conversational language rather than Boolean connectors. Returning to the search on resources and community care services, a Freestyle search could be couched in the following manner – 'Are resources relevant in identifying need for "community care services"'. The key search concept, community care services, is placed within quotation marks. Freestyle will then display the 'top 50 documents based on statistical ranking'. A breakdown of the statistics explaining why a document has a particular ranking is available (the **Why** command). The command **Where** reveals the existence of the search terms within each of the documents identified.

The advantage of this breakdown is that users can see which of the search terms are contained in any one document identified. As with a Boolean search the documents may be viewed using CITE, KWIC and FULL. SUPER KWIC shows a section of each document that most closely matches your search description.

The benefits of the Freestyle will depend on personal preference. This reviewer felt more comfortable using the traditional Boolean search techniques and considered that Freestyle did not provide any additional advantages. Those not brought up using Boolean language may find Freestyle easier.

In addition to ENGGEN, LEXIS also contains many other Libraries. The EURCOM Library contains EC/EU material including reported and unreported decisions of the Court of Justice of the European Community, Commission decisions relating to competition, European Community legislation, treaties, Commission proposals, and Parliamentary resolutions.

The case law in EURCOM includes:

- decisions of the Court of Justice of the European Communities since 1954 as reported in the *European Court Reports* (ECR)
- official English-language reports of the court transcripts of cases not yet reported in ECR including the Advocate-General's opinion
- European Commercial Cases from January 1978
- *European Human Rights Reports* from November 1960
- Unreported cases from October 1980
- Commission decisions relating to competition from November 1959
- Cour de Justice des Communautés Européennes (in French) from December 1954.

Legislation covered by EURCOM includes

- Basic Documents of International Economic Law
- *Journal Officiel des Communautés Européennes* (in French) from 30 December 1992
- European Commission legislation from 30 January 1980
- European Commission treaties from 19 November 1979
- European Commission parliamentary questions from January 1989
- European Commission National Provisions from January 1989
- European Commission Preparatory Acts
- European Commission proposals from January 1984
- European Commission parliamentary resolutions from June 1979
- European Community Law (CELEX database) including LEGIS, TREATY, PARLQ, NATPRV and PREP files
- Spicers Centre for Europe from January 1989.

Particular mention should be made of the inclusion of the comprehensive CELEX database which includes treaties, preparatory legislation, case law, national law implementing EC legislation and parliamentary questions. The ability to retrieve this information in full-text form and to use it alongside other UK and European Community material has provided LEXIS with a distinctive advantage over other databases and sets the standard for comprehensive coverage.

Comparative material is also available on LEXIS. Irish cases are found in IRELAND. This Library contains cases reported in the *Irish Reports*, *Irish Law Reports Monthly*, and *Irish Law Times*, and judgments of the Court of Criminal Appeal. It also includes selected unreported cases from July 1925. The Commonwealth Cases Library, COMCAS, provides access to case law from the Republic of Ireland and the British Commonwealth, including England, Northern Ireland, Scotland, Australia, New Zealand and Canada. This Library may be searched by country (or selected countries) or across all countries. If the user chooses to search all countries the results of the search may be displayed chronologically or according to country. LEXIS also contains a French law collection. This contains Libraries on French International Relations, French Laws and Regulations, French News, and French Public and Private Cases.

LEXIS also contains a considerable amount of American material that reflects its American origins. As well as federal and state data, the American collection contains specialist Libraries on areas such as Immigration, Insurance, Military, Taxation and Torts.

INTLAW LEXIS includes a useful collection of international material. The International Law Library provides comprehensive international law materials, including:

- EC/EU materials
- treaties and agreements
- Irish and British Commonwealth law materials
- topical and professional journals
- French law materials
- Chinese law materials
- topical publications
- US federal and state cases arising under international law.

LEXIS must still be considered a market leader as an all-embracing database providing full-text material for academics and practitioners. The new interface provides a more agreeable environment within which to work. LEXIS has responded to criticism that it was slow, cumbersome and user-unfriendly.

The Central Computer and Technology Agency Government Information Service

Government accumulates and produces vast amounts of information. For the lawyer, this information can be categorized as irrelevant, of background interest or of direct interest. The Government Information Service (GIS) Web site is a positive treasure trove of government information. Used carefully and very selectively by lawyers, GIS will produce useful information. The site is accessed at <URL http://www.open.gov.uk/>. Upon entering, the user is presented with a number of options. 'What's New on GIS' features a daily update on government information. For example, the entry for 19 December 1997 informs the user that the Lord Chancellor's Department issued a consultation paper on *Civil Procedure Rules – Service of Court Process Abroad*. This facility is quick and easy for those wishing to keep abreast of developments.

The Organisational Index contains an alphabetical list of public bodies and government departments that have Web sites (see Figure 5.1). Among the organizations which can be accessed using this index are HM Customs and Excise (which includes Budget Notices, Business Briefings and Notices and Leaflets); HM Land Registry; The Lord Chancellor's Department (information on a range of

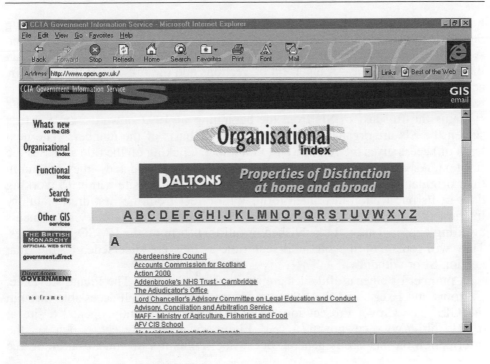

Figure 5.1   GIS Organisational Index

topics including Legal Aid, Family Matters and Magistrates); and the Public Trust Office. At present, the information held on each of the Web sites will vary. Some are very much in their infancy and contain only the minimal amount of information. Others are more comprehensive and will provide helpful information for lawyers seeking to access government information.

By using the GIS Topic Index the user has access to a wide range of government material. Acts of Parliament are now included on the GIS site and may be accessed through the Topic Index. By clicking on 'law and justice' the user is taken to a page that offers access to *Hansard* (Lords and Commons). The site includes debates from Session 1996/97. There is a helpful search feature which enables users to search either the House of Commons or the House of Lords or both, and also allows searching of individual aspects of parliamentary business (for example, written answers, Weekly Information Bulletin and Bills). Acts of Parliament may be accessed through the 'HMSO' option. The HMSO page may also be accessed through the Organisational Index. One encouraging aspect of the open government policy has been the amount of information published by HMSO now accessible through GIS.

The site contains all the Public General Acts in full form since the beginning of 1996 together with the Data Protection Act 1984 and the Disability Discrimination Act 1995. Unlike LEXIS, the Acts are published in their original form and are not updated. It is intended that Acts should be available on the site within ten working days of publication, although those with a more complex format may take longer. Acts are listed alphabetically according to year. By clicking on the name of the Act the user is taken to the Arrangement of Sections and the full text of the section is accessed by clicking on the section title.

A similar procedure applies for the statutory instruments (SIs). The site contains the full text of SIs from the beginning of 1997 onwards. On the first screen the SIs are organized into groups on the basis of the numbers. The next level of access gives the full title and SI number. Clicking on the title accesses the full text. As with the Acts of Parliament, the SIs are not updated – they remain in their original format. The intention is to have an SI on the site within 15 working days of its publication in printed form. With effect from the first draft statutory instrument published after 1 November 1997 all new draft statutory instruments awaiting approval are to be published in full-text form on the HMSO Web pages. They will remain on the site until such time as they are superseded by the final version SI or withdrawn.

A number of other useful sites are available on the GIS. The Inland Revenue, Customs and Excise and the Valuation Office Agency are all accessible through the GIS. The Crown Prosecution Service (CPS) has recently opened a site at <URL http://www.cps.gov.uk/> (see Figure 5.2). At present, much of the information on this site is general, but it does contain a document outlining the

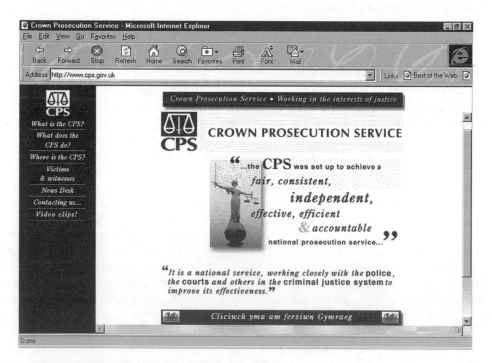

Figure 5.2   Crown Prosecution Service Web site

role of the CPS (including the Code for Prosecutors) and the CPS document on victims and witnesses.

The Court Service Web site is currently being developed, and the information it contains is patchy. Nevertheless, it will eventually publish Daily Lists, Practice Directions and landmark judgments of the Court of Appeal and the High Court. At the time of writing there is a selection of judgments that include *R* v. *Secretary of State for the Home Office ex parte Myra Hindley* and the *British Coal Respiratory Disease Litigation*.

The GIS will become an increasingly valuable site for lawyers. Parts of the site are already well developed and provide immediate access to those practitioners who do not enjoy the benefits of a nearby HMSO outlet. The search facility on the GIS is helpful, although it does tend to throw up too much information for the busy practitioner. The MUSCAT search engine enables users to mark results and then use the Improve or Expand features to generate more focused searches.

JUSTIS online and on CD-ROM

JUSTIS, produced by Context, enables access to a full-text database through a CD-ROM, an online database or a combination of both. The main advantage of the combination approach is that it reduces online charges for heavy users. Since the last edition of this *Manual* the content of JUSTIS has increased considerably, and new material is still being added. Amongst the materials currently being put on to the database are *The Common Market Law Reports*, *The Criminal Appeal and Sentencing Reports* and *Lloyd's Electronic Law Reports*. Table 5.1 shows the products that are available through JUSTIS.

Searching JUSTIS is relatively easy. On entering it the user decides whether to select a particular CD-ROM, connect to the online service or return to the last used database. On choosing the CD-ROM option, for example, the range of databases

Table 5.1 *JUSTIS databases*

BLISS	Bibliographic database of building and construction law
CELEX	Full text of EC legislation treaties and cases
European Commentaries	EC legislative information for businesses including the DTI's Spearhead
Electronic Law Reports	130 years of case law from the Council of Law Reporting
European References	EC bibliographic database
Family Law	Full text of *Jordan's Family Law Reports* since 1980
Industrial Cases	Full text of *Industrial Cases Reports* since 1972
JUSTIS Online	CD-ROM updates online plus some online only databases
Official Journal C	Full text of EC proposed legislation
Parliament	Bibliographic database of the publications and proceedings of UK Parliament
Statutory Instruments	Full text of UK Statutory Instruments since 1987
Weekly Law	Full text of the *Weekly Law Reports* since 1953

is revealed and the user selects one. Choosing the WEEKLY LAW REPORTS again presents users with a choice – this time, of the sector in which they wish to search. The options cover the full report, subject matter, ships' names, and cases, statutes and statutory instruments judicially considered.

Having entered the database, searching is relatively easy. The search phrase is entered into the Query Box. Five operators are available: AND, OR, NOT, WITHIN and NEAR. The WITHIN options allow searches within 25 characters either side, before or after. The NEAR option is a proximity search fixed at 40 characters.

A number of helpful devices are built into JUSTIS. The Field button enables users to search a particular section of the database. Using the WEEKLY LAW REPORTS Field facility users are able to confine the search to Title, Catchwords, Headnote, Citation, Counsel, Judgement, Order or Solicitor. The Index facility enables users to identify possible variations of the search term. The Index contains all the words in the database that is being searched. On choosing the Index button on the main screen users enter the 'Word root' – that is, the search word. JUSTIS then provides a number of 'Keywords' which are variations of the word root. These keywords will include variations in spelling and different tenses. Users can then select which of those keywords they wish to include in the search. In certain circumstances the Index facility can prove useful as a reminder of the variations which may exist. Index can be limited to a single field rather than the entire database.

Another aid to searching is the thesaurus facility that is available on some of the JUSTIS databases. If this facility is not available on a particular database the Thesaurus button is greyed out. On entering the search term, the Thesaurus will reveal a list of terms related to the search term. The hit list starts with the broadest references and these may be narrowed by working down the list and using the 'Related term' (RT) and 'Scope Note' (SN). Scope Notes provide further information on the term that is being searched. The thesaurus assists in identifying a more focused search and makes the user aware of the options that are available.

The results of a search are listed on the Titles screen. These may be saved, printed or displayed. Previous searches are listed in the History box and these may be saved for future use. Reading the document is aided by the Term and Find buttons: the Term button at the bottom of the screen allows the user to move between the occurrences of the search term; Find is a facility for searching words within the documents identified by the search.

JUSTIS is a database that has responded positively to the needs of its users. Although it is not as comprehensive a database as LEXIS, the material it does cover is made accessible by a friendly operating environment and the advantage of the CD-ROM/online flexibility. Its coverage is now more comprehensive than in its early days which makes it a worthy competitor of LEXIS for those whose potential usage is compatible with its content.

Current legal information

The hard copies of *Current Law* have been a regular feature of law libraries and practitioners' offices for many years. This comprehensive updating service has provided busy professionals with a concise up-to-date guide to recent developments in the law. Combining the comprehensive coverage of *Current Law* with the improved accessibility through electronic means greatly enhances what is already a valuable resource for the busy lawyer. Of course it must be recognized that the material in the electronic *Current Law* version is not full-text and simply acts as the gatekeeper for the full-text material. Nevertheless, this should not detract from the value of the database as a means of rapid updating and raising awareness of current developments. The Current Legal Information (CLI) service contains databases available in a range of different combinations on four separate discs. An Internet service is available as an add-on to CD-ROM subscriptions. The four discs available are:

- SUPER CURRENT LAW
  - Legal Journals Index
  - Daily Law Reports Index
  - Financial Journals Index
  - BADGER
  - Current Law Case Citator
  - Current Law Legislation Citator
  - Inns of Court catalogues
- COMBINED SERVICE DISC
  - Current Law
  - Legal Journals Index
  - Daily Law Reports Index
  - Financial Journals Index
  - BADGER
- JOURNALS INDEX DISC
  - Legal Journals Index
  - Financial Journals Index
- CURRENT LAW CITATORS DISC
  - Current Law Case Citator, 1989 to date
  - Current Law Legislation Citator, 1989 to date
  - Catalogues of the libraries of the Inns of Court
  - (The Case and Legislation Citators are updated monthly and are up to date to the current month.)

The following databases are currently available for access over the Internet:

- CURRENT LAW CASE CITATOR
- BADGER GREY PAPER INDEX
- LEGAL JOURNALS INDEX
- FINANCIAL JOURNALS INDEX

- CURRENT LAW CASES
- CURRENT LAW LEGISLATION CITATOR
- INNS OF COURT CATALOGUES.

Five databases make up the CLI:

- CURRENT LAW indexes legislation, case law, books and articles;
- the LEGAL JOURNALS INDEX indexes over 300 UK law journals and a number of international English-language publications;
- the FINANCIAL JOURNALS INDEX indexes articles on insurance, pensions and banking from 1992 onward;
- the DAILY LAW REPORTS INDEX summarizes all cases reported in *The Times*, *Financial Times*, *The Scotsman*, *Lloyd's List*, and the *Independent*;
- BADGER indexes and provides abstracts of supplementary legal materials such as articles from newspapers on law-related topics, press releases from UK government agencies, House of Commons *Weekly Information Bulletins*, statutory instruments, and the proceedings of the European Court of Justice.

Within its limited remit CLI is an excellent tool for the busy lawyer who needs to be kept up-to-date on a wide range of issues. It is easily searched, and the results provide a useful pointer to those who wish to research a particular topic in greater detail.

FINDLAW

There are a considerable number of US legal databases available online. FINDLAW can be found at <URL http://www.finelaw.com> (*sic*) and provides a comprehensive source of American legal material (see Figure 5.3). Included in the material that may be accessed through this site are the following:

- Laws: Cases & Codes:
  - Supreme Court Opinions
  - Constitution
  - State Laws
- State Law Resources
- Legal Practice Materials
- Consultants and Experts
- Legal Subject Index.

Searching this site is relatively straightforward. Searching for Supreme Court decisions on 'disability rights' requires the user to enter the Supreme Court Opinions options in the Law: Cases and Codes option. The search identifies a number of hits and allows the user to press the Highlight Hits button and be taken straight to the use of the terms in the cases identified. Topics can also be searched using the Legal Subject Index option. This provides a number of general subject headings, including 'Year 2000'. Entering the Civil Rights option reveals a further

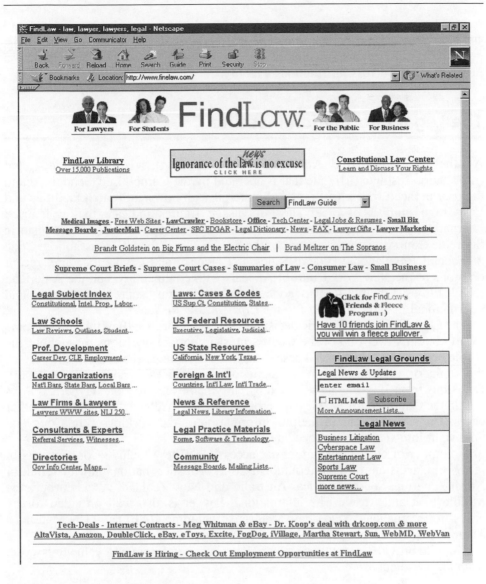

Figure 5.3   FINDLAW Web site

list of subheadings that includes 'Disabilities'. This reveals a useful crop of hits that range from the Americans with Disabilities Act Document Centre to the US Department of Justice ADA homepage.

The site also contains links to a number of other national and international legal sites. Using this facility allows subject searches to be made of many other jurisdictions including Canada, Europe and Asia. This is a very useful facility, especially for those practising or researching in the area of international trade.

FINDLAW is an exciting site to visit. Although the vast range of material and subjects covered mean that most people will only use a small part, it is, nevertheless, a serious attempt at making one-stop access to law within a jurisdiction and across jurisdictions a reality.

The Legal Information Institute

Another comprehensive American site well worth visiting is the Legal Information Institute (LII) site that is operated by the Cornell Law School. Again, the user is faced with a vast range of material with powerful search facilities and links to a number of other sites. Its usage figures indicate that it is used internationally. The sight contains the Institute's collection of recent and historic Supreme Court decisions, versions of the full US Code, the US Constitution, Code of Federal Regulations, Federal Rules of Evidence and Civil Procedure, recent opinions of the New York Court of Appeals with commentary, and the American Legal Ethics Library. It also contains other federal, state, and foreign and international material. It is host to the *Cornell Law Review*.

The LII collection of historic decisions (that is, before 1990) of the US Supreme Court contains over 600 of the Court's most important decisions throughout the whole period of its existence. These can be searched under the name of the parties, the topic or (very usefully) the name of the justices serving on the Court. Decisions from 1990 can be searched by party name and by topic. Hypertext links within the Court reports enable easy cross-reference to relevant legislation or other cases. The site also contains helpful information on the working of the Court and an insight into some of its procedures.

A number of other jurisdictions are accessible. These include Constitutions of the World, decisions of the International Court of Justice, national law material for North America, South America, Australia and New Zealand, Asia, Europe, the Middle East and Africa. The international lawyer is also well provided for by access to International Trade Law Materials (including GATT) and UN Materials. There is also a collection of Treaties Dealing with the Environment.

This site provides a wealth of material and will be of immense value to lawyers from all jurisdictions.

Conclusion

Legal databases, available either on CD-ROM or online, have continued to develop both in the quantity of the data they contain and also the quality of their search facilities. Clearly, they are here to stay and no doubt more specialist and generalist databases will appear. The choice for the ultimate user is difficult. However, he or she should consider a number of factors before deciding which one to choose. Cost must be a factor and, here, combinations of CD-ROM and online services prove to be attractive. Similarly, level of usage will be important, especially for the smaller practitioner who may only occasionally have recourse to an electronic database, although when it is used the subject matter of the search may vary from family law to the finer points of commercial law. This leads to consideration of the content of the database. To what extent does it come as one comprehensive package (as with LEXIS) or in discrete packages (as with JUSTIS)? Ease of use is becoming less of a problem as access becomes easier and more and more lawyers are being trained to search such databases.

American provision represents an exciting new development in increasing access to legal material. The very size of the sources and their easy and cheap accessibility illustrate the many benefits electronic information can provide. The Government Information Service site is perhaps the closest that the UK has to such a comprehensive and freely accessible site. Of course, accessing such a vast bank of material calls for further refinement of search skills – a demand that legal education must satisfy.

The move towards greater use of electronic legal databases will be hard to resist even for the most conservative of practitioners. Although many in the profession originally thought that such devices were a threat to their existence, it has now been shown that they are a valuable tool in representing the interests of clients and enhancing the quality of legal advice. Perhaps the next challenge is an electronic legal database that a layperson can use.

Database index

The following index contains references to all databases and electronic resources mentioned in the text as well as to the information providers, online vendors or CD-ROM publishers that make them available. Where appropriate, file names have been linked to databases. All databases are in upper case letters, as they are in the text.

ABECOR 201
ABI/INFORM 187, 191, 196, 198
ABREN *see* AUSTRALIAN BIOLOGICAL RESEARCH NETWORK
ACE *see* AUTOMATED CREDIT ENQUIRY
ACQUISITIONS MONTHLY INTERNATIONAL 206
ACS *see* American Chemical Society
ADP DATA SOURCES 205
ADP GLOBAL REPORT 191, 201, 205
AFX-UK 206
AGDOC (DERWENT WORLD PATENTS INDEX) 55, 56, 133
AGRIS 133
AICPA *see* American Institute of Certified Public Accountants
AIMS 195
AL IDRISI 5
ALTAVISTA 4, 5, 11, 18, 19, 143, 238, 239
AMDATA 206
American Institute of Certified Public Accountants 161
American Petroleum Institute Central Abstracting and Indexing Service *see* API ENCOMPASS
ANBAR MANAGEMENT INTELLIGENCE 196
API ENCOMPASS 109–113
APIPAT 44, 46, 55, 109–11, 128, 131–2, 134
ARMADILLO 168
ASAP PUBLICATIONS 196
ASSIST 128
Associated Banks of Europe Corporation 201
Association of UK Media Librarians 240
AUSTRALIAN BIOLOGICAL RESEARCH NETWORK 5, 7
AUTOMATED CREDIT ENQUIRY 198

BADGER GREY PAPER INDEX 257–8
BANKING INFORMATION SOURCE 192
BBC WORLDWIDE MONITORING FILE 193–5

BCC MARKET RESEARCH 179
BEILSTEIN ABSTRACTS 122
BEVERAGE MARKETING RESEARCH REPORTS 180
BIALL *see* British and Irish Association of Law Librarians
BIBLIOGRAPHIC DATABASE OF BUILDING AND CONSTRUCTION LAW 255
BILETA *see* British and Irish Legal Technology Association
BIOBUSINESS 133
BIOTECHNOLOGY ABSTRACTS 133, 136
BIS BANKING INFORMATION SOURCES 198
BLDSC *see* British Library Document Supply Centre
BLISS *see* BIBLIOGRAPHIC DATABASE OF BUILDING AND CONSTRUCTION LAW
Bloomberg 204
BLOOMBERG NEWS 204
BONDS 205–6
BONDSPEC 206
BOSTON GLOBE 230
BRIDGE CAPITAL MARKETS 204
BRIDGE CHANNEL 204–5
BRIDGE COMMODITIES 204
Bridge Data 204–5
BRIDGE EQUITIES 204
BRIDGE NEWS 204
British and Irish Association of Law Librarians 243
British and Irish Legal Technology Association 243
British Library Document Supply Centre 195, 196
Bureau van Dijk 162, 180, 187, 188–91
BUSINESS AND INDUSTRY 187
BUSINESS AND INDUSTRY ON THE WEB 191–2
BUSINESS AND MANAGEMENT PRACTICES 196
BUSINESS CENSUS 198
Business Communications Company 179
BUSINESS INTELLIGENCE PROGRAM RESEARCH CATALOG 195

CA SEARCH 36, 40, 44, 113–16, 132, 134, 136, 137
CA SEARCH *see also* CHEMICAL ABSTRACTS
CAB ABSTRACTS 10, 133
Canada Law Books, Inc. 126
CANADIAN PATENT REPORTER 126
CAOLD 114, 132, 137
CAPITAL DATA BONDWARE 206
CAPITAL DATA LOANWARE 206
CAPLUS 83, 114, 116, 137
CAROL 162, 166–7
CAS *see* CHEMICAL ABSTRACTS
CAS *see* Chemical Abstracts Service, ACS
CASES (LEXIS-NEXIS file) 248, 250
CASLINK 114
CASREACT 132, 138
CD/CORPORATE: EUROPEAN MERGERS AND ACQUISITIONS 206
CD/CORPORATE: US MERGERS AND ACQUISITIONS 206
CDB 46
CD-ROM MARQUIS WHO'S WHO PLUS 198
CDX *see* Credit Data Exchange
CELEX 251, 255

Central Computer and Technology Agency 252–5
Chadwyck-Healey 220, 226–7, 241
CHEMDOC (DERWENT WORLD PATENTS INDEX) 56
CHEMICAL ABSTRACTS 10, 43, 46, 67
CHEMICAL ABSTRACTS *see also* CA SEARCH
Chemical Abstracts Service 43–4, 69, 82–3, 110, 111, 113–16
CHEMICAL ENGINEERING ABSTRACTS 134
CHEMICAL PATENTS PLUS 44, 82–3
ChemPort 97
CHINAPATS 107, 136
CHINESE PATENTS ABSTRACTS 107, 138
CIB (file name) *see* INTERNATIONAL PATENT CLASSIFICATION
CITIBANK CHANNEL 207–9
Citicorp 191, 205, 207–9
CLAIMS 68–73, 132, 136, 137, 138
CLAIMS BIBLIO/ABSTRACT 68, 72
CLAIMS CITATION 138
CLAIMS COMPOUND REGISTRY 73, 138
CLAIMS COMPREHENSIVE 44, 68, 71, 72, 73, 126, 128, 131, 133, 134
CLAIMS CURRENT PATENT LEGAL STATUS 69, 72–3, 74, 78, 127
CLAIMS REASSIGNMENTS AND REEXAMINATIONS *see* CLAIMS CURRENT PATENT
     LEGAL STATUS
CLAIMS REFERENCE 69, 72, 73, 126
CLAIMS UDB 41, 46, 48
CLAIMS UNITERM 44, 68, 71, 72, 73, 126, 128, 131, 133, 134
CLAIMS/CITATIONS 69, 72, 131
CLI *see* Current Legal Information
COMBINED CHEMICAL DICTIONARY 122
COMBINED SERVICE DISC 257
COMCAS (LEXIS-NEXIS library) 251
COMMERCE BUSINESS DAILY 195
Commonwealth Cases Library *see* COMCAS
COMMUNITY OF SCIENCE 126
COMPANIES (AFX-UK) 206
COMPANIES HOUSE DIRECT 160–61
Companies Registration Office 158, 161
COMPANY ANNUAL REPORTS ON-LINE *see* CAROL
COMPUTER NEWS FULL TEXT 192
CONSUMER REPORTS 180, 192
Consumer Union 180
Context Ltd 255–6
Cornell Law School 260
Corporate Intelligence Service 43, 73, 75
COUNTRY REPORT SERVICES 201
Court of Justice of the European Communities 251
CPS *see* Crown Prosecution Service
CRC Press 122
Credit Data Exchange 198
CRO *see* Companies Registration Office
CRONOS 200
Crown Prosecution Service 254
CRRX (file name) *see* CLAIMS CURRENT PATENT LEGAL STATUS
CRXX (file name) *see* CLAIMS CURRENT PATENT LEGAL STATUS
CSO MACRO-ECONOMIC DATA BANK 200

CURRENT BIOTECHNOLOGY ABSTRACTS 133
CURRENT DRUGS 133
CURRENT DRUGS FAST ALERT 117–19, 133
CURRENT LAW CASE CITATOR 257–8
CURRENT LAW CASES 258
CURRENT LAW CITATORS DISC 257
CURRENT LAW LEGISLATION CITATOR 258
Current Legal Information 257–8
Current Patents Ltd 117–19

DAILY LAW REPORTS INDEX 257–8
DAILY TELEGRAPH, THE 178
DARC EURECAS 116
Data Resources, Inc. 199
DATAMONITOR MARKETLINE UK SNAPSHOTS 179
DataStar 5, 10, 117, 119
DATASTREAM/ICV 162, 199, 204, 205
DELPHION INTELLECTUAL PROPERTY NETWORK 27, 44, 52, 86–9, 109, 140
DERWENT CROP PROTECTION FILE 133
Derwent Information Services 27, 38, 50–61, 111–13, 119, 122, 127, 128
DERWENT JOURNAL OF SYNTHETIC METHODS 138
DERWENT PATENT CITATION INDEX 57–61, 131, 137, 138
DERWENT REACTION DOCUMENTATION SERVICE 132
Derwent Web site 140
DERWENT WORLD PATENTS INDEX *see also* WORLD PATENTS INDEX 27, 36, 38, 40, 41,
    43, 44, 46, 50–61, 67, 87, 109, 110, 111, 122, 127–8, 131, 132, 133, 134, 136–7, 138–9, 140
Deutsches Institut für Medizinische Dokumentation und Information *see* DIMDI
Deutsches Patentamt 105–7, 128
DGENE (file name) *see* GENESEQ
DIALOG 4, 5, 9, 10, 36, 38, 50, 52, 56, 57, 61, 62, 63–6, 69, 73, 78–82, 93, 94–7, 107–8, 109–10,
    126, 127, 135, 136, 138–9, 140, 154, 158, 178, 179, 196, 197, 198, 205, 220, 241
Dialog Corporation, The 7, 78–82, 162, 180, 187, 191, 210, 219, 228
DIALOG OneSearch 78
DIALOG QUOTES AND TRADING 205
DialogWeb 228, 231
DIMDI 4, 9
DIRECT MARKETING SERVICE 180
DJSM (file name) *see* DERWENT REACTION DOCUMENTATION SERVICE
DOE ENERGY 134
DogPile 5
DoubleTwist.com 122
DOW JONES 241
DOW JONES ENHANCED CURRENT QUOTES 204–5
DOW JONES HISTORICAL QUOTES 205
DOW JONES NEWS/RETRIEVAL 220
DOW JONES REAL-TIME QUOTES 205
Dow Jones Telerate 204
DPCI (file name) *see* DERWENT PATENT CITATION INDEX
DPIN (file name) *see* DRUG PATENTS INTERNATIONAL
DPINNS (file name) *see* DRUG PATENTS INTERNATIONAL
DRI COUNTRY DATABASE: UNITED KINGDOM 201
DRI COUNTRY DATABASE: US CENTRAL 201
DRI COUNTRY DATABASEs 200–201
DRI RISK MANAGEMENT DATA MODULE 201–3

DRI *see* Data Resources, Inc.
DRI WORLD FORECAST DATABASE 200
DRI/McGraw-Hill 200
DRUG DATA REPORTS 122, 133
DRUG MARKET – COMPANIES 192
DRUG MARKET – COUNTRIES 192
DRUG PATENTS INTERNATIONAL 119–21, 130, 132–3
DRUGS OF THE FUTURE 122, 133
DTAX (LEXIS-NEXIS file) 248
Dun & Bradstreet 153, 154, 158–60, 161, 168, 170, 180
DUN & BRADSTREET EXECUTIVES REPORT 197
DUNS ELECTRONIC BUSINESS DIRECTORY 197–198
DWPI (file name) *see* DERWENT WORLD PATENTS INDEX

EASY MAILING AND MARKETING APPLICATIONS 180, 187, 188–91
ECLATX 97–101, 125, 136
ECON (file name) *see* ECONOMIST, THE
ECONOMIC LITERATURE INDEX 201
ECONOMIST, THE 152, 226
EDGARPLUS 162
EDOC 45, 68
EIU MARKET RESEARCH 179
EIU VIEWSWIRE 193
ELECTRONIC YELLOW PAGES *see* DUNS ELECTRONIC BUSINESS DIRECTORY
EMMA *see* EASY MAILING AND MARKETING APPLICATIONS
ENCARTA 9
ENGGEN (LEXIS-NEXIS library) 248, 249, 250
Engineering Information, Inc. 109–11
ENTREPRENEUR'S GUIDE TO FRANCHISE AND BUSINESS OPPORTUNITIES 195
EPAT 97–101
EPIDOS 140
EPO *see* European Patent Office
EPO Web site 62, 140
EPRC Ltd 195
EPTEXT 98, 136
EQUIFAX INFOCHECK 161, 162, 198
ES (LEXIS-NEXIS file) 249
ESP@CENET 44, 93, 97, 109, 116, 137
ESPACE 93, 128
ESPACE FIRST CD-ROM 128
ESPACE GLOBALPAT CD-ROM 128
EURCOM (LEXIS-NEXIS library) 250–51
EURECAS 137
EUROLEX 244
EUROLOC 195
Euromoney 179, 195
Euromonitor 180
EUROMONITOR MARKET RESEARCH 179
EUROPATFULL 97, 101–4, 137
European Commission 251
European Patent Office 36, 44, 61–8, 93–7, 128
EUROPEAN PATENT REGISTER 97
EUROPEAN PATENTS FULLTEXT 94–7, 138
European Policies Research Centre 195

EUROPEAN REFERENCES 255
EVENTLINE 193
EXBOND 206
EXCITE 11, 18
EXECUTIVES 197
EXPERIAN 162, 198
EXPERIAN LINK 168, 170–73
EXPORT INTELLIGENCE SERVICE 193
EXTEL 162, 191
EXTEL EXAMINER *see* AFX-UK

FACTIVA 145
FAME *see* FINANCIAL ANALYSIS MADE EASY
FARMDOC (DERWENT WORLD PATENTS INDEX) 55, 56, 133
FILDATA S.r.l. 122
FINANCE AND BANKING NEWSLETTERS 192–3
FINANCIAL ANALYSIS MADE EASY CD-ROM 162
FINANCIAL FORECAST (WEFA) 200–201
FINANCIAL JOURNALS INDEX 257–8
FINANCIAL TIMES, THE 152, 174, 226
FIND/SVP MARKET RESEARCH 179
FINDEX 179
FINDLAW 258–60
FIZ Karlsruhe 105
FIZ Technik 101
FLUIDEX 134
FOREIGN EXCHANGE 205
FORTUN (file name) *see* FORTUNE
FORTUNE 152, 196
FPAT 43, 97–101
FREEDONIA MARKET RESEARCH 179
French Patent office *see* L'Institut de Propriété Industrielle
FROST AND SULLIVAN MARKET INTELLIGENCE 180
FT DISCOVERY 204
FT MERGERS AND ACQUISITIONS INTERNATIONAL 206
FT PRICES ON CD-ROM 204
FT PROFILE 174–7, 179, 198, 219, 200, 222–4, 226, 233, 236, 241
FT PROFILEWEB 223
FT REPORTS 192
FT REPORTS: ENERGY AND ENVIRONMENT 192
FT REPORTS: TECHNOLOGY 192
Funk and Scott 187

GALE BIOGRAPHICS 198
Gale Research, Inc. 198
GENESEQ 122–23, 133
GENOME 18
GERMAN PATENT REGISTER 107
GIS *see* Government Information Service
GLOBALPAT 93–4
Government Information Service 252–5, 261
GUARDIAN, THE 174
GUARDIAN, THE/OBSERVER 226
Hansard 253

HARVARD BUSINESS REVIEW 143, 196–7
HELECON ON CD-ROM 196
Hemmington Scott 197
HEMMINGTON SCOTT PEOPLE DATABASE 197
HM Customs and Excise 254

IAC BUSINESS APPLIED RESEARCH, THEORY, AND SCHOLARSHIP 196
IAC BUSINESS ARTS *see* IAC BUSINESS APPLIED RESEARCH, THEORY, AND
    SCHOLARSHIP
IAC COMPANY INTELLIGENCE 162
IAC F&S INDEX 187
IAC INDUSTRY EXPRESS 187
IAC MAGAZINE DATABASE 187
IAC MANAGEMENT CONTENTS 152, 196
IAC MERGERS AND ACQUISITIONS 206
IAC NEWSLETTER DATABASE 192
IAC PHARMA-BIOMED BUSINESS JOURNALS 192
IAC PREDICASTS 179
IAC PROMT 179, 187
IAC TRADE AND INDUSTRY DATABASE 187
IBM Corporation 86–9
IBM INTELLECTUAL PROPERTY NETWORK *see* DELPHION INTELLECTUAL PROPERTY
    NETWORK
ICC 161, 162, 180
ICC INTERNATIONAL BUSINESS RESEARCH 192
ICC KEY NOTE CD-ROM 179
ICC KEY NOTE MARKET RESEARCH 179
ICC SHAREWATCH 206
IDD Information Services 205
IDD LOANBASE 206
IDD M & A REPORTS 206
IFI CLAIMS Patent Services 68–73
IFICDB 138
IFIREP 73, 126, 137
IFIUDB 43, 69, 138
IMF DIRECTION OF TRADE DATABASE 200
IMF INTERNATIONAL FINANCIAL STATISTICS DATABASE 200
IMF *see* International Monetary Fund
IMSWORLD Publications Ltd 119–21, 130, 192
INDEPENDENT 226
INDUSTRIES 191
INFOLINK 168–70
Information Access Company 152, 153, 179, 187, 192, 196, 206
INFORMATION SCIENCE ABSTRACTS 132
INFOSEEK 11
INIS 132, 134
INKTOMI 4
Inland Revenue 254
INNS OF COURT CATALOGUES 258
INPADOC *see also* PLUSPAT 44, 54, 61–8, 75, 93–4, 107, 114, 119, 120, 129, 135, 137, 138, 140
INPADOC PFS/PRS 61, 62, 67
INPI *see* L'Institut de Propriété Industrielle
INSIDE CONFERENCES 195
INSPEC 10, 132, 134, 136

Institute for Scientific Information 6
INTERNATIONAL BUSINESS OPPORTUNITIES SERVICE 193
International Monetary Fund 200
INTERNATIONAL PATENT CLASSIFICATION 125, 136
International Patent Documentation Center 61–8
INTERNET GRATEFUL MED 6
INTLAW (LEXIS-NEXIS library) 252
INVESTEXT 192
IPC:CLASS CD-ROM 125
IRL LIFE SCIENCES COLLECTION 133
ISI *see* Institute for Scientific Information
ISMA 206–7
ISMEC 134
ISTA Inc. 109
ITALPAT 122

Japanese Patent Information Organization 38, 44, 107–9, 128
JAPIO *see* PATENT ABSTRACTS OF JAPAN
Johns Hopkins School of Medicine 18
JORDANS 161, 162
JORDANS SHAREHOLDER SERVICE 206
JOURNALS INDEX DISC 257
JUPITER MARKET RESEARCH 180
JUREP 127
JURGE 127
JURINPI 127
JUSTINFO Ltd 122
JUSTIS 255–6, 261

KEESINGS ON CD-ROM 201
KEESINGS RECORD OF WORLD EVENTS 201
KEY BRITISH ENTERPRISES 158
Knight-Ridder 210
KOMPASS 158

LEARN (LEXIS-NEXIS file) 248
Legal Information Institute 260
LEGAL JOURNAL INDEX 257–8
LEGIS (CELEX file) 251
LEGSTAT 62, 67
LEXIS-NEXIS 5, 43, 62, 75–8, 107, 125–6, 134, 142, 152, 161, 174, 178, 179, 187, 192, 193–5, 198,
    201, 204, 206, 219, 220, 224–5, 236, 241, 243, 244, 248–252, 253, 256, 261
LEXPAT 75–8
LEXPAT (LEXIS-NEXIS library) 126
LII *see* Legal Information Institute
L'Institut de Propriété Industrielle 68, 97–101, 117, 125, 127, 128, 136
LITALERT 127
LOS ANGELES TIMES, THE 178
LRNSTA (LEXIS-NEXIS file) 248
LYCOS 11

M & A EUROPE 206
MCCARTHY ONLINE 223
MCCARTHY PRESS CUTTINGS SERVICE 174

MAID plc 180, 181–6, 210, 241
MAIL, THE 226
MANAGEMENT AND MARKETING ABSTRACTS 196
MANAGEMENT HELPLINE, THE 196
MANAGEMENT TODAY 196
MARKET AND BUSINESS DEVELOPMENT 179
MARKETING AND ADVERTISING REFERENCE SERVICE 179
MARKETLINE UK SNAPSHOTS *see* DATAMONITOR MARKETLINE UK SNAPSHOTS
MARKETS (AFX-UK) 206
Markets and Industry (LEXIS-NEXIS library) 192
MARKINTEL 179
Markush DARC 117
MARPAT 41, 43, 114, 115, 116, 132, 137
MARQUIS WHO'S WHO 198
MARQUIS WHO'S WHO *see also* CD-ROM MARQUIS WHO'S WHO PLUS
MARS *see* MARKETING AND ADVERTISING REFERENCE SERVICE
MARTINDALE-HUBBELL LAW DIRECTORY 198
MATERIALS BUSINESS FILE 192
Media General Financial Services 206
MEDIA GENERAL PLUS 162
MEDLINE 5, 10, 20
MEETING AGENDA 193, 195
MEGAINSIGHT STOCKS AND INDUSTRIES CD-ROM 206
MERCK INDEX 122, 132
MERGED MARKUSH SERVICE 56, 117, 137
MERGERS AND ACQUISITIONS 206
MERGERS AND ACQUISITIONS (LEXIS-NEXIS library) 206
METACRAWLER 5
MGFS'S PRICE AND VOLUME DATABASE 206
MicroPatent 43, 44, 62, 128, 140
MicroPatent PATENT AND TRADEMARK WEB SITE 91–93
MicroPatent WORLDWIDE PATSEARCH 91–3, 109
Microsoft Corporation 9
MICROSOFT ENCARTA *see* ENCARTA
MINTEL MARKET RESEARCH REPORTS 179
MMS (file name) *see* MERGED MARKUSH SERVICE
MONEY MARKETS 205
MOODY'S 170, 173
MOODY'S DIVIDEND ACHIEVERS ONLINE SERVICE 206
MPHARM 137
MUSCAT 255

NAARS 161
National Library of Medicine 6, 10
NATPRV (CELEX file) 251
NEW YORK TIMES ONDISC, THE 174
NEWS ALERT 204
NEWS TRIBUNE, THE 238
NewsEdge 204
NEWSPAPERS ON THE WEB 241
NLM *see* National Library of Medicine
NME EXPRESS 122, 133
NORTHERN ECHO, THE 228
NORTHERNLIGHT 5, 11

NZ EXPLORER 5

OCLC FIRSTSEARCH 5
OECD MAIN ECONOMIC INDICATORS DATABASE 200
OECD NATIONAL ACCOUNTS DATABASE 200
OG 125 PLUS 128
OG PLUS 127
OMNI *see* ORGANISING MEDICAL NETWORKED INFORMATION
ONESOURCE 162, 197, 206
Orbit 10
ORGANISING MEDICAL NETWORKED INFORMATION 20
Ovid Online 5, 9
Oxford Molecular 122

PADE 101–4
PAIS INTERNATIONAL 201
PAPERBOY 231–2
PARLIAMENT 255
PARLQ (CELEX file) 251
PASCAL 132, 133, 134, 136
PAST *see* PATENT STATUS FILE
PATDPA 38, 43, 105–7, 137
PATE 101–4
PATENT ABSTRACTS OF JAPAN 26, 38, 40, 43, 67, 75, 83, 87, 93, 107–9, 132, 133, 134, 136,
    137, 138
Patent and Trade Mark Group Web site 140
Patent Information Users Group Web site 140
PATENT STATUS FILE 127
PATENTBIBLE 128
PATENTS OF RUSSIA CD-ROM 128
PATFULL (DIALOG OneSearch) 78
PATINTELLIGENCE 73, 75
PATIPC (file name) *see* INTERNATIONAL PATENT CLASSIFICATION
PATMG *see* Patent and Trade Mark Group
PATOLIS 44, 61, 109, 122
PATON/PAJ 109
PATOS 101–4
PATOS EPO 137
PATOSDE 101–4
PATOSEP 38, 101–4
PATOSWO 101–4
PCT GAZETTE 43
PCTPAT 97–101
PEOPLE (LEXIS-NEXIS library) 198
PERFECT INFORMATION 162, 206
PESTDOC *see* DERWENT CROP PROTECTION FILE
PHARM (file name) *see* PHARMSEARCH
PHARMAPROJECTS 122, 133
PHARMSEARCH 43, 44, 97, 117, 118, 131, 132, 136, 137
PHIND: PHARMACEUTICAL AND HEALTHCARE INDUSTRY NEWS 192
PHYSICS BRIEFS 132, 134
PIRA – PACKAGING, PAPER, PRINTING AND PUBLISHING, AND NONWOVENS
    ABSTRACTS 192
PIRA *see* Printing Industries Research Association

PIUG *see* Patent Information Users Group
PIUG-L Discussion List 140
PLASDOC (DERWENT WORLD PATENTS INDEX) 55, 56
PLUSPAT 45, 68, 94, 125, 136, 140
PLUSPAT *see also* INPADOC
Political Risk Service 201
PREP (CELEX file) 251
PRESTEL ON-LINE CITIFEED 204
PRIMARK 162–6, 199
PRIMARK GLOBAL ACCESS 162–6
PRIMARK/DOW JONES EQUITIES SERVICE 204
Primary Source Media 241
Printing Industries Research Association 192, 196
PROFOUND 180, 181–6, 201, 219
PROFOUND LIVEWIRE 204
PROQUEST DIRECT 220
PROSPECT LOCATOR 198
Prous Science 122, 130, 133
PSYCINFO 10
PSYCLIT 10
PUBMED 5

QL Systems 126
QPAT 44
QPAT-WW 44, 83, 86, 87, 88
QUEST ECONOMICS ON CD-ROM 201
Questel-Orbit 38, 45, 50, 51–2, 55, 56, 62, 68, 69, 70–71, 74, 83, 86, 94, 97, 98, 100–101, 107,
    111–13, 117, 118, 119–21, 122, 125, 127, 135, 136–7, 140, 179
Quicklaw 126

Raymond Morris Group Limited 168
RDS *see* Responsive Database Services
REGISTRY 114, 116, 132, 133, 137, 138
REGISTRY *see also* CLAIMS REFERENCE
Responsive Database Services 191–2, 196
Reuters 204, 212
REUTERS BUSINESS BRIEFING 145–6, 152, 174, 179, 187
REUTERS NEWS EXPLORER 204

S&P *see* STANDARD AND POOR'S
SCAN-A-BID 195
SCIENCES CITATION INDEX 122
SCIMA 196
SCISEARCH *see* SCIENCES CITATION INDEX
SCOTSMAN, THE 227
SDC WORLDWIDE MERGERS AND ACQUISITIONS 206
SEC ONLINE 161, 162
SEC *see* Securities and Exchange Commission (US)
Securities and Exchange Commission (US) 158, 161
Securities Data Company 206
SI (LEXIS-NEXIS file) 248, 249
SilverPlatter 5, 10
SOCIAL SCIENCE INFORMATION GATEWAY 5, 8, 20
SOSIG *see* SOCIAL SCIENCE INFORMATION GATEWAY

Special Libraries Association 240
Spicers Centre for Europe 251
STANDARD AND POOR'S 162, 170, 173, 191
STANDARD AND POOR'S REGISTER OF DIRECTORS AND EXECUTIVES 198
STARS 195
STAT (LEXIS-NEXIS file) 248, 249
STATIS (LEXIS-NEXIS file) 248, 249
STN International 4, 5, 10, 36, 38, 43, 44, 50, 52, 56–7, 58–62, 67, 69, 71, 73, 82–3, 84–6, 97, 101–4,
    105–6, 107, 109, 113–16, 119, 120, 122, 123, 125, 126, 132, 133, 135, 136, 137–8, 140
SUMMARY OF PROPOSED PROJECTS 195
SUPER CURRENT LAW CD-ROM 257
SUPERTECH 133

TDS Inform 198
TECHNIMETRICS EXECUTIVE DIRECTORY 197
TECHNIMETRICS SHARE WORLD 206
TED *see* TENDERS ELECTRONIC DAILY
TELECOMMUNICATIONS NEWSLETTERS 193
TELEGRAPH, THE 226, 229
Televisual Data 220, 227, 228
TENDERS ELECTRONIC DAILY 193
TENDERS ON THE WEB 193
TEXTLINE *see* REUTERS BUSINESS BRIEFING
Thompson Corporation, The 210
TIMES, THE 226, 229, 230
TIMES, THE, AND SUNDAY TIMES 174, 178
TOXLINE 133
TRADELINE AND TRADELINE INTERNATIONAL 205
TREATY (CELEX file) 251
TULSA 132, 134, 136

UAPT *see* United Association for the Protection of Trade
UK Department of Trade and Industry 193
UK MARKETING DATABASE 180
UKCURR (LEXIS-NEXIS file) 249
UKNEWS (FT PROFILE file group) 222–3
UKTAX (LEXIS-NEXIS library) 249
UN DEMOGRAPHICS 200
United Association for the Protection of Trade 168–70
United Nations 195
Universität Ilmenau 94, 109
University of North Carolina Online Resource for Journalists 241
US Patent and Trademark Office 26, 27, 44, 89–91, 128
US Patent and Trademark Office Web Site 140
US PATENTS FULLTEXT 44, 78–82, 138
USCLASS 126, 129
USPAT FULLTEXT 136
USPATFULL 41, 43, 82–3, 84–6, 137
USPTO PATENT FULL TEXT AND IMAGE DATABASE 89–91, 92
USPTO *see* US Patent and Trademark Office
USPTO Web site 116, 126, 137

VERITY 86–7

WAITER.COM 5
WALL STREET JOURNAL EUROPE, THE 174
WALL STREET JOURNAL, THE 152, 174, 178
WASHINGTON POST 178
WebCrawler 11
WEEKLY (LEXIS-NEXIS file) 249
WEEKLY LAW REPORTS 256
WEFA *see* Wharton Economic Forecasting Associates
WESTLAW 126
Wharton Economic Forecasting Associates 200
WHO OWNS WHOM 158–60
WHO'S WHO IN TECHNOLOGY 198
Wila Verlag/Bertelsmann Information Service 101–4, 128
WIPO *see* WORLD INTELLECTUAL PROPERTY ORGANIZATION
WIPO/PCT PATENTS FULLTEXT 93, 140
WORLD BANK BUSINESS OPPORTUNITIES SERVICE 195
WORLD BOOK MULTIMEDIA ENCYCLOPEDIA 9
WORLD CONSUMER MARKETS ON CD-ROM 179–80
WORLD DATABASE OF BUSINESS INFORMATION SOURCES ON CD-ROM 195
WORLD DATABASE OF CONSUMER BRANDS AND THEIR OWNERS 1997 ON CD-ROM
    180
WORLD INTELLECTUAL PROPERTY ORGANIZATION 27, 61–8
WORLD INTELLECTUAL PROPERTY ORGANIZATION Web Site 140
WORLD MARKETING DATA AND STATISTICS CD-ROM 179
WORLD PATENTS INDEX *see also* DERWENT WORLD PATENTS INDEX
WORLD PATENTS INDEX/APIPAT 38, 111–13, 132, 134, 136
WORLD REPORTER *see* FT PROFILE
WORLDWIDE PatSearch *see* MicroPatent WORLDWIDE PatSearch
WOTEXT 98, 136
WPAM (file name) *see* WORLD PATENTS INDEX/APIPAT
WPAMNS (file name) *see* WORLD PATENTS INDEX/APIPAT

YAHOO! 5, 143, 232

Subject index

Acts of Parliament (UK) 245, 246, 253, 254
advertising 178–79
African Intellectual Property Organization
   (OAPI) 31, 35
African Regional Industrial Property
   Organization 28, 35
aging *see* senior citizens
agriculture 48, 54, 118, 133, 201
Albania 28
Alert Manager 180
Alerting Bulletins 55
Algeria 28
All England Law Reports 244, 246, 248
American Institute of Certified Public
   Accountants (AICPA) 161
American Legal Ethics Library 260
American Petroleum Institute (API) 109
American Securities and Exchange
   Commission 158, 161
Analyze command 135
animation 10
Antigua & Barbuta 28
API *see* American Petroleum Institute
API EnCompass Industry Alert Bulletins
   109
Argentina 28
ARIPO *see* African Regional Industrial
   Property Organization
Armenia 28
art 134
Aurigin Workbench 89
Australia 28, 251, 260
Australian Biological Research Network 5
Austria 28, 61
Azerbaijan 28

Banking 192, 201, 207

Barbados 28
behavioural sciences 134
Belarus 28
Belgium 28, 61, 69
Benin 28
BILETA Report on IT for UK Law Schools
   243
biosciences 18, 132–133
biosystematic codes 49
biotechnology 118, 132–3
blocking software *see* filtering
bookmarking 143–4
Bosnia 28
Brazil 28, 61
Britain *see* UK
British and Irish Association of Law Librarians
   (BIALL) 243
British and Irish Legal Technology Association
   (BILETA) 243
British Library Document Supply Centre 195,
   196
browsing 9–10
building law 255
Bulgaria 2
Bulletin Officiel de Propriété Industrielle 99
Burkina Faso 28
business 23–4, 49, 135, 141–215
   biographical information 197–8
   news information 152, 157, 173–8, 196,
      197, 200, 204, 206, 220
   opportunities information 193–195

Cameroon 28
Canada 28, 37, 122, 126–7, 251, 259
CAS registry numbers (CAS) 69, 71, 111, 131,
   132, 137
Central African Republic 28

Central Patents Index see also Chemical Patents Index 52
Centre for Information Quality Management 154
Certificate of Correction 48, 72–3, 75, 88
Chad 28
Chemical Abstracts 36, 43, 46, 69, 71, 82, 83, 105, 107, 109, 110, 111, 113–14, 116, 131, 132, 137
chemical engineering 131, 134
Chemical Patents Index (CPI) 52, 131
chemistry 26, 27, 41, 43, 44, 54, 55, 56, 68, 69, 71–2, 82–3, 113–16, 124, 131–2, 133, 136, 137–8
ChemPort 116
CHI Research, Inc. 130
children 3, 19
China 28, 107, 252
Chinese language 93
Chinese Patent Office 107
citation indexes 124, 130–31
CLAIMS Thesaurus 73
clothing industry 134
Cluster command 137
clustering 89
command-driven systems *see* interfaces
Committee on Uniform Securities Identification Procedures 153
Common Market Law Reports 247, 255
Companies Registration Office 153, 158, 161
Company Code Manual 54
Company information 158–68, 197
competitive intelligence 135
computer science 132, 192
Congo 28
construction law 255
consumer behaviour 180, 201
controlled vs natural-language searching 11–13, 27, 45–6, 49–50, 53, 125, 127–9, 131–2, 143, 154
copyright 24
Cornell Law Review 260
Cornell University 260
Corporate Intelligence Service 43
Costa Rica 28
costs *see* pricing
Cote d'Ivoire *see* Ivory Coast
Council of Law Reporting 255
Cranfield Projects 14–15
Credit Card Management 198
Credit Card News 198
credit status information 168–73, 201
Criminal Appeal Reports 248, 255
CRO *see* Companies Registration Office
Croatia 28

cross-file searching 11, 36, 50, 54, 56–7, 136, 137, 138–9, 156, 221
Cuba 28
current affairs 217–41
Current Annotated Statutes 245
Current General Statutory Instruments 249
Current Law 257
Current Public General Acts 249
CUSIP *see* Committee on Uniform Securities Identification Procedures
Cyprus 28
Czech Republic 29
Czechoslovakia 29

Data Protection Act, 1984 253
database evaluation 10–11, 154, 219–22, 260–61
demography 199
Denmark 29, 61
Derwent Chemistry Resource 56
Derwent Classification Codes 56
descriptors *see* Controlled vs natural-language searching
Deutsches Patentamt 105, 107, 128
Development Business 195
direct manipulation 7–8
Disability Discrimination Act, 1995 253
Disabled Persons Act, 1986 245
Discovery interface 224
dissertations 11
document delivery 11, 92
Documentation Abstracts Journals 55
Dominica 29
DRIpro 201
Drug Price Competition and Patent Term Restoration Act 73
drugs *see* pharmaceuticals
DUNS numbers 153
Duplicate detection 50, 138, 156

earth sciences 132
ECLA *see* European Patent Classification
ECLATX classification codes 68, 136
Econometrics 199
economics 199–203, 251
Economist 226
Egypt 29
electrical engineering 132, 134
Electrical Patents Index (EPI) 52
energy 134, 136, 192, 204
engineering 23
engineering *see also* chemical engineering, electrical engineering, and mechanical engineering

England *see also* UK 251
English Reports 246
environmental sciences 132, 192, 260
EPIDOS 27
EPO *see* European Patent Office
Estates Gazette Digest 248
Estonia 29
Eurasian Patent Organization 35
Eurasian Patent Office 29, 35, 36, 44, 61, 93, 97, 117
European Communities 193, 245, 251, 255
   Official Journal 193, 247, 251
European Court of Justice 258
European Court Reports 247, 251
European Human Rights Reports 251
European Patent Bulletin 94
European Patent Classification 45, 99, 136
European Patent Classification Manual 125
European Patent Convention 35, 93
European Patent Office (EPO) 27, 29, 35, 45, 53, 68, 94, 109, 118, 125, 127, 128, 136, 140
   Bulletin 94, 98
European Patent Organization 140
European Patent Register 94
European Union 35, 247
Expand command 54, 154

FAM command 68
Family Law Reports 246, 248
FAMINPD command 68
FAMLIST command 68
FAMLISTE command 68
FAMSTAT command 62, 68
FAMSTATE command 68
File command 138
filtering 19, 157
financial derivatives 199
Financial markets 203–7
Financial Times 223, 226, 258
Finland 29, 61
food sciences 133
FPAT command 68
FPRI command 68
France 29, 43, 61, 69, 94, 99, 117, 127, 128, 252
Freestyle 250
free-text searching *see* Controlled vs natural-language searching
French language 18–19, 35, 36, 93, 94, 99, 101, 117, 125
FSORT command 138
furnishings 134

Gabon 29
Gambia 29
games 134
GATT *see* General Agreement on Tariffs and Trade
Gazette 246
General Agreement on Tariffs and Trade 26, 260
General and Mechanical Patents Index 52
geology 132
Georgia 29
German language 19, 35, 36, 43, 93, 94, 101–2, 104, 125
Germany 29, 53, 57, 61, 69, 94, 101, 104, 105–7, 117, 127, 128, 137
Get command 135, 137
Ghana 29
Global Patent Sources 27
Granada 29
graphics 10
Great Britain *see* UK
Greece 29
Guardian 226, 246
Guinea 29
Guinea-Bissau 29

Hansard 253
health care 192
HMSO 245, 249, 253, 254, 255
Hong Kong 29
Housing Law Reports 246
Human Rights Act, 1998 245
humanities 134
Hungary 29, 61
Hungarian language 125
hypertext 9–10, 87, 88, 213, 260

IAC Predicasts classification 153
IBM Technical Disclosure Bulletin 27
Iceland 29
ICIREPAT 27
IDPAT command 139
IMF International Financial Statistics 200
Incorporated Council of Law Reporting 246
Independent 226, 246, 258
Index to the Manual of Classification 125–6
indexing *see* controlled vs natural-language searching
India 29
Indonesia 30
Industrial Cases Reports 255
Industrial Relations Law Reports 246
industry information 187, 191–3

Information
 on demand 156
 seekers 1–4, 142–8, 150–51, 153, 155, 179,
  193, 203–4, 211–14
 science 132
 technology 132
INID 27
INPADOC *see* International Patent
 Documentation Center
INPI *see* Institut National de Propriété
 Industrielle
Insta-Vu 198
Institut National de Propriété Industrielle
 (INPI) 97, 99, 117
Institute of Information Scientists 140
Institute of Management 196
interfaces 3, 7–8, 13, 18, 20, 142–8, 151, 154,
 175, 199, 200, 211–14, 219–221, 222–8,
 248
Intermediaries *see* information seekers
International Court of Justice 260
international law 252
International Monetary Fund 200
International Patent Classification (IPC)
 codes 45, 55, 57, 67, 68, 71, 83, 98, 99,
 107, 109, 111, 116, 117, 125
International Patent Classification Manual 135
International Patent Documentation Center 61
International Technology Abstracts 56
International Technology Disclosures 27
international trade 259
intranets 145, 207, 209, 214
IPC *see* International Patent Classification
Ireland 30, 61, 251
Irish Law Reports Monthly 251
Irish Law Times 251
Irish Reports 251
Is it in Force? 245
Israel 30
Italian language 19
Italy 30, 61, 122
Ivory Coast 30

Japan 30, 35–6, 37, 38, 54, 55, 57, 67, 68,
 87, 93, 107–9, 118, 122, 128, 132, 133,
 139
Japanese language 93, 122
Japanese Patent Office 38, 44, 107, 109
Johns Hopkins University 18
Jordan's Family Law Reports 255
Journal Officiel des Communautés Européenes
 see European Communities, *Official*
 Journal

Kazakhstan 30
Kenya 30
keywords *see* controlled vs natural-language
 searching
Knight's Industrial Reports 248
Kokai 107, 132, 133, 134
Kompass classification 153
Korea, North 30
Korea, South 30
Kyrgyzstan 30

Latvia 30
law 24, 243–261
 case law 246–7
 education 243–4
 secondary legislation 245–6
 statutes 245
Law Reports 244, 246
Law Technology Centre 243
Lesotho 30
Liberia 30
Liechtenstein 30
Lithuania 30, 61
Lloyd's Electronic Law Reports 255
Lloyd's List 258
Luxembourg 30

Macedonia 30
Madagascar 30
Malawi 30
Malaysia 30
Mali 30
Malta 30
management information 196–7
Manual of Classification see US Manual of
 Classification
Manual of Patent Examining Procedures 27,
 128
MAP command 139
MAPPN command 36, 57
market research 179–80
market trading 199
marketing information 178–87, 196
Markush structures 41, 43, 56, 116, 117, 131,
 136–7
mathematics 132
Mauritania 30
mechanical engineering 132
Medical Law Reports 246
medicine 48, 132–3
..MEM command 125, 137
..MEMSORT command 135, 137
menu-driven systems *see* interfaces
mergers and acquisitions 206

messenger 56
metadata 143
metals 204
metasearch engines 5
Mexico 30
Moldova 30
Monaco 30, 61
Mongolia 30
Morocco 31
Mozambique 31
Multi-file searching *see* cross-file searching
multilingual aspects 18–19, 49
multimedia 10, 204, 221, 238
music 134

NAICS *see* North American Industry
    Classification System
Narin, Francis 130
NASDAQ 205
National Library of Medicine 6
natural languages *see* controlled vs natural-
    language searching
Neighbour command 54
Netherlands 31, 61, 68, 69
New Zealand 31, 251, 260
news *see also* business news information
    217–41
    events 235
    dates 235–6
    localities 235
    objects 234
    people 233–4
Niger 31
NIMEXE classification 153
NLM *see* National Library of Medicine
North American Industry Classification System
    153, 154
Northern Ireland 246, 251
Northern Ireland Law Reports 246
Norway 31

OAPI *see* African Intellectual Property
    Organization
Observer 226
Official Gazette of the USPTO see USPTO
    Official Gazette
Official Journal see European Communities,
    Official Journal
OPACs 3, 4, 13
Open Data Gateway 204
Organizing Medical Networked Information
    Consortium (OMNI) 20

paper industry 192

Paris Convention for the Protection of
    Industrial Property 38
Patent and Trade Mark Group 140
Patent Cooperation Treaty 31, 34–5, 43, 49, 53,
    56, 57, 61, 94, 98, 102, 105, 110, 128, 130
*Patent Information and Documentation
    Handbook* 27
*Patent Information from Chemical Abstracts
    Service Coverage and Content* 27
Patent Information Users Group (PIUG) 140
patent litigation databases 126–7
Patent, Trademark & Copyright Journal
    126
Patentblatt 105, 107
patents 23–140
    applications 24, 26, 27, 37–9
    codes 27–32
    data fields 33–49
    definition 24–6
    drawings 43–4, 55, 69, 71, 75, 78, 134
    laws governing 26
    patentee names 39–40, 62, 69
    prior art 33
Patents International 119
PCT *see* Patent Cooperation Treaty
PCT Gazette 43, 97, 98
personal credit information 198
Petroleum Abstracts 110
petroleum technology 109, 132, 134
pharmaceuticals 26, 48, 52, 54, 98, 117–21,
    124, 130, 131, 192
pharmacology 132–3
Philippines 31
physics 132, 134
Poland 31
polymers 55, 56, 72, 122, 131
Portugal 31, 61
Portuguese language 19
precision 14–17, 152–3, 179, 196, 234, 237
pricing 8–9, 10, 20, 52, 62, 89, 93, 120,
    148–51, 155–7, 211, 219–21, 223, 237
printing 192
Public General Acts (HMSO) 245, 253
publishing 192

Rank command 135
ranking 9, 50, 86, 90, 152–3, 213
real-time services 154, 156, 203–5
recall 14–17, 152, 196, 237
research and development 23
Research Disclosures 27, 56
retail trade 199
risk management 201
Romania 31

Russia 31, 128
Russian language 93, 125

Saint Lucia 31
science 23
*SCIMP European Index of Management
    Periodicals* 196
Scotland 246, 251
Scots Law Times 246
Scotsman 227, 258
Scottish Parliament 246
SDI 157
search evaluation 14–17
searching *see* information seekers
SEC *see* American Securities and Exchange
    Commission
Select (STN) command 135, 138
Selective Cooperative Indexing of Management
    Periodicals *see* SCIMP
Senegal 31
senior citizens 3
Session Cases 246
SIC *see* Standard Industry Classifications
Sierra Leone 31
Simon's Tax Cases 248
Singapore 31
SITC *see* Standard Industrial Trade
    Classifications
Slovakia 31
Smart Patents 89
SmartSelect command 138
social sciences 134
Solicitors Journal 246
sound 10
South Africa 31
Southern California Online User Group 20
Soviet Union 35, 115
Spain 31, 61
spamming 11
Spanish language 19, 93, 125
Sri Lanka 31
Standard Industry Classifications (SIC) 153
Standard Industrial Trade Classifications
    (SITC) 153
Statutes in Force 245
Statutory Instruments 246, 249, 254, 255
Stock Exchange (UK) 158
Sudan 31
Swaziland 31
Sweden 31, 61
Switzerland 31, 61, 94, 128
synonyms 3
SYSTRAN 19

Taiwan 31
Tajikistan 31
Tanzania 31
tax law 249, 252
Technical University Ilmenau 94, 109
technology 23
thesauri 54, 55, 69, 71, 73, 83, 111, 125, 126,
    137, 152, 219, 233, 256
time series 200–201
Times 226, 246, 258
Togo 31
toys 134
trade 199
training 4, 20
Transfer command 57, 138
Treasury risk management 199
Trinidad and Tobago 32
Turkey 32
Turkmenistan 32

Uganda 32
UK 32, 35, 53, 57, 61, 69, 117, 118, 128, 153,
    197, 198, 200–201, 206, 219–20, 222–4
UK Department of Trade and Industry 193
Ukraine 32
United Arab Emirates 32
United Association for the Protection of
    Trade (UAPT) 169
United Nations 195, 260
Universität Ilmenau *see* Technical University
    Ilmenau
US Manual of Classification 73, 75, 83, 90, 91,
    125, 128, 137
US Patent and Trademark Office 26, 27, 41, 44,
    71, 94, 126, 140
US SIC 153, 154
USA 26, 27, 32, 33, 34, 35, 37, 39, 43, 47, 48,
    53, 57, 61, 68, 69, 72, 73, 75, 78, 87,
    90–93, 94, 117, 118, 122, 124, 126, 128,
    131, 139, 153, 179–80, 197, 198, 201,
    205–6, 220, 247–8, 252, 258–60
user studies 3–4
US Patent and Trademark Office *see* USPTO
USPTO 26, 69, 71, 73, 128
    Concordance 71
    Official Gazette 71, 73, 92, 127
USSR 32
USSR *see also* Russia
Uzbekistan 32

veterinary science 133
video 10
Vietnam 32

Wall Street Journal 220
Web site evaluation *see* database evaluation
Weekly Information Bulletins 258
Weekly Law Reports 246, 248, 255
Wila Verlag/Bertelsmann 128
Welsh Assembly 246
WIPO *see* World Industrial Property Organization
Woodward, Louis 236–9
World Intellectual Property Organization 27,

35, 45, 99, 125, 140
World Patents Index 43
World Trade Organization 26, 38

Yellow Pages 153
Yugoslavia 32

Zambia 32
Zimbabwe 32